CRISTIANO AND LEO

Jimmy Burns is an award-winning journalist and author of eight other books. He was born in Madrid in 1953. He has reported for the *Financial Times,* the *Observer,* the BBC and *The Economist,* and was the *FT* correspondent in South America in the early 80s. His book on Argentina and the Falklands War, *The Land that Lost Its Heroes,* won the 1988 Somerset Maugham Award for non-fiction. When not in Spain, or travelling elsewhere, he lives in London.

www.jimmy-burns.com
@jimmy_burns

JIMMY BURNS

CRISTIANO AND LEO

#whoisthegreatest

PAN BOOKS

First published 2018 by Macmillan

This paperback edition first published 2019 by Pan Books
an imprint of Pan Macmillan
20 New Wharf Road, London N1 9RR
Associated companies throughout the world
www.panmacmillan.com

ISBN 978-1-5098-4914-7

Typeset by Palimpsest Book Production Limited, Falkirk, Stirlingshire
Printed and bound by CPI Group (UK) Ltd, Croydon, CR0 4YY

Visit **www.panmacmillan.com** to read more about all our books
and to buy them. You will also find features, author interviews and
news of any author events, and you can sign up for e-newsletters
so that you're always first to hear about our new releases.

For Julia & Miriam

CONTENTS

GREAT PLAYERS IN AN UNPREDICTABLE WORLD

It became part of a shared experience in the turbulent times we lived in that nothing is predictable, and anyone who claimed a crystal ball into the future was either naive or a fraud.

The world of football is of course not only unexceptional in this sense, but also owes its popularity to a rollercoaster of fortune and failure. Video Assistant Referee (VAR) may have brought some order to the previously arbitrary, and often mistaken and unfair, judgements of referees and linesmen (while also producing a frustrating interlude, or football's equivalent of *coitus interruptus*), but goals still continued in all sorts of unexpected ways; even the best could be beaten by the minnows, and sustained success could not easily be bought.

Nonetheless, when I signed off the first edition of this book, at the end of the 2017–18 club football season, I took a punt that one of the most enduring rivalries in world sport was not yet finished, if still reaching the end of a historic cycle. Ronaldo's widely speculated imminent departure from Real Madrid seemed to provide a bookend to nearly a decade when the intense competitive spirit affecting the Clásico encounters between Los Blancos and FC Barcelona had given the race with Messi – to be considered the greatest football player of all time – its special edge.

It was something that the usually tongue-tied Messi recognized in an unusually confessional interview he gave in March 2019, during which he admitted he 'missed' competing against Ronaldo in Spain.

'I miss Cristiano in Spain,' Messi told Radio C5N. 'It was lovely having him here, even though it annoyed me seeing him win so many titles. It would be great if he was still here.'

Lest we forget, this was Messi – a recognized genius of the game – speaking about another football legend, Cristiano Ronaldo: like him a five-time Ballon d'Or winner and breaker of numerous records. Both players began 2019 fit and similarly ready to scale new heights, with an enthusiasm that belied their relatively advanced ages, but for the first time in years, in different national leagues.

At the age of thirty-one, Messi kicked off the 2018–19 season at Barça – the second under coach Ernesto Valverde – for the first time wearing the club's first-team captain's armband, taking over the role following the departure of his friend and mentor Andrés Iniesta to Japanese club Vissel Kobe, who in turn had been preceded by other icons of the youth academy – Xavi and Carles Puyol.

Messi promised fans he would help win another Champions League trophy, then made an immediate mark in Barça's first La Liga game of the season against Alavés at the Nou Camp on 18 August 2018, with a clever free kick under the wall. As man of the match, he orchestrated and delivered a 3–0 victory, scoring a second great goal in stoppage time with typical strength and skill, taking down a pass from Suárez, holding off a defender and finishing at the near post. Barcelona's 6,000th goal in La Liga history and Messi's 384th!

By contrast, for all the summer hype surrounding his €100 million transfer a month earlier to Juventus, Cristiano's new season got off to a less impressive start. Despite twenty-three shots for the Turin giants in his first three Italian League matches, he failed to score.

But Italian national team manager Roberto Mancini predicted that Ronaldo would soon find his goal-scoring form once he adjusted to a different style of playing and defending to Spain, which left him with less space in the final third for him to find openings. And he was proved right, with Ronaldo showing his versatility, alternating as a winger and striker. Before the year 2018 was out, he had scored his thirteenth goal in Serie A since the start of the season. His goal in a match against Sampdoria came within two minutes of the start, as he picked the ball up on the left-hand corner of the box, controlled and fired it into the far corner, predatory and skilful. He later converted a penalty, making it 2–1.

By March 2019, Barça was well on its way to running away with La Liga and into the Champions League quarter-finals. Juventus too was well clear at the top in Serie A, and into the Champions League quarter-finals, while Real Madrid was out of Europe, trailing in La Liga and struggling, without Ronaldo, to compete with its Catalan rival. Such was the sense of crisis at Real Madrid that club president Florentino Pérez fired Santiago Solari and brought back Zinedine Zidane as coach in a belated recovery operation.

This update picks up on my prediction in the summer of 2018 that the story of two unrivalled geniuses of the modern game was entering the final period of their careers in top-flight football, with Ronaldo, the oldest of the two at thirty-three, arguably taking on the biggest challenge by switching clubs and leagues for the third time since starting up in competitive football as a teenager at Sporting Lisbon.

That is not to say that Messi necessarily faced an easier future by choosing to play his final years at competitive level at FC Barcelona, a club he had joined aged thirteen. It was a club that had become his home from home, not so much an exile but his psychological comfort zone, the club and city where he felt most at ease and where his talent flourished each season, like a perennial flower planted in the best possible soil.

It was a club that had over the years lost its inspirational manager Pep Guardiola and similarly legendary players like Xavi and Iniesta, and had become increasingly dependent on the Argentine-born star for its success – great as long as Messi could deliver, but not a limitless guarantee, unless and until a substitute of his quality and influence could be found. And yet Messi was surrounded by players at FC Barcelona who were not only inspired by him, but also played in a way that combined with and brought out his talent. On a good day Barça was not just Messi, but a class team act, with the team coalescing like a harmonious orchestra around its director and lead musician.

And here it's worth remembering that Messi is someone who lived and breathed his football as a player, but his genius has shown itself exclusively on the pitch, not off it. Barça provided Messi with his stage and a theatre, a club with a distinctive playing style and identity, and a powerful trademark as 'more than a club'.

FC Barcelona was a political and cultural entity as well as a corporation with a huge commercial ambition, as was underlined in a *Financial Times* weekend magazine report by sports writer Simon Kuper, published in March 2019. The article focused on the club's

'Innovation Hub', charged, as the writer put it, with 'helping to invent the future of football', with staff researching everything from players' diets to virtual reality to enable the club to be even more successful and make even more money, even after Messi's departure.

Club president Josep Maria Bartomeu said he considered the hub to be Barça's 'most important' project. 'The sportsmen of the future will perform much better than the ones now,' Bartomeu told Kuper. As the writer went on to claim: 'The officials didn't tell me everything, but they told me a lot. They know that football cannot be "solved" with algorithms, and that no robot will ever match Messi's genius; all they aspire to is to add something.'

In the 2018–19 season, politics not business still stirred a section of the Camp Nou stadium, which chanted the word 'independence' in Catalan after seventeen minutes and fourteen seconds of play in every home game. The outburst commemorated a key date in Catalan history, the year that Barcelona fell under the control of the centralizing Spanish Bourbon monarchy, whose latest King Felipe reigns today.

With local Catalan politicians put on trial in early 2019 for sedition by the Spanish state for declaring unilateral independence, Messi remained aloof from involvement in politics. And yet, growing up with the club over two decades, it was almost unthinkable he would wear the shirt of any other club, even if he had hinted on a number of occasions that he might see out some of his eventual retirement from top-flight football in his native Rosario, playing for Newell's Old Boys where he had been as a young boy.

And if there was something that had not changed, it was that Messi had neither the physique nor personality required for celebrity status, nor could he develop his brand across social media and the world of advertising and sponsorship as effectively as Cristiano Ronaldo had done – this was a brand that, like Beckham's, looked set to endure in business and advertising long after the Madeiran hung up his boots.

Real Madrid president Florentino Pérez made a calculated business risk in selling Ronaldo to Juventus, making a profit on the sale of him after nine years of service, and beginning the regeneration of an ageing squad. But while Ronaldo turned thirty-four in February 2019, he looked to be joining sports stars such as Roger Federer and LeBron James, who excelled in their mid-thirties. Certainly commercially, as the face behind the portfolio of CR7 brands, Ronaldo's stock seemed never to have been higher. No other athlete, according to *Forbes* magazine, made as much on endorsements, with an unrivalled global social media following also built up over the duration of a hugely successful sporting career.

Ronaldo had ripened into a brand of his own off-field as well as on it. It was because he had been showcased effectively while playing successfully not just at one but two clubs – Manchester United and Real Madrid – which resonated in the collective football imagination, each with a culture and business model that guaranteed a mass following across borders, and who found in Ronaldo not just a great player but one who knew precisely how to promote himself.

In the course of updating his story, I was struck by how, behind Ronaldo's transfer to Juventus, was the Italian club's hopes of mirroring the potency of brands of clubs that had greater success on the international stage, despite taking him on at an age at which most players would have been considered past their peak.

I visited Turin in the early spring of 2019. It's a small city with an imposing historic centre of baroque architecture and a wonderful view of the Alps, but hardly buzzing during a short break in Italian football games. The club and its fans were still savouring the experience of its extraordinary second-leg victory over Atlético Madrid in the last sixteen of the Champions League, where Ronaldo had played the role of hero and saviour after helping consolidate Juventus's unassailable position at the top of the Italian Premier A League.

I was initially struck by the orderliness and sobriety of Turin compared to other Italian cities, and by the relatively low-key presence of Ronaldo in shop windows, on billboards, and in newspaper kiosks, compared to his huge visibility in Spain when at Real Madrid and in the Premier League when at Manchester United, and while playing for his native Portugal.

Even in Juventus's atmospheric museum, the space devoted to Ronaldo was dwarfed by that given over to others considered by Italian fans as enduring legends. The pantheon of greats included those who had made the highest number of appearances, like Alessandro Del Piero, or the much-loved non-Italian John Charles, or those who made their mark as national heroes in other ways, like Paolo Rossi and the iconic goalkeeper Gianluigi Buffon, all of whom had sweated the club colours through great victories and similarly huge defeats before recovering again. As Juventus's official history album puts it: *Paradiso-Inferno – andata e ritorno*; on a return ticket from heaven to hell.

'We will move Cristiano Ronaldo from the room of the first team this season to join the room of legends when he becomes part of our history,' the museum's director told me.

Elsewhere, downtown, the relative absence of Ronaldo's image from Turin's streets was deceptive, as was the club's enduring nickname La Vecchia Signora, the Old Lady. The museum was vibrant and modern, as was the club's nearby headquarters, opened in 2017 and still in development. The 4,370 square metres of converted farmland and buildings on the outskirts of the city near the Allianz stadium, with its convergence of modern design – all black and white – and smooth surfaces, not unlike Ronaldo's branded CR7 hotels, was a statement of style and ambition by a club that drew its main fan base from outside Turin and across Italy, and had set its sights on a global market.

As Andrea Agnelli, a scion of the billionaire automotive family that has owned the club for ninety-five years and who personally signed the cheque for Ronaldo, told the *FT*'s Murad Ahmed on 16 September 2018: 'It was the first time that the commercial side and the sporting side of Juventus came together in assessing the costs and benefits [of a signing]. The opportunity of Ronaldo was thoroughly assessed…and it made sense, both on and off the pitch.'

On the pitch, Juventus as a team did not need Ronaldo to ensure its dominance of Italian football as the country's most successful club. When Ronaldo moved to Turin, the club had won seven consecutive Serie A league titles. It had, however, failed in recent seasons to clinch the Champions League, having lost twice in the previous four years in the final of the world's most prestigious club competition. Ronaldo, in contrast, has won the last three Champions League finals with Real Madrid.

Off the pitch, Juventus believed the player presented an unparalleled financial opportunity, described by executives as 'the Ronaldo effect'. The club was looking to use the global celebrity of Ronaldo to attract fans and corporate groups, with higher broadcasting money to follow. There were early signs that the bet was paying off, with the club's share price more than doubling in Ronaldo's first three months, raising its market capitalization to €1.5 billion. There was brisk trade in Ronaldo shirts, and ticket prices went up, causing unprecedented protests from fans who'd bought tickets for matches only to find Ronaldo was not actually playing.

Meanwhile, Ronaldo's social media drawing power resulted in Juventus gaining 10 million followers in the month of his signing at the club. With Serie A locked into broadcast deals until the end of the 2020–1 season, there was little immediate upside from any surge in viewers for Italian football, even though – unlike many of its Italian club rivals – Juventus plays to a packed house in a ground that it owns. Unsurprisingly, club president Agnelli was among those football senior execs who wanted to see European club football competitions being rearranged to involve more financially lucrative ties between big teams and few local minnows.

Ronaldo still played best on the big stage, and the hope was that he would help secure Juventus a permanent position in the top tier. Even if the search was on for the next global superstar, with the likes of Neymar and Kylian Mbappé in the sights of big clubs, it would take a long time to find ones of such enduring quality, performance and return on investment as Ronaldo and Messi, occasional controversies notwithstanding.

Juventus was preparing a tour of Asia in the summer of 2019, earlier denying a report in the *New York Times* that this had been chosen as a destination in preference to the USA, where their star player was facing allegations of sexual assault. Police in the state of Nevada had reopened an investigation into an allegation made by an American woman, Kathryn Mayorga, who said that Ronaldo had raped her in a Las Vegas hotel room in 2009 and later paid her $375,000 for her silence. Ronaldo and his lawyers repeatedly denied the rape accusation when it first emerged in October 2018 in the German magazine *Der Speigel*, after the player had transferred from Real Madrid to Juventus. Ronaldo was at Manchester United when he met Mayorga in a Las Vegas nightclub in June 2009, just before his record-breaking transfer to Real Madrid.

It was not the only cloud from his past hovering over him. In January 2019, Ronaldo was fined almost €19 million ($21.6 million) for tax fraud by a Madrid court, but avoided serving a twenty-three-month prison sentence after agreeing a settlement. In 2017, Ronaldo denied the accusation that he knowingly used a business structure to hide income generated by his image rights in Spain between 2011 and 2014.

Ronaldo left the Madrid court smiling, holding hands with his Spanish girlfriend Georgina Rodríguez, pausing to sign photographs. The player with a greater social media following than any other sportsman, rock star, actor or politician, struck a typically self-assured celebrity pose, seemingly determined not to allow the case to undermine either his popularity or his success, on or off the field. He was on his way back to Turin, determined to prove to local fans he was more than just a pretty face, while Georgina pursued her modelling career, posing in a bikini after signing for the Italian fashion company Yamamay in March.

Three months earlier, in December 2018, Real Madrid and Croatia star Luka Modrić was awarded the Ballon d'Or. It was the first time since 2007 that the award had gone to a player other than Cristiano Ronaldo or Lionel Messi, who came second and fifth respectively. However, any suggestion that either Ronaldo or Messi had been dethroned from the higher echelons of world football in any meaningful way proved premature.

Jimmy Burns
May 2019

PROLOGUE

April 2017. Real Madrid and FC Barcelona square up for the latest El Clásico. As the minutes tick away to kick-off, a capacity crowd of over 81,000 is packed into Real Madrid's sizzling Bernabéu Stadium, while a global audience of 600 million watches and listens through TVs, radios and computers in 185 countries, across every time zone on the planet.

And there, at the centre of the storm, are two players: Cristiano Ronaldo and Lionel Messi, the star attractions of the biggest club football show on earth, wearing their totemic initials and shirt numbers. Such is the interest in 'CR7' and 'LM10' in this, the 234th episode of the most legendary rivalry in football, that the attention of the forty fixed cameras in the stadium and two super-slow-motion rigs are exclusively focused on them.

The ongoing battle between these two hugely talented players is, of course, being played against the backdrop of one of the most enduring and politically charged rivalries in sport. It's Castile vs Catalonia, Franco vs the freedom fighters, expensive *galácticos* vs homegrown stars. With six rounds of games to be played, Barcelona find themselves three points behind leaders Madrid, who also have a game in hand. A win will bring Barcelona level on points, but defeat will allow Madrid to open up a six-point gap at the top of the table.

Cristiano Ronaldo comes out last of the Madrid players, the headliner, bouncing like a pogo stick. Pristine and swaggering.

By contrast, Lionel Messi comes out with his head bowed, shoulders hunched, expressionless, only briefly looking up and surveying the crowd through a black eye and from behind a beard. For him, the game comes at the end of a week of speculation that he is reaching the end of the season battered, worn out; Barcelona's loss to Juventus in their Champions League semi-final three days previously has proved the players have hit a wall, and not even their talisman is able to lift a team in urgent need of regeneration.

The game gets off to an explosive start. Within two minutes of the opening whistle, Ronaldo theatrically claims a penalty after FC Barcelona's defender Samuel Umtiti leaves a leg trailing in the box. Play on. Ten minutes later, Ronaldo tests Barcelona keeper Marc-André ter Stegen with a stinging drive.

Now it's Messi's turn. He nutmegs Casemiro and dribbles free in midfield, before the Brazilian recovers by hacking the Argentinian down. With each player seeking to land the first blow, Ronaldo strikes again, this time more powerfully, just inside the box, only to have his effort parried by the FC Barcelona keeper. With the pace of the match intensifying, Messi requires medical attention after Marcelo's elbow catches him in the mouth, producing a torrent of blood that looks worse than it is. And so it continues, end-to-end, engulfed in the roar of the crowd.

Midway through the first half, Gareth Bale pressures Barça stalwart Gerard Piqué into conceding a corner. Barcelona fail to clear it properly, Marcelo's deep cross is poked against the post by a stretching Sergio Ramos, and Casemiro bundles it over the line. A scruffy goal, but the Madridistas don't care.

Messi is still playing with a blood-soaked bandage in his mouth, and suddenly this seems to inspire him. He collects a perfectly cushioned pass from Ivan Rakitić and accelerates into the box – the ball perfectly controlled, his small frame almost brushing the ground as he changes direction – before finding the net with a precise left-footed shot. He nearly claims a second five minutes before half-time, when he pounces onto a loose ball and chips just wide of the goal. Just before the end of the half, there's time for him to somehow sidefoot just the wrong side of the post from a corner. Messi means business.

The second half continues in the same vein. A fierce Benzema header is saved by ter Stegen; Paco Alcácer's toe-poke is blocked by Keylor Navas in the Madrid goal.

It's time for Ronaldo to come back into focus. In the sixty-sixth minute, he attempts a stretching overhead kick which sails over the bar. Minutes later, Marco Asensio puts him through on goal, but he's off-balance and blazes over.

The heavyweights are still trading blows, unwilling to concede ground. But then, in the seventy-third minute, the ball bobbles to Rakitić just outside the Madrid box. With six defenders in front of him, the Croatian international turns inside onto his left foot and bends a perfect shot into the corner of the net.

2–1 Barça.

Five minutes later, Madrid's captain Sergio Ramos receives his fifth Clásico red card for a wild, two-footed challenge on Messi. It seems like game over, but then in the eighty-fifth minute, Madrid's forgotten man, the Colombian attacker James Rodríguez, somehow arrives at the near post unmarked and spoons a shot into the roof of the net. As the clock ticks into the second minute of stoppage time, it is somehow Real who look the more likely winners.

A brilliant change of pace allows Barcelona's Sergi Roberto some space in midfield and he finds André Gomes. The Portuguese slips the ball to Jordi Alba on the overlap, whose cutback falls into the path of – who else? – Lionel Messi. His low shot is unerring and the net bulges – the final kick of the match, his 500th goal for Barcelona. The Real Madrid fans are stunned into silence, the title race is back on. As he wheels away to celebrate, pumping his fists, he pulls off his shirt, holding it with arms stretched out to the crowd, still, as if his identity was in any doubt.

Of the several images of a memorable El Clásico, few will endure with such iconographic intensity as that of Messi, holding up his number 10 Barça shirt to the Bernabéu crowd.

The other slow-motion camera catches Ronaldo grimacing and lifting his arms to the sky with a look of frustration and disillusion. In the end, it was Messi's willpower, resilience and shuffling magic that prevailed, even in hostile territory where he was the enemy's main target.

Fans at the Bernabéu are even more exacting than those at Barcelona's Nou Camp. Perhaps, for those in the Spanish capital, the political and cultural identity of the club matters less than winning football. They expect and demand the best from their star players, as those at the city's nearby bullring do of the country's best matadors, not least in encounters with their historic rival. They are an excitable, polarized, visceral, tribally obsessive lot, and yet capable of showing respect when it is due, even to the sworn enemy – just as the bullfight crowd can rise to applaud a brave bull. Messi was the man of the match in that El Clásico of April 2017, the undisputed hero, and the Madridistas knew it.

Not even Messi knew what moved him to that act of defiantly showing off his shirt. A man not known for articulating his feelings, Messi says afterwards that he did it as a tribute to the few hundred Barça fans who had endured the game up in the gods. But it is a cathartic moment. Perhaps, after all, he has it in him to carry his team across the line, to justify the faith those fans show in those who wear the shirt.

In the end, though, both teams won the remainder of their games, meaning that it was Real Madrid who won the League, by just three points. Messi won the battle, but Ronaldo the war. Just a week later, after sealing the League title, Ronaldo lay on the pitch, overcome by joy at the final whistle, as Real thumped Juventus 4–1 to claim the European Cup. He had scored two goals, his forty-first and forty-second of the season. It wasn't enough to win him the Golden Shoe, though. That honour went to Lionel Messi.

Four months later, the Portuguese player was able to replicate Messi's Bernabéu gesture in the Nou Camp during the first leg of the Spanish Super Cup. Or at least perform his own take. After scoring a goal, Ronaldo stripped off his shirt to reveal his sculptured torso to Barça fans. Almost as if to say, of all the things that Messi can do, he cannot do that.

What separates genius from the good, or even great, is the ability to evolve with the passing of time; not just to endure, but to mature, to create anew and still be inspirational, to remain decisively a cut above the rest.

By the time he was seventeen, Wolfgang Amadeus Mozart had composed sublime music, including symphonies, sonatas, string quartets, masses, serenades and a few minor operas. The year leading up to his death in 1791, aged just thirty-five, was a period of intense production as well as personal rediscovery. During this time he composed some of his most famous works, including *The Magic Flute* and his unfinished *Requiem*.

As his rival Antonio Salieri puts it in Peter Shaffer's play *Amadeus*, 'Here again was the very voice of God.'[1]

This same ability to evolve is also present in sporting genius. Muhammad Ali was just twenty-two years old and still known as Cassius Clay when he became heavyweight champion of the world, but his most memorable fights came in his thirties: defeating George Foreman in Zaire, his three bouts against Joe Frazier, and, at the age of thirty-six, his victory over Leon Spinks that made him the first man to win the heavyweight title three times.

In June 2017, Rafa Nadal took possession of a special replica trophy to mark 'La Decima': his tenth French Open title. In terms of individual trophies won, Nadal had become as dominant on clay tennis courts as Usain Bolt on the athletics track, Tiger Woods in golf, Michael Jordan on the basketball court or Michael Phelps in the pool.

In top-flight football, as much as in any other elite sport, the awareness of mortality, the ease with which a player can go from their peak into a swift decline, from valued asset to beyond sell-by date, is often only too clear, sometimes with tragic consequences.

Among the greats, one thinks of George Best and Diego Maradona among those whose careers were cut short when they lost the desire for discipline, for improvement, for relevance, for regeneration. The all-too-brief white-hot intensity of their peak feels somehow part of their legend. Their relatively short periods of true excellence are in contrast to the more than ten years that Lionel Messi and Cristiano Ronaldo have not only repeatedly broken record after record with the consistency and volume of their goal scoring, but refigured what our conception of an elite footballer could be. Through it all, both have given football fans around the world unrivalled entertainment and joy with their unique abilities. It is arguable that we have become somehow numbed to their excellence. Had either one of them existed on their own, they would non-negotiably be the defining footballer of their generation.

Instead, the debate among millions of fans – over who should be considered the better player, and by logical extension, which of them is the greatest of all time – continues to rage in the background.

If one is looking for historic precedents for epoch-shaping rivalries in the world of sport, one thinks of another great cultural clash involving two great basketball stars, Larry Bird and Magic Johnson, and two great teams, Boston Celtics and Los Angeles Lakers. During the 1980s, this rivalry turned the NBA into a global blockbuster.

Johnson famously asserted that, for him, the eighty-two-game regular season was composed of eighty normal games, and two Lakers–Celtics games. For his part, Bird admitted that Johnson's daily box score was the first thing he checked in the morning. What made the Johnson–Bird rivalry so great was not just the players' excellence, but the way it involved a clash of personalities as well as cultures; between Hollywood flashiness and Boston/Indiana blue-collar grit. Less palatably, many in America loaded the country's racial baggage onto the players' backs.

Just as basketball did in the 1980s, twenty-first-century football has produced two differentiated megastars, playing for two great teams whose separate identities have been marked by history and politics, in a cultural clash that has extended over time.

This has not been a sporting rivalry in the classic sense of two individuals competing one to one, but they have converged across time and space as the central characters on football's global stage, carrying the weight of their clubs' and countries' history on their shoulders and inspiring each other to ever greater heights. Rarely has the hype leading up to the games in which they've both played led to disappointment, with some of the most memorable Clásicos becoming the equivalent of a heroic duel in which the other players on the pitch seem to fade into the background.

For some football fans, the question of who is better seems to tip over into an almost moral issue of what football is and how it should be played. Power vs guile, chest-thumping bravado vs head-bowed modesty, the arching leap vs the shuffling weave. It just feels right that they should hate each other.

That, publicly, they have always tried to show a mutual respect, and have never conceded that they consider each other as rivals, does not seem to matter. Indeed, it makes it even more fun to speculate. Rumours continue to abound that there is tension. Dutch legend Ruud Gullit called their relationship 'strange' when he saw them interact at the 2013 Ballon d'Or ceremony, and yet the year before they had reportedly 'hugged like children', according to Fernando Torres. When Spanish football expert Guillem Balagué, in his biography of the Argentine, reported that Ronaldo's nickname for Messi was 'motherfucker', Ronaldo released a statement on Facebook saying, 'I have the utmost respect for all my professional colleagues, and Messi is obviously no exception.' His own position is that it's pointless to compare them: 'Messi and I are as different as Ferrari and Porsche.'

However, they continue to live in each other's light and shadow.

The popular imagination defines them as each other's nemeses, even in the context of a nine-month club season and global international tournaments, and in doing so feeds one of the most dramatic and financially lucrative narratives of modern sport.

Ronaldo and Messi's cultural and social backgrounds, and their careers, could not be more different, but each has faced challenges from birth. Indeed, it is these differences and stumbling blocks that enriches and makes their biographies so fascinating to consider side by side, providing, as they do, a unique insight into the world of modern football.

There is the irony that although they have always kept their distance personally, perhaps no one can understand the pressures and demands of their lives better than the other.

This dual biography follows two separate and contrasting journeys, influenced by different personal circumstances and national cultures, from fraught childhood days and their troubled legacies, to the challenge of playing for the world's most successful clubs in the frenzied colosseums of the Santiago Bernabéu and the Nou Camp, and to competing for the biggest and most lucrative team trophies and personal accolades the game has to offer.

The narrative highlights the extent to which sport, and particularly football, has been transformed in the modern era. It chronicles the transformation of two child prodigies into highly paid superstars guided by accountants, agents and lawyers, playing before not just the crowds in the stadiums but a global audience that follows the epic contest on satellite TV, billboards, social media and the internet, and which is desperate to marshal evidence of one or the other's ascendancy.

I, for one, am not a great fan of statistics on their own – they reduce the game and players to the mechanics of a video game, lacking life and blood and soul. It ignores the fundamental nature of football – its sheer unpredictability – and the moments created by each player. Though they do it in very different ways, they both have the ability to leave players in their wake, not just beaten but entirely removed of purpose. I am yet to see a stat that successfully captures that.

However, since they have come to form part of many fans' judgement in the digital age, I will draw on statistics throughout the book.

As much as anything else, they are useful in quantifying the unremitting excellence that characterizes most of their time on a football pitch.

One of the reasons that the question of which of the two is the best remains unanswered, and is perhaps futile, is that neither player has lost his capacity to surprise us. Every time you think there might finally be an answer, that one of these football legends might have done something so brilliant that it confirms he truly is the world's best, the other one responds by doing something equally phenomenal. A strictly unprejudiced view is that for as long as Ronaldo and Messi can play top-level football, we should simply sit back and enjoy it. Later, when they have retired, we can think back on the glory days and the unprecedented endurance of their reign.

And that is because each has shown an extraordinary ability to evolve their creativity and contribution to their respective teams, as if the rivalry was as much with themselves as with the other. Their ability to constantly self-improve has left other, younger, claimants to the throne trailing, but this book is written as they both begin the slow physical wind-down that is the fate of all elite athletes.

The following pages trace their contrasting lives and their convergence as the unrivalled superstars of one of the greatest and most enduring sporting spectacles of our times. Its highs and lows, its light and shadows – the very human story of two thoroughly modern icons.

1. MADEIRA

The boy, according to the astrological profile, is born destined to defy and overcome the handicap of his immediate circumstances . . .

He likes to be alone, and values his independence more than anything, but can also enjoy being the centre of attention, which will lead others to suspect him of arrogance. In fairness he is an honest guy, if occasionally temperamental.

On 5 February 1985, Dolores Aveiro, a thirty-year-old, long-suffering wife and hard-working mother of three children – a boy and two girls – gave birth to her second son.

In her memoir, published in Portuguese in 2015 under the title *Mother Courage: The Life, Strength, and Faith of a Fighter*, Dolores tells a Dickensian story of her early life. She was born in 1954 in the fishing village of Caniçal, on the Atlantic island of Madeira. She was brought up in an orphanage after her mother died and her father abandoned her. In her early adult years, she suffered and survived poverty, domestic violence and cancer.

Aged eighteen she married Dinis, and had three children – Hugo, Elam and Katia – during her first four years of marriage. Then she fell pregnant for the fourth time. She went to see a doctor to ask whether she could terminate the pregnancy, but he advised strongly against it. Abortion was illegal in Portugal at the time.

Dolores emerged from her consultation deeply depressed. A neighbour told her about a recipe that might just help her abort without seeking medical help. It involved drinking boiling black beer and running until fainting. After considering the 'remedy', Dolores's Catholic upbringing and the doctor's advice about the medical and legal risk she would be taking won out.

Cristiano Ronaldo Aveiro was born at 10.20 a.m. in the Cruz de Carvalho hospital in Funchal, the coastal capital of Madeira. Weighing four kilos and measuring fifty-two centimetres, he was above average in size. 'With that size he will grow up to be a footballer', the gynaecologist told Dolores.

On both his mother and father's side, Ronaldo was descended from islanders of Portuguese stock. A paternal great-grandmother, Isabel Risa Piedade, had been born in Praia, the capital of the Portuguese colony of Cape Verde, off the coast of West Africa.

The Aveiro marriage was defined by the fact that Dinis had been an alcoholic since before Ronaldo was born, and was slowly killing himself while struggling to hold down any kind of job. This is turn meant that Dolores had to spend long periods working away from her children. In her absence, the youngest of the siblings, Cristiano, was looked after by his elder sister, Katia. She took him to school and brought him home at the end of lessons, and helped him with his homework.

The names that Cristiano Ronaldo's mother chose for him tell their own story: the first is an acknowledgement of her Catholic faith, the second is in deference to President Ronald Reagan.

Reagan, a blue-collar boy from Illinois, had worked as a sports commentator and actor before his meteoric rise in union politics saw him elected as governor of California. He then went on to become the most powerful man in the world.

In January 1985, Reagan had been sworn in for his second term as president after winning a landslide, and was well on his way to making more history by contributing to the breakup of the Soviet Union. Deep down, Dolores Aveiro longed for a fairytale rags-to-riches story of her own, one that would transform the misery of her marital life into something worthwhile.

On 25 April 1974, Dolores Aveiro was away working in France when Portugal liberated itself from decades of right-wing dictatorship, thanks to a Communist-supported, populist and largely bloodless military coup. It was popularly called the Revolution of the Carnations, given that its enduring image was that of soldiers with these flowers in the barrels of their guns, placed there by supportive civilians.

By 1985, the year of Ronaldo's birth, the power of the pro-Soviet Portuguese Communist Party, and radical leftism generally, had dissipated in the country. As part of its bid, together with post-Franco Spain, to join the European Union, Portugal had become a politically moderate state.

Madeira, which traditionally had been more conservative than the mainland owing to its dominance by absentee landlords and foreign – mainly British – business interests, had become locally governed by centre-right and traditionally Catholic politicians, led by those in the anti-Communist Social Democratic Party (PSD).

Revolutionary pledges of a Portugal where poverty would be eradicated and all men and women become as they were born – equal – had proved illusory, and with it disappeared Dolores's hope that the Aveiro family might emulate Ronaldo Reagan and reach the height of presidential power one day.

However, in a twist of fate, it was now that the destiny of Dolores Aveiro's fourth-born became sealed, thanks to the decision of his often absent father to make his friend, Fernando Sousa, the young boy's godfather. In 1985, Sousa was the captain of the local football club, Andorinha, where Dinis worked as an unofficial kit man, when not struggling to put in some hours as a municipal gardener close to the neighbourhood's main bar.

In contrast to his friend Dinis, Sousa was in good health and was content in his part-time amateur sporting role. Indeed, the two men's differing dispositions could be traced back to another twist of fate. Fernando had been saved from an experience that had proved traumatic for Dinis – a story I explored when I visited Madeira for the second time in 2016. It is to this story that I now turn, for without it one cannot begin to understand the redemptive nature of the life of Cristiano Ronaldo.

Late one afternoon in November 2016, I found myself being driven up a steep hill to a quiet and modest residential neighbourhood in Funchal. My destination was not far from Quinta de Falcão – the poor barrio where a former shantytown had been transformed into social housing units made of unpainted brick and wood. It was there that Cristiano Ronaldo had spent his childhood, in a three-roomed bungalow.

My guide was João Marquês de Freitas, a retired public prosecutor and influential fan and member of Sporting Clube de Portugal, often known in the UK as Sporting Lisbon. This institution would, of course, be where Ronaldo began his professional career.

For now, de Freitas's contribution to our story was in his service as an army colonel during the early 1970s, in the last days of Portugal's colonial presence in Africa – a protracted effort to hang on to its colonies of Angola, Mozambique and Portuguese Guinea, after armed independence movements had gathered pace in the 1960s.

As with many former colonial powers, the Portuguese have belatedly come to terms with the truth about those wars, but an enduring reticence about debating or examining the bad old days contributed to the neglect of the country's war veterans. As Barry Hatton, author of *The Portuguese*, writes: 'About 9,000 soldiers were killed and at least 12,000 wounded on the African battlefield. Like many armies, they were cheered when they left but forgotten when they returned.'[1]

I was thinking on this when my friend de Freitas volunteered to introduce me to former army colleagues in a war veterans' club. The club was located in a converted nineteenth-century ammunitions depot overlooking the bay of Funchal. The round building of thick stone and the surrounding land had the atmosphere less of an arms dump than a surreal Latin American hacienda – the kind one expected Zorro to jump in and out of, or a modern-day drug trafficker to hide in.

Inside the main building was a large, simply decorated room overhung with wooden beams, its walls covered with scenes of heroic military exploits. It had been renovated, like so many other areas of Madeira, with generous EU funds, and was a belated government response to the needs of thousands of veterans who had survived the military campaign but returned to civilian life either physically injured or psychologically damaged, or both, but who had been forgotten by society as a whole.

Those who fought in Portugal's colonial wars were destined, like the Americans who fought in Southeast Asia before them, to suffer long after they had ceased fighting because of poor medical and psychological support.

'Being in the war meant narrowly escaping death after seeing one's comrade in arms shot or blown up, or killing another human being because he was the enemy. Coming back, for some, was to feel abandoned by the society they had thought they were defending, and living haunted by nightmares that returned, time and time again, when you least expected them,' de Freitas told me.

The veterans' association secretary, retired Lieutenant Colonel

Teixeira de Sousa, then pulled out a small index card. 'Dinis Aveiro,' he read, 'Battalion Number 4910, Company number 3. Enlisted July 1974. Angola.'

Surviving veterans and their family members recall the last months of Portugal's late colonial wars as a horrific experience, made worse by a gradual breakdown of discipline and morale. Gida, a sixty-year-old woman, recounted how her late older brother had served with Dinis Aveiro in Africa. Her brother had told her about the day he had seen four of his closest colleagues blown to bits by mortar shells while they were on patrol: 'He reacted by dropping his rifle, and running away as fast as he could. He kept running and running until collapsing from exhaustion. He was later found by other Portuguese soldiers. When he returned to the mainland, every time he heard a cork pop, or a piece of cutlery hit a plate, he would dive under the table. He died without recovering from his mental breakdown.'

Other soldiers caught malaria, which left them barely able to move and shaking with bouts of heat and cold as the fever took hold. A generation of students or young working-class Portuguese were drafted into military service, most of them against their will. When not out on patrol or escorting trucks along roads studded with mines, they played cards, listened to rock music and smoked joints of local marijuana.

But most of all, they drank a lot of local beer which, unlike non-alcoholic beverages, was never in short supply. It was also essential drinking, because the local water was prone to be unsanitary and used only to wash and cook.

There is a surviving photograph of Dinis Aveiro from his time in Africa. He is sitting on the engine chassis of a car with his friend Alberto Martins. The thickset Martins, long haired and wearing sunglasses, wears an open, broad-collared shirt and bell-bottom trousers. In contrast, Dinis has short hair and is dressed in military fatigues. With a skinnier frame, he stares at the camera with deeply set eyes, unsmiling, tight-lipped, his torso even tenser than his face.

'The young soldiers out in Africa began to drink a lot,' Lieutenant Colonel de Sousa told me. 'Sometimes out of boredom, but mainly out of fear, as an escape, as a denial of an existence they couldn't handle. It was in Africa that soldiers became alcoholics. Those who returned to Madeira were particularly prone to addiction because the island – still very poor in the 1970s – had transformed its vineyards for domestic consumption as well as export. When they got back from the war, there was a lot of drink available and not much work.'

'We were told we were there to keep the peace, but we were caught in the crossfire of rival factions, fire-fighting, trying to put out one fire and having another one blow up in our face,' recalled another veteran, Fernando Luís, whose brother was in the same company as Dinis Aveiro.

After returning to civilian life, Luís refereed in the local regional football league, and of the days he crossed paths with Cristiano Ronaldo's father, one endures in his memory more than any other.

It was before a game, and Luís was changing into his referee's kit in the cramped, poorly equipped changing rooms that Andorinha shared with visitors. They heard a frantic thumping on the door and raucous cries of 'Let the people in! Everyone wants to watch this match! Let them in!'

It was Dinis Aveiro, blind drunk, as he often was.

Aveiro's increasingly irrational and tortured behaviour strained his marriage and distanced him from the few friends he had known from childhood, and those he had made prior to and during the war. And while the Andorinha clubhouse became a kind of second home to him for a while, he eventually squandered any respect anyone in the club might have had for him, beyond the fact that some held him indirectly responsible for putting Cristiano Ronaldo on the road to success.

If Ronaldo, in later years, could never bring himself to belittle or diminish his dad, it was because he owed his own motivation and ambition to making up for Dinis's failings. From a young age, Cristiano set about proving he could not only conquer demons, but draw strength from confronting them.

The tall bell tower of the Church of Nuestra Señora de Guadalupe looms over the hillside neighbourhood of San Antonio, and the adjacent, poor quarter of Quinta de Falcão, where Cristiano Ronaldo grew up. The church's most venerated icons are the local St Anthony, the Immaculate Conception, our Lady of Sorrow, the Crucified Christ, and last but by no means least, Cristiano Ronaldo, for he was christened there.

Fernando Sousa, the godfather who was spared the military draft, will never forget the look of despair, verging on anger, on the face of the local parish priest as he and his half-drunk friend Dinis arrived half an hour late for Ronaldo's baptism. The two men had spent the afternoon some thirty kilometres away at Andorinha's match against local rival Ribeira Brava – Sousa, of course, played as team captain, while Dinis filled in as kit man when not retiring to the changing rooms for a top-up from his bottle of rough wine.

Many years later, Sousa would try and make light of the fact that he and the baby's father nearly wrecked the entire ceremony. A less patient priest would have simply declared it null and void. Rather than blame Dinis's drunkenness, Sousa blamed the bad state of the mountain road they had had to drive along in order to get to Funchal.

'The match ended a bit later than we thought, we miscalculated the time it would take us. The priest was a patient type, thank God, but, more important, he was an Andorinha fan, so our excuse had his blessing in the end.'

Thus did football define the timing and nature of Cristiano Ronaldo's admission into the Catholic Church, as well as his destiny. It was there, in that church of white stone and dark timber, as she stood waiting, clutching her latest child in her arms, that Dolores finally came to terms with the fact that she could not depend on her husband for her son's wellbeing.

I had looked forward to my first meeting with Cristiano Ronaldo's godfather with some trepidation. Even though the player, in young adulthood, had given control of his career to his agent Jorge Mendes, part of me wondered if Sousa had survived in the family saga as something of an enforcer.

As it turned out, Sousa was no Don Corleone, but rather a genial if slightly bumptious pensioner, who arrived late for our meeting in a small car, blaming his lateness on the fact that the hotel I was staying in would not let him park because he wasn't a client, even though the owners were business partners of Ronaldo, his godson.

While he talked of having visited Madrid twice in recent years to watch Ronaldo play, Sousa seemed to have long since ceased to have regular contact with him. Nonetheless, he had been a major part of the formative years of his godson's life – the early years of hardship and family trauma, which never included the word 'abuse', but were underpinned by a redemptive gloss which no one on the island of Madeira was prepared to contradict.

'When you're born into poverty, a toy, any toy is steeped in magic,' I wrote in *Hand of God*, my biography of Diego Maradona,[2] who was given his first football aged three by his Uncle Cirilo. The Aveiro home in Quinta de Falcão had no mobile phones, games consoles, tablet computers, voice-recognition puppies or robot kits. But it did have a football, which Sousa gave his godson after he had given him a toy car and he had thrown a tantrum.

From an early age, Ronaldo showed a burning ambition to be the best, even though he knew that the odds were stacked against him, not least because of the remoteness and outsider status of the island where he'd been born.

In that respect, it's interesting to consider the long shadow cast by Eusébio de Silva Ferreira, the Mozambiquan-born Portuguese national, considered one of the greatest players of the twentieth century. Eusébio, as he became more popularly known, moved from his native Mozambique when it was still a Portuguese colony to Lisbon, where he played for Benfica and Portugal's national squad. A great inside-forward, Eusébio possessed a staggeringly effective right foot with flowing control and explosive acceleration, and could leave defenders trailing in his wake. He could also dribble and was good in the air. A superb athlete, he was graceful in movement as well as enormously powerful.

Closer to Africa than to the European mainland, and a natural stopoff point for those travelling across the Atlantic, the island of Madeira had always struggled with its identity. As a staging post for trade for centuries, its population became diverse and cosmopolitan for somewhere so remote. Yet that same trade only enriched the few, and the gap between rich and poor on the island has been profound since the seventeenth century. Both foreign settlers and Portuguese landowners built palatial houses with large manicured gardens, filled with exotic plants and flowers, contrasting with the poorer neighbourhoods' rudimentary huts, or, later, workers' bungalows and council flats subsidized by the state, such as the one in which Ronaldo's family lived.

Ronaldo's success has put the island on the map for new generations, and the pride that the island has in him is not just as a Madeiran but as a Portuguese citizen. He is part of both the island's and the nation's sense of self-worth, for Portugal has spent most of her history regarding herself as one of Europe's underdogs.

As Hatton points out in *The Portuguese*: 'A common sentiment among the Portuguese is that the odds are stacked against them, that they are playing a losing game with fate.' He quotes Fernando Pessoa, one of Portugal's greatest poets, who in 1928 described the nation as 'slumbering' since the maritime feats of the glorious Age of Discovery, its fate determined by foreigners, and, in Hatton's words, 'doomed to be a B-list country.'[3]

Fertile ground, then, for someone determined to defy the personal and social circumstances of his upbringing.

In his childhood, Cristiano played his first football games on the unpaved streets near his home, with stones piled up as goalposts, and sometimes only a wall as a teammate. The location of the neighbourhood, on a steep hill, meant that from an early age Cristiano would face arduous walks to school and back. With the strength of his legs and feet and his balance severely tested, he would make his way along rough, narrow paths, with a sheer drop on either side. Cristiano became streetwise and physically resilient.

'The street gives you cockiness. If you are born in a poor neighbourhood you step out, or they step on you. Cristiano was aware of that from the day he could walk,' recalled family friend Rui Santos, who was president of Andorinha, Cristiano's first football club.

There is one 'official' family memory that has the young Cristiano following his father – the kit man – as he carried a huge bag of balls around with him, and Sousa giving him one of them, with Dinis's blessing.

'Dinis was really proud of his youngest child from the first day he came into the world,' Sousa told me as we sat drinking coffee in Madeira's biggest shopping mall, ignored by the passing public. The 'godfather' clung onto those childhood memories, for they placed him, for a brief period, at the centre of the life of a future superstar.

'Cristiano was, in his childhood years, playing for Andorinha, rather like his father; thin, and very agile. Of course he didn't drink, but he also didn't eat much and when he played football he was very fast and moody.

'His dad called him the "little rat", because of the way he dribbled round the other boys. And Cristiano always wanted to win! He would argue with his teammates and cry if he missed a goal or the team lost.'

Ronaldo played for Andorinha for two years, when he was seven and eight. One of the local kids who played with him, Ricardo Santos, the son of the club president Rui, remembered that Cristiano was not particularly strong and was not the tallest of his group – although he was certainly not the smallest: 'He was good and could score goals and he always wanted to win, and yes he had a temper and would indeed burst into tears if he lost.'

Ricardo now trains young children, when not managing the clubhouse bar at the all-weather turf grounds Andorinha have built since the days Ronaldo was there. In his day, the local boys had to settle for a rougher, unturfed surface that the club shared with a school. While Ronaldo went on to become a major global sporting icon, Ricardo Santos stayed more or less in the place he had kicked his first football. It was unclear whether his reluctance to talk much about his childhood teammate stemmed from a scarcely repressed resentment at having lost out on the lottery of life, or loyalty to a former teammate.

By contrast, his father Rui is a small dynamo of a man. I met him at the foot of the main staircase in the municipal building of San Antonio Funchal, where he had been elected as the council leader. He asked me to wait while he settled a dispute between two social workers over a room that had been double booked, then took me up to his spartan office.

Rui Santos was only thirteen when the Portuguese Revolution broke out in 1974 – 'I felt the younger people were happy but the older people not so much' – so was also spared conscription and the subsequent trauma suffered by Dinis. He befriended Ronaldo's parents, and at one point offered them both work in his uncle's artisan wicker factory. He also witnessed at close quarters the deterioration of their marriage as Dinis's alcohol addiction grew, making it impossible for him to get full-time employment.

Meanwhile, as president, Rui spent many weekends watching Cristiano play his first club games for Andorinha: 'When he was a kid, his technique set him apart from the others. He learnt step-overs, was fast, and had a hunger for goal, although I would be lying to you if I told you that I knew then what he was destined to become,' Rui recalled.

But if Cristiano Ronaldo had yet to develop the physique and skills that would turn him into a superstar, it was only a matter of time before someone identified his potential, and that person was his godfather.

Compared to mainland Europe, football as popular pastime took root belatedly in Madeira. One of the island's more flourishing export businesses, that of wine, was run by well-resourced British families educated in English public schools, who had grown up playing rugby and golf. Unlike their nineteenth- and early twentieth-century compatriots in mainland Iberia and South America, the British in Madeira showed no interest in importing football. Thus football on the island developed more slowly, its following further handicapped by the mountainous terrain and poor communications and infrastructure which left many parts of Madeira isolated.

What it lacked in early foreign influence, however, it made up for with a strong sense of regional identity, underlined by a traditional insularity. The island's oldest surviving major clubs, Club Sport Marítimo and Nacional, were both founded in 1910, when Madeira felt the aftershock of political upheaval on mainland Portugal. In that year, the monarchy was overthrown and a republic proclaimed, but Portuguese football didn't keep pace with social change, and was destined for decades of underachievement, not least in Madeira.

When Cristiano Ronaldo was born in 1985, Madeira had little to boast of in football terms. Of the island's clubs, only Marítimo had managed to win the Portuguese championship, in 1926, and became Madeira's only permanent presence in the Portuguese League from the early 1970s.

By contrast, Nacional earned an early reputation less for its football than for its cultural eclecticism, spreading its thin resources across a number of locally popular activities like volleyball, hockey and swimming. One of the club's enduring legends was the athletic and strikingly handsome swimmer José da Silva, known as 'Saca', who set new 1,500 and 1,000-metre freestyle national records in the late 1940s, before seeing his popularity increase as a result of his long-distance swims, including a successful crossing of the English Channel.

In Nacional's official illustrated history, published in 2010 to commemorate the club's centenary, Saca is one of two club icons given considerable coverage. The other is Cristiano Ronaldo, who played in Nacional's junior teams for two seasons in the mid-1990s and who, a matter of weeks after signing, found himself taking a central place in the team photograph as captain.

The photograph shows Ronaldo standing stiffly, arms held behind his back like a military cadet and with a more intense, seemingly self-confident look than any of his teammates, from whom he seems aloof. In the image, Ronaldo already seems to define himself as someone who is the leader because he believes he is, and as someone on the road to the top. As he put it in an interview in 2010, recalling those early days at Nacional, 'I felt that I was different. Why? I don't know, maybe because I was more ambitious.'

In truth, he might have stayed on the island of Madeira, gradually fading into oblivion, had it not been for his godfather and mother deciding that the club they were fans of, Nacional – rather than its more historically successful and seemingly better-resourced rival Marítimo, which Dinis supported – was the next step up after Andorinha.

The traditional gap between Marítimo and Nacional had been narrowing for years, thanks to science professor turned football manager António Lourenço, who was appointed head of Nacional's youth development programme in 1978.

Learning from the experience of leading Portuguese mainland clubs like Benfica and Sporting, Lourenço convinced senior executives and other backers to help finance a significant investment in new training techniques, diet and medical assistance. The programme expanded the club's reach across the island's school system in a concerted effort to tap the largest pool of available talent, with the ultimate aim of Nacional producing a senior team capable of competing successfully in the upper echelons of the Portuguese leagues.

Thanks to Lourenço, by the early 1990s, when it came to deciding on Cristiano Ronaldo's next step up, there was little to choose between Marítimo and Nacional, and both clubs were interested. The fact that Dinis was actually a Marítimo fan counted for very little in the decision-making process, perhaps other than reinforcing Dolores's determination to stick to Nacional, on Fernando Sousa's advice.

One somewhat farcical version of what happened next has Bernardino Rosa, the head of recruitment at the Marítimo academy, missing an allegedly crucial meeting that had been arranged by Andorinha because of a poorly organized schedule. Nacional's representative was present, Rosa was not.

But, according to Rui Santos, the president of Andorinha at the time, the move to Nacional was a done deal, with or without the Marítimo meeting going ahead. The key factor was the friendship that Fernando Sousa had with senior officials and staff at Nacional, among them the youth coach António Mendoça, who had been scouting for talent and had expressed his admiration for Cristiano.

When I caught up with Santos more than twenty years later, he remained philosophical about how he had ended up handing over his star player. 'Nacional just had better resources to develop him as a player and allow him to make that next step,' he said. In fact, Santos not only had little say in the decision but the move didn't much matter to him at the time – he claims that no one on the island foresaw the superstar that Ronaldo would eventually become. The 'deal' involved a very modest transfer payment in Portuguese escudos, equivalent to about £1,500, and two sets of semi-complete cast-off football kits – shorts, socks and boots, but no shirts, as the clubs' colours didn't match.

'Dolores was the decisive factor,' Fernando Sousa told me, 'because she told me she wanted Nacional and she looked to me as the person who had Cristiano's best interests at heart, and as someone who protected him. That was my duty as a godfather.'

After arriving at Nacional aged ten, Ronaldo showed from early on his potential, playing seven-a-side and later eleven-a-side, often competing against boys from older teams. One youth coach there at the time, Pedro Talinhas, recalled: 'He was very good technically, he was very good with both feet. His objective was to score beautiful goals. He was fast, great at shooting, he was already powerful.'

His exceptional speed, dribbling and finishing were apparent to the youth coaching staff, but so was his resilience. As Mendoça recalled: 'Street football had taught him how to avoid being hit, side-step the opponent and face up to kids much bigger than he was. It had also strengthened his character – he was extremely courageous.'

By eleven years of age, Cristiano was also showing the emotional volatility that would come to be seen as a characteristic of his game.

'When Nacional was losing, he'd be playing and crying at the same time,' Talinhas recalled.

According to Talinhas, the player's 'troublesome temperament' included a lack of team spirit. From his early days at Nacional, he showed a tendency, once he had picked up the ball, to run with it and keep running with it, rather than pass it, with only one aim in his head – to score a goal. Coaching staff saw their main challenge as trying to get Ronaldo to see football as a collective sport, where each player, not just him, had a part to play.

At the same time, they recognized that Ronaldo's self-belief was a fundamental part of his character. It was a response he drew from within himself to the adversity that had haunted him from birth. It was not just that he had learnt to play football on the rough streets, and developed his stamina and physique walking up and down steep slopes. The fact that his father made a habit of turning up to watch him play at Nacional, but seemingly remained disconnected from what he saw, was both an embarrassment and an incentive to play better.

In his analysis of the internal dynamic forces which motivate creativity among iconic figures, the distinguished English psychiatrist Anthony Storr notes how ambition can sustain self-esteem and develop as a motivating force in response to deprivation of parental affection in childhood.

In Cristiano's case, there seems little doubt that his childhood was overshadowed by the alcoholism of his father, whose condition made him incapable of providing the support and encouragement his talented child craved.

In *Ronaldo*, the authorized 2015 documentary directed by Anthony Wonke, which was filmed with the support of Ronaldo and his agent Jorge Mendes, there are two striking images of Dinis: one a framed photograph of a gaunt, unshaven man with a vacant stare, hung on an otherwise undecorated white wall in Cristiano's Madrid home; the other a video clip of a similarly wasted figure, looking awkward and disengaged, but managing a smile and a token show of affection towards his son, in a rare glimpse of family life in the early days in Madeira.

The family life that Ronaldo experienced as a child was far from normal. As he himself recalls in that documentary: 'My father was drunk almost every day. It was very difficult to get to know him. I never had a connection with him. I feel frustrated he wasn't around more.'[4]

Cristiano Ronaldo would not only survive but draw strength from early hardships. His self-belief, based on a trust in his talent and hard work, fuelled his desire to seek 'the recognition and acclaim which accrue from external achievement'. Words written by Anthony Storr about the psyche of Winston Churchill.

Dolores Aveiro likes to tell the story of when Ronaldo fell ill with flu before the final of a regional competition. She wanted him to stay in bed, but he insisted on playing. 'If I feel too ill, they can always substitute me,' he told her.[5] They never did substitute him. He played and helped the team win the tournament.

At Nacional, Cristiano Ronaldo showed a tendency to argue with his teammates. The other boys put up with it only because he proved a prolific goal scorer, and he became a key element in Nacional's youth category success, with the team often beating opponents by a margin of nine or ten goals. Cristiano spent two years with the Madeiran club, enhancing his reputation on the island and catching the attention of scouts from the Portuguese mainland.

2. ROSARIO

If Bilbo Baggins had existed in real life, he may have shown a striking similarity to a young Lionel Messi. For Bilbo, in J. R .R. Tolkien's novel, is the most heroic of the hobbits, a diminutive, shy race nevertheless capable of great courage and amazing feats under the right circumstances. Bilbo's rites of passage were also made in exile, after moving from one mythical kingdom to another in search of his destiny.

The Messi legend had an inauspicious beginning. Unlike another stocky Argentine, who was to overshadow much of his adult career, Lionel Andrés Messi's birth on 24 June 1987, just a few minutes before six a.m., was not announced in mythical terms. For Lionel Messi there was not a star glowing in the southern hemisphere, as legend claims there was at Maradona's birth. Nor did Messi come out, like Diego, kicking, with his mother letting out a cry that many years later would be echoed by commentators around the world. GOOOOOOOL!

On the day Messi was born, many Argentines would have been celebrating the anniversaries of three icons – the births of the racing driver Juan Manuel Fangio and literary giant Ernesto Sabato, and the death of Carlos Gardel, the legendary tango singer. Despite these precedents, Lionel's birth was a mundane affair, with minimum excitement. Doctors had diagnosed foetal distress and had thought of delivering with forceps. It proved unnecessary. The third son of Celia Cuccittini and her husband Jorge was born without complications in Rosario's Hospital Garibaldi. Baby Lionel was small in frame – he weighed 3.6 kilograms and measured 47 centimetres, and had ancestral roots shared somewhere in that Middle Earth between Italy and Spain. His older brothers were Rodrigo and Matías. A sister, María, would come later.

Although Argentina was originally colonized by Spaniards, its growth as a modern nation was down to a mixture of mainly European immigrants, led by the Italians. By the end of the 1920s, Italians comprised about 42 per cent of the total influx of immigrants to Argentina. Rosario, the riverside city at the heart of the fertile temperate prairies, or pampas, where the Messis had settled, had seen its immigrant population mushroom in the second half of the nineteenth century, owing to the productivity of its surrounding land and the trade that went through its port, but also thanks to the expansion of the British-built railways, whose engineers and workers founded the country's first football clubs.

Rosario's population spoke Spanish with an Italian intonation, and generated a political, social and religious culture that was as much Italian as Hispanic in its intrigue, corruption and superstitions. Its most popular sport, however, had distinctly English roots. The city's two major football clubs, Rosario Central and Newell's Old Boys, were founded in 1889 and 1903 respectively – Central by English railway workers and Newell's by an English teacher from Kent, Isaac Newell.

The Messi ancestral tree, though, had grown from Catalan as well as Italian roots. His paternal great-grandmother had been born in Tragó de Noguera, a small municipality that was deliberately flooded as part of a Franco-era hydroelectric scheme. Messi's forebear, Rosa Gese, was long gone, having emigrated to Argentina in the 1920s. Other traces of Messi's Catalan ancestry survive. I was shown them by a retired teacher turned diligent local historian, Ana Miralles, about an hour's drive from the now-ruined Noguera, in the village of Bellcaire d'Urgell. It is there that another of Messi's paternal great-grandparents, José Pérez Solé, was born in the nineteenth century.

Bellcaire is a somewhat down-at-heel village; most of the young adults have migrated to northern Europe in search of work. On the day I visited, the village bar was occupied by unemployed barflies and pensioners, playing cards or collapsed over their wine jars. Not a romantic source of Messi's connection to Catalonia. It was in the ancient church, following a discovery of its hidden archive, that Ana Miralles had found a crucial birth certificate that allowed her to trace Messi's ancestors through various generations, until the two lines converged on a transatlantic liner called, appropriately, *El Catala* – the Catalan. It was aboard *El Catala* that Rosa Mateu I Gesé met José Pérez de Solé. The two settled in Rosario and had three children, one of whom, Rosa María Pérez, married an Italian immigrant called Eusébio Messi, grandfather of Lionel.

Catalan and Italian roots converged still further when Lionel's father, Jorge, married Celia Cuccittini, the daughter of Italian immigrants. Celia is named after her mother, Messi's much-adored grandmother and the woman he immortalizes by pointing to the heavens every time he scores a goal (she died in 1998).

It was Grannie Celia who used to reassure Messi when he was a mere toddler and holding his first ball, telling him not to worry about his small size, but to dream of becoming the best footballer in the world one day – as good as Diego Maradona, who a year before Messi was born had dazzled the globe during the World Cup in Mexico.

The recollections of boyhood teammates and grainy video footage leave little room for doubt that, from early childhood, Lionel Messi was possessed of enormous vitality and a natural talent for football. But, of course, he was also very small.

Almost as soon as he learnt to walk and run, Lionel found himself drawn into the improvised kick-arounds and matches that took place in the streets and square near his family home at number 525 Estado de Israel, an unassuming medium-sized house of painted concrete in a lower-middle-class neighbourhood of Rosario. The neighbourhood that Messi was born into was not one of the rougher ones of the Zona Sur, the south side of the city, but much of Rosario – a city of pervasive extremes – is a patchwork of speculative housing development and overlapping neighbourhoods, where social divisions are often not geographically delineated.

Lionel was part of an intimate group made up of his brothers Rodrigo (seven years older), Matías (five years older) and his cousins Maxi (three years older) and Emanuel (one year younger) Biancucchi, both of whom went on to become professional footballers. Lionel and the others used the patio of his house as a training pen, and the walls of nearby houses to practise passing and goal scoring. The little group provided a protective circle for Messi; while he was conscious from an early age that he was smaller than the others, they noted in him courage and skill that was based not on any natural physical superiority, but on a determination to be tough in spite of his lack of height and muscle.

The Messi brothers' father, Jorge, looked on whenever work allowed, and went to watch all his sons play in competitive matches, taking a particular interest in Lionel from his early days at a local youth team, for it was soon evident that he had a special talent with the ball.

It was Grandoli Football Club, not far from the banks of the Paraná River, in a rough, working-class neighbourhood on the outskirts of Rosario, where Messi played between the ages of five to almost seven. The club, funded by local parents, was the brainchild of Salvador Aparicio, a retired railway worker who thought organized football – with training, games, and a local league cup to compete for – might be a good way of keeping some of the local kids out of trouble.

Grandoli was within walking distance of the Messi family home. Football proved a social leveller, bringing Lionel together with children of more deprived backgrounds, who were on a poorer diet and lived in makeshift shanties of scrap metal, loose bricks and cardboard – dwellings much like Maradona's childhood home in Villa Fiorito, a suburb of Buenos Aires.

Many goals were scored, first at Grandoli and then at Newell's Old Boys, which he joined at just six years of age. Early footage shows Messi during his first year with Newell's, dribbling the ball through a team of players of similar age but twice his size. During the six years Messi played for Newell's, he scored almost 500 goals as part of a team that achieved a legendary reputation and became known as La Máquina (The Machine).

Messi's birthright, it seemed, was to be invincible. La Máquina swept all before them, going unbeaten for three years in seven-a-side games, and then, after they had graduated to the eleven-a-side format at age eleven, winning competitions in both Argentina and Peru. His teammates remember Messi losing his normal reserve when someone didn't pass him the ball when he wanted it, or when he missed a chance. But if Messi seemed insatiable in his hunger for goals, neither his courage nor his skill were alone sufficient to deliver on his ambition to grow up, as his beloved grandmother dreamed for him, to be a player as good as Maradona.

The people of Rosario felt a particular sense of collective humiliation after the Falklands War of 1982, for its main association with it was not a heroic one. The president of Argentina, General Leopoldo Galtieri, who had sparked the war by plotting and leading the invasion of the islands, was earlier in his career the officer in charge of an infamous military battalion based in Rosario, known as Battalion 121. It was one of the military units, following the coup of 1976, that was involved in the torture and disappearance of thousands of civilians.

Lionel's father, Jorge Messi, did his military service in his late teens, during the bloody regime of the juntas. He then applied for and got a job on the shop floor of Acindar, a steel company founded during the Second World War, which grew in the post-war years into a major state enterprise managed by the Argentine military and their civilian allies.

Following the collapse of the military regime after the Falklands War, General Galtieri was among several military officers given heavy prison sentences for human rights violations. Evidence produced by state prosecutors included the repression of trade union activists in some of the factories owned by Acindar, and the illegal detention, torture and execution without trial of numerous political dissidents by army units like Rosario's Battalion 121.

Army veterans from those years of internal repression claimed that conscripts doing their military service simply followed orders, and that the torture and summary executions involved smaller numbers of specifically tasked killers. There is no suggestion that Messi's father was one of the killers.

The main factories of the military industrial complex, including those owned by Acindar, were taken out of the control of the Argentine armed forces and privatized after the restoration of democracy in 1984. By then, Jorge Messi had risen from the factory floor to secure a well-paid job as supervisor. The neighbourhood where he and his family lived had for years grown under the shadow of Battalion 121 – the buildings and playing fields of its large military compound dwarfed the primary school where the Messi children were sent.

Then, as now, Rosario was a town where you were well advised to watch your step, and not just on the bumpy football turf. In its modern history, the sprawling riverside port had gained a reputation for living dangerously. Nicknamed 'the Chicago of the South', it had become a centre for the modern slavery trade and international drug trafficking, when not the setting for periodic political protest and violent repression by the state.

It was a town which was nonetheless proud of its relatively modern cultural legacy and its enduring passion for football. It had produced three of Argentina's most popular singers – Fito Páez, Litto Nebbia and Juan Carlos Baglietto – and one of the country's most talented literary figures, the cartoonist and writer Roberto Fontanarrosa, who created the gaucho Inodoro Pereyra, a nobly spirited if luckless cowboy, and also wrote lyrically about football.

Among the players who began their career in Rosario was the World Cup winner and later director of sport at Real Madrid, Jorge Valdano. Rosario is also the town that produced two of the most famous coaches in Argentine football history – César Menotti and Marcelo Bielsa. 'There are other more cultured cities,' Menotti commented once, 'but in Rosario what matters more than anything else is football. Rosario loves football.'[1]

Both Menotti and Bielsa, each in their own way, made of football a refined art, both in the way they talked about the sport and the carefully choreographed team tactics and creative individualism they encouraged. Bielsa is popularly known as El Profesor – such is his cerebral approach to the game, and his tendency towards eccentricity. Among his disciples is Pep Guardiola who, just before his time as coach of FC Barcelona, famously disappeared on a three-day 'retreat' with Bielsa in Argentina, during which the two men did nothing other than drink, eat and talk incessantly about football.

The passion for football in Rosario has also combined with the city's edge to produce one of the most violent local club rivalries to be found anywhere in the world – that between Rosario Central and Newell's Old Boys. When Messi was growing up in Rosario, as part of a family united in its unquestioning support for Newell's, football there gained its reputation as much for what occurred off the pitch as on it, with its modern history tainted by the corruption and violence that characterized economic life and local and national politics.

The historic rivalry between Newell's and Rosario Central has often deteriorated into gang warfare between rival fans, who go by the names respectively of Leprosos (Lepers) and Canallas (Scoundrels). The origin of the terms was Newell's Old Boys' request at some point during the 1920s that Rosario Central play them in a benefit match to raise funds to fight leprosy, of which there were still cases occurring in northern parts of Argentina and other neighbouring Latin American countries. The request was turned down by Rosario Central, as the club suspected that the funds might be misappropriated, although Newell's put down the rejection to sheer bloody-mindedness.

From that moment, Newell's fans called their rivals 'scoundrels', and the Central fans hit back by calling Newell's 'lepers'. The terms would regularly dominate local murals, which in turn delineated the club loyalties of specific neighbourhoods. Territories, which some-times cut across each other, were aggressively defended by fans of one club or the other as part of a permanent communitarian civil war, with club organizations mirroring each other in their lack of transpar-ency and accountability and in the way they disposed of assets or invested in players and property – all of which was closely linked to the drugs trade and money laundering throughout the 1980s and 1990s.

Such was the bad blood in local football during Messi's childhood that the clubs even disputed the legacy of Rosario's most famous political icon – Ernesto Guevara de la Serna, more popularly known as Che Guevara. Guevara was born in Rosario into a middle-class family, but the family did not live there for long before moving north to Córdoba, where Ernesto went to school and later studied medicine.

In his biography of Guevara, the left-wing Argentine author Hugo Gambini – himself an ex-guerrilla fighter – claims that the young Guevara became a fan of Rosario Central simply because the club name included the name of his birthplace, and because he wanted to be different to most of his classmates, who were supporters of Buenos Aires giants Boca Juniors and River Plate. He recounts El Che answer-ing with delight whenever he was asked where he was from: 'I am a Rosarino', ignoring the fact he knew almost nothing about the city and had certainly never seen the team play.

In 1952, Guevara, then a twenty-four-year-old medical student roughing it with his friend Alberto Granado on a Norton 500 motor-bike, had a chance meeting with the future Real Madrid star Alfredo Di Stéfano when the Argentine-born player was playing for Millonar-ios, the Colombian club. Granado and Guevara, unshaven and unwashed after many days on the road, asked Di Stéfano for tickets to a football match in the capital Bogotá, a request the player was only too happy to comply with after taking pity on what he took to be two out-of-luck fellow Argentines. So it was that – for one time only – the world's most famous guerrilla fighter and one of the best players in the history of football appeared in the same stadium.

The early home-video shots taken by Jorge Messi of his third son playing his first football games show an undersized boy, dwarfed by the others of the age group, defiant and determined, seemingly intent on replicating Maradona as he picks up the ball and dribbles end-to-end, the ball stuck to his foot.

Jorge, never far from his boy whenever he played matches, filmed the young Lionel playing so frequently partly because his son showed little interest in anything else. Jorge was also consciously building up a record of his youngest son's genius as a prime asset, and as part of an investment in his and the family's future.

When he was a part of La Máquina at Newell's youth section, Lionel was brought on at half-time during a first-team League match and, before an astonished crowd, gave an exhibition of his skills, juggling the ball from one foot to the other with a dexterity which instantly convinced one of his first coaches, Quique Dominguez, that he was something special. The year was 1996, and Lionel Messi was nine years old. The prodigy's profile was already growing.

Others began to think of another genius when they saw the tricks the little Messi could perform with the ball. During a victory parade of the Newell's first team, when Messi did his party piece and played with the ball like a juggler, the stadium chorused '¡¡Maradó, Maradó!!'

Thus, from an early stage, did the Messi story seem destined to have as its point of reference that of an earlier legend. Back in 1971, Maradona, aged ten, was brought on at half-time during a first division match between Argentinos Juniors and Independiente, also to show off his tricks.

In 2016, I met Quique Dominguez in Rosario. The son of a Syrian immigrant, he was as portly in his retirement as he had been when a coach. (For his part, Messi saw in his coach a reassuring if slightly overweight father figure. He used to call Quique 'Father Christmas.') Quique retained the engaging informality of an Arab street trader, one unspoilt by conceit, despite the fact he had played a not insignificant role in the story of a football icon.

'My first eye contact with Leo Messi was during that half-time period, when I saw this undersized boy with a ball bigger than his head, doing little tricks so that it never fell from his boots. I thought, This guy is a magician, not just a football player. Within two years I was his coach, and that of the brilliant so-called Class of 87. Everyone was talking about how brilliant they were, and that was because there was one player in particular who was quite simply out of this world. But I was also struck by just how small he continued to be compared to others. In the changing room, he would always put his shirt on with his back to us. I later realized that he was trying to hide from us how fragile he looked, for I saw his chest. It was very sunken.'

The young Messi did not look, as Maradona had at the same age, an unwashed urchin, escaped from a piece of wasteland. His skin was lighter, his long hair better groomed; not a shantytown kid at all but one who had just taken a break from school lessons to put on the oversized Newell's football kit, which hung from him like a drenched overcoat.

One film clip shows Messi playing in a sports centre where Newell's youngsters played seven-a-side. The boy Messi plays with the confidence and poise of an adult player, even if his shirt and shorts are too big for him. The sight of this boy's love for the ball filled Quique and others who watched with a sense of a future, a belief that Argentine football had the capacity to continue to nourish itself, invent something new.

Looking back over those years, Messi would insist he didn't have any idols when he was a child, but did follow the fortunes of Pablo Aimar. The statement seemed a deliberate effort not to be drawn into comparisons with Maradona, a god few Argentines believed or wished could be dethroned in the mythological pantheon. Aimar was a good player, although obviously lacking the sublime skills of Maradona. What made Aimar a more acceptable role model for the shy, retiring, football-obsessed Messi was that he was a model professional, not identified with the celebrity and drugs culture in which Maradona immersed himself after Mexico '86.

Much like the young Cristiano Ronaldo, and the young Maradona before them, Messi did not like losing or not getting his way. He would throw little tantrums when playing cards, or when he didn't feel like going to school, or when he missed a chance on the pitch. A famous Messi family story is that of the young boy getting locked inside his house alone by mistake, just before he was due to head off to play in a match. He broke a bathroom skylight, crawled through it and climbed down to the street rather than miss the match. He arrived at the game to find Newell's two goals down with only a few minutes left. Messi was quickly subbed on, and scored two in a rapid-fire comeback, including the winner.

As one of his teammates at the time, Gerardo Grighini, would later recall in an interview with the Argentine newspaper *Perfil*:

'Messi was a real son of a bitch, but in the good sense of the term. Because when he played he was terrifying: he would take the ball and run past any opponent he wanted. Once, when we were playing in a youth game, Clásico against Rosario Central, he scooped the ball over the same defender – a classic sombrero trick – five times during the match, and maintained possession each time. You could hear the defender's dad, out of sheer frustration, screaming, "Kill him, kill him." He didn't, of course. He couldn't have done so even if he'd wanted to.'[2]

Young Lionel was not only having to develop mental fortitude on the pitch. When Messi had first started playing at Grandoli, his mother would stay behind to deal with the domestic chores, in between her hours at a magnet manufacturing workshop. With Jorge also often working long hours, it was his beloved grandmother, Celia, who had accompanied Lionel the fifteen blocks from home to the sports ground and back again. All the while offering encouragement and support to the slight child. He was just ten years old when Celia was diagnosed with Alzheimer's. The degenerative disease drained her mentally and physically, and she died just short of Messi's eleventh birthday. Lionel was so distraught that at her funeral he clung to her coffin, weeping uncontrollably. 'For Leo, it was like losing a part of himself,' wrote one of Messi's earlier biographers, the Catalan journalist Toni Frieros.[3]

One more story from this period has come to seem significant. It has the ten-year-old Messi playing Nintendo at a friend's house with a group of other boys. Before the game began, the friend would produce football shirts with different club colours, and each of those present was free to choose his favourite colours to wear while they played. Messi always chose those of FC Barcelona.

3. RITES OF PASSAGE: RONALDO

In 1986, the year after Cristiano Ronaldo was born, Portugal signed up to the European Economic Community, stimulating a consumer bonanza and accelerating the country's embrace of a liberal parliamentary system, and changes in social mores.

By 1996, Portuguese football was ready to enter a new stage in its history, with one of its biggest clubs taking a serious punt on a player – not from the mainland or one of its African colonies, but from Madeira, an island better known for its wine and its plants than any aspect of its local sports.

Fernando Sousa was that player's godfather, who had recommended Ronaldo to his friends at Nacional's academy. Sousa decided to contact a friend, João Marquês de Freitas, after Cristiano's mother had suggested her son's best hope of a decent future was in making money as a football player, and pursuing his career on the Portuguese mainland.

De Freitas was an influential Madeiran lawyer, who worked as an attorney for the Portuguese state. His network of contacts on the Portuguese mainland extended to Sporting Clube de Portugal, the Lisbon club of which he was a passionate supporter. De Freitas was on good terms with all the senior directors and technical staff, thanks to his long service as the president of Sporting's fan club in Madeira.

As described in the first chapter, Nacional had grown as a sporting entity during the 1980s and 1990s, but still lacked the resources of the big clubs on the mainland. If football was to offer a potential escape from Cristiano's adverse family circumstances, Sousa and Dolores Aveiro agreed that they would have to embrace the opportunities de Freitas's contacts offered. If Cristiano failed to impress in Lisbon, they would think again, but at the time it was all that was on offer. As a player he seemed to be among the best of his age group, but remained unknown and untested in a more competitive environment.

In 2016, I caught up with de Freitas in Madeira. He chose as our meeting point the Hotel CR7, in Funchal, the first of a chain branded with Cristiano Ronaldo's initials and shirt number, and owned by the player in a joint venture with the Portuguese international hotel group, Pestana.

The CR7 is predictably themed around the player and his lifestyle; his image is liberally replicated in different pictures, sculptured logos, and football shirts along passageways and on room walls. Hotel services include a Ronaldo-branded fitness programme. All this, just twenty years after de Freitas's first encounter with a poverty-stricken Cristiano Ronaldo had opened the door into the young prospect's future.

'I was sitting in my office in Funchal one morning when a policeman who was on duty came to tell me that there was a man with a boy who wanted to see me,' recalls de Freitas. 'It was Fernando Sousa, who I knew from his days as a player with Nacional. By his side was a boy who I remember striking me as being from a poor background, not particularly tall for his age, and very thin.'

When he asked Sousa about the boy, he was told that the youth team of Nacional had just won the championship on the island, and that young Cristiano Ronaldo had played a key role in its success, and was the player in the team with the greatest talent and commitment. De Freitas trusted Sousa's judgement, and agreed to contact Aurélio Pereira, the director of Sporting's youth academy and a hugely respected figure in Portuguese football.

Pereira was destined to go down in history as the man who added Ronaldo to a list of talented Portuguese footballers initially trained by Sporting, a list that includes Paulo Futre, Luís Figo, Simão Sabrosa, Ricardo Quaresma, Nani and João Moutinho. But his initial reaction to de Freitas's approach was one of caution. He thought that it was a big risk for the club to commit itself to a child of barely twelve years old, who had not yet appeared on his scouts' radar screen. As a favour to de Freitas, whom he respected professionally and as a friend, he agreed to take a closer look.

For his part, de Freitas thought it best that both he and Sousa consulted further with Cristiano's mother, Dolores, before taking the next step:

'I knew already about the father's alcoholism and wanted to reassure myself that I was not introducing another problem into the Aveiro household. I needed consent. Dolores's only concern was the money side, as she couldn't afford to pay for Cristiano's passage to Lisbon for the trial. I told her not to worry, as I would pay for the return flight.'

So the young Ronaldo was put into the temporary care of a stewardess for the hour-long flight to Lisbon, with an identity tag around his neck. In a rare show of unity, both his parents, along with his sisters and his brother, saw him off. He would later recall seeing his whole family crying, and he himself shed tears once the plane had taken off.

In a 2017 piece on Usain Bolt for the *Observer*, the US-born professional basketball player turned author Benjamin Markovits wrote that, 'Athletes, maybe even more than other people, depend on the myths they can tell about themselves.'[1] The departure from Madeira on his first ever trip abroad took on a mythical dimension in Ronaldo's own recollection, a rite of passage that marked the end of anonymity, and his propulsion down the road to fame and fortune.

As recounted by Ronaldo himself in an early memoir, his mother made the decision for him to live away from her at the age of twelve; she didn't want the reason for him not to be a footballer to be her or her husband. He remembers the tears starting to pour from his eyes as the plane took off and, even though he knew it was temporary, described it as 'the most difficult period of my life'.[2]

It is of course unclear the degree to which financial motives played their part in his journey to the Portuguese mainland, but the adult who arranged the trip was keen to let me know that totally abandoned he was not. Indeed, the origin-myth story that the young boy Ronaldo flew to Lisbon on his own, cast adrift in the world, does not quite match the recollection of de Freitas, who told me he accompanied Cristiano on the flight: 'As it happened, my wife was due for a hospital check-up in Lisbon, with her flight and mine paid for by the government, so she and I flew there and stayed with friends in Bucelas,' a small town near Lisbon.

Whatever the exact logistics of the journey, it's clear that for a boy of his age, who had never left his home island, this was a defining experience.

Ronaldo spent the night in the residence adjacent to Sporting's old José Alvalade stadium. The next day, de Freitas took him on a guided tour of the club's facilities before handing him over to one of the coaches, Osvaldo Silva, for a trial training session. 'This boy is spectacular,' Silva reported once the first training session had finished. 'He is a diamond but a rough one. All he needs is working on. I have no doubt we have the making of a great player.'

Two days later, de Freitas received a call from Aurélio Pereira, who told him: 'This kid is very good. In fact, he is so good that the first-team players have been turning up at the training sessions to watch him play.'

Ronaldo was left in Silva's hands for further training and observation. It took a formal report by Pereira to convince the club that the boy was worth having. 'Cristiano is a player with an exceptional talent and a very developed technique. Of particular note is his ability to take on and beat an opponent, either from a standing start or at pace. He has a great variety of dribbling tricks and he is very good with his feet, fearless and daring.'

The question that then arose was over how Ronaldo could be valued. 'Sporting were owed money by Nacional, because they'd signed a player from Odivelas FC who had previously played for a Sporting youth team,' Pereira later recalled. 'The amount was around 25,000 euros, and Nacional proposed paying the debt off with Cristiano Ronaldo. I agreed after watching the player in Lisbon during a trial. I soon realized it was a good deal for us, despite the accountants calling me crazy.' It would not take long for Nacional's football executives to realize how cheaply they had allowed Madeira's greatest ever talent to slip away.

Ronaldo's first contract with Sporting was signed in 1997, after Pereira had flown to Madeira and reassured Dolores Aveiro that the club would take good care of her son. Terms agreed included paying her travel expenses for three trips to Lisbon a year, and an annual wage for her son of 10,000 euros, to be paid into a family account. As part of the deal, the club paid for trips to Funchal so he could visit his family, or they could come and visit him.

I caught up with Pereira in April 2017, during a football conference in Lisbon organized by Sporting. This personable, quietly spoken man also seemed unsullied by his brushes with fame and his own immense reputation. One of football's 'nice guys', he was unboastful about his contribution to Ronaldo's career, remembering those early days with the natural affection any ordinary teacher feels for his prize pupil, but claiming little credit for himself.

'It was very difficult for Cristiano at his young age to come to Lisbon from Madeira with his social and family background. We knew he had talent but that there was a lot of work to do in terms of developing him physically and psychologically.

'Working on the psychological aspects was fundamental . . .

'He came feeling separated from his father – a person he loved naturally as a son but also felt himself rebelling against, escaping from, because of his alcoholism.

'In the early days in Lisbon he was very homesick. He missed his family, the other boys teased him about his Madeiran accent, which really annoyed him – he felt he didn't have any friends.

'But on the pitch, everyone was impressed by his personality. Not just myself and the rest of the technical staff but the other kids. It was as if a UFO had landed on us. He not only played better, but in a way we hadn't seen before. From the outset he showed an extraordinary passion for the game, and a real desire to improve himself in every training session, every game. He wanted to be a professional. We couldn't become his parents but we could offer him a family that he could feel part of, integrated with, and where he was respected as a human being.'

The Sporting youth academy was an institution that prided itself on nurturing talent and allowing it to grow with only minimum interference, usually whenever it was felt necessary to ameliorate some of the more negative traits of character. 'We didn't want Ronaldo to feel bullied or repressed. We saw he was an individualist and we tried to teach him that there was no point in dribbling the ball if there was no outcome for the team. All the time his self-confidence grew. He began to say "I am the best." And he believed in himself . . . What caught my attention was the energy he put into his game, his natural skill, his willpower and confidence in everything he did.'

Others who had direct contact off the pitch with a still physically immature Ronaldo during his early days in Lisbon also recognized a restless, if determined, spirit: 'He seemed skinny like all the other kids, although he was pretty highly strung,' recalls María José Lópes. 'He couldn't keep still. He always seemed in a hurry to get to training on time.' María José was one of the cleaners in a rundown hostel near the Marquês de Pombal square, which the club rented in those days on behalf of its sixteen youngest charges, prior to the more comfortable modern residence that Sporting inaugurated as part of its new youth academy in 2002.

Conditions were so cramped in room 34, which Ronaldo shared with three other boys, that María José remembered him opening the door and just managing to squeeze past his bed, the headrest of which was against a bidet, by the only window.

Perhaps unsurprisingly, Ronaldo did not find his early years away from the island he had been brought up on at all easy. But he would also later recall this time as formative, his character developing as he fought and achieved something better for himself, on his own merit, so that his later success was a seamless continuation from childhood.

Moving to Lisbon allowed him to move on from the even more difficult part of his life that preceded it – that of a bruised childhood in Madeira marred by his father's disruptive alcoholism and his parents' growing separation from each other and those around them.

Lisbon was liberating. An early Portuguese documentary would show an unnamed roommate at Sporting's youth academy recalling how, 'When we were young lads we would spend a lot of time chasing girls and also playing ping pong, which Cristiano would go on playing until he won.'[3]

But it wasn't all fun and games. Sundays were particularly tough for the young Ronaldo, for the youth academy did not play football that day. 'It was when the lads spent time with their families,' recalled Madeiran-born Leonel Pontes, who was one of Ronaldo's early coaches at Sporting. 'Everyone except Cristiano, who had no one who visited him. I would bring him to my home to share a meal with my family. I used to talk by phone with his mother, who told me that Cristiano was sad, that he cried whenever they talked with each other. When he was with us he never cried.'

Others remember Ronaldo as a somewhat self-obsessed young boy who did not take kindly to criticism from his peers and was very much out for himself. At one point, his petulance became so critical that another coach, Luís Martins, decided to discipline him by excluding him from the team for an away tie in Madeira. Ronaldo would remember it as the worst punishment he experienced in his life:

'I left him behind in Lisbon because he had to learn a lesson: this was that his teammates were as important as the coach and the club staff, and that they deserved greater respect from him. He used to get really angry, blaming the others for teasing him about his accent. His mother understood the action we took. She was also supportive of the club's decision.'

The decision was a big risk, especially considering that in his first few months in Lisbon, Ronaldo's homesickness had become so bad that a deepening depression affected his concentration. The club felt it had no option but to fly him back to Madeira and let him finish the season playing for Nacional. It seemed, for a while, that the dream of stardom that his mother had encouraged in her son had simply been tilting at windmills.

But within a month the sense of doom and gloom was lifted, thanks again to Ronaldo's godfather, Fernando Sousa, who forced a reality check as a way of raising spirits in a family summit he held with Dolores. According to Dolores, her boy suffered *saudades*. It is a word the Portuguese use for a feeling that they consider a national cultural trait, but which has no easy translation. At its most literal it conveys a deep sense of melancholy, but it is, as author of *The Portuguese*, Barry Hatton, has noted, 'a bittersweet emotion, its expression of loss, pain, sorrow, also carrying hopes of a better tomorrow, expressing desire as well as memory.'[4]

It is seen as a deep part of Portugal's identity, emerging from its history as a land of explorers, resonating through those who left and those who stayed on the mainland. Hatton sees it as a key ingredient of close-knit Portuguese society within the neighbourhood communities known as *bairrismo*. He draws attention to the tens of thousands of Portuguese emigrants to return each August for month-long holidays with their family in a tradition knows as *matar saudades*, literally 'killing off the feeling of *saudade*.'

Sousa, the godfather, killed off Ronaldo's feeling of *saudade* and put him back on track to his destiny:

'I told Dolores, "That's enough *saudades*. Ronaldo has got to go back to Sporting. He holds the key to the fortune of the family, and the family has to be strong, like him."'

'I told Dolores, "I will take care of everything. I have faith in Cristiano. He is going to be a great player." Then I rang Pontes, the coach, and said: "Can I send him back?" and he said yes. Ronaldo never again suffered *saudades*. From then on he became focused on his football.'

Some weeks later, the club official who had risked his reputation on bringing him to Lisbon, Aurélio Pereira, asked the boy straight: 'Do you want to go on crying to your mother or do you want to play football?' Ronaldo's answer was unequivocal: 'Football.' It is a story familiar throughout the world where children and sport are concerned, but the pressure put on a homesick boy to focus exclusively on football must have been immense.

By then, Ronaldo's school notes had shown an improvement. But more importantly to the club, he was growing as a footballer, physically as well as mentally, in defiance of those who had teased him because of his size. As Ronaldo would later recall: 'I remember the first time I heard one of the kids say to another kid, "Did you see what he did? This guy is a beast." I started hearing it all the time. Even from the coaches. Then somebody would always say, "Yeah but it's a shame he's so small."

'It's true, I was skinny. I had no muscle. So I made a decision at eleven years old. I knew I had a lot of talent, but I decided that I was going to work harder than everybody else.'[5]

Such was his singlemindedness that for a while he would leave his room before dawn, climb over a nearby wall and scale a roof before slipping into the club gym unnoticed, through a back window. There he would use weights and a running machine to build up his muscles and stamina. 'He was a bit of a rebel as well as a perfectionist, to the point that he would even measure his speed against cars at traffic lights. But he was too young to do so much training out of hours – we had to put special locks on the door and windows of the gym,' Pereira recalled.

As head of the youth teams, Pereira was an important influence on Ronaldo, not just as a coach but as a mentor, who saw part of his responsibilities as infusing in his young charges a sense of character, while ensuring that football became part of their soul. As he told journalist Guillem Balagué: 'We made them understand that making mistakes is part of the learning process. We needed to plant the seeds that would bear fruit later on. That's the football education that Cristiano Ronaldo received.'[6]

He was not an easy boy to handle. In the local day school, where the club paid for his lessons, he was popular with his classmates but gained a reputation for behaving badly. As Ronaldo himself recalled of those early years: 'I was not thick but I was not interested in school. I was expelled after I threw a chair at the teacher. He disrespected me.'[7]

By contrast, when supported by Pereira and Leonel Pontes at the Sporting academy, Ronaldo overcame his homesickness and found his compass. The 'cry-baby' period lasted just a few months. By his second year at the club, he had begun to earn a respect among his peers, sharing duties such as being a ball boy during first-team matches at the old José Alvalade stadium. The small payments the boys got would be spent on a shared pizza and a movie after the match.

'He was already a leader as a twelve-year-old, just like he is now; it didn't matter what the game was,' Pontes recalls. 'We were closely matched in table football, but in table tennis he would always beat me, he had great technique and I used to laugh as he tried to show how he did it.'

As the youth team prospect became a teenage trainee, he once again showed himself to have greater talent and self-belief than his peers. At age fourteen, he was already playing with boys at least a year older for Sporting's under-seventeen team. One of Ronaldo's older teammates, Hugo Pina, recalled in an interview with Sky TV that 'he wanted to do the lot, irrespective of his age: he wanted to take free kicks, corners, penalties . . . he was a year younger than us and we thought: "What the hell do you want?" And we got angry with his reactions and his demands, but at the end of the day we could see that he was better than us. Eventually we gave him the ball and looked on in awe. It was much easier to win games with him.'[8]

Pina accompanied Ronaldo on a number of holidays to Madeira. His enduring memories are of waking up in the morning to find that Cristiano was already playing with a ball. He would later train by putting weights round his ankles and running up Funchal's steep hills, before playing some more football with his island friends.

By this time, aged fourteen, Ronaldo had no doubt that he had the ability to play professionally, and agreed with his mother that he should cease his education in order to focus entirely on his football. However, one year later, a medical check-up showed up a congenital heart murmur, which caused a quickening of the pulse during rest periods. It was corrected by non-intrusive laser surgery and not widely publicized at the time, but would later be absorbed into Ronaldo's official history – not as a sign of fragility, but, on the contrary, as yet another example of his resilience.

One evening, Ronaldo and a group of other Sporting prospects were attacked on a Lisbon street by a gang wielding knives. The club legend has it that the streetwise Ronaldo, formed in the poorest neighbourhood of Funchal, was the only one to hold his ground and fight off the aggressors. The skinny boy from Madeira was finding his feet.

4. LITTLE BIG MAN: MESSI

Growth hormone is a hormone essential to growth and development. It is produced in a gland at the base of the brain called the pituitary gland . . . If a child does not have enough growth hormone, then the speed of growth is much slower and final height is reduced.

Society for Endocrinology

Lionel Messi was nine years old when his parents realized that his only hope of following a lucrative career as a professional footballer was to follow the doctor's advice. That the boy had immense talent no one doubted, but this boy wonder had also been diagnosed with a hormonal growth deficiency. If left in the hands of mother nature, his stature and build would remain diminished to such an extent as to put him at a distinct disadvantage to others of his age group, or older, when it came to adult competitive football.

Messi, aged nine, measured 1.27 metres tall, which was about 10 centimetres shorter than the average height for a boy of his age. If his size had been limited by genetics, there would have been little any doctor could have prescribed to alter his ordained adult size. But the fact that Messi had a hormonal deficiency meant that science had a solution.

At hand was Dr Diego Schwarzstein, an Argentine endocrinologist who had moved back to Rosario after working in a practice in Barcelona from 1989 to 1994. He was a long-term fan of Newell's Old Boys, and was trusted by the club with overseeing the physical development of its child players. It was the club that first suggested a check-up for the child who seemed to be, by a considerable margin, the best among his peers, but who was also simply very small for his age. He was nicknamed 'La Pulga', the flea, because his size belied the enormity of his impact on the game, at least while it was played among kids.

'Don't worry, one day you will grow to be taller than Maradona. I don't know if better, but certainly taller,' Schwarzstein told Messi after he had first met him, accompanied by his parents, at his private clinic in Rosario. The date of that first meeting was 31 January 1997, never forgotten by the doctor, as it was his birthday.

Manufactured growth hormone, patented by a US drugs company, had been commercially available since the 1980s, but was still not widely in use in Argentina, and it was expensive. Schwarzstein had learnt more about the drug in Barcelona, a city that has always prided itself on its pioneering medical practices as well as its innovative art. The treatment involved a daily injection into the fat underneath the skin, normally in the evening, to fit in with the body's natural cycle for producing growth hormone. Messi's parents were assured that the treatment was a relatively straightforward one, with a positive outcome a great deal more likely than any lasting side effects. 'Messi was one of about every 20,000 in the Argentine population born with a growth hormone deficiency,' Schwarzstein would recall years later.

In fact, research into hormone treatment was far from conclusive, and other members of the Argentine medical profession would remain far more cautious in their approach to the issue. Seven years after the Messis had their first meeting with Schwarzstein, one of Argentina's leading sports journalists, Julio Marini, worried that his young son was much smaller than most of his peers, and sought advice from a specialist in Buenos Aires. Marini never forgot the conversation that ensued. He was told that there were too many potential risks: problems with bone structure, with muscles, with ligaments; even a risk of tumours on skin tissues.

There and then, Marini and his wife made up their minds not to go for the treatment. The doctor's words had shocked them both. For the sports journalist, the meeting would later raise thoughts of Messi, and the risk his parents had taken. 'My first thoughts were of course about my son and having to accept the doctor's advice. But later it made me think of Messi, and now I question whether the treatment was justified in his case simply because of the great football player he ended up being.'

It's worth recording here that Messi was not the first Argentine football legend to count on medical assistance for his physical development. Diego Maradona was eight years old when Francisco Cornejo, his trainer at Cebollitas, the youth team of the Buenos Aires club Argentinos Juniors, took him to see 'Cacho' Paladino, a doctor of dubious reputation who specialized in building up the bodies of boxers with a mixture of unspecified drugs and vitamins. Paladino was also employed by another local football club, Huracán.

When Maradona visited him, he was put on a crash course of unidentified pills and injections, Cornejo told me: 'Diego was so small when I took him to see Paladino that he didn't seem strong enough. I wanted Paladino to round him off, get him fatter and bigger. So I asked the doctor to give him vitamins and other things to help him develop. "Cacho," I said, "you fix him, this boy is going to grow up to be a star."'

I remember meeting Paladino while researching my biography of Maradona. He was a large man with a gruff, no-nonsense approach to life that had endeared him to several players and managers. He had become involved with Maradona at a time when no specialized training existed for the profession of 'sports' doctor, and when the footballing and boxing authorities in Argentina had yet to develop an effective way of policing the methods and prescriptions with which doctors could treat athletes. Paladino didn't blink when he told me: 'When I finished with him [Maradona], he was like a racing colt.'

Maradona first saw Paladino in 1968. While Maradona's later substance abuse as an adult is now widely known, the player himself always denied that he ever drugged himself to improve his performance. Two decades or so later, sports health had become altogether more sophisticated and, in Messi's case, far more transparent. His growth hormone treatment required him to inject himself each evening with a pen-like instrument that was easier to handle than a syringe, alternating the location between arms and legs. Schwarzstein takes pride in his reputation as one of the people who helped facilitate Messi's rise to stardom, insisting that the injections were unobtrusive and had less effect on Messi's skin than a mosquito bite.

In an interview with Irish journalist Richard Fitzpatrick made available for this book, Schwarzstein remembers the young boy as initially introverted: 'He was a very nice child. He wasn't shy – when you broke the ice, when you started talking with him, usually football was the initial topic he talked a lot about – but he was introverted. It's one thing if you prefer to keep things to yourself. Another thing is feeling anxious about expressing your feelings, being afraid about not saying the right thing. Then there is being introverted, preferring to keep things to yourself. Leo is not shy. He's introverted. He's reserved.'[1]

Messi's youth teammates recall him as open and outgoing, but only among a close circle of friends. Beyond the football pitch he was less at ease with the wider world, distrusting it, perhaps. The treatment, never fully explained or justified at the time by his parents, beyond to those who needed to know, separated him more from his wider peer group, made him feel distinct and different. It would be surprising if he inwardly questioned the nature of his parents' love for making him endure it. In fact, he engaged with the treatment, as if offered a magic potion, and the challenge it presented to his self-esteem seemed to nourish in him an even greater determination to focus on the thing he loved and could do well at – football. By undergoing the treatment, Lionel Messi drew on his strength of character, as well as the helping hand that science could provide.

The programme required regular dosage monitoring and review of the most appropriate injection device, up to and beyond the age of sixteen, the age at which growth 'catch-up' is expected to have been achieved.

Messi carried his hormone-boosting kit in a small case, which he would take with him on school trips and visits to friends' houses. Some would watch with a mixture of disbelief and pity as the young boy injected himself. There were times when he cried and couldn't train because of the pain. As Franco Falleroni, one of Messi's boyhood teammates, recalled, the needle was very thin and the length of a fingernail. He would visit Falleroni's parents' house, put the pack in the freezer, take it out, and then inject himself in the thigh.

The decision to give the treatment the go-ahead was made by Messi's parents after they had weighed up the hopes they had for the child against the health risks involved. The risks were also financial. The cost of a month's supply of the hormone was $1,300, which Messi's father initially covered with the medical insurance provided by his employers at Acindar, the metallurgical company, and with the help of two local friends, who worked as football agents in Rosario.

However, as the twentieth century reached its end, Argentina – a country rich in natural resources but historically prone to political and economic instability – sank into its deepest crisis in living memory, under centrist president Fernando de la Rúa of the Radical Civic Union party. A loss of confidence in the government's ability to tackle a soaring public-sector deficit, plus high unemployment, led to a run on bank deposits, which in turn led to the highly unpopular *corralito* – an official ban on the withdrawal of savings.

In a climate of political disintegration, there was even briefly talk of Maradona standing for the Argentine vice-presidency on a joint ticket with his friend, the former Peronist president Carlos Menem, despite the latter facing prosecution over an illegal arms exports scandal.

The crisis left the Argentine working classes condemned to abject poverty, and middle-class households struggling to pay their bills. The latter group included the Messis, particularly when Acindar cut the medical insurance that paid for Lionel's treatment, and threatened to make his father Jorge redundant.

Initially, Jorge turned to Newell's Old Boys for support. The club was not a happy ship at the time. Its president, local businessman Eduardo López, had turned the club into a fiefdom since being elected in 1994.[2]

The needs of the Messi family were judged far less of a priority than those of the *barras bravas*, the violent fans who acted as López's enforcers, and as less important than the shady deals struck for the transfers of older players. Jorge Messi's request for financial support was granted grudgingly, with the club soon underpaying what the injections cost or missing payments altogether.

Increasingly worried for his son's future, Jorge Messi approached Buenos Aires giants River Plate, to see if they would be interested in buying his son from Newell's and paying for his treatment. According to Federico Vairo, one of the River Plate youth coaches at the time, Messi put on an impressive performance at a trial training session, nutmegging opponents much taller than him, showing off his dribbling skills, and scoring a goal just like the many he had got used to scoring in Rosario.

But the club's youth department refused to see Vairo's glowing description of Messi as a 'mixture of Sivori and Maradona' as a reason for taking the boy on, and the matter went no further. Senior executives claimed they could not afford the risk inherent in signing up this undersized boy, just because his father claimed he was a child prodigy.

The full reasons why both Newell's and River Plate refused to give the Messi family a helping hand remain a subject of unresolved controversy to this day. Vairo blamed vested interests that ex-River players had in another club – Renato Casarini – that supplied young players to River's academy. Veteran Argentine football writer Julio Marini believes that, despite the country's financial crisis at the time, both Newell's and River Plate had the resources to invest in Messi, including his treatment, but simply underestimated his potential: 'The fact remains that no one at Newell's or River Plate has ever assumed responsibility for letting Messi slip through their fingers. In Argentina, everyone wants to claim credit for a success story, but none will confess to a major error of judgement; no one has ever said "We made a mistake."'[3]

Whatever the reasons for Argentina's clubs rejecting Messi, by the turn of the new millennium, the Messi family were ready to consider an approach from further afield. Enter FC Barcelona, stage right.

Josep María Minguella brokered some of FC Barcelona's most successful signings, including major stars like Hristo Stoichkov, Diego Maradona and the Brazilians Romário and Rivaldo. Now in his seventies, the media-savvy Minguella has lived and breathed Barça since he was aged five, when his father – another fanatic – made him a life member of the club.

I first met Minguella in the mid-1990s to talk about Maradona, whose contract with FC Barcelona he helped negotiate in 1982. We've kept in touch ever since, exchanging periodic notes about Spanish and South American football, with our conversation enlivened by the subject of the enduring legacy of Johan Cruyff and Lionel Messi.

In 2016, I visited Minguella at his home in the hillside Barcelona neighbourhood of Pedralbes, where live the rich and powerful of the Catalan capital. What was now his retirement home was more tranquil than when I had first visited it to talk about Maradona, when it had doubled up as an office, but the building retained its understated grandeur as it spread out across an overgrown tropical garden populated by parrots of different species.

Researching this book had prompted a personal invitation from

Minguella to join him at a street-naming ceremony in honour of the late Johan Cruyff, who had died six months earlier. The event was the idea of a fanatical Cruyff fan, Francesc Llobet, the young mayor of the small village of Vallfogona de Riucorb, population ninety-six, which lies nestled in the foothills of the Pyrenees. The date was 9 September 2016, in honour of the number 9 shirt that Cruyff had first worn when he joined Barça from Ajax.

'Johan Cruyff changed a country and FC Barcelona. He taught us to lose our fear as a club and as a country and left an enduring mark as a player and as a coach,' the young mayor told the gathering, attended by a group of Cruyff loyalists led by the former Barça president and pro-Catalan independence politician Joan Laporta.

After the ceremony, Minguella and I shared a lunch of snails and roast pork in nearby Guimerà, the medieval village where he was born, before driving back to Barcelona, feeling all the better for having honoured the legendary Cruyff, and discussing Messi, a player who owes part of his success to the Dutchman's influence at FC Barcelona, and Minguella's mediation.

Minguella shared his story thus: 'When the financial crisis hit Argentina and the Messi family, I was working flat out as an agent, and had several top players on my books. A friend of mine, an Argentine lawyer called Juan Mateo Walter, rings me and says, "Look, there is this incredible kid from Rosario I have for you."

'I thought he might be sixteen or seventeen, but then Juan says, "He is twelve going on thirteen." My first thought was, Fuck me, what I am going to do with a kid so young? But he showed me a video of a boy who seemed to have the ball attached to his feet and a huge hunger to get it into the net and I said, "OK, let's see what I can do." It was February 2000.'

In September of that year, Lionel and his father Jorge flew into Barcelona, their flight and accommodation paid for by Minguella. The agent had spent the intervening months preparing a plan, which he hoped would seduce both the Messi family and FC Barcelona, as it was tailor-made to reconcile the player's and the club's best interests.

The Messis were put up in the Catalonia Barcelona Plaza, a four-star hotel with a seasonal rooftop pool and terrace and panoramic city view. The hotel manager was the son of one Barça legend Domingo

Balmanya, and had secured Minguella a special VIP deal for his Argentine guests.

The suite where the Messis stayed not only had twenty-four-hour room service and all mod cons, but also featured a magnificent view over one of Barcelona's biggest squares at the foot of the picturesque Montjuïc hill and across to the city's majestic Monumental bullring, whose neo-Mudéjar facade had been designed by Domènec Sugrañes i Gras, a friend and disciple of Antoni Gaudí. For the Messis, this first experience of the economically vibrant and culturally diverse capital of Catalonia, a region from where their ancestors had come, must have been incredibly attractive, and contrasted with the doom and gloom they had temporarily left behind in Rosario.

Minguella knew a lot about the power of football in Catalonia, and in particular FC Barcelona. He had also learnt much from his experience of handling other Latin American players, not least the fact that while they found the Mediterranean climate of Barcelona agreeable, they also found the more nationalistic among the Catalans too closed-minded, and easily grew homesick.

Maradona remembered his stay at Barcelona as 'the unhappiest period of my career', with particular misery setting in over the first Christmas he found himself away from Argentina. Minguella wanted, as only he could, to soften Messi's landing into what was for him uncharted territory.

For Messi, the mere thought of stepping onto one of Barça's training grounds for a trial was like an encounter with wonderland. However, Minguella remembers it as a personal gamble which got off to a bad start.

FC Barcelona had just elected a new president, the hotelier Joan Gaspart, who showed little interest in Messi when Minguella mentioned the boy to him. Despite Minguella's track record as the man who had brought Maradona and other key players to FC Barcelona, Gaspart pointed out to him that when Maradona was signed in the summer of 1982, he was in his early twenties and had just played in a World Cup as a star player in Argentina's national squad. Many of Minguella's greatest hits had been of a similar age and had also had major club and international experience before their Barça signings.

By contrast, Messi was not even a teenager and was barely known outside Rosario, where the closest he had come to playing for the first team at Newell's Old Boys was kicking a ball around at half-time as light entertainment.

Gaspart's main concern was the poor form of his club's first team when compared to Real Madrid, who appeared to have guaranteed themselves a golden period after embarking on an unprecedented spending spree, kicked off with the PR coup of snatching Luís Figo from FC Barcelona themselves, a defection which caused enduring chagrin for both Barça officials and fans.

With Real Madrid's rich and politically influential new president Florentino Pérez boasting about the club's new era of *galácticos*, Gaspart had little time to focus on an investment in an underage Argentine who was undergoing a growth hormone treatment programme.

'I remember Gaspart saying to me, "Look, your job is to help me win La Liga, not try and convince me to pay for an underage, underdeveloped kid from Argentina I have never heard of. Anyway, if and when he grows up and plays for the first team, I won't be president any more,"' Minguella recalled.

As things turned out, Gaspart was right on the latter point, as his presidency proved short-lived – three years – a great deal shorter than the rule of his predecessor, the enduring José Luís Núñez, whom he had served loyally as vice-president for twenty-three years.

But Minguella felt frustrated and angry with Gaspart's perspective, and thought it reflected the general bad governance and lack of vision then affecting FC Barcelona. Minguella's doubts about Gaspart formed part of a widely shared view inside and outside the club that Barça had entered the doldrums after the golden years of Cruyff as a player and later manager, with allegations of dubious transfer deals and overpricing of certain players, and a relatively poor record in Europe under Louis van Gaal.

'While they resisted the idea of Messi, Gaspart and his junta that summer went ahead with five disastrous deals, selling our star Figo to Real Madrid and buying de la Peña, Gerard López, and from Arsenal Overmars and Petit – a complete waste of money on overrated players who had no potential of improvement, of bringing added value to a team that was in crisis,' says Minguella.

Gaspart was not the only person that Minguella had trouble with. There were others with influence on the club's coaching and transfer policy – like the two veterans Migueli and Asensio – who told Minguella: 'Sure this kid plays some beautiful football like Maradona, but they are going to kill him – he is only twelve kilos, they are going to kill him if he stays this size.'

And then there was a family affair. Jorge Messi was restless. He was without a job or prospects and the two clubs in Argentina he had trust in had betrayed him. As for his son, there was a risk that cutting off his hormone treatment – due to lack of funds – could be prejudicial to his wellbeing and damage him mentally and physically. While thousands of Argentines were escaping from their country's crisis by emigrating to the then economically prosperous Spain and setting up new roots, his own son was holed up in a hotel without even an offer on the table.

Back in Rosario, friends and neighbours, feeling in the dark, were asking as to Lionel's secret whereabouts. As his boyhood teammate, Franco Falleroni later told the Barcelona-based Irish journalist Richard Fitzpatrick: 'A month passes without seeing Messi. We were training and there was no sign of Messi. We were asking, "What's up with Messi?" My dad rang up the Messi house. Messi's mother answered. My dad asked, "What's up with Leo? He is not coming to practice." She said he couldn't because he was ill. Another week went by and then another. They kept saying he hadn't recovered.'

After a month or so of waiting for a decision from FC Barcelona which wasn't forthcoming, Jorge Messi packed his bags and flew back to Argentina with his son, to await better news and formulate another plan. As meetings continued without any formal resolution, Messi continued playing for Newell's youth team, winning the Apertura championship (a competition lasting the first half of the season), and finishing as the top scorer.

As Falleroni remembered it: 'He came back, looking a little more developed. It was strange. We were asking him, "Leo, are you OK?" and he said, "Yes, I'm better." Sometime afterwards we were training, and his mother came and said, "Let's go, Leo. We have to go." "No," he said, "I want to stay a little longer with the guys, with my friends." But his mother grabbed him by the arm and took him away. He never showed up again. A week later we found out he was in Barcelona.'

After the Messis' first departure from Barcelona, Minguella felt the whole situation disintegrating in his hands, and urged Jorge to be patient. Then he decided to play a final card. He approached FC Barcelona's sporting director, the veteran player and coach Charly Rexach, who agreed to watch Messi play in a trial with some of the other youth coaches. The Messis returned to Spain.

One of the coaches, Xavi Llorens, thought he recognized a young version of Maradona as he watched Messi. 'You could see that the ball was attached to his foot like a claw. He was very fast, and he ran with his head down, and looked as if he didn't know where he was going, but of course he did know. He showed he had peripheral vision already in those early days. He could see the move he had to play in advance.' But other observers were worried that the boy still had to develop Maradona's natural strength and self-belief. There was no majority opinion, but there was Rexach, cast in the role of *deus ex machina*.

'Charly (Rexach) watched Messi and was converted to his cause. Charly said: "I don't know what we are going to pay him but we have to make sure we keep this kid,"' Minguella told me. 'That was the first step towards having Lionel Messi at FC Barcelona, although quite honestly none of us then could have ever imagined just how far the kid was going to go or the trouble we were going to face in getting him signed up.'

Bringing Messi to Barcelona from Argentina, and keeping him there on terms his father and Argentine agents would accept and which the club felt it could afford, proved a logistical and financial challenge.

FIFA regulations stipulated that when a player under eighteen was transferred from his native country, he had to be accompanied by his parents. Jorge also insisted that in Barcelona, Lionel must live with his family rather than board at the youth academy where he was to be trained up to first-team level. This meant the club paying for an apartment and helping Messi's parents find work, in addition to funding Lionel's training and school lessons.

By December 2000, there was still no decision from Barça, and the Messi camp issued an ultimatum. Ruben Horacio Gaggioli, a businessman from Rosario who had been living in Barcelona since the late 1970s, was representing the young player together with his colleagues in Rosario. They allowed rumours to reach FC Barcelona that other major clubs, such as AC Milan, Atlético Madrid and Real Madrid, were showing some interest. Although there was more bluff to this than substance, the ploy succeeded in focusing minds in Barcelona.

Just before Christmas 2000, Rexach met Gaggioli and Minguella for lunch at the private Pompeya tennis club. There the following was written, in Spanish, on a paper napkin: 'In Barcelona on 14 December 2000 in the presence of Minguella and Horacio, Carles Rexach, technical director of FCB, commits to the signing, in spite of opinions to the contrary, of Lionel Messi, as long as the figures previously agreed are respected.'

Or so the legend goes. A photograph of the alleged napkin was shown to Richard Fitzpatrick by Gaggioli, who says he kept the original in a bank safety-deposit box. It is scribbled informally, by hand, with the full names of those allegedly present not given and no counter-signature from a notary to give it legal status. Contractually, the napkin is worthless, but mentally it proved an invaluable stopgap.

Then, in early January 2001, the club's youth director, Joan Lacueva Colomer, and Joaquim Rifé, the director of La Masia, FC Barcelona's youth academy, drafted between them a contractual note, under which the player would have his hormonal treatment paid for, earn a decent wage plus additional payments for image rights, and that guaranteed an annual wage for Jorge. While the contract specified that Jorge would be employed by Barna Partners, a company that supplied security staff for the club, Jorge would in effect become self-employed, spending as much time as he wanted near his son, representing his interests, and, in the early days in Barcelona, doing occasional admin working at Minguella's agency's office. The Messi family relocated to Barcelona in February 2001, but the contractual situation was still unresolved.

A formal agreement between Messi and FC Barcelona was not drafted until March 2001, and its implementation was delayed by several weeks, much to the despair of Jorge. The first payment due to Messi and his father was triggered only after Jorge had written a pleading letter to Gaspart in early July 2001.

So what was happening all this time between the legendary napkin memorandum and the final contractual signature? Not a very pretty story, but perhaps a predictable one, of protracted wheeling and dealing. The majority of the FC Barcelona board, including Gaspart and some of the coaches, had still to be convinced by

Minguella and Rexach that the boy was worth it, especially after demands from Jorge that he and his family would be given better terms and conditions than those offered to other entrants of La Masia.

The demands weren't limited to the stipulation that Leo would not live at La Masia like many other youngsters, but in a comfortable flat paid for by the club, large enough to accommodate father, mother and siblings. There were also travel expenses to be paid for the Messis' comings and goings from Argentina, and the cost of Lionel's continuing hormone treatment.

In contrast to Gaspart's early reticence, Minguella and Rexach's key ally at the highest level of the club was Joan Lacueva Colomer. Colomer lobbied hard for the Messi deal, while Gaspart and his faction fixated on signing another rising Argentine star, nineteen-year-old Javier Saviola, from River Plate. Continually introducing the subject of Messi to a board whose president had eyes focused on Saviola was like throwing a hand grenade into a picnic. Or, as Colomer put it, 'The club was fire-fighting and we were starting another fire.'

Colomer found himself rounded on by other directors, who rained insults on him and alluded to his former employment by Espanyol, the rival Barcelona team that historically had been considered anti-Catalan. But Colomer was persistent and argued passionately: 'If you don't support me,' he told the doubters, 'you will be committing the biggest mistake in the club's history.' He prevailed.

In 2010, four years before he died, Colomer was asked in an interview by the Spanish newspaper *El País* how he saw his role in the history of Messi. 'I did my job. That is what I was paid for. There were things that had to be done or else Messi would have left us,' he recalled with typical modesty.[4]

5. LISBON STAR: RONALDO

Sporting's first-team coach László Bölöni will always be my first point of reference, because he was the one to launch me into professional football.

Cristiano Ronaldo, *Moments*

In the 2001–2 season, Cristiano Ronaldo made his first serious mark on football history, if initially on a modest scale, by becoming the only player in the history of Sporting Clube de Portugal to play for the club's under-16s, under-17s, under-18s, B team and first team in one season. It was indicative of an extraordinary career trajectory to come, but also marked the culmination of an intense period of self-development for the skinny kid from Funchal, and a way-marker in Portuguese football history.

Nineteen ninety-eight, Ronaldo's first full year with the Sporting academy, saw Portugal fulfil the criteria to join the launch of the euro in 1999, José Saramago being awarded the Nobel Prize for Literature, and the country host the final world's trade fair of the century, Expo '98, coinciding with the five hundredth anniversary of Vasco de Gama's pioneering passage to India.

The reputation of Portuguese football was also in the ascendancy, with its rising international star personified in Luís Figo. Thirteen years older than Cristiano Ronaldo, Figo had risen through Sporting's youth ranks before his career took off at FC Barcelona, which he joined in 1995 for around £2 million. Figo was considered the leader of the so-called 'golden generation' of Portuguese players, a maturing group who had won the under-20 World Cup in both 1989 and 1991. Not since Eusébio's exploits at the 1966 World Cup in England had the country had an internationally recognized star, but the golden generation provided a glut of them, and revealed an increasingly confident country from a footballing point of view. As well as Figo, other

Portuguese players of the group who made their mark in Europe included Rui Costa, Paulo Sousa, João Pinto and Fernando Couto.

At Barcelona, Figo won a reputation as one of the most admired players since Cruyff: reliable, effective and committed to the cause as a team leader, hugely creative on the wing, and a brilliant goal scorer, often cutting in and linking up with the midfield. Few at Barça would easily forget Figo's contribution to FC Barcelona's victory over Real Madrid in the Clásico at the Nou Camp in March 1997, coached by Bobby Robson and his assistant José Mourinho. In total Figo would win two League titles, two Copas del Rey, a UEFA Cup and a Cup Winners' Cup at the club, as well as the Ballon d'Or in 2000, but he is as remembered for his departure from the club as much as for anything he did on the pitch.

Barça fans will never forget or forgive Figo's transfer to Real Madrid in the summer of 2000, for the then world record transfer fee of £37.4 million, the first of Florentino Pérez's *galácticos*. His first visit to the Nou Camp in a white shirt, in the autumn of 2000, provoked such an uproar from the local fans that play was temporarily suspended. Among chants of 'Judas', 'mercenary' and 'scum', Figo was removed from corner-taking duty to avoid him getting too close to the terraces. When he returned again in 2002, a pig's head was thrown at him from the stands.

Whatever catharsis or revenge some Barça fans felt they gained from their extreme reaction, for many Portuguese watching the matches it left a bad taste, a reminder of the prejudice they felt Spaniards had always harboured against their neighbours. At international level, Spain, regardless of region, had historically resisted being measured as an equal with Portugal, choosing instead to ensure that her neighbour's inferiority remained the order of the day, south of the Pyrenees.

Whatever the socio-political interpretation of the transfer and its fallout, making the move required immense bravery and self-confidence on the part of Figo himself. An indirect example set, perhaps, to the then teenager whom destiny had marked out as Figo's successor for both club and country.

In Portugal, the popularity of football persisted through the end of one century and into the beginning of a new millennium, and Sporting, like their Lisbon rivals Benfica and northern powerhouse Porto, had money to invest. The upturn in Portugal's post-EU entry economic activity and the upcoming hosting of Euro 2004 meant that the club's José Alvalade stadium would be rebuilt. Investment in youth training also became a priority for the club, and after the golden post-war years had been succeeded by a title drought lasting nearly two decades, the policy began to bear fruit with a League win in 2000.

Twenty years had passed since Eusébio had retired, and nearly thirty since his heyday as a Benfica and international player, without anyone emerging to challenge his unrivalled reputation as a 'national treasure'. But, as Figo and the rest of the golden generation's stars continued to rise, the search for a worthy successor was well under way and major Portuguese clubs were increasingly prepared to look to their youth teams to build winning sides.

As he recalled in later years, it was around this time that Ronaldo felt his destiny beckoning, like a story foretold. 'When I was fifteen, I turned to some of my teammates during training. I remember it so clearly. I said to them, "I'll be the best in the world one day."

'They were kind of laughing about it. I wasn't even on Sporting's first team yet, but I had that belief. I really meant it.'[1]

Sure he did, but you could have forgiven his teammates for being a little cautious. If few details of his on-field life during his first two years in Lisbon form part of the official Ronaldo narrative today, it is because he took time to mature from the skinny, homesick adolescent who struggled to adapt, and to prove he had the physique as well as the psychology to develop into a star.

Indeed, as mentioned in Chapter Three, in the summer of 2000 he was not even allowed to play for about three months, after a routine medical check by the club doctor revealed that the young Ronaldo had a heart murmur and needed surgery. His mother, Dolores, was warned that – if untreated – the condition risked bringing her son's football career to an early end. She didn't need much persuasion to sign the authorization forms, as she later revealed in an interview: 'I had to fill in a mountain of paperwork so that they could admit him and do some tests. Eventually they decided to go ahead with the procedure . . . Before I knew what was really going on, I was really worried that he might have to give up football.'[2]

If there is a certain mythologized drama surrounding Ronaldo's childhood, worthy of the Brazilian TV soap opera or *Telenovela* that millions of Portuguese speakers have lapped up for decades, it is the mother–son relationship that is the most enduring aspect.

In more recent chapters, both would star in a series of advertisements for the Portuguese telecoms firm MEO. One of these, released in April 2017, charts Ronaldo's life from early days in Lisbon to Real Madrid legend. Emotional exchanges via a mobile phone, beginning with Ronaldo as a young child, are intercut with scenes of him as an adolescent playing in Sporting colours – we get a brief glimpse of an already tall but skinny teenager darting down the right wing, and cutting in to score an impeccable goal.

'A few days after the procedure [on his heart],' Dolores says, 'he was back in training with his teammates. He could run even faster than before.'

It is only from the 2001–2 season that we have any surviving records giving insight into why the club felt Ronaldo was good enough to promote so rapidly through the different category youth teams to the reserves, and finally to the first team. For four years after Ronaldo arrived in Lisbon for his first trial, aged eleven, he led a life of relative anonymity in the Portuguese capital, largely unknown by the outside world. Only in September 2001 did a Portuguese TV channel – Sport TV – compile the first report on the player, focusing on his life off the pitch when, as a later commentary on YouTube puts it, 'he did not have a Porsche, a Ferrari and a Bentley but bought tickets to travel by metro.'[3]

The documentary shows a young, confident Ronaldo already displaying his speed, step-overs and dribbling skills in training with unidentified older players, some of whom he tells us play for the Portuguese national team. The camera follows Ronaldo into the cramped boarding house where the club housed young players before inaugurating a modern, well-equipped residence at their new academy. Despite his humble lodgings, Ronaldo tells his interviewer that he has put the early days in Lisbon behind him, when he was teased by other boys about his Madeiran accent, and is now enjoying mixing it with older players and earning a modest salary. The image conveyed is of a personable, self-assured, good-looking lad who has fought hard to make a new life for himself, overcoming the poverty he was born into.

In April 2001, four months prior to his TV report being aired, a breakthrough in his career had come when Ronaldo, advised by lead-ing agent José Veiga, himself fresh from negotiating Figo's move to Real, had signed his first professional contract. It was worth €2,000 a month and included a €20 million release clause.

But the relationship with Veiga proved short-lived, after Ronaldo and his mother were approached the following year by an emerging challenger to Veiga's reputation as the top Portuguese agent, a man who would become inextricably linked with young Cristiano and come to define the next era of football business – Jorge Mendes.

Despite his coup in securing Figo's record transfer from Barça to Real Madrid, and also being involved in Zinedine Zidane's subsequent move from Juventus to the Spanish club, Veiga's influence in Portu-guese football was beginning to wane. It was built on his strong links with Porto, but in 1998 the club ignored the agent's advice and sold one of its stars, Sérgio Conceição, to the Italian club Lazio, rather than go for a deal Veiga had lined up with Spanish side Deportivo de La Coruña, where Mendes was also developing an interest. The disagree-ment between Veiga and Porto turned into an acrimonious row, which allowed Mendes to step forward and strengthen his hold on Portuguese football, as well as develop his links with top clubs in Europe.

Twenty years older than his most illustrious client, Jorge Mendes had grown up in the rundown industrial district of Moscavide, on the banks of the Tagus estuary in the east of Lisbon, an area then domin-ated by the massive Petrogal gas and oil company plant where his father worked.

The family lived on a housing estate built for Petrogal workers. His mother weaved straw hats and baskets at home. At weekends, Mendes took the number 28 bus to Fonte da Telha beach, where he sold his mother's pieces when not making money by selling old clothes at flea markets. One of his friends had a stall nearby and made around 500 escudos per day. Mendes was making ten times that amount. He seemed destined to be an entrepreneur, always on the lookout for the best deal and how to maximize its potential.

During the summer, he worked in a Cornetto factory, where his assigned task was to hold the cone at the end of the process, to ensure the ice cream was not wasted. He joked to his friends that he had the most important job of all.

Unusually for working-class kids at the time, Mendes also had access to a grass football pitch at his father's workplace, fifty metres away from his apartment, and when that was busy, he joined his friends for three-on-three games in the nearby cobbled square, using benches as goals. He played for the Petrogal youth club and for a while dreamt of becoming a professional.

After his brother's wife died, he moved, aged twenty, from Lisbon to Viana do Castelo in northern Portugal, to be near his sibling and nephew. There he began playing for a lower-league side, Vianense. However, Mendes's focus was soon on developing a new ambition – that of being a successful businessman. In 1989, he opened a video store called Samui Video in a deserted shopping mall.

'I knew it was a ghost mall, but it had one thing I needed: there was plenty of parking space,' he later told the Portuguese media network SIC. 'I earned much more with the video store than playing for any team. It might have been the idea that changed everything for me.'[4]

Nonetheless, he retained and developed his ties with the football world, moving from Vianense to the second-division club Amadores de Caminha in the small town of Caminha, a few kilometres north of Viana do Castelo. His new club only trained at night, which allowed Mendes to continue running his video business by day.

He was then invited to play for Varzim, a first division club near Porto, but turned the offer down and went instead to play for third division Lanheses, between 1991 and 1994, which was also based at Viana do Castelo. He made it a condition of his contract with Lanheses that he also be given the concession to manage the advertising space at the club ground, his first football business deal.

He gave up playing when he was thirty. 'I loved playing, but, if the truth be told, I was not a great player. I was just an average player,' he recounted in a 2012 documentary on the Portuguese TV network SIC called *Jorge Mendes: The Super Agent*.

In 1991, he bought a popular discotheque called Club Alfândega in Caminhas, near the Spanish border, and there he met professional players from Braga, Porto and Vitória de Guimarães, all first-division northern Portuguese clubs. It was here that, in 1995, he met Nuno Espírito Santo, the reserve goalkeeper of Vitória de Guimarães.

At the beginning of the 1996–7 season, Nuno wanted to move from Vitória de Guimarães to FC Porto, with dreams beyond that of moving to Spain's La Liga, but a dispute between the two clubs was preventing the transfer. Mendes had an idea of his own. He wanted to fast-track Nuno's entry into La Liga by having him sign for Deportivo de La Coruña, the Galician club that at the time was experiencing a golden period of football success, and was in the market for star signings.

Legend has it that he drove the 300 kilometres from Viana do Castelo and waited for days to speak to club president Augusto Lendoiro – a leading figure in Spain's right-wing Popular Party and a man with a reputation as one of the toughest negotiators in Spanish football. Mendes felt up to the challenge of dealing with him. When Lendoiro eventually agreed to see him, he was persuaded to sign Nuno. 'The emotion he puts into things, the way he transmits them, it makes it very difficult to say "no" to something he proposes,' Lendoiro recalled years later.[5]

Mendes, it is claimed, did not take a commission from the Nuno deal, but it did wonders for his reputation as an agent. From thereon he began to make significant strides in building up his client base among Portuguese players and coaches as a launch pad for global expansion.

A major fork in the road came in the late 1990s, when, as previously noted, he took advantage of a fallout between Porto president Pinto da Costa and the leading Portuguese agent of that period, José Veiga. Another Mendes client, Costinha, joined Porto from Monaco, and others – Jorge Andrade and then Deco – followed. Meanwhile, Veiga continued to hold on to a not insignificant stable of players, like Luís Figo, Nuno Gomes and Fernando Couto.

For a while it was an amicable division of labour and business between two highly ambitious agents. That all changed in the summer of 2002, when the pair took the same flight from Milan to Lisbon. A report published in the Portuguese paper *Record* on 15 October 2002 explained what happened next: Mendes approached Veiga to ask him about rumours that Veiga had allegedly started. What these rumours were has never surfaced in the public domain, but whatever was alleged must have been considered sufficiently damaging to the reputation of one party or the other, given what ensued.

A fight broke out between the two and they grappled with each other on the floor, Mendes on top and Veiga grabbing his tie. In the confusion, Mendes picked up Veiga's phone, which had fallen onto the floor, with the apparent aim of checking his client list and latest phone calls.

It was also around this time that Mendes must have approached one of Veiga's most promising young clients, and that September, Dolores Aveiro, the mother of seventeen-year-old rising star Cristiano Ronaldo, ended her contract with Veiga and joined up with Mendes. At the start of the 2002–3 season, Ronaldo and his mother informed Veiga that his agreement with them was not being renewed because he had shown an alleged 'systematic lack of interest' in improving the terms of the contract. Thus started an enduring professional and personal relationship between Ronaldo and Mendes, whom the player would come to regard as both a close friend and father figure.

Jorge Mendes: The Super Agent portrays Mendes as a personable, sentimental, down-to-earth sort of guy, looking at old family portraits and enjoying reunion dinners with old mates, even if he does spend much of his time on his mobile, keeping up, like an obsessive, with his work. But there is a more complex character behind his suave dark looks and easy, charming smile. He is both ruthless and ambitious, and a tough negotiator: traits without which he would not have developed into one of football's most famous super agents.

From early on in his career, Mendes has provoked fear and loathing, as well as a great deal of respect. A profile of him by Ben Lyttleton in *FourFourTwo* magazine, published in May 2016, quoted his lawyer, Carlos Osorio de Castro, as being 'adamant that Mendes always acts within the law: "He's obsessed with being lawful." Others simply say he is honest, transparent, and brilliant with relationships', writes Lyttleton.[6] Senior executives of three Spanish La Liga clubs – Real Madrid, Atlético de Madrid and Valencia – told me unreservedly that he was the best in the business, quite an accolade given the traditional superiority many Spaniards feel towards the neighbouring Portuguese.

In the end, Mendes has built his reputation on being very good at representing the best interests of his clients, being a calculated risk-taker as well as consummate deal-maker, and on winning the trust of one rising star in particular and keeping it once he had become a legend. 'Jorge's greatest virtues are that he is honest, sincere and professional,' Ronaldo told the SIC documentary. 'Everything he has was well earned. Nobody works as much as he does. If you look at the market, at the clubs he works with, the players he represents, the transfers he makes, he's number one without a doubt.'[7]

On the purely playing side, it was Romanian coach László Bölöni who, in his first season as Sporting's first coach, 2001–2, progressed Ronaldo's career by calling him in to train with the first team when he was still only sixteen.

It proved a steep learning curve, as Ronaldo took time to adapt to a more demanding environment, and to show off why he was worth it. As his biographer Guillem Balagué puts it, 'the very worst script was being played out: he was going unnoticed.'[8] To be so near to the path to success and yet unable to reach it must have been incredibly frustrating for the young Ronaldo.

An initial report by Bölöni was hardly complimentary. In fact, it was largely negative, claiming that Ronaldo had 'no tactical awareness as an individual or team player' and was 'selfish, and lacking mental strength and concentration'.

Only four months on, as Balagué describes, did everything suddenly begin to click, as Ronaldo recovered his self-confidence and became increasingly assertive, daring to nutmeg a veteran player, flicking a sombrero and 'dribbling aplenty'.

As reported in another biography by Luís Pereira and Juan Gallardo, in one training session Ronaldo was rebuked by his teammates for tackling an older player too hard – they called him 'kid' and told him to calm down. 'We'll see if you call me that when I'm the best player in the world,' replied Ronaldo.[9]

That time had yet to come. The team was simply doing too well without him. Sporting ended its first season coached by Bölöni by winning the Portuguese treble – the League, Cup and Super Cup. But the dynamic between player and club was about to change.

As Bölöni prepared for his second season, he was aware that his first-choice striker, Jardel, wanted to leave the club, and was therefore looking for another attacking player for his squad, with no budget to buy one on the transfer market. He decided to take a punt on Ronaldo, switching him from his traditional striker's role, a position he had played through his childhood and youth team years, to left wing, thus giving the team greater mobility in their counter-attack during the 2002–3 season.

That summer of 2002, Ronaldo distinguished himself in a number of friendly matches against foreign and Portuguese teams – impressing with his speed, ball control and ability to beat opponents, including using his height to good effect when climbing for headers. Bölöni had even told sceptical Portuguese media that he was destined to be better than Eusébio or Figo.

Sporting had a long tradition of nurturing highly rated players – especially wingers, like Paulo Futre, Simão Sabrosa, and perhaps the best of them all, Luís Figo. The previous year, another one of those magical wingers, Ricardo Quaresma, had had his breakthrough season, astounding the crowd with his skills. But Portuguese journalist Pedro Marques, who followed Sporting closely at the time, recalled: 'I remember people saying: "Sure, Quaresma is great, but there's another kid who will soon make it into the first team who is breaking records at youth level." They were talking about Cristiano, and when he did get into the first team in 2002, I understood what they meant.'

On 14 July, Sporting's first home game of the season at the old José Alvalade was a friendly against Olympique Lyonnais. In his first professional appearance in a ground he first glimpsed as a ball boy, Ronaldo scored a goal that was disallowed, and the match ended in a 1–1 draw. But the Portuguese media had already started to take notice of the cheeky, self-confident, versatile young Madeiran in their midst. 'This boy is one to watch. He knows how to lose his opponents. He can dribble and he has a nose for goals,' reported the Portuguese sports paper *Record*.[10]

Within days, Sporting had drawn 2–2 in another friendly against Paris Saint-Germain. Ronaldo had three shots at goal, and provided a menacing presence on the wing for most of the match. It wasn't exactly showtime, but the local media were in the process of realizing that Ronaldo was not a player who wanted to stay out of the limelight for long, such was his determination to realize his potential. 'The fans have yet to see the real Ronaldo. This is just the beginning,' he told journalists after the match.

A short sequence posted on YouTube immortalizes the best goals scored by Ronaldo while at Sporting in the 2002–3 season. Compiled by GM Productions, it shows him already displaying the repertoire of trademark tricks that would earn him a global following. Whether running on either wing or down the middle, Ronaldo, aged seventeen, is shown using his pace, athleticism and ball-control skills to outplay his opponents.

On 3 August, Ronaldo came off the bench in the last fifteen minutes of a friendly match against Real Betis. This time he scored the winning goal in injury time, making it 3–2. Exploiting a defensive mistake, Ronaldo stole the ball with a back-heel, then brings it back in front of him before dribbling round the Betis goalkeeper, Toni Prats, who has rushed off his line. Then, on the left edge of the box, and from a tight angle, Ronaldo aims for the goal and lobs it in, beating the defender who has tracked back and made a desperate attempt to deflect the shot.

The journalist Pedro Marques later recalled: 'His amazing pre-season goal against Betis was all the proof I needed: showing fantastic pace and composure, Ronaldo beat the keeper to the ball and, from a difficult angle outside the area, curled a beautiful shot into the top corner with his right foot. Sporting had a star in the making.'[11]

'The exceptional goal that Cristiano Ronaldo scored against Betis put this seventeen-year-old from Madeira on his way to stardom,' wrote the Portuguese sports paper *A Bola* shortly afterwards, when assessing Sporting's prospects for the coming season. 'Over the last month, he has proved he can be the next big thing at the club.'

A 'work of art' was how another Portuguese newspaper described it.[12]

Despite being national champions, as is often the way, Sporting did not enter the 2002–3 Champions League at the group stage; instead they had to face Inter Milan in the qualifiers. With some important players absent through injury, the tie allowed Ronaldo a further opportunity.

Ronaldo was on the bench for the first leg of the qualifier with Inter, on 14 August 2002, and came on for Spanish midfielder Toñito in the fifty-eighth minute. 'Much of the talk before the game centred on another Ronaldo, the Brazilian, and his absence from the Inter squad that night. As for Cristiano Ronaldo, only seventeen at the time, he'd had a great pre-season for Sporting, scoring his first goal for the club a couple of weeks before in the 3–2 friendly win against Betis,' recalled Marques. 'The media and the fans were starting to talk about him as the next big star out of the club's academy, but no one expected him to become so important so quickly. I remember when he entered the field, midway through the second half, I heard a supporter near me saying: "This is the kid I was talking to you about. Just wait and see." So there were already people eager to see him play.'[13]

Despite the anticipation, Ronaldo struggled to make his mark. He made a couple of dribbles down the right, to the delight of the crowd, but nothing decisive enough to help Sporting break the deadlock. The game finished 0–0, with Sporting then losing the second leg 2–0 in Italy and failing to reach the group stage. The main criticism from the Portuguese press was that he didn't pass enough or combine with other players, that he played too much as an individual. With more senior players then returning to fitness, it would be a few months before he was deemed ready to play a League game. This time he was picked from the start against Moreirense, and this time he grabbed the opportunity with both hands.

It is the thirty-fourth minute of the game and a Sporting counter-attack is in full flow. Ronaldo picks up a clever back-heel from Toñito just beyond the halfway line. With a burst of speed, he beats an attempt to bring him down from behind and uses a soon-to-be trademark step-over to leave another defender for dead, before easily beating the goalkeeper, João Ricardo, with a perfectly angled shot into the bottom corner. In doing so he has become Sporting's youngest-ever goal scorer. He is seventeen years, eight months and two days old.

Cristiano Ronaldo instantly takes his shirt off, revealing a youthful but athletic build, runs over to the stands and throws his arms in the air in triumphant recognition of the fans' collective euphoria, before turning and receiving the hugs of his teammates. In less than a minute, Ronaldo has defined a public persona that is destined to become a football icon and global celebrity brand: sheer talent expressed in what the Portuguese TV commentator described as a 'monumental goal', accompanied by preening showmanship and the insatiable desire to make the moment all about him.

He goes on to score a second goal, taking Sporting to a 3–0 win, with a powerful header that shows his height, strength and accuracy in front of goal, adding them to the acceleration and dribbling technique he has already displayed that are further components of his stardom.

He tells journalists that his goals are dedicated to his family, especially his mother, who has joined him in Lisbon. Dolores – a woman of nervous disposition despite a proven record of coping with some tough challenges in her personal life – could barely cope with the first glimmer of a star-studded future. Such was the emotion she felt watching him from the stands that day that she hyperventilated and fainted, breaking her front teeth.

As Ronaldo will later choose to remember it, Dolores suffered this because of 'the emotion, the pride of seeing her son fulfilling himself both professionally and personally'.[14] He basks in the parental recognition that he had been deprived of in his childhood.

In his post-match interview, he goes on to thank his manager, Bölöni, for taking the big risk of playing him. He promises his fans that he will work very hard to live up to the trust they have invested in him, and he hopes he will succeed. Adrenalin pumps through his veins. Few players have so much to say after just one match so early on in their careers. Ronaldo is just a few months into his eighteenth year but he is already acting like a superstar. Extraordinarily self-confident, but a lone warrior nonetheless, with the weight of history on his shoulders, and more ego and self-belief than Eusébio had shown in his entire career or Figo had yet shown in his.

Sporting ended the 2002–3 season with one evident light shining amidst the general doldrums. The club had been knocked out of the Champions League, UEFA Cup and the Portuguese Cup early, and trailed behind both their arch rivals Benfica and José Mourinho's Porto in the League. To add insult to injury, Porto had also been triumphant on the continental stage, winning the UEFA Cup. However, one thing was considered worthy of record by local commentators: Cristiano Ronaldo, the star of Sporting's youth academy, had outshone the rest of the team. 'I passed from anonymity to be in the newspaper headlines, which were already suggesting names of clubs interested in me,' he would later recall.[15]

José Mourinho was among those impressed by the seventeen year old's performances, commenting that summer, 'The first time I saw him I thought: That's van Basten's son. He is a striker, but above all a very elegant player, with great technical quality and movement.'[16] Lest we forget, Marco van Basten was, in the words of the Dutch football chronicler David Winner, 'the greatest and deadliest forward of his generation of terrific footballers'.

For his part, László Bölöni remembers, over the two seasons he worked with Ronaldo, having to rein in the young Madeiran's tendency to show off his technical skills, particularly by over-elaborating his step-overs or holding on to the ball with his extended dribbling, when a pass to a teammate might have proved more effective.

'At the beginning, I had to fight against some permanent exaggerations and correct some things,' Bölöni told *France Football* magazine after Ronaldo secured his third Ballon d'Or in 2014. 'But preventing him from dribbling would have been crazy. The essential part of my job was to find and maintain a balance . . . Was he ready? Yes, he did not lack the courage nor the desire to improve.'[17]

But it would not be the Romanian who would oversee the next phase of Ronaldo's development. After Bölöni bowed out as manager of the Portuguese club, his replacement at the start of the 2003–4 season, Fernando Santos, assumed that honour would be his, declaring in an unequivocal statement that 'Ronaldo is a key player as far as Sporting is concerned.'

Santos, while Lisbon-born, was not among the top tier of European managers, and his low profile meant that he struck some fans as an odd choice to take over at Sporting at a time when one of its emerging stars needed careful grooming, and would present any aspiring boss with a challenge. No one at the time could have guessed that Santos was destined to become one of Portugal's most celebrated football coaches, and achieve immortality over a decade later when he guided the national side to victory at Euro 2016.

Soon after taking up his role as Sporting Lisbon's manager for the 2003–4 season, Santos found in Cristiano Ronaldo a more forceful and ambitious personality than he'd anticipated, and his pledge that he would make the starlet central to his planning came back to haunt him. Rumours soon began circulating that Ronaldo felt restless after his breakthrough season, during which he had started in only eleven out of his twenty-five games – something he saw, with characteristic humility, as the main reason for the team's faltering performance.

By June 2003, Ronaldo had not only become Sporting's likely

starting striker and greatest hope, but had gone on to distinguish himself at the renowned Toulon under-20s tournament, with Portugal winning the competition that always attracted the interest of major clubs looking for young talent. Even before he became the youngest of the winning finalists, Ronaldo declared in an interview: 'I'm very pleased to hear many important clubs are interested in me. My dream is to play in Spain or England; they're the best leagues in Europe.'

It didn't take a rocket scientist to realize that the most lucrative deals for any aspiring star player were to be found not in Portugal, but in Spain and England. The hugely ambitious Jorge Mendes was certainly well aware that this was the case. Forged by the iron will created in his troubled childhood, and the discipline imposed by the Sporting academy, Ronaldo by now had an additional prop: his increasingly powerful agent. With perfect timing, the hottest property in Portuguese football and its most ambitious agent had come together, and were heading for the global stage.

6. GROWING PAINS: MESSI

The large comfortable flat that the club paid for was on a long, lively avenue called the Gran Via Carles III. The apartment was conveniently located within easy walking distance of one of Barcelona's most popular department stores, El Corte Inglés, and the Nou Camp. It contained four bedrooms, two bathrooms, a kitchen and a balcony that led to a landscaped garden and community swimming pool, which the Messis happily shared with their neighbours in their early days in Barcelona, when the young Argentine was still far from being a celebrated public figure, still a shy person who rarely drew attention to himself off the pitch. The same could not, perhaps, be said of Jorge Messi.

The agreement signed by Messi in March 2001, after he and his father had returned to Barcelona, guaranteed that young Lionel would be paid an incremental salary reaching the equivalent of €600,000 as he progressed through the youth categories to the first team.[1] An astonishing commitment to make to a thirteen-year-old child. FC Barcelona had also agreed to fully cover Messi's growth hormone treatment, on the advice of the club doctor, José Borrel, who had seen Messi's medical notes and had no doubt that the key to Messi's future as a professional player lay in it continuing, for a then unspecified period.

The contract was negotiated, by Minguella, among others acting for FC Barcelona, and Messi's father. Only later did it emerge that Jorge Messi had also signed a separate contract with a firm of agents based in Rosario – represented there by Martin Montero and Fabian Soldini – giving them an agreed percentage of any ensuing image rights as Lionel developed as a professional player.[2]

Montero and Soldini were well known to the Messi family, as they represented several Rosario-based players, among them Leandro Depetris, who had recently transferred from Newell's to AC Milan, and Maxi Cuccittini, an older first cousin of Lionel on his mother's side, to whom Messi had been close since early childhood. After playing as a youth with Newell's, Maxi played for San Lorenzo de Almagro before going on to play for clubs in Paraguay, Mexico and Brazil.

I caught up with Martin Montero in the autumn of 2016 in Rosario, one of the few inhabitants of the city prepared to balance his respect for Messi as a player with a more critical view of his father. A long-running legal action taken by Montero and Soldini against Jorge Messi for alleged breach of contract, which Messi senior contested, remained unresolved, with local judges perhaps reluctant to pronounce in any way that might damage the reputation of the city's most famous and universally admired icon.

When I met him, Montero was working for ADIUR, a sorting house for young players dreaming of becoming famous like Messi one day. The premises, in one of the more rundown neighbourhoods of the city's notorious Zona Sur or South Side, seemed deliberately aimed at imposing a reality check on any star-struck youngster from an early stage. A small football pitch made up of rough turf was enclosed by a block of council flats, its perimeter a high fence topped by barbed wire.

With his portly build, ruddy face and bloodshot eyes, Montero would not have been out of place running a small grocery store. His cramped office was decorated with rusting, unidentified silver trophies and broken filing cabinets, the only hint of glamour a passing reference and introduction to his wife – I mentioned I needed treatment for pain in my lower back and she runs a popular aquatherapy practice, in a building owned by César Menotti, the coach who had taken Argentina to World Cup victory in 1978 and managed FC Barcelona in Maradona's time.

'The story is clear as daylight,' according to Montero. 'We had made international headlines in the summer of 2000 by negotiating the transfer of Leandro Depetris, a twelve-year-old from Newell's Old Boys, to AC Milan. We also represented a cousin of Messi called Maxi Cuccittini. Then Maxi's father, Messi's uncle, tells us one day: "My nephew Lionel plays really well, you should check him out." So we went and saw the boy Messi playing at Newell's. He was very small but he was a nice boy, a divine boy, clearly the best and he was passionate about his football.

'We talked with his dad, Jorge, who said he wanted to get his son a trial, to see if he could move to a bigger club. We said we'd see what we could do . . . so we got in touch with Minguella in Barcelona, who we knew, and we told him we have this real talent and could we bring him over for a trial . . . so within a week we travelled: me, my partner Soldini, Messi and his father, to Barcelona. They did the trial . . .

'We had no dealings with River Plate . . . I don't know what happened there but he did go for a trial . . . While he was still at Newell's and after he arrived in Barcelona we paid for his injection course at \$890 per month. Part of it was paid for by his father's employers, Fundación Acindar, the other half by ourselves – Fabian Soldini and Martin Montero.'

I asked Montero if Jorge Messi had been motivated by the need to escape from Argentine football, its uncertainties, its corruption, its lack of prospects at club level. His answer was sanitized, or perhaps influenced by a touch of nationalist pride. 'Football here in Argentina isn't complicated. It has its virtues and its defects just like European football – a lot of good things, and not so good. No, I think Messi's father wanted the experience of a new life – and when a club like Barça shows interest in you, it's an added motivation. When Barça appeared on the scene Lionel was thunderstruck.'

So what was the case against Messi's father all about?

'He denies our existence in the official story – but the fact is that we signed a contract, like when one does a property deal, before a notary on 18 October 2000, which gave me rights of attorney to manage the professional career of Leo with Soldini. We worked for six years on Messi's behalf before the father broke off the relationship, without paying us.'

Montero was visceral in his criticism of Jorge Messi and his wife, both of whom he feels conspired in a betrayal of trust. As for Leo . . .

'Me and Soldini have great affection for the kid. Early in 2016, Soldini was with Leo in Barcelona at his home . . . but when you bring up the subject of money, of what his father owes us, he doesn't want to know. He doesn't face up to the problems. He is a boy who doesn't want problems. He says, "No, that's a problem for my father to deal with." . . . There is a judge overseeing the case but it's difficult for any judge in Argentina to rule against the Messis.'

*

By the spring of 2001, the entire Messi family had relocated to the Gran Via Carles III apartment, and Leo was settling in to life at La Masia. The converted traditional stone farmhouse, named La Masia as it is Catalan for 'home', was first used as a base for young players in 1979, and in the intervening years had developed into one of the world's foremost club academies. The La Masia name is part of the club's identification with a local culture that sees itself as distinct in language and history from the rest of Spain, and which had suffered under the Franco-era repression of Catalan nationalism.

The club's slogan, *mes que un club* – more than a club – is also part of this mythology of Barça playing a political role as a representative democracy, owned by members who elect their president, and an artistic role by playing the game with a refined and creative style.

This politicization of a sporting entity was perhaps not one of the club's pull factors for the Messis, however. Escaping from the financial chaos and turbulent politics of Argentina, the family were initially happy to enjoy the relative stability and economic benefits of Spanish democracy. Despite their Catalan ancestral roots, they were less inclined to engage with what they feared might threaten their integration as Spanish-speaking immigrants: the potentially volatile historic campaign for Catalan independence.

The independence movement had been growing since the long presidency (1980–2003) of the first post-Franco elected Catalan regional president – Jordi Pujol – as Catalonia gained more autonomous powers under the Spanish constitution than at any time since the Spanish Civil War. Pujol had emerged as a leading figure of the nationalist Convergència y Unió grouping during the last year of the Franco regime, developing close ties with FC Barcelona at all levels of the club and pressing for ever-greater powers for Catalonia from the nascent democratic state.

While Pujol was in power, Catalonia's immigration policy tilted towards North Africans – mainly Moroccans – rather than Latin Americans. Cheap North African labour was regarded by employers as more suitable for the fruit, vine and olive harvests than the socially mobile, more skilled Latin Americans (although the influx has led to the near ghettoization of the Muslim community in Catalan towns like Lleida, potential breeding grounds for militant Islamists). The immigration policy drew criticism from unionist politicians in Madrid and non-nationalist Catalans, who claimed that Pujol favoured North Africans over Spanish-speaking Latin Americans because he believed they would be more willing to learn Catalan.

Drawing on his experiences of the resistance and repression of Catalan identity, Pujol had declared in one of his political manifestos that FC Barcelona was a folkloric manifestation of the Catalan people, 'a reserve we can draw [on] when other sources dry up, when the doors of normality are closed to us'. In other words, he saw it as a political and social vehicle to be used when necessary, along with other 'manifestations' of cultural identity. Other Catalan politicians followed, and continue to follow, his lead.

Catalan politics provoked a certain tension in the Messi family. After Messi was signed up by FC Barcelona, he and his father Jorge found themselves drawn inevitably into the protective environment of the club, with its collective identity forged round a sporting ideal of excellence along with the perks and benefits that were enjoyed by players and staff. By contrast, Leo's brother Hugo had stayed in Rosario with his grandparents, and his mother Celia struggled to play the family matriarch and make new friends in Barcelona. Her stay, and that of her oldest son Matías and her daughter María Sol, proved short-lived.

Matías missed his girlfriend in Rosario, while Celia became increasingly concerned with the effects of the local education system on María Sol. Learning in Catalan was a compulsory part of the curriculum, but with Spanish as her native language, María Sol found it difficult (as did the rest of her family) to learn Catalan, which sounded like a mixture of French and Portuguese but had none of the global reach of either, and which many Spaniards and Latin Americans considered a dialect rather than a language. Their return to Rosario in the summer of 2001 provoked the first breach in the Messi family history.

Far from making them feel integrated, Catalan politics had made them feel outsiders, not just as immigrants, but simply because their first language had always been and continued to be Spanish. As Jorge Messi later told the Catalan sports journalist Sique Rodriguez: 'It was a very hard change. The customs, the idiosyncrasies, the values, the food . . . everything was different. We had to start from scratch. Practically from zero. Even the language was different.'[3]

Life was not particularly easy for Lionel either in those early months. His status as an underage foreign player allowed him to play in regional matches and friendlies, but not in any national competition in Spain. That clearance was pending, as he awaited a full licence from the Spanish football authorities, which was delayed because Newell's Old Boys took their time in submitting the necessary papers. It would take almost a year for the technicalities to be resolved. The boy had borne the weight of his family's hopes and sacrifices on his back, all based on the future his footballing abilities could deliver, and now he wasn't even allowed to properly play.

La Masia provided the kind of safe haven and education that the young Messi needed to nurture his talent and his and his family's ambitions, even as the family divided geographically. In Messi's time La Masia – now replaced by a more modern facility – was innocuous and self-contained, in stark contrast to the looming presence of the nearby Nou Camp and the expansive city of Barcelona that spread out in every direction. Its interior was simply decorated and furnished with touches of functionality, like the small number of computer screens intruding on an otherwise spartan space.

The pervading sense of austerity and discipline was not unlike that of the Benedictine monastic fathers of Montserrat, the mountain shrine outside Barcelona where the Catalan Virgin, her face darkened by the flames of votive candles over centuries, which remains a key place of pilgrimage for many Barça fans.

As the former hockey player turned sports director at La Masia Carles Folguera explained to me, 'It's important that a pupil who comes to our academy knows that his talent is on a hiding to nothing unless it is accompanied by values such as commitment, discipline, solidarity and comradeship.'

Discipline extended to a zero-tolerance policy on class absenteeism, drugs, alcohol and uncontrolled web browsing. Today, lectures are given by outside specialists on subjects that range from the destructive nature of cocaine to the security risks of social networking.

'We try and get our kids to understand that simply because you have 800 "friends" on Facebook, this is not a guarantee of support and loyalty. Trust is knowing that a friend is not going to take a picture of you in the bathroom and distribute it round the world. It's a question of privacy and respect,' Folguera told me when I visited La Masia in 2010, shortly before it moved to its new, larger premises.

Messi, together with other famous alumni including Pep Guardiola, Andrés Iniesta, Xavi Hernández, Cesc Fàbregas, Gerard Piqué, Sergio Busquets, Pedro, Victor Valdés and Carles Puyol, retained an enduring respect for their teachers and for a building that stands to this day by the main entrance to the Nou Camp, marked by the statue to Joan Gamper, the Swiss-born founder of FC Barcelona.

In any one year, some 100 teenagers were attached to La Masia after being selected, with their parents' agreement, for an education that included the national curriculum but which placed a special emphasis on a philosophy of sporting excellence and ethical conduct.

The school, far from being an infallible production line for talented young players, was a meticulously organized system for sifting the wheat from the chaff, with only a small number of pupils in any year destined to break through into top flight football, even fewer of them destined for FC Barcelona's own first team.

A team photograph from the early 2000s shows three players who broke through: Cesc Fàbregas, easily recognizable without a beard; Gerard Piqué, a giant among minnows; and then the smallest in the group, his attention not on the camera but talking to a teammate, a scruffy-haired Leo Messi. Diligence and talent would take all three to the very top, but in late 2001 Leo's registration status meant he was still unable to play in competitive, national matches.

'I would see Messi at the youth games not even sat on the bench, but in street clothes because he was not allowed to play in certain matches,' remembers Jaume Marcet, a Catalan journalist who covered the young Barça players in those days. 'He had come all this way to play and he was unable to.'

Such circumstances might have defeated a weaker character. But Leo, like his father, was determined to succeed – playing for FC Barcelona was a dream come true. As Jorge told the UK journalist Pete Jenson, 'Just as the bright kids want to go to Harvard, Messi wanted to go on trial with Barça.'[4]

A fellow La Masia resident at the time, Victor Vázquez, recalled: 'The first days he sat in the corner and never said anything. He was very shy until one day Piqué, Cesc and myself went over to talk to him.' By the following year, Messi had won over his teammates, and was an inspiration. 'You looked forward and you saw Messi,' Vázquez told Guillem Balagué. 'And you said, "Fuck me, mate, I know we are going to do something good here."'[5]

Messi's experience of La Masia was that it encouraged his talent to flourish in an environment that was both safe and diligent. The young Argentine soaked up Barça's system of play and culture, while giving it a new dimension with his own style and attitude.

As Messi recalled for Jordi Llompart's documentary *Barça Dreams*: 'It was hard at first when I arrived in Barcelona because I was only thirteen and had left everything behind – my family, my friends, my country. The truth is that it was difficult. But I am lucky that I landed in Barcelona, and in La Masia, and found myself living and playing alongside great kids who treated me really well from the start. I spent almost all my days with them. And that made things easier for me.'[6]

Still, there were some of the teaching staff in his early days at La Masia who were not entirely convinced even then that Messi had the talent, let alone the build, to have a real future in top-flight professional football. They suggested that he might be better suited for five-a-sides. Carles Folguera did not share in that line of thinking. In his view, Messi's shyness and underwhelming physique belied a hidden fortitude that defined his character.

A significant turn in Messi's fortunes came when he was finally enrolled by the Spanish Football Federation in February 2002, freeing him up to play in all the competitions that FC Barcelona were involved in. He and his father were also joined in Barcelona by his older brother, Rodrigo. The 2002–3 season was one that would endure in La Masia's history books, with that under-16s team going on to win an unprecedented treble in their category – the Spanish Cup, the Catalan Cup and the League. Messi scored thirty goals in thirty-seven games playing as a second striker, supported by the creativity of Cesc Fàbregas in midfield and Gerard Piqué rallying the defence. The team are acknowledged as Barcelona's greatest ever youth side and became known as the 'Baby Dream Team', with Messi making a very distinctive mark from an early stage.

'Messi came alive when he was on the pitch,' recalled Albert Benaiges, who oversaw Barça's youth development at the time. 'Everybody said that he was really special. But he had great qualities that you very rarely see – this incredible change of pace and the ability to run with the ball so close to his feet.'[7]

Josep Minguella remembers dropping in one Saturday morning to watch the Barça youth team play. 'It was a really brilliant show. I remember I sat there watching it with Messi's father and his brother, Hugo, who was in Barcelona visiting. The game had already begun when we were joined by a member of the FC Barcelona board of directors with overall responsibility for youth development. At half-time he asked me if I could introduce him to Messi's father, so he could congratulate him on his son's performance. It was the first time he had seen Messi play and had no idea who he was. This showed just how ignorant the highest echelons of the club had been about his potential.'

But Messi didn't single himself out in what was first and foremost a remarkable team: 'Piqué was our chief, *el jefe*,' he later recalled. Fàbregas remembers one of the early matches that the Baby Dream Team played together: 'The opposing players for some reason had it in for Messi, and Piqué came to blows with some of them in Leo's defence, getting a red card as a result.' The act is indicative of the camaraderie that La Masia had instilled. He added: 'I began at La Masia aged nine with Gerard, and we were twelve years old when Messi turned up. If at that time anyone had told us that we would one day reach the first team and be surrounded by other great players, the three of us would have said "impossible". Perhaps one of us, two at the most, but three? No way.'[8]

But just as he had been with Newell's record-breaking class of '87, Lionel Messi was the star. Another memorable team photograph of the period from the Barça archives shows Messi with a football clutched between his boots, and his face covered in a plastic protector. It was taken during what became known as the Game of the Mask, the final of the Catalan Cup in 2003, in which Messi played with a broken cheekbone. Wearing the mask annoyed him so much that he took it off, prompting his substitution for his own safety, but only after he had scored two goals to secure victory.

Messi's eventual registration with the Spanish federation and stellar performances during his time in the youth teams triggered another tug-of-war for his services. Messi's residential status made him eligible for Spain's national youth squads, but then Argentine Football Association president Julio Grondona pre-empted any attempt by the Spanish authorities to select him. Grondona enlisted Messi to play for Argentina's under-17s team, ensuring that Spain would not be able to call him up.

According to Vicente del Bosque, who in later years managed the Spanish national team to European and World Cup glory, an attempt to select Messi as a Spanish youth international was made by senior officials of the Spanish Football Federation as early as 2002, when the player was only fifteen. FC Barcelona were apparently well disposed to the idea, but Messi, as he always did when it came to complex decisions off the field, deferred to his unofficial agent, his father Jorge, who blocked the move.

'The Spanish federation contacted the club through the manager, who then talked to the kid, but in those days he was even more tongue-tied and mumbled something about letting his father deal with it,' del Bosque told me in 2016.

I asked del Bosque why the Spanish authorities didn't try harder to get Messi before Grondona moved in, for surely it would have changed the history of international football, and made Spain's period of international dominance endure even longer.

'Those in the Spanish federation who went looking for Messi in 2002 knew from reports that he was a good player, but they could not have imagined that he was going to become the player he became. There were lots of good young kids around with potential. It wasn't easy. It seems they didn't realize that one of them was going to turn out to be quite amazing.

'As it turned out it was a bad decision for him, that did not help his career in any way. Just look at the last time Argentina won a World Cup – or how often they've won the Copa América since he's been in the team. Not once – he just doesn't have the players around him.'

If Messi had become a Spanish international, he would have ended up playing alongside not just the best of FC Barcelona but also the best of Real Madrid, and a sprinkling of other players, who produced the most entertaining and successful football by a national team in a generation. 'Yes, you could say we would have liked having Messi in the team,' del Bosque told me, with characteristic understatement.

It's another example of the influence Jorge has always had over his son's career, often to the point that Leo's own attitude to off-field matters has been hard to discern. But perhaps this owes as much to Messi's singleminded determination to succeed on the field of play. Years later, Jorge Messi told the Spanish TV sports programme *Informe Robinson* about the insecurity his family felt in those early days in Barcelona: 'One day I asked Leo: "Well, what do you want to do? Because the decision is yours, if you want to go back to Argentina, then we'll go back."

'Leo looked at me, and he said: "No, I want to stay, I want to play football in Barcelona and want to play in the first division for Barcelona." That was Leo's decision, it was his decision: nobody forced him into anything.'[9]

7. INTO THE MARKET: RONALDO

From the early years of Cristiano Ronaldo's childhood, Dolores Aveiro had always encouraged her son to find substitute father figures, men she felt she could trust and who could compensate for the failings of her husband.

Jorge Mendes, for his part, saw in Cristiano's talent that same rough diamond the player's early mentors had identified – with a personality and ambition that needed careful, if firm, handling. That someone would also require business acumen, if the full financial potential of his prize client was not to be squandered.

In Mendes, Cristiano Ronaldo found himself an agent who was more than a match for a new generation of big-money club presidents when it came to distinguishing between expression of interest and speculative bids, between tentative offers and firm ones. The business of modern football is not like a normal corporate tendering process, where each interested party presents a sealed bid, but rather a game of cards, with players hiding or showing up to suit their interests, a game of bluff and counterbluff in which sectors of the sports media are complicit – for nothing sells better than a good transfer story, however baseless it ends up being.

Mendes was a master when it came to exploiting the football market for his and Ronaldo's benefit. He had the strength of character and empathy to deal with the self-possession of the ambitious, extroverted and physically beautiful young Cristiano Ronaldo. He became a genuine adviser and mentor, as well as trusted friend, rather than a Svengali figure seeking to manipulate or control the player through some mesmeric or sinister influence. Both personalities were destined to complement each other in the brave new world of elite football dominated by a handful of global super-brands.

This was a world in which, since the beginning of the millennium, national teams had been eclipsed by the inexorable rise of multinational clubs like Real Madrid, FC Barcelona and Manchester United. For talented players, their agents and their clubs, globalization and ever-increasing TV money meant that selling or being sold to the highest bidder was competing forcefully against traditional ties. Everything now seemed to have a price, even loyalty to one's roots. Local culture and even tribal loyalties appeared to matter increasingly less than the business of winning the most lucrative deals, whether they be sponsorship, merchandising or TV.

As David Goldblatt writes of this modern period, beginning in the 1990s, in his seminal history of football, *The Ball is Round*: 'The Queen of Hearts had surely been reading the European sports press at the turn of the millennium. Here she would have found ample material for practising the absorption of the implausible, the contradictory and the bizarre. Had she been steeped in the cultural norms of an earlier generation of European football, the daily digest would have seemed incomprehensible.'[1]

A watershed moment was the European Court of Justice ruling in 1995 in favour of the Belgian player Jean-Marc Bosman, who challenged the restrictions placed on footballers from European Union countries playing within the national leagues of Europe. The ruling allowed professional football players in the EU to move freely to another club at the end of their contracts, in accordance with the new competition rules established by the EU's single market in 1992. This meant players could demand ever-higher salaries and bonuses, whether they were renewing a contract or moving on, as clubs fought to avoid losing their assets for nothing. This in turn inflated transfer fees, creating an elite group of clubs able to financially out-muscle those with less commercial clout. All of which was music to agents' ears.

In Spain, fertile ground for a global mass following had long since been sown by FC Barcelona and Real Madrid, not least because a rivalry that was fuelled by high-voltage politics and commercial interests had translated into a self-serving duopoly, at least at national level. When it came to forming the teams with the biggest foreign stars or investing in homegrown talent with the biggest potential, the two clubs were in a Spanish market of their own.

Initially, the extent to which the post-Bosman player market and global commercialism was shaping football was most evident on the Real Madrid side of the divide, particularly after the construction magnate Florentino Pérez won the club presidency for the first time in 2000. Over four seasons, he took advantage of the speculative and overheated Spanish economy to sell off high-value real estate belonging to the club at a huge profit, and built Real Madrid's marketing strategy around the purchase of at least one major new international star per year, who could appeal to consumers across frontiers.

Real Madrid developed its 'brand' as a global club of *galácticos* – superstars – with record transfer deals led by the Portuguese Luís Figo and the Frenchman Zinedine Zidane in 2000 and 2001 respectively, before Brazilian Ronaldo Luís Nazário de Lima – the original Ronaldo – was also signed in 2002. Next on their list was Manchester United's David Beckham.

Not only did the players guarantee that millions in new merchandise would be sold, they also enabled the club to improve its TV and sponsorship contracts.

Further north, by 2003, Manchester United had established themselves as the pre-eminent English football club, and as a global football brand. Since the foundation of the Premier League in 1992, they had won eight of the eleven titles and been runners-up on another two occasions. On-field success was enabled by staggering growth off it. Between 1992 and 2002 their turnover grew from £25 million to £175 million. In the first five years of the Premier League, from 1992 to 1997, the club generated income of £249 million, of which £69 million was spent on its wage bill and £66 million reported as profit. 'This performance would be good by any standard; in the football industry, where most clubs have reported a pre-tax loss, it was dazzling,' noted a report by Stefan Szymanski of Cass Business School in London.[2]

It wasn't just financial performance either: as the millennium turned, they had established themselves as the pre-eminent club in England, with three successive League titles, off the back of their treble-winning season in 1998–9. A third place finish in 2001–2 to an upwardly mobile Arsenal team was a reality check, but they had flexed their muscles by acquiring Rio Ferdinand for a world record fee. Throughout this phenomenal period of financial growth and sporting success, United's most prized asset was widely recognized as their manager, Alex Ferguson. In football terms he was a rarity – and alone among the British managers – in not only surviving but flourishing in the new globalized era. As the football scout Greg Gordon wrote on Quora after Ferguson's eventual retirement in 2013: 'He has been able to flourish as a manager who can mix consistent and consistently applied old-fashioned inter-personal values with the mental acuity to innovate and not just move with the times but shape them, creating a whole host of successes in wildly different circumstances and contexts.'

Ferguson was the only manager to flourish in both the pre- and post-Bosman eras to any real degree. His success straddled the transition from 'working-class boys' to cosmopolitan superstar players, agents and international twenty-four-hour media. His influence ensured that United jostled with Real Madrid and FC Barcelona, and a handful of others, at the front of the queue whenever a rising star was ready to step into the big time.

Throughout the 2002–3 season, the rumour mill listed FC Barcelona, Real Madrid, Arsenal and Manchester United among the clubs interested in Cristiano Ronaldo. In reality, neither of the two Spanish clubs was a serious runner.

The FC Barcelona of summer 2003 was entering a new era under young president Joan Laporta and his vice-president Sandro Rosell, both of whom had their minds and club funds focused on the €30 million signing of Brazilian Ronaldinho, as well as on a new manager in Dutchman Frank Rijkaard, and the exploitation of an unprecedented supply of brilliant homegrown talent, among them Leo Messi. Barça did also move for a young Sporting player, but that was Ricardo Quaresma, seen as closer to the finished article.

Real Madrid were flush with funds but were fixated on David Beckham, a player the marketing department believed was needed to expand the Spanish club's commercial interests in the USA and Asia, specifically Japan and the ever-expanding Chinese market.

Among the English clubs, it was Arsenal that were the first to show real interest in Cristiano Ronaldo, making a characteristically tentative approach in January 2003. Talks were held in Lisbon between Mendes and Arsenal's representatives, and Ronaldo even visited London with his mother, where the club became enthused with him and he with the club.

Arsène Wenger, the Arsenal manager, would later recall that Cristiano warmed to the cultural transformation the Frenchman had achieved at the Gunners. The Madeira-born teenager, who had grown up in mainland Portugal, came across as a player who would easily manage a new life in the UK, adapting to its language and customs. He was also a striker who was fast and managed the ball with flair and skill, and would fit in well with the creative and cerebral Wenger regime. As Wenger revealed years later, the manager even went as far as to present Ronaldo with an Arsenal shirt with the number 9 and his name on the back.

However, money and tactics contrived against Arsenal. The cost of the construction of the new Emirates Stadium left the club unable to raise their initial offer after it was deemed too low by Sporting. Another season of domestic development looked likely from the club's perspective, hence their new manager, Fernando Santos, planning a team around the teenager in summer 2003. But then Real Madrid got their man, Beckham, and Manchester United were left with a space to fill on their right flank.

United's assistant manager at the time was Portuguese Carlos Queiroz, who was also represented by Jorge Mendes and had close contacts with Sporting, where he had been head coach from 1994 to 1996. When he was recruited by the English club in 2002, he had successfully lobbied for a cooperation agreement between the two clubs, covering coach and player training, and made a point of recommending that his new club sign Cristiano Ronaldo.

The assistant manager's first few months at Manchester United were overshadowed by the widening of the rift between Ferguson and Beckham, which had been opening ever wider since the player's celebrity marriage to Victoria Adams, popularly known as 'Posh' as a member of the pop group the Spice Girls. The first major and widely publicized row between the two had occurred in February 2000, when Beckham missed a training session and claimed it was because his son, Brooklyn, was ill with gastroenteritis. Despite the alleged illness, Victoria attended a fashion gala in London. Ferguson was furious that Beckham had agreed to babysit ahead of a crucial League match with Leeds United, their nearest title rival. Ferguson fined Beckham £50,000 (the equivalent of two weeks' wages at the time) and left him out of the Leeds match.

Two months later, Ferguson was in secret contact with Luís Figo's agent, José Veiga, to explore the possibility of transferring the

Portuguese player from FC Barcelona to United – perhaps even swapping him for Beckham. The idea came to nothing after Figo became the prime target of Real Madrid's president Florentino Pérez.

Ferguson then put any plans to sell Beckham on hold, calculating that he would face a huge backlash from United fans and the media if he allowed Beckham to leave when the Englishman's star was rising high at both club and international level. During that summer's European Championships in Holland and Belgium, Beckham's occasional flashes of brilliance struck one of the few positive notes in a generally mediocre campaign by England. 'He has no ego. He is prepared to be a general if that is needed, and also a soldier if that is needed,' commented the then England manager Kevin Keegan.

Beckham's England star perhaps reached its zenith with his free kick against Greece, three minutes into added time, which secured England's qualification for the 2002 World Cup in Japan and South Korea. Manager Sven-Göran Erikson called it the most important goal of his career as a manager. The contrast with Ferguson's reaction could not have been more stark. Asked for his comment on Beckham's goal, the United boss darkened and scowled before telling journalists: 'The media has gone over the top as usual. You do not care a damn about us. It is all about selling newspapers for you people. You do not have to pick up the pieces, pick a team and bring your players back to earth.'

His comment was followed by a decision to drop Beckham from the next United game and to continue dropping him, off and on, in subsequent weeks, which may have resulted from a dip in the player's form, but which certainly made Beckham feel unfairly treated.

It was the beginning of the end of Beckham's time at United, an end eventually realized when Real Madrid signed him for £24.5 million in 2003, leaving fans and shareholders of the English giants wondering how the gap he was leaving as a player and global brand could ever be filled. But when one door closes, another opens, especially with Mendes and Queiroz oiling the hinges.

On 7 August 2003, newly Beckham-less Manchester United fulfilled a long-standing invitation to play Sporting, in a match marking the inauguration of the Portuguese club's new stadium in Lisbon, the rebuilt Estádio José Alvalade.

Manchester United's jet-lagged players landed in the Portuguese capital feeling exhausted after a three-week pre-season tour of the United Sates, played largely for commercial reasons and beginning just after they'd yet again won the League. The fanfare given to the inauguration of a new stadium and the enthusiasm of the 50,000 fans belied the appalling condition of the turf – it was a new pitch, but the grass was poorly drained and cutting up in places.

Nevertheless, Ferguson fielded a strong team and had every expectation of winning. The team had won all its games in the US against strong competition – AC Milan, FC Barcelona, Juventus and Bayern Munich. But that day in Lisbon, Sporting beat them 3–1. The match was brought alive by the performance of an eighteen-year-old boy from Madeira whom none of the Manchester United players had ever encountered before, but who was not unknown to the boss and his assistant.

Ronaldo's reputation as the hottest prospect in Portuguese football, well promoted by Mendes in his early dealing with Manchester United and other clubs, was growing, a year on from making his first appearance as a professional and two weeks away from his debut with the Portuguese national team.

The quality of the player, with his lightning runs and repertoire of step-overs, was evident from early on in the game. If there was one moment in the match that defined it, it was in the first half, when Ronaldo picked up the ball and turned John O'Shea inside out, before firing a dipping shot at goal that Fabien Barthez could only parry.

'I thought, Bloody hell,' recalled Gary Neville, who was watching the match at home and paying particular attention to how Ronaldo, playing on the left, was tormenting his deputy at right back. 'When you're watching a player who you would usually play against, you look much more closely, and it's very rare to see that level of movement and speed. Only a few people are capable of timing a run like that, inside the full-back and centre-back – and the speed of it.'[3]

Poor O'Shea, tasked with marking Ronaldo, was left so outclassed and outrun by the teenager's dribbling tricks and sheer speed that he returned to the dressing room at half-time exhausted, before being substituted in the second half. 'He did give me a roasting,' O'Shea later conceded.

Within minutes of the game's conclusion, Gary Neville was texting his younger brother Phil about Ronaldo. Phil, who played that day, had been struck initially by Ronaldo's appearance – scrawny yet carefully groomed. His brightly coloured boots, his carapace of immovable hair with its blond highlights, the metal brace in his mouth: carnivalesque, eccentric, egocentric. 'He was obviously someone who liked himself,' recalled the older Neville.

Other United players shared Gary's enthusiasm: 'Scholesy [Paul Scholes], Butty [Nicky Butt] and I were saying, "We have got to sign this guy," because, remember, we had just missed out on Ronaldinho. So we needed to sign a top player,' said Rio Ferdinand.

Ferdinand and his teammates Gary Neville and Ryan Giggs asked Ferguson in the dressing room whether he was going to sign Cristiano. The boss was initially non-committal. Then, after the match was over, when the players were changed and back on the coach waiting to depart for the airport, word came that assistant manager, manager and chief executive were trying to broker a deal. 'So we weren't pissed off about being late,' Ferdinand recalled.[4] In his memoirs, Ferguson describes the Man United players in the dug-out during the game exclaiming, 'Bloody hell, boss, he's some player, him.' Ferguson replied, 'It's all right. I've got him sorted.'[5]

Ferguson met Ronaldo and his agent Mendes in an office at the new stadium, agreeing to pay a £12.24 million transfer fee – considerably more than the £8 million Sporting executives claimed Real Madrid were prepared to pay for him.

Then Ferguson told Ronaldo: 'You won't play every week. I'm telling you that now, but you'll become a first-team player. There's no doubt in my mind about that. It'll take time for you to adjust. We'll look after you.'[6] Ferguson would keep his word.

Five days after the match, on 12 August, Manchester United formally announced to the London Stock Exchange that it had completed the signing, with the Portuguese teenager signing a four-year contract. Ronaldo said: 'I am very happy to be signing for the best team in the world, and especially proud to be the first Portuguese player to join Manchester United.'

Ferguson claimed an agreement had been in place to sign the player 'months ago', but that his club quickened their pursuit when it became clear other clubs were also chasing him: 'We have been negotiating for Cristiano for quite some time, but the interest in him from other clubs accelerated in the last few weeks so we had to move quickly to get him . . . It was only through our association with Sporting that they honoured our agreement of months ago.'[7]

Ferguson had indeed been on the case since Queiroz had joined Man United in 2002, and had followed up his assistant manager's recommendation by sending his chief scout Jim Ryan to Lisbon to take a closer look at Ronaldo.

Ryan returned and told Ferguson: 'Wow, I've seen a player. I think he is a winger, but he's been playing centre-forward in the youth team. I wouldn't be waiting too long. At seventeen someone will gamble.'[8]

Sporting wanted to keep him for two more years. Ferguson initially suggested a deal that would have him transferring to Manchester United at the end of that period. The final details of a deal, bringing forward the transfer and agreeing on price and commissions, were thrashed out by Ferguson and Mendes, and remain a matter of dispute.

As the *Guardian* investigative reporter David Conn revealed in an article published in January 2011,[9] documents and statements filed in a court case in Porto raised questions about which agents actually worked on the deal, how much they were paid and why United paid £12.24 million when it was rumoured Sporting Lisbon had been discussing a fee of €6 million with other English clubs, including Arsenal.

In the court case, Mendes's company GestiFute was sued by the English agency Formation for half the fees the Portuguese agent allegedly earned on the Manchester United contract, and other deals. In his defence, according to documents seen by the *Guardian*, Mendes said United did not pay him at all and that his fee was paid by an Italian agent, Giovanni Branchini. The Football Association, through which clubs must pay all agents' fees, is understood to have stated, in a court-ordered disclosure, that United did indeed pay 'another agent' – not Mendes – £1 million. The agencies eventually reached an out-of-court settlement, with GestiFute paying Formation a substantial undisclosed sum.

Whatever the detail, it was the outcome that was to remain fixed in history. As Conn points out, Manchester United's 'signing of a callow, improbably talented Cristiano Ronaldo in August 2003 was a defining moment for the Premier League and modern football itself, heralding a dazzling new superstar for a fledgling millennium.' He adds: 'For the eighteen-year-old's agent, former nightclub owner and semi-professional footballer Jorge Mendes, Ronaldo's arrival marked his entry into football's big time.'

Ronaldo would later claim that he had been a fervent follower of Manchester United's treble-winning team. He called putting pen to paper on the Man United deal 'a dream' fulfilled. Mendes called it a 'moment of unique happiness'. The player suggested they should go and celebrate with champagne that evening, but Mendes said he was too busy and had to get to work on some other deals. Ronaldo ended up celebrating alone – but held no hard feelings against his agent and friend.

Toasting his future by himself, at probably the last moment in his life when he could sit in a bar without being recognized, it must have all felt a long way away from the skinny little boy who ran up the hills of Quinta de Falcão. Things were about to get really interesting.

8. THE DWARF: MESSI

On 16 November 2003, FC Barcelona played a friendly match away against Portuguese club Porto, for which the Catalan club was paid €250,000. The match marked the inauguration of Porto's new Estádio do Dragão, built to be ready for the European Championships the following year, just like Sporting's new José Alvalade.

Having worked under two managers at Barça, Bobby Robson and Louis van Gaal, José Mourinho had taken Porto to Portuguese League, Portuguese Cup and UEFA Cup glory during the 2002–3 season. A game between this rising force and a traditional continental power-house seemed a fitting inauguration for the stadium, but it would also produce an even more important debut.

Lionel Messi had much to prove as, aged sixteen years and four months, he stepped out in the seventy-fifth minute to play for the first team of FC Barcelona, one of the world's great sporting institutions.

Messi would later reflect on this game as a major breakthrough in his career, calling it a 'childhood dream come true' in a Barça TV programme specially made to commemorate the tenth anniversary of his debut. That season, he played for a record-breaking four other Barcelona teams at various youth and reserve levels on his way to the first team.

Playing alongside him that day was an earlier product of FC Barcelona's youth team, Xavi Hernández, a player who was to have a major influence in mentoring Messi's professional development at the club. Xavi had not long met Messi at the time, since the two had never overlapped at La Masia, and the two were barely on first-name terms, moving in different social circles. But Messi had been given the best of references by a close friend of Xavi's, a long-term coach of the youth teams called Sergi Alegre. A few weeks earlier, over a lunch they had together, Alegre had told Xavi: 'You know there are some really good young players coming up, but there is a young Argentine lad among them and you can't imagine how good he is. He is spectacular. You will see.'[1]

Years later, Xavi would recall the first time he and Messi shared a training pitch: 'I realized he was different from the first training rondo we played together. Leo seemed to have something which is really difficult to achieve: he understood the game, he could pass and dribble regardless of who he had by him or in front of him, even the best defender that faced him understood that.'[2]

In a personal tribute to Messi on receiving his fifth Ballon d'Or in January 2016, Xavi wrote a growing tribute in *El País* about the first season they played together in the first team. He describes him as 'educated, respectful', a 'humble lad'. He said that though you could tell Messi knew inside that he would be a good player, Xavi knew there were all sorts of ways it could go wrong.

The decision to bring Messi into the first team regularly was taken by Frank Rijkaard, Barça's new manager, who had been appointed that season as part of a major shake-up at the club, aimed at rescuing it from the doldrums into which it had sunk at the start of the new millennium, going four seasons without winning any title.

A native Amsterdammer, as a player Rijkaard had distinguished himself during two golden eras of European club football. He built his reputation as a great defensive midfielder during the 1980s playing for Ajax and the Dutch national team under Johan Cruyff. In the early 1990s he played for Arrigo Sacchi's AC Milan during one of the Italian club's many glory periods, when it won the League title and two European Cup crowns. He finished his playing days back at Ajax, where over two seasons he helped lead them to a League title and European Cup.

In the European Championships of 2000, the Dutch team he coached delighted the crowds with fluid and attacking football, but were beaten on penalties by Italy in the semi-finals. Rijkaard resigned immediately afterwards. He was next appointed manager of the Netherlands' oldest professional club, Sparta Rotterdam, for the 2001–2 season. Questions were raised about Rijkaard's relaxed manner against a backdrop of tightening financial constraints. Sparta were relegated for the first time in their history and Rijkaard departed soon after. He spent the next few months on his second sabbatical in three years, working on a book about how to run a football club, which he never finished.

While the new president of FC Barcelona, Joan Laporta, had promised during his 2003 election campaign to bring back some of the joyful, Dutch-inspired creativity and success Barça fans had enjoyed with Cruyff, first as the Flying Dutchman player and then as manager of the 'Dream Team' that won the club's first ever European Cup in 1992, the choice of Rijkaard to deliver on the promise, on Cruyff's recommendation, was a gamble.

In many ways, Rijkaard as player and coach had come to personify the 'neurotic genius' of Dutch football, as its chronicler David Winner describes it in *Brilliant Orange*; seemingly forever poised between brilliance and a penchant for self-destruction, with the capacity to reach great heights but also to tumble without fulfilling their potential.

When Rijkaard arrived at Barça, the club was in a mess. Louis van Gaal's second spell in charge had gone spectacularly wrong and care-taker managers in Antonio de la Cruz and Radomir Antić had guided the club to the embarrassingly low final League position of sixth in 2002–3.

The tired presidential regime of Joan Gaspart had come to an end and a new, reforming president, Joan Laporta, had been elected. The latest South American star, the Brazilian Ronaldinho, had been signed from under the noses of Man United in a €30 million deal with Paris Saint-Germain, but it was hard to imagine what was to come.

Laporta was a young lawyer who had helped found a movement of fans determined to bring about a radical reform of the club after decades in which it had been under the authoritarian control of a construction magnate, José Luís Núñez. Laporta had campaigned for the presidency with the support of one of the club's most enduring icons, Cruyff, on a pledge to greater accountability and transparency in the running of the club's affairs and of reviving the club's fortunes by investing in both homegrown talent and foreign players capable of competing with the stardom of Real Madrid, and with style. Youth-team star Messi, of course, ticked every box; if you wanted to find a player who was the antithesis of a *galáctico*, Leo was your boy.

In that friendly in November 2003, Messi immediately caused Porto problems with a series of dazzling dribbles which showed off his Argentine skills as well as the extent to which he had yet to mature as a Barça player. He fluffed two chances at goal. The first involved him losing the ball to the keeper after overrunning it. The second had him choosing to pass the ball in front of an open goal after beating the keeper. Porto ended up winning 2–0.

Journalist Cristina Cubero recalled seeing Messi walking past the press area after the match with his head bowed, crouched, almost too embarrassed to look anyone in the eye. 'I have always said that he has all the strength he needs on the pitch, but off it he shrinks,' Cubero told Guillem Balagué.[3]

Rijkaard praised Messi at the post-match press conference: 'He's got a lot of talent and a very promising future,' he told journalists. Watching the game from the dug-out, the Dutch coach felt that Messi was still on a learning curve, and would have to adapt himself to the style of play he was developing at Barça.

For his part, Ronaldinho famously told his teammates that Messi would go on to be a better player than him. The two became friends, with the older Brazilian referring to his protégé as 'little brother', which must have helped as he made the move into the first team. Later, the flamboyant playboy's influence would be more problematic, but it was key in this early period. Messi would never forget how generous Ronaldinho was with him: 'The first day I was in the dressing room with the first team, Ronaldinho made me sit next to him and that made it all easier,' he recalled.[4]

When Messi first arrived in Barcelona he was so small that his feet didn't touch the ground when he sat on the bench. Gerard Piqué recalled he was so small that he was initially relegated to a lower category – the B Juniors, where his teammates gave him the affectionate nickname of *enano*, 'the dwarf'. It seemed to make him even more determined to score goals, even if he suffered physically when he was caught by players bigger than him. Injuries in his early days included a broken leg and the broken cheekbone for which he refused a protective mask.

Thanks to the growth hormone treatment, by the age of sixteen he had grown to 1.70 metres, at which point his treatment and growth stopped. He had reached the height projected for him at the start of the treatment, and was two centimetres taller than Maradona. To have carried on the treatment as an adult would have put his heath at risk, and raised the potential of him being engulfed in a doping scandal.

It is worth recording here that Human Growth Hormone (HGH) – both in and out of competition – is listed under section S2 of the Word Anti-Doping Agency's list of prohibited substances and methods. As the WADA website points out, the major role of HGH is to stimulate the liver to secrete Insulin-like Growth Factor – IGF-I – which in turn stimulates production of cartilage cells, resulting in bone growth. It also plays a key role in muscle protein synthesis and organ growth.

'Some of the effects attributed to HGH, which may explain the attraction for its use as a doping agent, especially in power and endurance sports, include the reduction of body fat (lipolysis), the increase in muscle mass and strength (anabolic effect), as well as its tissue-repairing effects (recovery) on the muscular-skeletal system,' the website states.

The agency goes on to warn that side effects for HGH abuse can include diabetes in prone individuals; worsening of cardiovascular diseases; muscle, joint and bone pain; hypertension and cardiac deficiency; abnormal growth of organs; and accelerated osteoarthritis. If untreated, many of the symptoms described can significantly reduce life expectancy.

The use of HGH is banned in almost all sports, amateur and professional. Although Section 46 of FIFA's anti-doping code contains provisions for a therapeutic use exemption of a banned substance when that substance is considered medically essential, it remains unclear whether FC Barcelona ever felt it necessary to ask for such a waiver.

After the treatment had been discontinued, Messi followed special diets to help maintain his fitness, and focused his training on building up the muscle mass in his legs and strengthening his body generally in order to compete against players taller and stronger than him – but his skill showed an increasing refinement, as the star player in him matured.

'I've seen games where for ninety minutes it looked as if he was playing one against eleven, and he kept getting kicked, but we only won 1–0, or drew 0–0, or we lost 1–0. He's a fantastic dribbler, but he was making leaps forward by seeking variation in his game: one time you dribble, another time you give the ball back and go deep. He was becoming more effective by doing less,' Rijkaard told football journalist Simon Kuper in 2008.[5]

The *pibe*, or native Argentine boy, who had learnt his dribbling techniques in the street and on rough open spaces in Rosario, would go on to absorb some European passing and tackling techniques on his path to becoming a complete player.

On the personal front, his main reference point remained his father Jorge, with whom he continued to share the four-bedroom flat in the Gran Via Carles III. As well as overseeing him as a parent, Jorge was now becoming increasingly involved in representing Leo in all dealings with the club and outside agencies.

His mother Celia travelled to Barcelona twice a year, but still lived in the family's home in Rosario with her second son Matías, five years older than Leo, and her daughter María Sol, six years younger. Leo remained in daily contact with his mother via the internet and mobile phone, and always looked forward to her next visit – he had struggled to come to terms with his parents' living in different cities, however amicably it presented itself. His idea of a good dish was the Argentine-style breaded veal Milanesa his mother cooked him, as she had done from early childhood, and drinking the traditional green tea, or *mate*, she brewed for him.

The oldest of the four Messi siblings, Rodrigo (seven years older than Leo) abandoned his dream to become a football star early on, and instead settled with his girlfriend Florencia in Barcelona, where he was to take an increasingly key role, together with his father, in handling Messi's affairs.

Back in Rosario, it was Matías who seemed destined to be the black sheep of the Messi family. He had been born in 1982, five years and a day before Leo, whose face he later had tattooed on his left arm. Matías's early promise as a footballer had crash-landed after he was dropped from Newell's Old Boys' youth academy after a season. An unstable working life had followed, during which he had become best known for his alleged connections with Rosario's violent radical football fans, the thuggish local *barras bravas*, whose organized criminal networks pervaded Argentine football.

The public record of Matías's alleged involvement in criminal activity dates back to 2000, when he was allegedly involved in a robbery.

That was followed by an alleged assault a year later and an accusation of threatening behaviour in 2002. The charges were dropped in each instance, but Matías would continue to get into trouble.

It was not easy to grow up in your kid brother's shadow, as Leo's brother Rodrigo, another failed footballer, admitted. 'We didn't adapt very well,' he told Spanish TV's *Informe Robinson* in 2011. 'It was a problem, we were united [as a family] but one person did something and the others did nothing. Therefore we all suffered in different ways.'[6]

By contrast, Messi's life as it developed in Barcelona was a life less ordinary, meaning that he lived it on his own terms, not how others might have expected, and remained undaunted by the success of others, still less by his own achievements.

The generation of 1987 spent two and half years together before Cesc's departure to Arsenal in September 2003 and Piqué's to Manchester United the following year. Despite his growing reputation as one of the best young players that Barça had ever had in its history, and while showing enormous respect for the senior players, Messi remained both far from star-struck and eager to keep out of the limelight.

When not indulging in his lengthy daily siesta, Messi's favourite habit was playing video games. His best friends from La Masia were Victor Vázquez and Luís Calvo. They would tease him, calling him *enano* – dwarf – whenever Messi beat them at PlayStation, which was almost always. He played with a focus and passion that only his own real-world football could emulate. Messi would tease them back by breaking into the Argentine slang they found difficult to understand.

Messi was still a little big man, a teenager growing up, not remotely interested in the business of football yet but with star potential – a tempting target for exploitation by Argentine agent Rodolfo Schinocca, a one-time player with Boca Juniors who was handling Leo's image rights in 2004, at the behest of Jorge, before the player shot to fame.

'Was it difficult to sell Messi's image then?' the Argentine journalist Leonardo Faccio asked Schinnoca years later. 'I had to reinvent the business. In those days the image of a successful footballer was David Beckham,' Schinocca replied.[7]

In 2004, the English international was twenty-eight, in his first season at Real Madrid following his record-breaking transfer deal, and widely regarded as the biggest marketing phenomenon in the history of the sport.

In the same year, Messi was still 'an adolescent with acne', as Faccio puts it, and Schinnoca might have thought of airbrushing his image to make it more attractive. Instead, he promoted his adolescent traits. The first advertisement to feature him was shown in Argentina, not Spain, and had him promoting hamburgers, fizzy drinks and video games.

'He was very humble,' Schinocca told Faccio. 'He always used to tell me: "The only thing I want is to have a house in Barcelona, and another one in Rosario."'[8]

In 2007, Schinocca would have a widely publicized falling out with the Messi family, and Leo's image rights were eventually wrested from the agent in a move subsequently contested in court. In 2004, however, there was nothing controversial about Messi's life. He retained his essence: shy of publicity but confident in his own talent.

As Jorge Valdano would reflect long after Messi had come to dominate football headlines, 'Messi only produces headlines with his feet.'[9]

In the spring of 2004, with just twenty-three minutes of first-team football under his belt, those headlines were yet to come. But the clamour for 'the dwarf' to take a starring role was becoming ever louder.

9. THE RED LEGACY: RONALDO

George Best called it the most exciting debut he had ever seen.

There had been other high points in recent Manchester United memory: Paul Scholes scoring both goals against Port Vale in United's League Cup win in September 1994, Ruud van Nistelrooy's brace against Fulham in his first full League game in August 2001. But eighteen-year-old Cristiano Ronaldo's debut at Old Trafford on 16 August 2003 in a Premier League match against Bolton Wanderers was certainly an event most of those watching would not easily forget.

A few old veterans at the game compared him to Best. 'There have been a few players described as "the new George Best" over the years, but this is the first time it's been a compliment to me,' replied the legend.

In the sixty-sixth minute, Alex Ferguson substituted Ronaldo on for Nicky Butt. The new arrival made an instant impact, dancing around defenders, running with the ball and showing off an athleticism and skill that forced his teammates to raise their game. As Best noted, Ronaldo showed he was genuinely two-footed; beating players with ease and putting in dangerous crosses with his left or right. 'Another thing I liked about Ronaldo against Bolton was how he dealt with the physical side. As soon as he came on, he was clattered from behind but he just got up and got on with the game, it didn't faze him at all,' Best commented.[1]

Ryan Giggs later remembered Ronaldo coming on for the last half-hour of the Bolton game and 'dazzling a tired defence with a brilliant display of pace and skill'. It was that, allied to the physique – 'he looked more twenty-eight than eighteen,' Giggs recalled, 'he was tall and strong and very impressive to look at' – which mattered.[2]

Ronaldo had been given United's legendary number 7 shirt, previously worn by George Best, Eric Cantona and David Beckham, among others. The fans saw elements of all three flashing before them – his dribbling, speed and feints (Best), his vision and range of passing (Beckham), his self-confidence verging on arrogance and sheer flamboyance (Cantona). United executives saw a celebrity in the making, with his good looks combining with his talent to make him an exciting marketing tool, and thus a good replacement for Beckham. As long as Ferguson believed in him.

There were, of course, other characteristics on show which suggested more than a touch of narcissism in Cristiano's personality, something that would not always fit in a place like Manchester, yet still he impressed. As Paddy Harverson, a life-long United supporter who was the club's head of communications at the time, recalled of his appearance in the Bolton game: 'He had that stupid haircut with funny things in his hair, and lots of spots, but he showed immediate courage on the ball, demanded it time and time again, and every time he was fouled, he just got up again. He was unbelievably brave and the fans fell in love with him instantly. He demonstrated in a very short space of time, in just a few minutes, that he was a Manchester United player. Not everyone does that.'[3]

The new United signing drew a standing ovation from the 70,000 fans that packed Old Trafford that day, but he could have been jostling for a wing berth with an emerging talent elsewhere. Different pieces in the complex puzzle of the international transfer market had only just been fitted into place. David Beckham, Cristiano Ronaldo, Carlos Queiroz (United's assistant manager was about to replace Vicente del Bosque as manager at Real Madrid), Alex Ferguson and Jorge Mendes, as well as three major clubs, Manchester United, Real Madrid and FC Barcelona, were all very much part of the manoeuvring and calculation that would have a major impact on the business of football in the years ahead.

It's worth recording here that protracted transfer negotiations over Ronaldo during the spring and early summer of 2003 had involved, at one stage, FC Barcelona: 'Mendes offered us Cristiano and Nani as part of a package, €18 million each,' recalled Alfonso Godall, a senior Barça executive. 'By that time we had bought Ronaldinho and didn't have all that much spare cash, but we were looking to find it when Mendes closed the deal with Man United.'

Imagine Messi playing alongside Ronaldo. Awesome possibilities never realized form part of FC Barcelona's history, as when the club could have had Di Stéfano playing alongside Kubala, but lost the former to Real Madrid, but the 'what if' of Ronaldo playing alongside

Messi brings into sharp relief just how ingrained their roles as footballing yin and yang have become. Can you imagine one passing to the other, the two of them celebrating a goal together? It's impossible to tell what might have been had Ronaldo moved to the Nou Camp – perhaps the two players would have inhibited each other's development rather than thriving together. In any case, while Leo continued his careful development at Barcelona, eighteen-year-old Cristiano set about building on his impressive debut.

Ronaldo's star had risen in the small Portuguese League but, without the security and family environment that Barcelona had provided Messi with, he was transferred to a foreign country where they spoke no Portuguese and the weather was cold and damp for most of the year. Not Lisbon, let alone semi-tropical Madeira.

Ronaldo had a lot to prove in the tough, competitive English Premier League, not least at a club like United, one of the giant names of global club football, with a huge tradition and history made up of legendary players, many of them homegrown and moulded in youth teams; much like FC Barcelona, but without the politics.

The only Portuguese to have made much impact on United's history before Ronaldo arrived was the great Eusébio, and he only by virtue of being part of the Benfica side that Best, Charlton, Law et al. had defeated to win United's first European Cup in 1968. When Ronaldo was transferred to United, he was an unknown quantity to many local fans, and few could have guessed his burning ambition to claim Eusébio's crown as Portugal's greatest ever player, and much more besides. He carried the weight of history on his shoulders, both footballing history and his own past, but they already seemed broad enough to bear the burden. At Manchester United, he could also draw inspiration – on the pitch and off it – from the two number 7s who had preceded him.

During the 1990s, United had regained their reputation for entertaining, swashbuckling football with the arrival of the Frenchman Eric Cantona, a controversial but hugely skilled operator. Cantona had a fierce temper, and sometimes showed a distinct lack of enthusiasm for winning the ball back. But he earned the respect of his teammates for his talent on the field – his deadly finishing, control of the ball and creative passing could turn a game round in an instant. His charismatic leadership inspired an emerging generation of young thoroughbreds, who got used to the idea of being the best and winning.

The flamboyant Frenchman was responsible for many things during his time at United: he broke the team's sense of insularity; he also taught them a thing or two about the power of the media and sponsors, and the way that marketing could be exploited. In commercial terms, he set an example which David Beckham and, after him, Cristiano Ronaldo followed.

After joining the club aged fourteen, Beckham made his debut appearance for Manchester United in 1995, aged nineteen, when the club was well into its revival under Ferguson and Cantona was in his pomp.

Beckham was conscious from his early days at Manchester United of having joined one of the most famous and exciting clubs in the world, where all the players involved, whatever their age, were made to feel part of the family as long as they remained subject to Ferguson's regime. The manager retained the Calvinist work ethic of the Glasgow shipyards, arriving at his office at 7.30 each morning and overseeing every aspect of how the club was run.

Beckham won promotion to the first team in a hugely competitive environment where the disciplinarian and driven Ferguson regime required full commitment, best performance and results. There was a theory, which every player found himself confronting one day, that after leaving Ferguson's Old Trafford there was only one way to go, and that was down. (Ronaldo was to prove that wrong, of course. His arrival at Old Trafford was a breakthrough in his career and his years there were formative. His eventual departure, far from being the end of the road, represented a giant step to superstardom.)

Beckham's departure from the club followed the breakdown of his relationship with Ferguson, a process that had begun with his marriage and reached a controversial climax in his final season, with a much publicized dressing-room bust-up that left Beckham with a cut above the eye, inflicted by a flying boot. By then, Beckham was a marketing machine. As Ellis Cashmore has written in his analysis of Beckham as a cultural phenomenon, his marriage turned the football star into an all-purpose celebrity: 'The synergy produced in the fusion of two performers, each drawn from different spheres of entertainment, created new and perhaps undreamed of possibilities in marketing, merchandising and promotions in sport, pop, fashion, and eventually patriotism.'[4]

All of this jarred with Ferguson, of course, and precipitated the player's departure to Real Madrid. In more ways than one, Beckham paved the way for Ronaldo.

In his autobiography, Alex Ferguson devotes an unusually unqualified section of praise to Cristiano Ronaldo. Even after he had left for Real Madrid, Ferguson looks back at the Madeiran's time in Manchester with pride and gratitude, for it coincided with the manager's most successful period of his final years before retirement. In a book that settles scores with many of his starring players who left, it is noticeable that Ferguson acknowledges how mutual their relationship was. He describes how necessary the 'special talent' was at that point in their history which he describes as a 'lean spell' in the middle of the decade:

'We helped Ronaldo to be the player he was and he helped us recapture the excitement and self-expression of Manchester United teams.'[5]

Ferguson played a key role in helping Ronaldo settle in Manchester and mature while he was there. While over the years he had been a paternal figure for young British and Irish players coming up through the youth teams, he knew enough about overseas players at other clubs to know they did not always easily adapt to English weather, humour and general lifestyle. He was also well briefed enough on the particularities of Ronaldo's family background to realize that the first Portuguese player ever to sign up for Manchester United might struggle with his first experience of living in a foreign land, and needed sensitive handling, not least because of his young, impressionable age.

Around the time of the move to Manchester, visits to Madeira had brought childhood traumas back to haunt Cristiano Ronaldo. It was the vox populi among family friends, and in the neighbourhood where he had been brought up, that his father Dinis's drinking problem was getting completely beyond his or anybody else's capacity to control.

Dinis couldn't stop drinking. His periods of sobriety over the years had become less frequent and briefer, and always with a psychosis commonly felt by unreformed addicts – he was engulfed by the tide of the overpowering necessity to drink. He had panic attacks and thought that he would die if he didn't get that drink inside him.

Word had also reached the English media that there was a lurking scandal inside the new United signing's family, with echoes of the most notorious football-related struggles with alcohol immortalized by Best, Adams and Gascoigne. Soon after Cristiano arrived in Manchester, a leading tabloid dispatched a photographer to Madeira with the sole purpose of trying to snap Dinis Aveiro out of his mind, on one of his drunken binges. Word reached a family friend soon after the photographer alerted a local journalist to his assignment, and Dinis was kept under wraps for several days, until the photographer, on this occasion, left the islands seemingly empty handed – at any rate, no embarrassing pictures emerged.

With his father's mental and physical health deteriorating after years of alcoholism, Ronaldo used part of his increased wealth to fund a new house in Madeira, in an attempt to help Dinis and reconcile his parents. 'Ever since I was a boy, I had a dream: to build a large house for me, for my family and also for my friends; a space that is not just a house but rather a home, where I can feel really comfortable,' Cristiano later recalled.[6]

Ronaldo's insecurity, masquerading as a need for privacy together with an obsession with family, was rooted in the memory of his parents' separation and the need he felt to overcome the sadness of his childhood. Dinis moved into the lavish new house with one of his daughters, but within weeks he had been hospitalized in Funchal suffering from liver and kidney problems. The new-found family wealth seemed to have had little impact on his alcoholism, but it did provide Cristiano's brother, Hugo, with an opportunity to break the cycle of his own substance abuse problems.

As the firstborn of his siblings, Hugo's early years had coincided with Dinis's military service in Africa, and his adolescent years with his father's growing alcoholism. Without the talent at football of his younger brother, Hugo stayed in Madeira, left school early and fell into a life of addiction – drugs and alcohol. Hugo started using hard drugs in the late 1990s, when Cristiano was fourteen and already embarking on a football career with Sporting Lisbon. His mother Dolores realized that Hugo needed help and took out a loan in order to send him to a specialist clinic for treatment. But Hugo failed to stay clean and, two years later, he needed a second course of treatment. Cristiano, by then earning more, helped pay for it.

After Ronaldo moved to Manchester and was joined by his mother there, Hugo gave up his job as a painter and decorator to work as his brother's aide, dividing his time between Madeira and England.

Having his family around him, a set-up encouraged by Ferguson, helped Cristiano to settle in to life in Manchester. Dolores was first to move into the spacious and comfortable home the club had rented for Ronaldo – a converted farmhouse in Alderley Edge, the quiet village near Manchester popular with players. The neighbourhood had fashionable shops and eateries on the edge of picturesque Lancastrian countryside, and easy access to both the club's training ground and the city centre.

Dolores was not entirely happy there, missing her friends and the warmth and exuberant vegetation of Madeira. However, she stuck it out for three years, during which time she saw her son adapting to and absorbing life at Manchester United, not because he felt he carried the club in his DNA – which he didn't – but because he was driven by an ambition to be the best player ever, and because Jorge Mendes had convinced him that this was the best club to be at that stage in his career.

'Ronaldo was not born a Manchester United fan like, say, Beckham was. He saw United as a platform to develop his enormous talent,' said Paddy Harverson.

The vanity of CR7 – as Mendes's agency would soon begin to brand Cristiano Ronaldo – was evident from early on in his time at United, largely because he spent so much time in front of the mirror. In the dressing room, teammates would tease him about it. 'He always hogged the mirror in the changing room, and some of the other players – Scholes, Giggs, Ferdinand – would get involved in a lot of piss-taking,' Paddy Harverson recalled. 'It might have cowed a lesser individual at that age, but he was street smart. He was not intellectually gifted or academic but he was a bright guy who knew from early on, instinctively, how to adapt to the English dressing-room culture – and that, from a kid from Madeira who arrived without speaking English but fitted in, was quite an achievement.'

Many children of alcoholics have fallen under an addictive parent's shadow, developing similar personality traits and addictions, but not all, by any means. Many, having lived with years of secrecy and shame, consciously try and lead very different lives. Ronaldo was a virtual tee-totaller, recognizing the negative impact Dinis had had on his brother Hugo, and fearing that he too carried a potential demon in his blood and that even a drink or two might set him off on the road to perdition.

The self-confidence he displayed in his early appearances at Old Trafford showed him to be a natural leader and a potential superstar on the pitch. His inspiring runs, effortless step-overs, expertly timed passing and powerful strikes at goal all caught the eye on the training ground and on the pitch.

Largely unknown when he arrived, and preceded by some of the greats of English football, the first challenge he faced was to win over the demanding and in many cases sceptical United fans. But then, as Ferguson remarked, 'Old Trafford had a tradition of building up heroes quickly.'[7] Ronaldo's evident talent and idiosyncratic personality had an immediate impact on fans and in the dressing room.

His relatively sober, self-possessed lifestyle was one aspect of his personality that actually created a certain distance between him and some of his British teammates in those early months. The other was the closely related evidence of his narcissism, which was out of step with the club's team ethos and which challenged the macho culture that had long prevailed in English football.

The young Cristiano, from his early days in Manchester, had a personality that grated with some teammates and broad sections of the media, because it was seen to be different from the norm in its seeming grandiose sense of self-importance, entitlement and arrogance. As Ferguson later recalled, in the early days at Manchester United, Ronaldo 'showboated a lot, on field as well as off it . . . There is no doubt that he acted a bit. His earliest lessons were in a theatrical footballing culture.'[8] The Leicester City striker James Scowcroft tells of how his manager Micky Adams told him to try a 'welcome to England' challenge on Ronaldo: 'I did what he asked, but he was twenty yards away before I'd finished the tackle.'[9]

Manchester United's history was hardly short of showmen, but players became legends because of what they delivered, not the way they acted. Ronaldo's self-belief from his early days at Manchester was extraordinary, but it would take time for his performances to keep pace with the posturing. The opening months of the season began to suggest a player who was the worst thing a foreign import could be: all mouth and no trousers. In the first instance, though, it was to be his passion, rather than his skills, that began to turn the tide.

It was a turbulent first few months of the new season for United, as they defended their latest League crown in the midst of relentless controversy on and off the field; not least of all, the latest episode of what some commentators had dubbed the enduring soap opera of their rivalry with Arsenal.

This acrimonious and protracted rivalry had been intensifying since the formation of the Premier League in 1992, since when, all but one League title had been won by one or the other team (the exception being Blackburn Rovers' successful title bid in 1994–5).

In its collective talent and sheer competiveness, as well as its indiscipline and occasional thuggery, the rivalry surpassed anything that the young Madeiran had experienced while at Sporting, even if his childhood and adolescence had had its rougher edges beyond the field of play.

The latest fractious and perhaps most brutal encounter between the two teams had taken place on 21 September 2003, with Ronaldo very much a part of it. It was dubbed the 'Battle of Old Trafford' by the press. Arsenal's captain, Patrick Viera, was sent off for two bookings, the second for a challenge on Ruud van Nistelrooy which the Dutchman made a large meal of.

When the Dutchman then failed to convert a disputed penalty kick just before the final whistle, all hell broke loose. Van Nistelrooy was jostled and taunted by several Arsenal players, and a fight soon broke out. Despite being a relative novice when it came to understanding the idiosyncratic culture of English football, Ronaldo was one of the first United players to throw himself into the punch-up, ostensibly in support of his Dutch colleague. The youngest player on the pitch at eighteen, Ronaldo's reaction surprised some United fans, who – up to that point – had seen him as a bit soft for the English game. But this was the kind of dust-up Ronaldo had experienced as a young teenager in the backstreets of Funchal and Lisbon.

Now, at Old Trafford, getting his hands dirty on behalf of a team-mate earned him respect in the dressing room and from the terraces. Once it was all over, it was the Arsenal combatants who incurred the heaviest punishments arising from the 'battle': a three-match ban and £20,000 imposed on Martin Keown, and further fines, totalling £275,000, and bans totalling nine games imposed on Lauren, Ray Parlour, Patrick Vieira and Ashley Cole. Identified as the main United culprits, Ronaldo and Ryan Giggs were also found guilty of misconduct by the FA, but received much lighter fines of £4,000 and £7,500 respectively, and escaped bans.

Although Arsène Wenger at one point protested that his players were the victims of 'trial by Sky [TV]', by general consensus it was Arsenal who deserved unqualified criticism, and Ronaldo emerged with his reputation untarnished. As journalist Henry Winter put it: 'Arsenal may have worn yellow yesterday but they were tainted with red. The face of the beautiful game was ravaged with scars and tears.'[10]

Ronaldo would not always be thus exonerated of blame. During that first season at United he tended to over-elaborate on the ball and exaggerate his falls when challenged. Ferguson recalled a slightly hysterical edge to Ronaldo's amateur dramatics in early training sessions at Carrington, when he had a habit of letting out a terrible screech whenever he was tackled, which was often. But the response of those around him helped him adapt and improve.

'The players would give him pelters. He soon learnt not to make that kind of racket,' Ferguson remembered. 'His intelligence helped. He was a smart boy. Once he realized the players would not be a willing audience for his screaming and amateur dramatics in training, he stopped. Over time it erased itself from his game.'[11]

His theatricality was in no small measure a response to his burning desire to be noticed, the need some naturally gifted players have to show off their talent, but he was determined to get to a point when what he showed off was of such brilliance that everyone who watched him would be in awe of his talent.

But, as he was advised by Carlos Queiroz in his native Portuguese, the onus was also on him to apply his talent. 'You're only a great player when people outside the club start recognizing you as such. It's not enough to be a great player to us at Manchester United,' Queiroz told him before departing for Madrid to join David Beckham. 'When you start delivering the passes, delivering the crosses at the right time, people won't be able to read you. That's when the great players emerge.'[12]

In that infamous match against Arsenal, which ended in a goalless draw, just weeks into his first season, you see Ronaldo in part as a victim of Wenger's defensive tactics, with his opponents reading him and knowing when and how to interrupt his runs. But critics who accused him of falling over too easily also failed to recognize the extraordinary speed with which the tall teenager moved on as well as off the ball, and his body's natural susceptibility to losing its balance at the slightest contact. Footage from that first season suggests there was no single match in which he played where he didn't make some significant contribution. On 1 November 2003, ten games into his first season at Manchester United, Cristiano Ronaldo finally opened his account in the Premier League. With only fifteen minutes of the game at home against Portsmouth left, Ronaldo replaced the Uruguayan international Diego Forlán, and five minutes later he took what would come to be seen as one of his trademark free kicks – curling it at an angle from the left, over the wall and into the net.

He finished his opening season with an impressive eight goals in thirty-nine appearances and, watching back over those performances, now you can see the stirrings of those characteristics that will become iconic. That particular high angle of his feet as he cuts in from the right against Tottenham, before pinging a drive off the inside of the far post, the long hang of the leap for his headed goal against Birmingham, the sheer vicious power of his goal against Aston Villa; like the loosely gelled hair, it feels not quite under the full Ronaldo control yet.

The season ended with him wearing a new pair of golden boots against second-tier Millwall in an exciting FA Cup final in Cardiff's Millennium Stadium. Manchester United won 3–0. Cristiano opened the scoring. For all the obvious flashiness, Ronaldo showed in this match how far he had matured as a player since he had arrived in the Premier League, and what a key component of the Ferguson project he had become.

The FA Cup has a history of top clubs being beaten by smaller ones, often because star players find it difficult to feel incentivized either by the contest or the tournament itself – but this was not such an occasion. Manchester United worked hard and showed imagination to win their eleventh FA Cup, their effort personified in Ronaldo, whose evident exhilaration and enjoyment at playing in an FA Cup final was contagious.

Just before the interval, nineteen-year-old Ronaldo danced in front of Millwall's combative player-manager, thirty-seven-year-old Dennis Wise, to nod Gary Neville's searching cross down and in. The eighteen-year age gap between the young predator and the veteran midfielder showed in Ronaldo's mental sharpness and physical grace in front of goal, contrasting with Wise's somewhat predictable and plodding physicality in defence. It was symptomatic of a match in which, as Ferguson acknowledged, Ronaldo demonstrated that his individualistic repertoire had a richer seam than simply the obsessive step-over of his early days in a United shirt, including a rabona cross with his right foot that made the commentators laugh with incredulity.

While van Nistelrooy collected the man-of-the-match award for scoring the other two goals, Ronaldo would have been a more deserving winner in the view of some commentators, like the *Guardian*'s Kevin McCarra, who described how at home he seemed in the game, how he 'luxuriated in the occasion'.[13]

'Cristiano was particularly outstanding,' commented Gary Neville. 'I think Ronaldo can be one of the top footballers of the world.'[14]

Ferguson was especially pleased, saying that Ronaldo had cut out the 'bit of the Portuguese thing' about him and was now developing really well.

During his first season at Manchester United, Ronaldo had surpassed all expectations as a player, showing extraordinary talent as well as a rapidly growing maturity on the pitch, and picked up his first trophy. His contribution to the team's success was recognized in him being named the Sir Matt Busby Player of the Year, a trophy awarded by the club's fans.

To cap it all, he'd been selected for Portugal's Euro 2004 squad, the nation's first home tournament.

10. EURO BLUES: RONALDO

Despite his successful landing in Manchester, Ronaldo still had much to prove as a Portuguese international. In the summer of 2004 he faced a big test when the European Championships in Portugal presented the underachieving home team, and its bright new star and emerging celebrity, with an unprecedented opportunity to shine in front of a global audience.

One of the tableaux in the opening ceremony showed the ships of the Portuguese explorers disappearing into the flags of all nations. While aimed at reminding people of Portugal's impact on the development of human history in the age of discovery, it was inadvertently a reminder that Portugal as a nation had never, since the sixteenth century, lived up to its mythology of greatness.

Before the tournament began, Portugal were considered one of the favourites, and had the backing of the entire nation. Porto was packed with people waving national flags and cheering for the opening match, and an enormous tide of supporters followed the coach as it carried Ronaldo and his teammates to the stadium. Throughout the tournament, the whole of Portugal seemed to stand still every time the home team were playing.

Expectations of victory were high. Portuguese sides hadn't lost in Lisbon, where most of their games would be played, for seventeen years, not in Sporting's Alvalade or in Benfica's Estádio da Luz. They were also the host nation – something which was a deciding factor in previous European tournaments: for Spain in 1964, Italy in 1968 and France in 1984. And the Portuguese had three of the most gifted players in Europe. Together with Ronaldo were the captain and Real Madrid superstar Luís Figo, and Deco, the naturalized Brazilian who had been a key figure in José Mourinho's ambitious Porto team, which had won the UEFA Cup and the UEFA Champions League over two seasons. Deco was soon to transfer to FC Barcelona, having been voted UEFA Club Footballer of the Year. Of the three, it was Ronaldo who had yet to win the hearts of a nation. Only Sporting fans venerated him as the natural heir to the retired legend Eusébio – a player who had always been claimed by the other Lisbon club, Benfica.

The team had been managed for over a year by Luiz Felipe Scolari, who had taken Brazil to World Cup victory in 2002. Like Alex Ferguson, the Brazilian Scolari had already made an important contribution to Ronaldo's road to stardom by introducing him gradually into the national side in 2003, helping mould the rough diamond into a member of the team.

'Just like Sir Alex Ferguson, Scolari knew he had to be patient with Ronaldo, help him grow as a man, polish him as a player, work on him like a master jeweller might,' recalled Scolari's biographer, José Carlos Freitas, in his book *Luiz Felipe Scolari: The Man, The Manager*.[1]

Scolari believed United's star in the making was immature, exuberant and selfish, but also a prodigy as far as technique and skill were concerned. During Portugal's preparations for Euro 2004, Scolari had adopted the 'softly-softly' approach to Ronaldo, gradually introducing the teenager into the big time.

In his book, Freitas wrote: 'Evidently much of that work [helping Ronaldo settle in Manchester] had been done by Sir Alex Ferguson and especially Carlos Queiroz . . . But for the few days that Scolari lived with Ronaldo during the Portuguese team's preparations, he took the opportunity to get to know him, to talk to him and to make him see that although he was an exceptionally talented player in the team, he would be just another member.'[2]

Freitas describes the day Scolari first met the rising star: Ronaldo was wearing a baseball cap back to front, sunglasses and headphones. 'Like any other adolescent he was convinced that he was the centre of the world and couldn't care less about the advice of any manager. For months, during Euro 2004 preparation games, Scolari felt there were some communication issues.'[3]

Scolari, however, encouraged Figo to play a 'silent part' in Ronaldo's development, ensuring that the two players complemented rather than competed against each other, using a variation on the symbolic '7' that was destined to become so totemic in Ronaldo's iconography. 'The position of right wing belonged to Figo, as did the number seven shirt,' Freitas writes. 'Cristiano was given the number seventeen, the second number seven, the second Figo.

'Figo's attitude towards Cristiano was more like that of captain and teammate than as a veteran leader preparing his replacement. Ronaldo looked up to Figo, but he also had the attitude of someone who was ready to take on the mantle and be even better than him . . . and Figo knew it . . .'[4]

Scolari was manager of Portugal from 2002 to 2008, and the Brazilian later insisted that it was Figo's guidance during his first couple of years in the national team that set Ronaldo on the path to greatness.

'Of all the players I coached while at Portugal, there was one that was especially important for Cristiano Ronaldo, that was Luís Figo,' Scolari recalled in an interview with Omnisport, the live sports website.

'When Ronaldo started with the national team, the first one to help him was Figo. He was the first player to challenge Ronaldo to dribble and shoot, to score goals, to play his own game, to keep working all the time and become a better footballer.

'Figo took a position, saying, "My son, try again, keep trying. If you see the situation is difficult, I will give you a hand, and if you make a mistake I have everything ready, so calm down, but you have to try."'[5]

At Euro 2004, Ronaldo and Portugal got off to a bad start. In the opening game against Greece he was brought on as a substitute when his team were losing 1–0, only for them to concede a second goal by giving away a penalty. He later scored a header in stoppage time, but it came too late to save a match that Portugal lost 2–1.

By contrast, after Portugal had defeated Russia 2–0 in their second game, Ronaldo put on a brilliant man-of-the-match display in the decisive group game with Spain. Ronaldo mesmerized his Spanish opponents with his high-speed runs down the right wing and through the centre, his skilful footwork and abrupt changes in direction, and, of course, his step-overs. He also created two great chances for Figo – one with a wonderful pull-back pass, the other with a superbly delivered cross – but both ensuing shots at goal were blocked. It was Nuno Gomes who grabbed Portugal's winner just before the hour mark. The Spanish team, containing several future teammates, were torn apart.

By this stage of the tournament, Ronaldo was being held up not just as one of the most talented young players of the tournament, but had the newly acquired status as a Portuguese teenage heart-throb, his naked torso gracing local newspaper front pages and magazine covers and his smooth young Adonis face, airbrushed of its acne, plastered over billboards and TV ads.

Portugal went on to beat England in a quarter-final penalty shoot-out, the outcome on such a knife-edge that Ronaldo's mother, watching the match from the stands, fainted, before thousands of English fans walked away wondering if they might have won had Ronaldo not been bought and developed by Manchester United.

Next it was Holland's turn to suffer Ronaldo's brilliance, when the player scored his team's first goal with a header off a Figo corner, a replica of his goal against Greece in the first game. Portugal won 2–1, and had made it through to the final.

But at the Estádio da Luz in Lisbon on Sunday, 4 July 2004, it all went belly-up for Ronaldo and for Portugal. Portugal's second encounter of the tournament with Greece – 80/1 outsiders before the tournament began, who had ground out a series of deeply uninspiring, narrow victories – proved a lacklustre match, with the only goal scored by Angelos Charisteas in the fifty-seventh minute, and Ronaldo missing two chances at goal. One of them, his side's best, was thwarted by the Greek goalkeeper Antonios Nikopolidos, after a perfectly placed pass by Rui Costa. The other, shooting over the bar after finding space in the penalty area, generated a collective 'Ahhh!' from the crowd, as if the whole nation had issued its final gasp, audible on the pitch. The party Portugal had planned for was abruptly cancelled.

Ronaldo stood in the centre circle and wept. As Jonathan Wilson, reporting for the *Financial Times*, wrote: 'Portugal, after seventeen years without defeat in Lisbon, had lost the one that really mattered, beaten 1–0 by Greece in the final of Euro 2004.'[6]

After wiping away his tears, Ronaldo was the only one ready to speak out among the dejected Portuguese. He was the player the world sports media seemed most interested in, showing the extent to which his move to Manchester United and his appearance in the tournament had raised his marketing potential.

'We had a fantastic team and we have played a great tournament and we don't deserve to lose like this,' Ronaldo insisted. He was upset, he said, because he was 'an ambitious person' and he wanted to be 'the champion of Europe at nineteen years of age.

'I have to move on,' he told the assembled media. 'I have to look forward. There will be many other opportunities to win in Europe throughout my career, and make up for this huge disappointment.' The young man had now identified another chapter for his mythology, one that would be more than a decade in the writing.

11. FIRST TEAM CALLING: MESSI

After giving Messi his debut in the friendly against Porto, Rijkaard waited nearly a year before calling Messi up again for the first team. By then, Messi had demonstrated an increasing improvement in his performance playing for the youth teams and for FC Barcelona's C and B teams. His progress was reflected in his first professional contract, signed on 4 February 2004, which lasted until 2012 and contained an initial buyout clause of €30 million. When he made his debut for Barcelona B in March 2004, his buyout clause automatically increased to €80 million.

Throughout the spring, summer and autumn of 2004, without the competitive pressure of playing in the first team, Messi found the time and space to develop in a way that preserved him for the future, not burning himself out before he had fully matured, as he himself later recognized.

'Rijkaard took it step by step without rushing. Often I would say to him that I didn't understand why I wasn't called up to play. I'm grateful he knew what was best for me,' Messi acknowledged in a 2014 documentary about his life and times, directed by Álex de la Iglesia.[1]

Messi was also carefully handled by FC Barcelona's trainers and doctors, who tried to ensure that his development as a player and his body growth were kept in balance. While his training regime focused on building up muscle in his legs and strengthening his lower body, it also involved carefully monitored resting periods to avoid the negative impact of overexertion.

Although things hadn't gone exactly to plan in Rijkaard's first months in charge, with the club falling to twelfth place in La Liga and some fans demanding his resignation, as the season went on, Barça made up eighteen points on Real Madrid in the second half and, despite finishing as runners-up, it felt as if there was new momentum gathering. That summer saw players like Deco, Samuel Eto'o and Ludovic Giuly sign, and youth team prospects like Victor Valdés and Andrés

Iniesta promoted to the first team. A little under a year after his first-team debut in a friendly, on 16 October 2004 Messi made his League debut in a Barcelona city derby against Espanyol, coming on in the eighty-second minute.

Those who were there remember the mumbles of astonishment as this long-haired youth with red cheeks, this 'child' in the number 30 shirt, came on to the pitch. With the only goal of the game scored by Deco early in the first half and the game petering out, many saw the break for the substitution as the ideal moment to try and beat the rush and leave. The Barcelona-based German writer Ronald Reng described what happened next:

> With two of Espanyol's defenders – and no space whatsoever – in front of him, he simply dribbled between them, the ball stuck to his feet like a sixth toe. It was just eight inconsequential minutes at the end of a game, but his debut in professional football had me and the stranger on the terrace next to me instinctively shaking hands, with all the pathos of men who believe they have witnessed an event that has bound them together for ever. We were there. We had seen him. We all know that overwhelming feeling when we see a footballer for the first time and are struck by the conviction that we have never seen anyone like this.[2]

Messi's League debut at the age of seventeen years, three months and twenty-two days made him their then youngest competitive debutant. That night, Messi went home with his father to his flat a few streets away from the Nou Camp and sat remembering what it had been like.

And yet Rijkaard was not a coach to be rushed. His careful nurturing of Messi continued with what other players took to be almost Buddhist placidity. Messi only feels football: 'When I have the ball at my feet, I don't think, I just play. On the football field, my only thought is: Give me the ball! I don't invent dribbles. I don't work out any moves. Everything simply comes from instinct.'[3]

As Ronald Reng has pointed out: 'the invisible achievement of the Messi story is how his coaches have tactically channelled the instinct of this genius without Messi himself realizing it.'[4]

Messi owed his professional kick-start to his Dutch coach, as he generously acknowledged in an interview eight years later. Messi told an Egyptian TV station in March 2016 that it was Rijkaard who made the most important coaching contribution to his career. 'All the coaches I had at first left me things, but I think the most important thing in my career was Rijkaard.'[5]

Rijkaard initially used Messi – both in training and in his early game-time – on the right wing, which the left-footed teenager took initially as a punishment, and took time to adapt to. In the youth teams, he was used to playing centrally, being the fulcrum, receiving the ball constantly from deep and turning to run at defenders. From his early days in Rosario he had always played on the left flank or in the centre, behind the strikers. But putting the left-footer on the right meant that he could cut inside. It was time-tested football wisdom, but Messi saw it as a demotion, pushing him away from seeing enough of the ball. He essentially refused to play wide right in the youth teams.

In the 2004–5 season, Messi debuted in three competitions in his first five matches for Barça's senior team, with mixed results. After the electrifying La Liga cameo against Espanyol, his first competitive start came eleven days later in the Copa del Rey, on 27 October 2004, against the minnows UDA Gramanet, a third division side.

Messi was lined up in a decidedly second-string attacking three, alongside Henrik Larsson and Ludovic Giuly, but with the key players Xavi, Iniesta, Rafael Márquez and Carles Puyol all included in the team. Messi failed to make his mark as Barça suffered an embarrassing 1–0 defeat, with the press quick to note the lack of effective attacking play.

Messi then made his debut in the UEFA Champions League against Shakhtar Donetsk in December 2004, when Barça were already guaranteed a top-two finish in the group. He played the full ninety minutes on that occasion, but failed to have much impact on a match that Barça lost 2–0. This was to be his only experience of playing in European football that season, as he was left out of the squad for the round of sixteen, where Barça were knocked out by Chelsea.

He remained a bit-part player for the rest of the season, playing only seventy-seven minutes for the first team, but regularly for the B team, where he wore the number 9 shirt and regularly dominated games.

Then came a point in the season when any doubts that may have hovered over Messi as a player were lifted, with a performance that confirmed Messi was destined for stardom.

'The goal that started the Barcelona legend' was how the BBC headlined Messi's contribution in the game on 1 May 2005, against Albacete.[6] Coming on as a late substitute for Samuel Eto'o, Messi took just minutes to account for himself to the Nou Camp.

Albacete were a badly resourced and lacklustre club; not a team used to finding a cherished place in the history of stars. But their thirty-fourth match of the 2004–5 La Liga season became part of their far more illustrious opponent's folklore.

The visitors came to the match fighting off relegation after losing ten out of their last eleven fixtures. Barça had maintained their lead at the top of La Liga for six weeks, and their big rivals Real Madrid were poised not far behind them in La Liga, determined to take advantage of any slip-up. Short of capacity, some 80,000 spectators made it to the Nou Camp that evening to see the home side crush the visitors, and with style.

It didn't quite go according to script initially. Albacete played a defensive game, which proved frustrating for an attack made up of Ronaldinho, Eto'o and Deco. Eight yellow cards between the two teams underlined the fractious nature of the game. It was only in the sixty-sixth minute that Eto'o scored the first goal.

Since his debut against Espanyol, Messi had played five games for the first team, but only for a few minutes, and had no goals. Up until that point, it had been Ronaldinho and Eto'o who had formed Rijkaard's preferred main strike force. The game was still in the balance, with Barça still leading 1–0 with three minutes plus injury time left to play, when Rijkaard gambled by substituting Eto'o for Messi, much to the chagrin of the Cameroonian, who shrugged off the comforting hand of one of Rijkaard's backroom staff and stormed down the tunnel.

Ronaldinho approached Messi who, despite the muscle he'd been adding to his frame with intensive training, still had the look of a child playing dressing up in his oversized kit, and told him he was going to set him up to score. 'Tomorrow it will be you on the front pages,' the grinning Brazilian told the earnest-looking young Argentine.

Shortly afterwards, Ronaldinho picked up a pass on the right wing and dribbled effortlessly past a defender before feeding a beautiful pass to Messi, who beat the goalkeeper only to have the goal disallowed for offside. A replay suggested it wasn't, but Messi had to settle for having his scruffy long hair ruffled patronizingly by the goalkeeper – or so it seemed.

A few minutes later, like an action replay, Ronaldinho audaciously scooped the ball over two Albacete defenders for Messi. He let it bounce, and with a remarkably cool finish lobbed it over the goalkeeper. Like all great players, Messi controlled the moment. It was as if time stood still for him, or rather that he had more of it than everybody else. The goal generated a celebration that few watching the game inside the Nou Camp stadium or live on TV would ever forget. Ronaldinho gave Messi a piggyback ride – the older star paying homage to his young pretender, and in the process introducing *el pibe*, the Argentine street kid, to the world stage. It was as if the *barrio* of Rosario and the Brazilian *praia* had come together in a celebration of football played at its most instinctive and joyous.

The Nou Camp was engulfed in euphoria, with fans chanting Messi! Messi! – a moment that his father Jorge counts among his most treasured memories. Messi entered the dressing room at full time to a collective embrace and cheering. The Albacete players teased their goalkeeper that – in concentrating on Ronaldinho – he had forgotten about the 'little fella'.

The next day Messi was eating with his family, when Maradona – seemingly just woken or still awake after a long night – rang him to add his own personal good wishes, and convey how much he had enjoyed the goal.

Messi would remain eternally grateful to Ronaldinho for those halcyon days, when his Brazilian teammate and 'guardian' selflessly gave him the encouragement he needed to progress in his professional career.

As Messi told Barça TV in an interview on the tenth anniversary of Ronaldinho joining the club: 'Ronaldinho was the star of the team. I learnt a lot at his side. I'm grateful for the way he treated me from the first moment; he was a great help to me because I had never been in a changing room like that, and with me being the way I am, well, it made everything much easier for me.'[7]

That season, 2004–5, Rijkaard's Barça won La Liga for the first time in five years and Messi found himself among the celebrating players, and among the happiest. As the victory bus made its way through the city, Messi could be seen with a huge smile on his face, larking around with the Brazilians Ronaldino and Thiago Motta and the naturalized Portuguese Deco, the social lifeblood of the squad at the time. The Brazilians affectionately called Messi *irmao*, 'little brother' in Portuguese, although Messi was fast growing out of being anybody's mascot.

Two months after the Albacete game, the journalist Simon Kuper watched Messi play in the World Youth Cup, in which he scored two penalties in Argentina's 2–1 victory over Nigeria in the final. 'My main memory is his second penalty,' Kuper wrote in his book *The Football Men*. 'Some penalty-takers wait for the keeper to dive, before choosing the other corner. But Messi just needed the keeper to shift his balance fractionally on to his right leg, before choosing the other corner. My neighbour in the stands was the world's leading expert on youth football, the ancient, birdlike Dutchman Piet de Visser . . . He inevitably exclaimed: "Maradona!"'[8]

Family circumstances were also changing. The day of the victory parade had seen Florencia, wife of Messi's older brother Rodrigo, give birth to a son, Agustin, who was to become Messi's much-loved nephew, and a new footballer in the family. It was as if his career and family were putting down roots all at the same time.

12. MANCHESTER DAYS: RONALDO

Fans who expected Ronaldo to continue his form from the previous season's FA Cup final soon realized that the disappointment of Euro 2004 had seemingly put the brakes on. There were still flashes of brilliance in the early months of the 2004–5 season, but it seemed hard for him to put the various elements together into a sustained run of form.

It was December before his first goal, and he would score only one more before he produced an entire performance that suggested he was capable of impacting the biggest games. This was on 1 February 2005, during a highly charged encounter with Premier League rivals Arsenal at Highbury.

In the history of the intensifying rivalry between the two clubs during the Wenger/Ferguson era, the game had a particularly epic quality. Just a season after the 'Battle of Old Trafford', this game would be remembered as the 'Battle of Highbury' – reminiscent of the violent match between England and Italy in 1934. This time around the match was preceded by ugly scenes in the tunnel, and on the pitch before the first whistle.

The two captains, Roy Keane and Patrick Vieira, had squared up before a ball had even been kicked, after the Frenchman apparently announced that he wanted to break Gary Neville's legs. Then the captains refused to call heads or tails for the toss, let alone shake hands, forcing referee Graham Poll to select one side of the coin for each of them.

In addition to the off-field melodramatics, it was a match almost made to measure for a talent and personality like Ronaldo, with a lot of free-flowing football that allowed him to show off his speed, athleticism and ball control, and a lot of tough tackles testing his resilience. Although Arsenal initially looked the stronger of the sides and took the lead twice in the first half, Ronaldo was in inspirational form, scoring a brace in the second half, the first goal bludgeoned in from an acute angle after he was fed by Ryan Giggs, the second stabbed into the net from two yards after Giggs had floated a superb ball in from the right. United eventually won 4–2, in spite of going down to ten men, with Ronaldo's goals turning the game in their favour.

However, over the following months there was bitter disappointment for Ronaldo as he failed to make any impression on a second leg match in the last sixteen of the Champions League against AC Milan, and United were defeated 2–0 on aggregate. They limped home third in the League, eighteen points behind the winners Chelsea, and though they reached the FA Cup final and played well, with Ronaldo scoring in the three successive rounds leading to the final, United lost against Arsenal on penalties, after the game had ended after extra time at 0–0.

It was a game in which United dominated and Ronaldo permanently threatened, with his perfectly weighted cross – after he had skipped past Lauren on the left flank – squandered by an unmarked Scholes; two free kicks narrowly missing the target, and a curling corner just blocked by Vieira. It felt very much like a season of what-ifs. He had featured heavily throughout the season, playing fifty times, and scoring nine goals, but there were mutterings that perhaps, as they'd suspected all along, he just didn't have the end product. All those step-overs and rabonas were useless if they didn't score goals or win games.

That summer, there were loud whispers that Real Madrid were looking at Ronaldo, but nothing came of them; so, as the following season began, it felt as if the Portuguese very much had something to prove. However, the beginning of the following season also proved challenging on and off the field and, as the autumn days darkened, there was the sense that events off the football pitch might derail his season completely.

Firstly, while away with the Portuguese national team, he received the devastating news that his father Dinis had died from illnesses relating to his alcoholism.

Ronaldo was in his hotel room watching a movie when Luiz Felipe Scolari, the coach, accompanied by Luís Figo, the captain, told him the news. His initial reaction was one of shock. 'I had no feeling. My head felt like a balloon that was suddenly deflated. I could not think about anything. Absolutely nothing,' he later recalled.

Then he told Scolari he wanted to stay and play: 'I am going to play a game in honour of my father, I will play for him.'[1]

On the day of the match, Ronaldo's behaviour created a strange atmosphere in the dressing room. Out of respect, the other players kept quiet, until Ronaldo told them not to act strangely just because of him. He asked them to crack a joke or two, and then did what people were used to seeing him do in the dressing room, when he wasn't checking himself out in the mirror. He began to play with the ball. Then he played in a match that ended 0–0. For all the bravado, no one, not even Ronaldo, was in the mood for a goal.

Ever since his childhood, Ronaldo had had to live with his father's alcoholism, although he clung on to and later idolized the better moments. He cherished having Dinis accompany him on his days playing football as a schoolboy. This myth of childhood innocence endured in his memoir. He always claimed to have loved Dinis, despite admitting, after his father's death, to being 'outraged by his physical appearance'.[2] While Dinis was alive, Ronaldo's feelings towards him were awkwardly balanced between embarrassment and despair on the one hand, and on the other a determination not to allow the dysfunctionality he brought to family life destroy it completely.

Then on 20 October 2005, the *Sun* ran a front-page story alleging that he had been involved in the rape of a woman. A separate story broke in the *Sun* ten days later, alleging that Ronaldo's cousin, Nuno Aveiro, had been involved in the rape, holding the woman down while it took place. Both men strongly denied the allegations and, although they were questioned by police, no charges were brought.

In the middle of this, legendary club captain Roy Keane, a player who Ronaldo would later say was a massive influence in his young career, left to sign for Celtic.

It felt as if everything negative came together on 6 December 2005. Ronaldo became the scapegoat when United were knocked out of the Champions League, beaten by Benfica and ending bottom of the table in the first group stage.

As Rio Ferdinand remembers it in his autobiography, Ronaldo was so concerned with putting on a good show for the Portuguese to justify his move to United that he forgot to play as part of a team. None of the tricks came off and Ferguson was furious at the final whistle saying, 'Playing by yourself? Who the hell do you think you are?'[3]

Ronaldo was upset and cried afterwards in the changing room, as he had sometimes done before – but he had the strength of mind to ride the storm and bounce back, just as he had done all his life. And Ferguson was a reader of personalities. There were some players who would not have taken that kind of treatment, but Ronaldo used it to motivate himself or, as Ferdinand put it, say, 'Right, I'll fucking show you . . .'

It is worth noting that these off-pitch events would be enough to destabilize any twenty-year-old, and that in the context it was perhaps harsh to interpret his poor form as relating only to too many step-overs, but Ronaldo was later extremely complimentary about Alex Ferguson's support while his father had been ill.

Ronaldo could never be accused of lacking a work ethic, or not using adversity to his advantage. From the early days at Manchester United, his manager and teammates had been impressed by how he worked his socks off and battled opponents. Quinton Fortune tells the story of how Ronaldo would finish training, strap on some ankle weights and go back on to the pitch to work on his step-overs. The players would laugh at him and he would laugh at himself.

'Injustice was never far from the judgements formed around him. But he changed,' Ferguson recalled. 'He had that wonderful courage and confidence in his own ability. He elevated himself, in my mind, and in those of the other United players, to a point when those around him were in awe of his talent.'[4]

If the relationship with Ferguson was like that of father and son, it was one that was carefully managed to bring out the best in the player, and this was mutually understood. As Gary Neville recalled: 'He wasn't above being left out of the team. [Ferguson] encouraged him to show his ability and flair but didn't pick him every match.'[5]

The top brass at Manchester United were monitoring the situation closely. If there was regular controversy on the pitch at Old Trafford, there was also a history of periodic scandal or unwanted attention beyond it, often outside of the club's control, from the heady George Best days of sex and booze and his later tragic alcoholism, to David

Beckham's regular appearances in the showbiz pages, and the falling out with Ferguson prior to his departure for Madrid.

But in Ronaldo's first season, he had built up a small, intimate circle of friends he trusted almost as much as his mother – his cousin Nuno, his sister Katia and his brother-in-law Ze, along with a Portuguese expatriate friend called Bruno. He also received occasional visitors from Madeira and Lisbon, including those who had known him from his Sporting schoolboy days, like Carlos Pereira.

The Ronaldo clan, so goes the image encouraged by the club and his agent, lived a life most ordinary together, spending their spare time playing PlayStation, tennis, table tennis and card games, with the occasional dinners out. Ronaldo, when not playing football, spent long hours training or in the gym, or swimming, a sport he had enjoyed since childhood in Madeira, an island where champion swimmers were hugely admired.

In Ronaldo's first season, media attention had in fact been focused on one of his United teammates. Twenty-three-year-old English international Rio Ferdinand was immersed in intense adverse publicity after being dropped from the England squad for missing a drugs test – an omission that eventually led to an eight-month ban in 2004. It would have served as a cautionary tale for the young Ronaldo, a reminder of how easily even one of the most popular of United's players could be the subject of scandal and vilified by the tabloids.

It is perhaps not surprising then that Ronaldo never developed George Best's reputation for hedonism, nor did he allow any relationship he might have had to impact negatively on his relations with the club management, as had happened with Beckham. Indeed, the detail of Ronaldo's private life was carefully screened from media scrutiny, even when he allowed the world to get a little closer to who he really was. Behind the scenes, he often showed a different side.

Paddy Harverson told me of an exchange he had with Cristiano in the corridor of a hotel the night before the team played in a European tie.

'I was looking for my room when I heard this cat meowing round the corner, apparently in distress. I went to where the sound had come from and there discovered Cristiano on his own, clearly showing off that he was a very good animal mimic. He was nineteen and with spots and he was being mischievous outside his room for no apparent reason. I just laughed, then asked him, "What the fuck are you doing?" And he just winked, because his English wasn't that good, and then wandered off . . .'

Throughout this period of burgeoning media attention and development on the pitch, Cristiano's ego was kept just about in check by Ferguson and his United teammates. Ronaldo was teased by his colleagues because of his hairstyle and the self-consciously fashionable clothes he wore, even to training. The club was not without a history of dedicated followers of fashion – George Best had led the way in the 1960s, and Beckham had taken up the mantle with a vengeance. And then there was Ronaldo. 'Cristiano always looked immaculate, always wanted to have very clean boots, perfect training kit, perfect hair, the best clothes even into training,' recalled Gary Neville.

Once his English had improved and he had got more used to the dressing-room culture, and forever growing in confidence, Ronaldo took such banter on the chin, and deliberately caricatured himself to make the others laugh.

There was also a much less brash side, as evinced by a visit he made to Banda Aceh, one of the areas most devastated by the 26 December 2004 tsunami, six months after the disaster.

There he met a seven-year-old Indonesian boy who had been rescued after surviving on his own for nineteen days. The boy was found, barely alive, wearing a muddied and half-torn Portuguese national shirt. This prompted an invitation from the Portuguese Football Federation to have him visit Lisbon so he could meet Ronaldo, his hero, for the first time. In the media spotlight, the boy declared himself a United fan. Ronaldo subsequently contributed a not insubstantial sum to help the post-relief effort. This was to set a pattern for the future: more discreet contributions to charitable causes, many of them unconnected to any marketing subplot.

Rather than allowing himself to go off the rails, as the year turned, he seemed to find renewed focus, scoring a goal on New Year's Eve against Bolton Wanderers and finding form over the next few months. Having scored only four goals in the first half of the season, he went on to score another eight. When you watch footage from that period now, you begin to see that familiar set of the shoulders, as he cuts in from the left or right, the defenders scrambling backwards. And then there are the goals – his 'howitzer' of a goal against Portsmouth that almost seems to swerve through the goalkeeper, and one against Wigan, following which he took his shirt off in his now trademark celebration. Although the season ended in disappointment for the club, Ronaldo entered the summer in good form and with a World Cup to look forward to.

13. THE RISE OF THE HOBBIT: MESSI

On 24 June 2005, his eighteenth birthday, Lionel Messi signed his first contract as a senior team player. It made him a Barcelona player until 2010, so would run two years less than his previous contract, but his buyout clause increased to €150 million. He wedged his foot more firmly in the first-team door two months later during the Joan Gamper Trophy, Barcelona's pre-season competition.

Messi returned from the U20 World Cup a conquering world champion. He was immediately thrust into a promotional tour of Korea, China and Japan, where he enjoyed the steadying influence of Sylvinho, the former Arsenal left-back, who became increasingly important as a more sensible, grounded mentor than Ronaldinho. Sylvinho has spoken in many interviews about how Deco and Ronaldinho tried to look after their junior companion on and off the pitch.

It was 24 August 2005 when the side, coached by Frank Rijkaard, entertained the current Serie A champions, Juventus. The game featured the likes of Ronaldinho and Deco, as well as Zlatan Ibrahimović and Alessandro Del Piero in opposition colours, but it was Messi who grabbed all the attention. 'Messi's solo runs, killer passes and shots on goal shone through against one of the finest defences in world football, with players of the calibre of Fabio Cannavaro and Patrick Vieira,' wrote the journalist Carlos Faneca in a blog posted at the time on FC Barcelona's official website.

Fabio Capello, the then Juventus coach, later commented that he had never seen such a quality player of such a young age. 'He's got flair, speed, everything, I love him.'[1]

Some speculated that he had been especially fired up by his recent unfair sending off on his senior debut for Argentina, only lasting for two minutes before his flailing arm in response to a foul by a Hungarian player was adjudged to have been a deliberate attack. Messi had been absolutely devastated by what had happened.

Whatever the reason for his captivating performance on that

August evening against Juventus, it was one to make the football world sit up and take notice.

As the chant of 'Messi, Messi, Messi' resonated again around the Nou Camp, Capello caught up with Rijkaard and asked cheekily if he might arrange a transfer to Juventus. 'You have to protect a talent like this. Tonight he was phenomenal,' replied the Dutchman, evidently still determined to look after his young charge and try to keep his feet on the ground. In the first few months of the season, it was in the Champions League where Messi seemed to thrive.

In the second match of the Champions League group phase, against Udinese on 27 September 2005, Messi was in the starting line-up and went on to help Ronaldinho dismantle the Italian team, before 90,000 spectators at the Nou Camp, beating them 4–1.

Veteran Barça chronicler Ramon Besa of *El País* had no hesitation in declaring Messi as man of the match, even though Ronaldinho scored a hat-trick and he scored none.

Analysing Messi's growing maturity as a player and his contribution to the teams' success, Besa commented that the player 'surprises us in each match because of his capacity to create danger in every area of the pitch, and because of the ease with which he interprets the game . . . Fearless and fast, with great change of rhythm, Messi is playing the role in his team that Ronaldinho played when he first arrived.'[2]

In fact Rijkaard still felt he was a player in development, and that Ronaldinho had a great deal still left to offer. Nonetheless the comparison between the two, in favour of the younger Argentinian, did not go unnoticed.

A few weeks later, on 3 November, in a Champions League game against Panathinaikos, Messi scored his first goal in the Champions League, which his coach Rijkaard pulled out for special praise. Messi pressurized the centre-back into a soft back-header, then stole in before the goalkeeper, lifting it over him and scoring. What was noticeable was the nous with which he anticipated the mistake – the cheek of an ambitious teenager, but also demonstrating a disarming skill and self-confidence worthy of a veteran star.

In spite of his misgivings, Rijkaard allowed himself to be persuaded by his coaches that Messi was ready to start the biggest game of the League season, and on 19 November 2005, when FC Barcelona visited Real Madrid at the Santiago Bernabéu for their first La Liga encounter of the season, Messi was told he would be starting. The two sides were just one point apart in the fledgling La Liga table, with Rijkaard's Barça having amassed twenty-two points from their opening eleven games, behind an unlikely usurper, the Pamplona club Osasuna. It was almost taken for granted, given the virtual duopoly the high-spending rivals had established in modern times, that the title race would be decided between them, and the first Clásico of the season would give an early pointer as to where the balance of power lay.

Barça won 3–0, and this Clásico would forever be remembered for the standing ovation that the home crowd gave Ronaldinho. But it has also entered the history books as the match in which Messi made his Clásico debut, and he did so with a performance which gave Madridistas every reason to take notice of him, and feel threatened.

The team line-ups were a study in contrasts and club identity. Real Madrid, coached by Vanderlei Luxemburgo, were at the high point of their *galáctico* era, with a team that included Zinedine Zidane, the Brazilian Ronaldo and David Beckham. However, both sides had homegrown players with a deep-seated awareness of what the game between these two historic rivals meant. Real Madrid had Iker Casillas and Raúl, and although the heart and soul of Barça's team were Xavi and Carles Puyol, veterans of La Masia, Barça's undisputed talismans were the three foreigners: Ronaldinho, Samuel Eto'o, who had been snubbed by Real Madrid as a teenager, and Messi, the new kid on the block who had much to prove still.

Messi started the game as a right-winger, forming an attacking trio with Ronaldinho and Eto'o. All three got off to a strong start, menacing Real Madrid from different angles, although Los Blancos' defence initially held up. With fifteen minutes of the game gone, it was Messi who set up the first goal. The ball glued to his feet as he dribbled on the right wing, he cut in and caused havoc in the Madrid defence before feeding Eto'o, who hit it home.

Barça continued to dominate: 'Carles Puyol played with his heart on his sleeve and his hair in his eyes as usual; Xavi Hernández moved the ball with ludicrous pace and precision; Leo Messi simply ran Madrid ragged,' wrote Sid Lowe.[3] But it was Ronaldinho who was the star of the show, scoring a goal of sublime creativity and effortless execution that personified that year's Ballon d'Or winner at his best.

Picking up on the halfway line out on the left, he danced his way around Sergio Ramos and Helguera before wrong-footing Casillas with a disguised shot that beat the goalkeeper at his near post. Twenty minutes later he scored his second, showing off a similar style and swagger, once again leaving Ramos for dead and sidefooting past Casillas.

Then those of us who were there that night in that monumental stadium experienced something extraordinary happening, an unexpected and dramatic climactic turn. As Casillas shrugged in resignation and Ronaldinho celebrated with his trademark samba and toothy grin, the Real Madrid fans spontaneously rose to their feet and broke into unanimous applause.

Prior to this game, the last visiting Barça player to get an ovation at the Bernabéu had been Diego Maradona, twenty-two long years ago earlier. Thanks to Ronaldinho, Messi was discovering that it was possible to at least equal the mighty Diego, if you happened to play for Barça, and you had the ambition. By then Ronaldinho had become part role model, part older brother, and also a friend. Two months earlier, Messi had bought and moved into his first house in the town of Castelldefels, just a few blocks away from the Brazilian.

In February 2006, Messi made an important contribution to Barça's away victory over Chelsea in the last sixteen of the Champions League, a match full of drama on and off the pitch. José Mourinho, by then ensconced in the Premier League, caused a major row by falsely claiming his team Chelsea lost because of complicity between the referee and Rijkaard.

But there was another, perhaps more enduring, image of that encounter – that of Messi's skill and strength of character, as well as physical resilience, as the Chelsea players focused on trying to break up his every move, sometimes brutally, as with the foul that earned Asier del Horno a red card. As Santiago Segurola, the Spanish football journalist, later recalled: 'That game showed me something about Messi, above all; the fear he inspired in his opponents.'[4]

Messi's later teammate, Thierry Henry, was among those whose eyes were opened that day. While at Barça there had been those acutely aware of his extraordinary ability long before he made his professional debut in 2004; Henry admitted that it was after watching him in action in that first-leg game against Chelsea that he realized how special he was. 'Chelsea kicked him all over the place in that Champions League game at Stamford Bridge. But Leo just kept picking himself up and running at them again and again,' Henry told the Spanish sports newspaper *MARCA*.[5]

Later Messi said in an interview that the Barcelona players hated Chelsea more than Real Madrid and said their behaviour made the infamous rivalry between Boca Juniors and River Plate look tame.

In the second leg at the Nou Cap, twenty-five minutes into the game, he collapsed on the pitch, with a pulled muscle in his right thigh. The first major injury of his career followed on from a previous injury, a week earlier, to the top of the femoral bicep in his right leg. While the first injury had kept him out of action for twelve days, this one – almost certainly because he had tried to accelerate his return – would keep him away from the training ground for seventy-nine days.

While there are no scientific tests that can explain muscular injuries, physiotherapists suggest that some are preventable through a combination of better diet and training techniques. One early biographer, Guillem Balagué, suggests that while FC Barcelona were not at that point monitoring players as diligently as they would do after Guardiola took over as coach, there was no evidence of drug or alcohol abuse. Messi himself retained an Argentine adolescent's craving for traditional food: *empanadas*, breaded veal escalopes and ravioli, along with Coca-Cola. As Balagué puts it, 'It wasn't a case of too much partying, rather one of order. Or lack of it. In his eating, in his personal timetable.'[6]

Although he was to miss a large chunk of the season, Messi's performances up to that point helped inspire and motivate his fellow players. The team, led by Ronaldinho, went on to achieve an impressive trophy haul. They retained La Liga and, on 17 May 2006, Rijkaard's Barça played the Champions League final against Arsenal in Paris.

Hard as the decision was for Rijkaard to take, in the end the Dutchman came to the conclusion that it was too great a risk to Messi's own physical wellbeing and the team's own prospects to have him play. Barcelona won 2–1, despite going behind, only the second time they had ever won the trophy.

When the game was over, Messi was so upset that he walked straight off the pitch and into the dressing room and refused, despite urgings from Rijkaard and his technical staff, to join the celebration. This was not the first nor the last sulk that Messi got into, but it perhaps exemplified more than any other incident his idiosyncratic character. At one level it seemed the kind of hissy fit typical of the kind thrown by an immature, spoilt kid. But it also seemed to reflect the obsession of a person who instinctively lives and breathes football, drawing life from the talent he knows he carries within himself, while easily falling into a very dark place when he is denied his ultimate expression of existence.

Interestingly enough, Messi's reaction reflected Maradona's when – at the similar age of eighteen and playing for the club Argentinos Juniors – he was told by César Menotti that he was being left out of the Argentine national team in the 1978 World Cup, being held in Argentina. Menotti told me that he had received medical advice that Maradona's muscular structure was still in the process of development and that he, as he put it, 'risked suffering a bad foul and being crippled for the rest of his career'.

In time both medical staff and Messi himself would draw an important lesson from the injury he had suffered in the lead-up to the Paris final of 2006. For both club and player had perhaps not sufficiently monitored the diet and fitness regime that Messi should follow once his hormone treatment had come to an end. While difficult to prove beyond reasonable doubt, his injuries may have sprung from his body having to adapt too quickly to physical changes as it faced the new challenges thrown up by Messi's rapid ascendancy from youth to first-team player.

It would take Messi several years to admit in a rare example of openly shared reflection that perhaps it was the kid in him still that stopped him from showing the kind of solidarity that teams like Barça expected from players, old and young. 'I realize now that I should have enjoyed that final match more, more than I did, for the moment that it was. I don't think many players get the chance to be able to win the Champions League. I was very young and didn't want to celebrate. Then Ronaldinho, Deco and Motta brought me the cup, and that is a very beautiful memory. Today I regret not enjoying it more on the pitch, although afterwards I did. I was there, and it is something very special,' Messi commented for a special Barça TV documentary aired for the first time on 21 July 2013.[7] The film was made to coincide with the tenth anniversary of Ronaldinho's famous official presentation in front of 25,000 fans at the Nou Camp. The programme was entitled *Quan el Barça va recuperar el somriure* (When Barça got its smile back).

Though nobody realized it at the time, that Champions League final was the zenith of Rijkaard's career and the peak of Ronaldinho's Barcelona career as well. As Messi was called up to the World Cup squad, still lacking in match fitness, the only way was down.

International Break

14. DIEGO'S SHADOW: MESSI

Messi's senior international career had got off to a decidedly shaky start only months beforehand, with that red card against Hungary after just two minutes. And though nobody really thought it had been fair, Messi had ended up crying in the dressing room and there were those who thought he simply wasn't mentally strong enough yet for the demands of international football.

He also did not distinguish himself particularly during the 2006 World Cup qualifiers, although coach José Pékerman described him as a 'jewel' after a match against Peru, during which he won a crucial penalty that secured his team's victory. He later suffered from a hamstring injury that nearly kept him out of the tournament, and his lack of match sharpness meant he began and ended the tournament on the bench. His absence from the team, and Pékerman's tactics, were blamed in the Argentine press for the quarter-final defeat by Germany.

The defeat was all the harder to bear given the expectations raised by Argentina's earlier 6–0 thrashing of Serbia, considered by many commentators to be one of the finest performances by any national side in years. It would be forever remembered for the twenty-five-pass move that led to the second goal. Eight Argentine players were involved, including the veteran captain Juan Pablo Sorín, but Messi was not one of them. He did come off the bench in the seventy-fourth minute for Maxi Rodríguez, assisting Crespo for the fourth goal, and two minutes before the final whistle scored the first World Cup goal of his career. This made him the youngest scorer in the tournament and the sixth-youngest goal scorer in the history of the World Cup. TV cameras pointedly captured Maradona, watching the game from the stands, rising to his feet, and signalling that the move was worthy of his approval.

In the words of Andreas Campomar, author of ¡Golazo!, a history

of Latin American football, 'a decade on from Maradona's ignominious retirement, Argentina was still looking for a new messiah.'[1] With
his star rising in European club football, it seemed only a matter of
time before Messi was considered Diego's successor in the Argentine
team, although he was destined to be blamed more regularly by his
fellow countrymen for its failures than celebrated for its less frequent
successes.

The comparisons, which had begun almost as soon as Messi had
kicked a ball, were perhaps inevitable, but only became more intense
and critical once Messi had broken into the national team. Diego
Maradona had led his country to World Cup victory in 1986, during a
decade when he had been far and away the central and most admired
figure of the national squad. Maradona was thus a messianic talisman
to whom a whole nation looked up and, for all his off-field decadence,
was judged a genius, beyond being good or evil. 'Diego went on an
extraordinary journey from his roots in poverty to his condition as a
people's hero,' wrote Jorge Valdano in *Fútbol: El Juego Infinito*, 'in
which millions of people projected themselves through the work and
grace of their idol and saw achieved what they thought impossible.'[2]

It was the international projection of an Argentine success story
that endeared Maradona to his fellow countrymen. To them, he
seemed to make up for so many failings in their own history. Maradona provided Argentines with a sense not just of identity but also of
escape. They saw purity in his play, and called it poetry.

As Campomar writes in *¡Golazo!*, once Maradona left the field of
play his supposed resurrections would be legion – young player after
young player was burdened with the expectation of being Diego
reborn. Amongst the unceasing and often undistinguished parade of
'New Maradonas', Ariel Ortega and Juan Román Riquelme both stood
out, but they too would fall short.

From even before Messi had been fast-tracked to the FC Barcelona first team, Julio Grondona, president of the Argentine Football
Association (AFA) and a leading figure in the FIFA hierarchy, had
updated the earlier glowing report he had received about the 'boy
from Rosario', and identified him as the future key player for a national
side with a worldwide following. Not only was Grondona convinced
of his unique talent, but he also saw in the quiet, withdrawn Messi
a player he could deal with rather better than the explosive and

unpredictable Maradona – hence the part he played in bringing Messi into Argentina's under-20s squad and blocking Spain's attempt to get him into their red shirt.

As for Messi's commercial potential, this was underlined prior to the World Cup in Germany by his signing of a new contract with the German sportswear company Adidas, who also happened to be sponsors of the Argentine national squad. The move proved controversial within FC Barcelona, for it involved Messi breaking his contract with Nike, the club's main sponsors. Among those most displeased was Sandro Rosell, the former Nike executive and vice-president elect of FC Barcelona, who had strongly encouraged Messi's promotion into the first team and had developed what he regarded as good personal ties with both the player and his father.

Adidas's first commercial with Messi featured prominently during the tournament in Germany, and showed him drawing a small doll playing football with much bigger dolls, and the player describing his dream of being recognized despite his size. A poster campaign had his face appearing in major football cities around the world, and a pair of boots was designed for him with the inscription of 'The Hand of God' and the date of 22 June 1986, when Argentina had played against England in the quarter-final of the World Cup in Mexico.

The campaign was not universally popular. Within the Argentine squad, some of the veteran players considered it presumptuous of Messi's promoters to equate him to Maradona. Back in Barcelona, it further fuelled the sense of betrayal felt by Rosell, who felt that Messi would be better served by Nike – a company he considered to be more in touch with the growing youth market and which was developing a successful promotional campaign with Cristiano Ronaldo (and for whom he had worked in the past).

The campaign also perhaps added to the sense that Messi's tournament was a let-down, and that he was underused for most of the tournament by Pékerman. Argentina's defeat by Germany brought back memories of the 1990 final in Rome, when Maradona's Argentina – defending the crown they had won four years earlier in Mexico – lost to the German team 1-0 after a controversial penalty award, with players and officials from both sides trading punches on the pitch. The difference was that while Maradona was then blamed for

Argentina's defeat, it was now Pékerman who found himself criticized for keeping Messi on the bench.

Inevitably, the what-if version of history asks what would have happened if Messi had played. Would the World Cup of 2006 have turned out to have been his crossing of the Rubicon; might he have scored the winner in the final and thus held up the trophy at a younger age than Diego in Mexico, forever escaping from Maradona's shadow?

It's a stretch. Brand Messi still had some way to go before dethroning Maradona, not least in the eyes of his countrymen. Nevertheless, it was from that moment onwards that the debate ended on whether Messi should or should not be left on the bench. He became an automatic starter in the national team, whoever the manager happened to be.

15. WORLD CUP TRAUMA:

RONALDO THE WINKER

Ronaldo came into the 2006 World Cup in Germany keen to kick on from his strong end to his club season and desperate to wipe out the sad memories of the Euros two years previously. However, for millions of English fans, his role would be immortalized not so much for anything he did with the ball, but for the wink he gave after his Manchester United colleague, England's star Wayne Rooney, was sent off in the two nations' quarter-final match on 1 July.

England, under the management of the Swede Sven-Göran Eriksson and captained by Real Madrid's David Beckham, approached the match with a not entirely unjustified optimism that they were on their way to the final, and had a good chance of winning the tournament.

Hopes rested on the talent of Rooney who, at twenty, was already reaching a high point in his club and international career, and was widely regarded as one of the best English players of modern times. Portugal, on the other hand, rested their hopes on Ronaldo, who – thanks to Ferguson's careful management – had matured into his own version of stardom.

After Rooney had been signed in the summer of 2004, the players had developed a mutual professional respect and regarded each other as good mates, even if the lean, self-pampered Madeiran and stocky Scouser presented a very odd couple. The Premier League's version of the beauty and the beast fitted into the stereotyping of English and Mediterranean football culture of sectors of the English media.

As noted in an article by John Vincent in *Soccer and Society*, pieces written at the time about Rooney emphasized 'his northern working-class roots in the construction of his hegemonic hypermasculinity and role as a "patriot at play"'.[1] By contrast, by the end of his third season at Manchester United, Ronaldo had replaced Beckham as the club's most daring marketing tool, and was still frequently seen as a narcissist by the English press, easily lampooned as the Derek

Zoolander of the Premier League. Quite apart from scoring goals, and his assists, and a general aspiration to be the best player on the planet, Ronaldo was also a fashion statement: a handsome man who checked himself frequently in the mirror, a strutting metrosexual image of naked torsos, hair products, diamond earrings and adverts for tight jeans and tighter underpants. The jug-eared Rooney, while also racking up big endorsement deals, was already losing his hair.

The signings by Manchester United of Rooney and Ronaldo as teenagers was a case study in physical and mental contrasts, but also a key part of Alex Ferguson's regeneration of United. After Beckham's departure, Ferguson's plans had been to assemble a group of young players who could develop over a number of years, with the experience of older players like Giggs, Scholes and Gary Neville to help the process.

Ferguson had seen the promise of the Rooney–Ronaldo double act developing from their first season together, 2004–5, when, as he recalled it, despite losing the FA Cup final against Arsenal on a penalty shootout, his team 'roasted' their opponents with twenty-two shots at goal. From there on Ronaldo and Rooney had confirmed themselves as essential parts of the Ferguson project, and seemed to recognize in each other a teammate on the way to the very top.

It was because they knew each other so well that they felt they could exploit each other's weaknesses on the international stage; Ronaldo's propensity to play-act, and Rooney's no less notorious short fuse. The first half of the World Cup quarter-final had Rooney trying to get Ronaldo yellow-carded for diving, but it was Rooney who came off second best in the mind games.

After a frustrating game, in the sixty-second minute Rooney was battling for possession with three Portuguese defenders when he seemed to be pulled back by Chelsea's Ricardo Carvalho, who was on the floor. Rooney's patience snapped, and he trod on Carvalho's groin. At first, Argentine referee Horacio Elizondo seemed to hesitate, but then, with Rooney trying to push off his Manchester United teammate, the referee was confronted by a gesticulating Ronaldo. A straight red card followed. Moments later, TV pictures showed Ronaldo winking towards the Portugal bench as a furious Rooney, surrounded by the anger of English fans, made his way off. As a final 'insult', Ronaldo would later net the decisive spot-kick as Portugal again triumphed on penalties.

From pop stars to TV commentators, English football fans were furious with Ronaldo's role in the sending off, and incandescent over his wink. Singer Liz McClarnon recalled: 'Everyone in the room was fuming, saying, "I can't believe he's done that. Oh my God!"'[2] Former England captain Alan Shearer told millions of BBC viewers: 'I think that there is every chance that Wayne Rooney will go back to the United training ground and stick one on Ronaldo.' The *Sun* quoted an unnamed source saying Rooney would 'split [Ronaldo] in two' when they next met. The newspaper also released a Ronaldo dartboard, so England fans 'could get revenge on football's biggest winker'.[3]

In the seething aftermath of the match, Ronaldo seemed close to calling it quits as far as the Premier League was concerned. The world was his oyster, and a move to Real Madrid or FC Barcelona, both of which continued to be interested in him, would have been a step up in profile and step away from the lion's den. He had won an FA Cup and League Cup from three promising, if not entirely satisfactory, seasons at Old Trafford, scored twenty-seven goals – some of them great – in 137 games, if also getting tangled in showy step-overs and a frustrating lack of end product. It had also been three seasons since United had won the League – José Mourinho's Chelsea seemed all set to be the dominant force of English club football for years to come, having won two titles in a row – and they hadn't come close to winning the Champions League.

'I'm not going to stay at Manchester United,' Ronaldo told the Portuguese media. 'After what happened with Rooney I can't remain there. In a couple of days, I will have my future sorted out. I don't want to stay in England.'[4]

But for a defiant player so concerned with his legacy and career narrative, to leave under a cloud would have been way off-script. Rooney, once he had piped down, was also in conciliatory mood, telling Cristiano that while he was furious at being sent off, he bore no grudge against him, and they should put the incident behind them in the interests of playing on for United. Later that summer, after the World Cup, Rooney is thought to have been in periodic phone contact with Ronaldo to urge him not to quit the club, and reassure him how important he was to United.

If only others' reaction had been so generous, Ronaldo would have had cause for celebrating his best international tournament to date. In Portugal's semi-final against France, his first touch in the opening seconds was greeted with a shattering and genuinely shocking chorus of jeers from all parts of a 66,000-capacity crowd. This was not just English supporters in possession of tickets, having hoped to watch their own team in the semi-final; French fans were happily joining in, and those of other nations.

Ronaldo nonetheless proved the major threat to the experienced French side, the best player by far in an otherwise unimpressive Portugal performance, particularly in the first half, when he produced a moment of magic to enliven a somewhat lacklustre game. In the thirty-eighth minute, on the left touchline, he got past two French players and ran almost thirty yards into the penalty area, only to have his shot deflected away by a diving Lilian Thuram challenge.

But the flashes of Ronaldo's genius, and the fact that he emerged as one of the game's outstanding players in a losing side, was insufficient to win forgiveness, that evening at least.

The BBC's Phil McNulty's response was one of the more balanced to come out in the English press, as he pointed out that Ronaldo was exactly the sort of player England would kill to have in their team, but noting the 'amateur dramatics – actually, let's call it diving – that earned him the contempt of thousands inside this space-age home of Bayern Munich'.[5] Even he wondered if that would be the end of his time in England, and mused that there was a fantastic player in there, if only he could escape from his prison of step-overs, feints and dives.

Zinedine Zidane's first-half penalty decided the game, and Ronaldo cried in Munich – as he did after Euro 2004 – and was seemingly further punished by not getting the tournament's Best Young Player award, which Rooney, among other United and Portuguese players, thought he deserved. But he also showed the kind of resilience that would help him get through the following challenging weeks, when fans – not generally United ones – booed him, and the tabloid media had several field days of thinly veiled racist abuse against him, painting him as a treacherous foreigner who had conspired against the club and nation to which he owed his wealth and celebrity.

16. KICKING ON: RONALDO

The aftermath from the wink seemed to rumble on and impact the whole of the club, as the press began to criticize Manchester United's entire transfer policy, with the *Guardian* describing it as 'lumbering across a dancefloor at 1.45 a.m., trying to get off with anything that moves'.[1] There had been rumours of various Spanish clubs making bids for Ronaldo, though none had materialized.

In August 2006, in his first game since the World Cup, Ronaldo got a taster of the broad mood among English fans when Manchester United played away in a pre-season friendly against Oxford United, but he also showed off the strength of his personality and the import-ance of the support he got from Ferguson and his team.

In a drunken atmosphere at the Kassam stadium, Ronaldo was heckled as he came off the team bus, jeered during the warm-up, hissed when his name was called out in the pre-match line-up announcement, booed every time he touched the ball and cheered when he lost it. At times, it felt as if Ronaldo had been turned into a panto villain. Only he knew just how far he was facing a make-or-break period in his career, and he reacted the only way he knew how – by reminding everyone just how good he was, without having to act.

He scored two super goals in United's 4–1 win. The first a superb volley off a cushioned lay-off by Louis Saha, his second a similarly killer twenty-yard shot into the bottom corner. At the end of the game, United fans rose as one to give him a standing ovation, and Ferguson singled him out for special praise.

The boos and verbal insults he encountered in almost every match he went on to play for Manchester United in the 2006–7 season served to strengthen his resolve to be the best. Ronaldo emerged from the World Cup with a more mature personality, and seemingly more determined than ever to train harder and improve his skills as a player. He'd returned after the summer looking as if he'd spent his entire break in the gym, in contrast to an overweight Rooney.

As Gary Neville recalled: 'Physically, he changed from a boy to a man. It was like he left as a featherweight and returned as a light heavyweight. That brought him a level of power he didn't have before. His power output increased through his body strength. And in the course of that summer his decision-making seemed to have improved as well. Before, he would cross or go one-on-one rather than pass.' Neville also insisted that the wink controversy was a media confection which barely registered with the English players. 'All's fair in love and war on the pitch,' he insisted. 'You give out and you take. I went and swapped shirts with Ronaldo after that game [the quarter-final].'[2]

Ronaldo says the media pressure after the 2006 World Cup helped him develop his own defence mechanism. The furore over the wink was 'not very pleasant', he said. 'But to tell the truth it did me some good. With this, I grew wiser and it ended up turning a problem into something that helped me mature. Whenever we get over-confident we stop listening to criticism about ourselves.'[3]

After the defiant performance against Oxford, he seemed to be distracted by the boos in some early fixtures, but then a brilliant goal against Reading on 23 September seemed to mark a turning point. He dominated the game with a performance of powerful, direct running that the opposition players seemed utterly unable to stop. The full-back on his side, Graeme Murty, described tackling him as 'like running into a brick wall'.[4]

He lit up the Premier League in November with a spectacular free kick against Portsmouth, which became a YouTube favourite. As the *Observer*'s Paul Wilson remarked, however many times goalkeeper David James might have watched the replays, and wondered what else he could have done to counter the strike, it was 'not about bend or disguise with Ronaldo's free kicks, it is all about speed, power and placement'.[5]

The boos were on a diminishing scale with further man-of-the-match displays at Chelsea and Everton. For the first time in his career, Ronaldo backed up performance after performance. Beginning with a goal and an assist in the Manchester derby, Ronaldo scored three successive braces over the Christmas period against Aston Villa, Wigan and Reading to send United top of the table. The sight of him attacking a full-back at speed, those lightning step-overs and changes of direction, him bending the ball into the bottom corner, came to define that period. It was as if his opponents were only operating at half speed. His sheer physicality, whether it was his pace, the power he hit his free kicks with, or the leap he seemed to get when challenging for headers, made it seem sometimes as if he was playing against younger kids in the park. In December and January the Portuguese won the League's Player of the Month award, becoming only the third player (after Dennis Bergkamp and Robbie Fowler) to do so in consecutive months.

In the second leg of the quarter-final of the Champions League, he scored his first goals in the competition, when Manchester United dramatically recovered from a 2–1 first leg defeat by crushing Roma 7–1 at Old Trafford. His first was bludgeoned past the keeper at his near post, who was surprised by the pace on the shot. His second slid over the line after a pinpoint cross from Giggs.

In the first leg of the semi-final against AC Milan at Old Trafford, he tormented opposition players all over the pitch as they resorted to cruder and cruder challenges to stop him, before he squeezed a header from a corner past the Milan keeper, Dida. United won 3–2 with a last-gasp Wayne Rooney penalty, but it was the Italian club that ended up going through on aggregate after a Kaká masterclass saw them win 3–0 at the San Siro.

It nevertheless proved to be a breakout year, as Ronaldo broke the twenty-goal barrier for the first time and won his first Premier League title – Manchester United's first in four years. The season had been an extraordinary, defining period for him, from World Cup turmoil and subsequent abuse by English fans to prolific goal scorer, Premier League champion and peer recognition with the PFA Players' Player of the Year and PFA Young Player of the Year awards. The threats of quitting had paid off in a more literal sense as well. During the season, Ronaldo penned yet another deal designed to keep him from heading to Spain, worth a cool £120,000 a week.

Life was just getting better for Ronaldo. From the first year after his arrival, Ronaldo and Ferguson always had a bet going on the player's goals tally for the season. The bet suited Ronaldo, who had developed an obsession with statistics, principally as a record of his own achievements. It also humoured Ferguson, owner of racehorses and a man who had a reputation for enjoying a flutter. The first season the target was ten (Ronaldo lost), then fifteen (Ronaldo lost). 'On both occasions I tried to pay him. He refused to take a penny,' Ronaldo recalled in *Moments*.[6] In the 2006–7 season, Ronaldo had raised the stakes to £400 and had won the bet by February. His fifteenth goal of the season came with the eighty-seventh-minute winner in a 2–1 come-from-behind victory at Fulham. It was a carbon copy of the goal he had scored against Reading earlier in the season, cutting inside from the left before bending the ball across a helpless keeper. This time, it was Ronaldo who refused to accept Ferguson's money. The gesture was indicative of the immense respect Ronaldo had for his coach. 'He taught me the basis of football,' Ronaldo would later say of Ferguson.[7]

The end of the season saw him win every individual League award possible. The wink no longer seemed to get much coverage.

17. THE NEW MARADONA: MESSI

Of all the ways in which the various World Cup disappointments that the Barcelona squad felt were processed, perhaps none was more instructive than Ronaldinho and Messi's approach.

Observers close to Messi worried that Messi's peripheral involvement could have damaged the young man mentally. But, far from pushing the self-destruct button, Messi threw himself fully into the next stage of his career and, from adversity, Messi drew strength, his presence and importance in FC Barcelona growing in the season 2006–7. The Brazilian, meanwhile, never really seemed the same after becoming something of a scapegoat for his country's failure.

By contrast, Messi's star continued to be on the ascendancy, even if FC Barcelona entered a period of decline, signalled by a 2–0 defeat by Fabio Capello's Real Madrid at the Bernabéu in the first Clásico of the 2006–7 season, in October. During that campaign, Messi scored seventeen goals in thirty-six games. Looking back on those goals now, it still often appears as if the groundsman's teenage son has wandered on to the pitch. He still seems adolescent, loping, his hair permanently in his eyes. Even the lightning-fast changes of direction seem to carry a sulkiness. But if physically he still seems undeveloped, his brain is clearly on a different level from almost everyone around him. His opponents seem several moves behind him, chasing shadows. He can often be seen pointing where he wants the ball played by a teammate, opening his body to say 'here.' When it comes to scoring the goals, it is the coolness that marks him out; he often simply sidefoots the ball past the goalkeeper. Again and again, he pops up on that right-hand side of the penalty area, sweeping the ball into the net with his left foot.

However, there were still peaks and troughs. He continued to be plagued by major injuries, and a metatarsal fracture sustained on 12 November 2006 kept him out of action for three months. He recovered in time for the last sixteen of the Champions League against Liverpool, but he was effectively marked out of the game; in early March

2007 Barcelona, the reigning champions, went crashing out of the competition. In La Liga, his goal contribution actually increased towards the end of the season: eleven of his fourteen goals came from the last thirteen games. On 10 March 2007, at the Nou Camp, he scored his first hat-trick in a Clásico. Spain's big two approached the game with every reason to feel demoralized after getting knocked out of the Champions League. But instead the players, with Messi the best among them, seemed to find renewed energy in what – against all odds – turned into one of the more exciting Clásicos of the modern era.

The word before the match was that these were two teams in a funk, but the game began with three goals in the first fifteen minutes. Ruud van Nistelrooy powered in a deflected cross from just outside the box for Real, only for Messi to sneak in wide on the right and side-foot an equalizer. Then a foul on Guti in the penalty area allowed van Nistelrooy to score from the spot. Another loose ball in the box allowed Messi to crash the ball into the roof of the net for his second. Both keepers were on brilliant form, making world-class stops throughout. It seemed a game-changer, if not game-ender, when Barça's young homegrown defender Oleguer was sent off just before half-time for a second yellow card.

Rijkaard removed Eto'o and played with only two forwards, an off-form Ronaldinho and Messi. Madrid dominated the second half and seemed set for victory when the gloriously sweat-banded Sergio Ramos leapt highest and headed their third. But Barcelona came again, and Messi salvaged the draw in stoppage time with a wonderful strike. Ronaldinho wriggled clear on the left, turning inside and holding several challenges off before curling the ball infield with his right foot. Without breaking stride, with quick feet, perfect balance, and a disarmingly cool head, Messi collected the ball five yards outside the penalty area, burst past Helguera and the final despairing lurch of Sergio Ramos and then hit the ball low to the left of Casillas. As the ball goes in, even Capello can be seen acknowledging the goal, shaking his hands together in admiration.

For all the gloomy pre-match forecasts, this Clásico had turned into a scorcher, with three goals in the opening quarter of an hour, a red card and penalty, and thirty more shots at goal, including Messi's third on the brink of full time.

At aged nineteen, Messi had yet to shrug off the nickname El Mudo – 'the mute one' – with which he'd been dubbed by some of his less respectful colleagues in Barcelona's youth team. There was no doubting the accolades after this match, though. Just one word, 'MESSI', splashed repeatedly across the front pages of the sports media in Barcelona. No one was in any doubt, in Catalonia at least, that he was well on his way to being the best player in the club's history. The headline in the Madrid sports daily *AS* proclaimed, '¡*Viva el fútbol!*' Messi was the main cause for celebration, much against the tribal instincts of most Madrid fans.

The point earned was enough to send Barça top that night. It was also the catalyst for a run of ten wins from the last twelve La Liga games of the season for Real Madrid. The two sides finished level on points, seventy-six apiece, but the draw at the Nou Camp (coupled with Real winning on home soil earlier that season) meant the Bernabéu club were crowned champions on the head-to-head ruling.

But with Ronaldinho in decline, and Eto'o now considered the third-choice striker by Rijkaard, it seemed that the Messi era at FC Barcelona was well under way. That March, the club had declared their long-term faith in him, and put a new value on him as their key player when he signed a seven-year contract which increased his salary over the period from €1.7 million to €6.5 million, with a €150 million release clause.

The following month he had immediately dispelled any doubt that he might not be worth it, scoring a spectacular goal in the first leg of a semi-final Copa del Rey encounter against Getafe at the Nou Camp. To those Barça fans who claimed that Messi was on his way to becoming the new Diego Maradona, he seemed to provide a watertight case – with a near carbon copy of one of the greatest goals in World Cup history. The similarity between Messi's strike against Getafe and Maradona's run through the England defence in the quarter-final of the 1986 World Cup seemed only too apparent but, just in case, Catalan television played them side by side on a split screen.

Messi, still only nineteen, picked up the ball inside his own half and, keeping it so close to his boots as to make it seem glued, proceeded to carve his way through the Getafe side, with the effortless movement of a racing skier in a slalom. A series of swerves and feints beat five defenders – Paredes, Nacho, Alexis, Belenguer, García – and finally the goalkeeper, Redondo. The goal became the talk of world football.

'It seemed a hybrid had been born: Diego Messi or Leo Maradona,' wrote the doyen of British La Liga commentators Sid Lowe.[1] 'So, you can copy a work of art, after all,' wrote the widely respected Spanish football writer for *AS*, Alfredo Relaño. He compared Messi to Elmyr de Hory, who forged famous paintings but always put the signature upside down. 'This was a replica, with the same path, the same acceleration with every touch, the same pauses and feints, always escaping on the same side. The only difference was Messi finishing with his right foot – that was the upside-down signature,' Relaño wrote.[2]

And yet, for all the hype, commentators seemed to have overlooked how the two goals were separated by the very different context and circumstances in which they were played. Messi's goal came in a one-sided match between Barça and one of the lesser clubs of La Liga. The event was a semi-final tie of the King's Cup, a tournament that – for political reasons – many of the more radical Catalan nationalist Barça fans refused to recognize or get too excited about.

As Maradona himself would argue, the challenge he had faced in 1986 had been much greater: a World Cup quarter-final against a decent English side with the memory of the Falklands War still fresh in the competing national psyches. Maradona was determined to avenge his country's humiliating defeat, and the deaths of hundreds of young Argentine soldiers. It gave the occasion in the Azteca stadium a huge emotional, cultural and political charge, as well as a sporting one, and dwarfs that game against Getafe.

In fairness, while the Getafe goal has a huge following on YouTube and has often been used as an example of Messi at his best, it is worth recognizing, as Guillem Balagué has done, that Messi scored that goal hundreds of times when he was in the lower ranks and in the Barcelona B team, and after the Getafe game went on showing his ability to break from deep and run with the ball, dribbling past whatever came in his path, up to and including the goalkeeper on a good day, often against much tougher competition. What that goal in Getafe displayed was skill, conviction and authority of a kind that left everyone watching with the sense that there was nothing even the best of defences could do to stop such a player in such form. It is an enduring example of football played at its best.

Around the world, articles were written about the boy from Rosario, this 'flea', this 'devil', this 'anti-Beckham'. He was a man without tattoos or piercings, who turned up to interviews in clothes that appeared to be borrowed from an elder relative, but of whom Samuel Eto'o said that watching him play was like watching a cartoon, while his Argentina teammate Gabriel Milito described him as unlike any other player in the world.

When asked if he aspired to be the best player in the world, Messi replied: 'Well . . . it would be nice, but it's not an obsession.'

18. CLOSE ENCOUNTERS:

MESSI VS RONALDO

In July 2007, Ronaldo was joined at Manchester United by another young Portuguese star from Sporting Lisbon, the winger Luís Carlos Almeida de Cunha, otherwise known as Nani, in a €25 million transfer deal. The son of poor immigrants from the Cape Verde islands, Nani spent his childhood living in one of Lisbon's shanty neighbourhoods before being scouted by Sporting's youth academy aged sixteen while playing for local club Massama.

When Manchester United were negotiating his transfer, assistant manager Carlos Queiroz – who had come straight back to the club in 2004 after his brief stint at Real in 2004 – travelled to Lisbon to seek reassurances from Aurélio Pereira, the director of the youth academy, that the player had the character to adapt to a new life in northern England. He wanted to know about Nani's mentality, and if he could handle the pressure of playing for United.

'He didn't want to know if he had good feet. He knew all about that. He wanted to know about his personality, how he could cope with a different country and a different team,' Pereira later recalled. 'It was a big responsibility for Carlos Queiroz because it was a €25 million deal and he wanted to be absolutely sure. I calmed him and said that, yes, he was buying a complete player.'

United, of course, had the perfect mentor for Nani, and Cristiano Ronaldo played a not insignificant role in helping his compatriot settle down as best he could in his early days in Manchester, sharing his house with him for a while. The role of protector drew the Madeiran further out of himself. Nani struggled to communicate with other, English-speaking Manchester United players, but found solace and empathy in the company and advice offered by his more experienced Portuguese teammate Ronaldo – a Madeiran with Cape Verdean ancestry who had experienced a rough childhood of his own and had learnt the rules for survival in a foreign land.

'There was a phase when I was living at Cristiano's house and it was very good. There were always cheerful people and we had everything – swimming pool, Jacuzzi, tennis, ping pong,' Nani recalled in an interview with the *Daily Mail*'s Chris Wheeler.[1]

Only later did Nani struggle to cope with solitude, when he moved to a house of his own. He would also find it hard to win over fans, and win a place in the team, ironically due to the sensational form of Ronaldo.

The rise of the Madeiran's star accelerated in the 2007–8 season, with an important factor in his success being the part played by the Manchester United coach René Meulensteen in one-to-one training. It was the Dutchman who stayed behind to work with Ronaldo early in the season, when he was suspended for three games after being sent off against Portsmouth. He taught him to be less predictable, improve his teamwork while, at the same time, to better exploit goal-scoring opportunities rather than squander them with excessive showmanship, as Meulensteen later recalled in an interview with the *Telegraph*'s Henry Winter:

'I knew what Ronaldo wanted. He wanted to be the best player in the world. I told him: "I can help you with that. There's nothing wrong with your work ethic, it's a wave pushing you forward."'[2] Meulensteen described drawing a diagram for Ronaldo, separating out the tactical, including awareness, understanding and decision-making, and the physical, of which Ronaldo was especially endowed, including pace, strength, stamina and agility. There was also a section for personality, which included mentality and attitude. Finally there was the technical: passing, shooting, turns and other skill moves. He asked Ronaldo what his strongest section was and he replied 'skills'. Meulensteen then advised him to work on his one-touch and two-touch play in order to make him a more unpredictable player who opposition players would find it harder to defend against. Meulensteen addressed another issue. 'I told him: "The problem is also your attitude and therefore your decision-making. At the moment you're playing to put yourself into the limelight, to say look at me, how good I am. Therefore, Mr Ronaldo, you are doing a lot that doesn't mean anything for your teammates." He accepted this. I said: "You need to score more goals. Targets, aims."'[3]

The pair worked intensively together, studying videos of Alan

Shearer and Thierry Henry to improve his output ever further. Meulensteen defined three action zones for Ronaldo to focus on – No. 1: in front of goal, No. 2: either side, No. 3: outside the area. Ronaldo became deadly in all three.

When Meulensteen asked Ronaldo how many goals he thought he could score in 2007–8, the Portuguese boldly said between thirty and thirty-five. 'I think you can score forty,' said Meulensteen.

That season was to see Ronaldo complete one of the most remarkable periods of high performance the English game has ever seen. And again, it began in adversity, when in the second game of the season against Portsmouth, Ronaldo was sent off for an attempted head-butt. He was fined by the club after being banned for three games. If there were worries that he might sulk or feel hard done by, his return to the team showed the opposite to be true. The 'wee show-off', as Ferguson had once characterized him, found a performance level to rival anything seen before or since, scoring thirty-one goals in thirty-four League appearances and another eleven in the cups and European competitions. In the first European game of the season, United were drawn against Sporting Lisbon, a game that could have led to a similar performance as the one against Benfica, which had drawn the hairdryer treatment from Ferguson. Instead it drew a performance of focus and discipline. Ronaldo scored a low dipping header, declining to celebrate, and United went on to win the game.

Over the next forty-odd games, he scored every type of goal. From the leaping headers that were becoming his trademark – one particular goal against Roma typifies this, as he seems to hang in mid-air for several seconds, several feet above the Roma players, before the ball rockets into the net past a despairing keeper – to tap-ins, long-range screamers and Exocet free kicks, including one against Newcastle that looked as if it had been fired from a cannon. Afterwards he turned to the crowd and almost seemed to shrug, with a look on his face that said 'not bad'. The bravado and showmanship was still there, but it was finally being backed up by awe-inspiring performances. Looking back at those goals now, it's amazing how often that change of direction, the Cruyff turn or step-over inside the flailing defender, was followed by the ball bending into the top or bottom corner. Defenders seemed to bounce off him; he had an extra yard of pace and vastly more mental acuity. The ball always seemed to be breaking into his path, or popping up at the far post as he arrived. There was a national debate over what the secret to his free kicks was and whether they were possible to stop. It was the quality of his interplay with Carlos Tévez and Wayne Rooney that drew most admiration, as it felt for the first time he was playing as an integral part of a team.

For Ronaldo and his team, it felt like the right time to assess the whereabouts of brand CR7. Four years after arriving at Manchester United, Ronaldo agreed to the publication of a ghost-written memoir entitled *Moments*. It was heavily illustrated, with photographs of him off the field outnumbering those of him as a player, and dominated by publicity shots, with the text admitting to a 'fondness for advertising'. It seemed aimed at confirming the player's celebrity status, while underlining his huge marketing potential.

Cristiano had shown himself to be a natural in front of the cameras, like Beckham, ever since his profile had rocketed during Euro 2004, although he claimed to have had to learn the trade. The first advertising contract he signed after his arrival in Manchester was with the Portuguese financial group BES. It had him kicking a ball several times and seeing it swerve away each time, until he finally scores and brings the net down – an image of ultimate success born from hard work and practice.

His first modelling experience was with the London trademark Pepe Jeans. 'It was totally different from everything I had done until then in advertising. I saw it as another personal challenge, because I had to pose side by side with a professional model, who was used to the cameras, unlike me,' he wrote, modestly.[4]

The Pepe Jeans ad showed him against a backdrop of an industrial wasteland in Barreiro near Lisbon, lounging, torso exposed, on an inflatable armchair, alongside a young woman reclining on the ground in high heels and black bikini, both in a pose suggestive of post-coital relaxation and yet strangely disengaged from each other's presence, as if they formed part of a collage. Other publicity shots that made their way into *Moments* focused on him as a sporting Adonis, his good looks and physique often displayed, with him dressed only in briefs or tight swimming trunks, seemingly at ease with a sexualized posing that would appeal as much to gay men as straight women.

Advised and encouraged by Jorge Mendes's now multinational agency, he willingly took on advertising assignments and relished the experience. Drawing on the marketing example of Beckham, he sold a range of commodities, from fashionable clothes to non-alcoholic drinks, all the while reminding us of his self-deprecating sense of humour, his athleticism and skill as a sportsman, and the trophies won at United.

Despite carrying an ankle injury as the season drew to a close, Ronaldo would also do something that would come to accrue massive symbolic significance: play in a game against Lionel Messi.

On 23 April 2008, the twenty-three-year-old Madeiran went head to head with the twenty-year-old Argentine for the first time during the first leg of a Champions League semi-final at the Nou Camp.

This was the fifth competitive encounter between the two clubs in modern football history, with the expectation of it being a classic, as memorable and full of drama as the first tie played in March 1984, when Ron Atkinson's United, captained by Bryan Robson, faced a Barça coached by 1978 Word Cup Winner César Menotti, and with a young Diego Maradona in its illustrious ranks.

The latest encounter had United and Barça fielding Ronaldo and Messi, two of the most exciting players to have emerged in a generation, and contenders for their first Ballon d'Or as Players of the Year, after finishing second and third in the 2007 voting. Each had already marked themselves as important entries in the histories of their clubs, both as play makers and goal scorers. Ronaldo was already seen by many of his own countrymen as the best Portuguese player since Eusébio, while at Barcelona Messi was seen as the 'new Maradona', who would finally live up to the billing, and had been dubbed 'Messiah' by the press.

In the run-up to the game, each player commanded respect if not fear from the opponent, because of the speed, resilience, vision and skill on and off the ball that they had shown in recent seasons. If there was a difference, it was one of context: Barça were approaching the game on the back foot after going through two seasons without silverware, while Manchester United were on a roll, heading towards their second successive Premier League title and hoping to clinch the Champions League, nine years after last winning the European crown.

But the focus of millions of Spanish- and English-speaking fans that evening was on Ronaldo and Messi. While the rivalry would not assume its most epic proportions until both players played in La Liga, the prospect of watching the two most exciting players of their generation in their first physical encounter was thrilling.

From the moment they stepped out on to the Nou Camp turf, in the middle of their team lines, the TV cameras quickly picked out the two opposing players. The contrast in their physiques was striking – Messi, small and ragged, with his shoulder-length hair topped by a somewhat unfashionable headband, still looking as if he had dropped in from a youth kickabout in his native Rosario, and with no interest other than going out and getting stuck into the game. In the other line, Ronaldo: tall, lean and bronzed, every bit the celebrity sportsman, evidently basking in the glow of the cameras and the stadium lights. Before them, one side of the stadium displayed a massive mosaic with the blue and claret Barça colours.

The fans' famous mosaics had their origins in a game against Real Madrid on 7 March 1992, when Johan Cruyff had led out the Dream Team that would win the League and the club's first European Cup a couple of months later. Now, sixteen years on, the hopes of most of the 95,000-plus fans inside the stadium were pinned on the young Argentine, who seemed poised to usurp the crown currently worn by Ronaldinho. The atmosphere lost none of its decibels as the home crowd belted out their battle hymn of heroic aspiration and solidarity.

> The whole stadium
> loudly cheers
> We're the blue and claret supporters
> It matters not where we hail from
> Whether it's the south or the north
> Now we all agree, we all agree,
> One flag unites us in brotherhood.
> Blue and claret blowing in the wind
> One valiant cry
> We've got a name that everyone knows:
> Barça, Barça, Barça!
>
> Players, Supporters
> United we are strong.
> We've achieved much over the years,

We've cheered many goals
And we have shown, we have shown,
That no one can ever break us.
Blue and claret blowing in the wind
One valiant cry
We've got a name that everyone knows:
Barça, Barça, Barça!

The match got off to a dramatic start, with Ronaldo at the centre of it. Two minutes into the game, his goalwards header was handled by Messi's compatriot, Barça's Argentine defender Gabriel Milito, and a clear penalty awarded. Ronaldo unhesitatingly stepped up to the spot, only to thrash his kick wide of the goalkeeper's left-hand post, provoking delirium among the home fans and total dejection among the United fans who occupied a small portion of the stadium.

Ronaldo barely had an impact on the rest of the game, with United finding it difficult to set up attacks, leaving him, Carlos Tévez and Wayne Rooney isolated up front. Ronaldo claimed afterwards he had been handicapped by being played as a striker rather than on the wing – when Barcelona dominated possession for long periods it reduced his ability to get involved and play a more decisive role.

Among the more menacing players was Messi, but it was a game of missed chances for him too, with his only shot at goal blocked before he was substituted halfway through the second half of the 0–0 draw. The first meeting of the two future greats was, then, something of a damp squib.

Fourteen minutes into the second leg at Old Trafford, the only goal of the tie came not from Ronaldo or Messi, but from a spectacular twenty-five-yard strike by veteran Paul Scholes, which secured Manchester United's progress to their first Champions League final since 1999. The victory had added poignancy and significance for the club, coming on the fiftieth anniversary of the Munich air disaster. But the tie also marked an inauspicious first Champions League encounter between Ronaldo and Messi, over the two legs.

Ronaldo was not on his best form at Old Trafford either. By contrast, Messi was the real danger man for Barcelona, pinning United back with his slalom runs at goal. Messi was frustrated by the resilient defence of a team normally noted for its attacking verve, but even in defeat emerged as the man of the match. It was indicative of the shifting balance of power and mood in Barcelona ranks, Messi as the bright spot amid a season of overall disappointment.

For Ronaldo, the tie was a rare personal blip in a spectacularly successful season and calendar year. He went on to score the defining goal that secured Manchester United the League on the final day of the season against Wigan, making up for that miss in Barcelona. It was his thirty-first goal of the League campaign, enough to make him the first winger to win the European Golden Shoe. Gary Neville later recalled in his memoir that he felt he owed Ronaldo his championship medal in a way he had only done previously with Peter Schmeichel and Eric Cantona in 1995–6.

The season ended on an even higher note, with Ronaldo making his mark in United's victory in the Champions League final in Moscow. Ronaldo scored the first goal, another of his gravity-defying leaps above an awestruck Chelsea back line. It was his forty-second goal of the season in all competitions – exceeding his own pre-season expectations, but matching those of René Meulensteen.

After Chelsea's Frank Lampard equalized on the stroke of half-time, the match went to a penalty shootout. Ronaldo had his kick saved by Petr Čech, who wasn't fooled by Ronaldo's stuttering run and attempts at mind games. The game ended in sudden death, when Nicolas Anelka's penalty was palmed away by Edwin van der Sar. United were kings of Europe again, and Ronaldo had his first trophy for being the Champions League's top scorer. The enduring image of the celebrations that rainswept night is of Gary Neville, elder statesman of the United team, who didn't feature, with his arm round Ronaldo, punching the air. Ronaldo is in tears, overcome by the occasion, the relief that his missed penalty did not lose United the game, and the realization that at twenty-three he has won the biggest competition in club football.

However, almost as soon as he was off the pitch, the rumours started that Real Madrid were going to sign him. It was to be a transfer battle that would threaten to overshadow his Euro 2008, in the same way Messi's summer would be hijacked by his appearance at the Olympics. But first, Leo had to limp his way there.

19. RONALDINHO'S FAREWELL: MESSI

For Messi, as for many millions of Barça fans, the era of Ronaldinho and Rijkaard ended not with a bang but a whimper.

The summer of 2007 had seen plenty of optimism, as Thierry Henry, Yaya Touré and Éric Abidal arrived with big fees and reputations. But their season began with a goalless draw against Racing Santander and never really seemed to recover. Especially in the away fixtures, they looked unfit, unfocused and increasingly lacking any kind of attacking impetus. Ronaldinho looked uninterested in playing with his teammates, and again and again he could be seen throwing his hands up in the air in frustration, as he seemed on a different wavelength to those around him.

Looking back on this era at the club, I remember reading a prescient online comment by Bruno Garcia, a Brazilian Barça fan who seemed to capture the essence of Ronaldinho as the loner who played for the crowd, not the team, and liked to entertain. As Garcia pointed out, in Portuguese there are different verbs that translate as 'to play' – for a competitive game like football it's *jogar*, for frivolous clowning around it's *brincar*:

> Ronaldinho stopped *jogar* and started to *brincar* more and more. That came accompanied by drinking, smoking, chasing girls, late nights at the club – the lifestyle of a student or artist, not of a professional athlete.
>
> Like everything in life, that had a cost: he could not run as much, he could not focus as much and could not perform at the same level any more. So, once he could not *jogar* to the same level, but was very admired for the way he did that, he started more and more to *brincar* – creating beautiful stuff, but completely useless.[1]

Messi himself, while promoted as the club's new star, struggled to maintain fitness during the 2007–8 season, and the team's overall performance reached one of the low points of his career. It frequently felt as if he was being patched up and sent out on to the pitch, such was his growing importance. Though his talent burned ever brighter, he still made the runs and scored goals. Indeed over the course of the season he played more games (40), scored more goals (16) and made more assists (13) than the previous one.

But it felt like a season defined more by the chances he didn't take. So many times he was forced to create the chance himself, beating two or three opponents until he was taking the shot off balance, exhausted by the energy of getting there. Debates over his fitness, and the right way to handle him, seemed to overshadow discussions of his performances.

Indeed, in March 2008, even Rijkaard's enjoyment of his side's progression to the UEFA Champions League quarter-finals, after they had eliminated Celtic, was tempered by concern about Messi's latest injury. A torn muscle in his left thigh forced the team's new star to abandon the game in the thirty-fourth minute and miss the next six weeks of competitive football.

It was the third time in three years that Messi, aged only twenty, had suffered the same injury, the last occasion being the previous December against Valencia, which had ruled him out of the following week's clash with arch rivals Real Madrid. Inevitably, the injuries raised questions over whether they might be in some way connected to the growth treatment that Messi had undergone as an adolescent.

There was no conclusive evidence of cause and effect one way or the other and, anyway, it was not an issue that FC Barcelona were prepared to discuss publicly, although Rijkaard after the Celtic match was forced, under intense questioning, to defend the club's medical services. 'To doubt that they are doing their best is an insult,' he said. 'The medical staff and the club in general are working to prevent these sorts of problems.'

Club captain at the time, Carles Puyol, criticized the media scrutiny, while unwittingly exposing the extent to which the Dutch manager may have also been to blame for the injury for not standing up to that scrutiny, and not adequately protecting the Argentine, on whose shoulders Barça's eventual recovery from the doldrums seemed to rest. Whatever the cause, there were some in and outside the club who felt that Messi was somehow too fragile for the rigours of regular first-team football. Nobody doubted his talent, but was his to be a tragic story of a career let down by his body?

Rijkaard had left Messi out of Barcelona's 4–2 defeat at Atlético Madrid in La Liga the previous Saturday, drawing widespread criticism from commentators. The club's medical staff announced that they had advised Rijkaard to leave Messi out, but in the build-up to the Champions League fixture against Celtic, there was a unanimous call from the media for Messi to be recalled.

'The doctors spoke and said there was a risk of injury and you [the media] put pressure on him to play, saying that he always has to play,' Puyol said. 'Now we're all left to regret the decision. On Saturday there was more risk than today, but if he hadn't played and we had got a bad result I'm sure you would have said it was because he wasn't on the pitch.'

In the crossfire of blame and counter-blame, not one comment of criticism was aimed at Messi himself, indicating the special status of untouchable that the player had already achieved within the club, and which was destined to be reinforced in the following years as a succession of managers adapted their systems and squad rotation to suit his wishes.

The club's anxiety over Messi's wellbeing had been underlined months earlier, when senior club executives had become increasingly concerned with Ronaldinho's private life in Barcelona. An internal investigation discreetly carried out for the board showed that Ronaldinho had drawn Deco and a rather more innocent Messi into some of his off-pitch partying, to such an extent that it was affecting their fitness and concentration when playing.

Senior club executives kept the full details of their findings secret, and allowed the media to focus on Ronaldinho and Rijkaard, as this offered some protection to Messi, a player in whom the club had real hopes for the future, but whose personality was judged not mature enough to be able to withstand the pressure of a media assault.

After limping out of the Champions League after not scoring against Manchester United, the end of the Rijkaard era and Messi's personal experience of it had its most emblematic humiliation at the Bernabéu in May 2008, when Bernd Schuster's Real Madrid, having already secured the League championship, thumped Barça 4–1. Worst of all, tradition in Spain dictated that Messi, along with his teammates, would be required to give the newly crowned champions a guard of honour, or *pasillo*, prior to kick-off.

For Rijkaard there was worse to come, as he faced a barrage of questions about his own responsibility in the subsequent press conference. He looked like a rabbit caught in headlights, any deference due to him as Barça manager lost completely, as if the success of the earlier seasons had belonged to someone else, to another club, to another century.

Though publicly he refused to say he was quitting, privately he admitted that his time was up. A few days later, Barcelona announced that he would not be the manager beyond the end of the season. He was to be replaced by untested B team manager, Pep Guardiola. Top of his agenda was sorting out the future of the misfiring Ronaldinho, and working out how to get the best out of Messi.

Meanwhile Messi was about to become embroiled in the very public club vs country tug of war that was playing out in various courts relating to his appearance at the Beijing Olympics later in the summer. As the European Championships in Austria and Switzerland loomed, it seemed as if both Cristiano and Leo had big decisions to make.

20. EURO 2008: RONALDO UNDER PRESSURE

Such had been the volume of rumour emanating from Real Madrid that Portugal's first match against Turkey when Euro 2008 started almost seemed like a side issue to the assorted press. It felt as if every interview involved a question on the winger's future. In the event, Ronaldo took all the uncertainty around his future and channelled it into a supremely effective performance. He had a long-range free kick tipped on to the post and had a hand in both goals, scored by Pepe and Raul Meireles, as he flew up and down each flank. In the second half he was even given the captain's armband. It continued the excellent form that had seen Luiz Felipe Scolari's side qualify with something to spare.

Their next game saw them up against the Czech Republic. After Deco opened the scoring early on, everything seemed to be going well before an equalizer from a diving header by Libor Sionko saw them go into half-time level. In the second half, again Portugal looked impressive, as Ronaldo scored one second-half goal, a low drive that went in just inside the post, and then squared a pass for Quaresma to tap into an empty net.

Such was the positivity around their performance that Ronaldo went on to say if they continued their form they had a good chance of winning the competition. There were those who speculated on whether defeating two of the lesser-fancied sides in the competition justified those claims. Those doubts seemed sensible when Portugal lost their third group game to Switzerland. Scolari made eight changes, and Portugal looked the better side for much of the game, but in the last twenty minutes, Yakin scored from a slotted finish and a penalty. Although it was very much a second-string side, it wasn't the ideal preparation for their next game against Germany. Their manager Joachim Löw had crafted a solid, physical side that seemed to tower over most of the Portuguese players at the beginning of the match. Much was made before the game of the German player Arne Friedrich, who would be up against Ronaldo and who was said to have a rudimentary attitude to defending. It was the hot-blooded Portuguese, all one-twos and delicate interplay, vs the physical heft of the Germans. In the end Germany took the lead with a brilliant team move that ended with Bastian Schweinsteiger tapping home after a sweeping passing move. Four minutes later, terrible marking from a free kick saw Miroslav Klose double their advantage. As Portugal poured forward, they looked increasingly vulnerable to counter-attacks, until Ronaldo broke into the box and his saved shot was swept in by Nuno Gomes. As the half came to a close, Ronaldo seemed to be taking things by the scruff of the neck. The second half was untidy and dominated by scrappy challenges and fouls, which seemed to distract Ronaldo from his own performance. After the Portuguese goalkeeper Ricardo failed to deal with another free kick into the box, in the sixty-first minute, Michael Ballack knocked the ball in.

Portugal huffed and puffed and got a second goal in the eighty-seventh minute, but Germany held on to win. The story was that Portugal's terrible defending had cost them the game and that perhaps the pressure on Ronaldo from his country's reliance on him and the constant transfer rumours might have been too much.

Germany went on to be beaten in the final by Spain. The Spanish team were beginning to employ the style of play that would become synonymous with Barcelona under Guardiola, a style to which Messi would become so central.

However, before that could happen, Barcelona needed to know where he was.

International Break

21. THE BEIJING OLYMPICS AND MARADONA

Argentina's campaign for an Olympic title in Beijing in 2008 was notable for three things: confirmation of the extraordinary talent of the Barcelona youngster Leo Messi, a controversy over his participation that suggested he might not be as shy and retiring as everyone thought, and the looming presence of living legend Diego Maradona.

Messi's talent might never have got a chance to shine if Barcelona had had their way when, on 6 August, just days before Argentina's opening fixture against the Ivory Coast, Barcelona won a decision against FIFA in the Court of Arbitration for Sport, which said they were under no obligation to release their players for the Olympics. This was just the final turn in a saga that had unfolded as claim and counterclaim for the IOC, AFA and FIFA about who held the power. In the end it transpired it was Messi, who quietly forced through his participation, having long harboured ambitions of winning a gold medal, as the team had four years before in Athens.

During the Argentina under-23s squad's first match against the Ivory Coast, Messi scored the opening goal and assisted another in their 2–1 victory. Following a 1–0 win in the next group match against Australia, ensuring their quarter-final qualification, Messi was rested for the game against Serbia, which his side won to finish first in their group. Against the Netherlands in the quarter-final, he again scored the first goal and assisted a second strike to help his team to a 2–1 win in extra time. After a 3–0 semi-final victory over Brazil, Messi assisted the only goal in the final as Argentina defeated Nigeria to claim Olympic gold. Along with one of the permitted over-age players, Juan Román Riquelme, Messi was singled out in the official coverage as the standout player from the tournament's best team. And yet the person who saw Messi as his natural dauphin was not about to take a low profile.

It was during these Olympics that Maradona took a symbolic step towards realizing his dream of managing the national squad. When Argentina won gold, he rushed down into the changing rooms and joined in the high-profile celebration with the players, as if he was already their coach, even though the hero of the hour was actually Sergio Batista, the manager of the squad.

And yet for Batista, a veteran of the 1986 World Cup, who had recently taken over the responsibility for the youth divisions of the Argentine Football Association, Maradona was not so much a potential rival as a useful ally and scout.

In the aftermath of the Olympics, while Batista for a period faded into the background, Maradona kept in touch with several of the gold-medal-winning players, including Messi, thanks to his friendship with Gabriel Heinze and his personal ties with Sergio 'Kun' Agüero, the then-partner of Maradona's youngest daughter Giannina, and father to her child.

The relationship between Maradona and Messi was an interesting one.

The first time Maradona ever spoke to Messi was in 2005, during his first season with FC Barcelona's first team, when he scored his first La Liga goal against Albacete. Messi was at home having lunch when he received the phone call, during which Maradona congratulated him for playing well in a string of games and encouraged him to look to the future and keep on scoring.

Then, in August of that year, Messi found himself in Buenos Aires, participating in the rather whacky, unpredictable *La Noche del 10*, a hugely popular TV show that Diego presented. Maradona had embarked on a financially lucrative career in TV a year earlier, after recovering from the latest of a series of near-death health scares related to his cocaine use and overeating. He had re-emerged in public after having gastric bypass surgery, having his stomach stapled by a Colombian doctor, and being put on a strict diet of lightly mashed, easily digestible foods, and no alcohol.

Diego's opening TV show had him and the Brazilian legend Pelé exchanging personally autographed national shirts, heading a ball at each other for a minute and playing and singing a tango song – Pelé on guitar, Maradona on vocals.

The ratings had subsequently flagged after Maradona had veered from light entertainment into politics, calling George W. Bush a murderer and doing a fawning and wordy interview with Fidel Castro – mercifully cut from its original five hours.

Then the producers thought of the young Messi. No matter that – in contrast to Pelé and Castro – he had nothing much to say. They set the programme up so he could do the one thing he was passionate about, which was play football – and what's more against Maradona. The programme almost always featured Diego playing football-tennis with his guests. On this occasion it was him and Enzo Francescoli, the Uruguayan-born River Plate star and a veteran of Diego's vintage, against Messi and Carlos Tévez, the emerging young thoroughbreds. Once again it made a great show, with the two sides growing in their determination to win, although characteristically the most heated moments – contesting rules and points given away – involved the bullish Tévez and Diego.

Diego's team ended up losing 10–6, his only loss in the whole run of the series, yet there was no sense of humiliation or gloating displayed on one side or the other. One can only imagine how Ronaldo might have reacted in the same circumstances, beating Di Stéfano or Eusébio or even Raúl. But this was Messi, who had always looked at Maradona not as his nemesis but as his mirror (when it came to playing), and Maradona, whose resilient sense of self-belief had survived worse setbacks in his life and who, even in 2005, saw his own future in Messi's, not competing for the title of best player in history – for Diego felt beyond such comparison – but as his coach.

'I've seen the player who will inherit my place in Argentinian football and his name is Messi,' Maradona said. 'He is beautiful to watch – my kind of player in our blue-and-white jersey. He's a leader and is offering classes in beautiful football. He has something different to any other player in the world.'[1] One might note the emphasis on eventual succession, rather than dethronement. For Maradona, his own personality would always be unsurpassable.

As Fernando Signorini, the physical trainer of the Argentine national squad who worked with both Maradona and Messi, told me: 'Physically and technically there is much in common but there is a gulf between the two when it comes to personality. Messi was not born like Diego was in a shantytown, nor did he have to fight for survival from an early stage. As a young teenager Diego was playing for the youth team of Argentinos Juniors, getting up at four in the morning to go and play in an away game across the country, on pitches that had no decent changing rooms, let alone hot water or lighting, and where you had to face growing violence from the fans. Messi, at the age of twelve, was taken to Barcelona where he was put in a glass house and protected.'

On the pitch, on their best days, Maradona and Messi produced football as a sublime art form of individual creativity. As Jorge Valdano, retired footballer turned brilliant wordsmith, puts it: 'For Diego, the ball was a painting brush; for Leo, a high precision tool. Diego loved the ball and played with an emotion that made him and those who watch him happy; Leo loves the ball like a surgeon his scalpel, and when he finishes his work we marvel at the efficiency, precision and imagination with which he transforms the game. Any game. Almost all games.'

And yet compare Maradona and Messi off the pitch, and they are no longer part of the same coinage but as different as heat and cold. 'In this territory,' Valdano goes on, 'Maradona is born into a time of great social demands, who goes on crying out his rebellion, feeling himself a representative of those who do not have a voice. He divides the world between friends and enemies with an expressiveness that leaves no one indifferent.'[2]

But Messi, by contrast, 'does not switch on the loudspeaker of fame to express his rebellions, if he has any. For him, all that matters is football, because he was born in a time when capitalism anaesthetized everyone and because his personality is far from being, at least publicly, volcanic.'

Although he might not have been volcanic, Messi's quiet determination to play at the Olympics was a clear marker that he was determined to do things his way, and left Barcelona in no doubt of who held the power when it came down to it.

As the summer went on, another indication of just how powerful elite players were when it came down to deciding their futures was playing out halfway around the world.

22. CENTRE STAGE: RONALDO

As Cristiano spent the summer stewing over Portugal's exit from the European Championships, it seemed as though not a day went by without another story reporting that his signing for Real Madrid was imminent. Manchester United went so far as to lodge an official complaint of tapping up with FIFA, which Real Madrid denied. But still the drip, drip, drip of rumour seemed to be never-ending.

However in August, after a long heart to heart with Alex Ferguson, Ronaldo made a very public statement that he would be staying, vowing to fight for the shirt with 'the same desire and dedication as I always have'.

After forty-two goals in the previous season, and a clean sweep of individual awards, plus the distractions of the summer, it seemed logical that the only way was down. He began the season unfit, after surgery on his ankle, only returning in October, and by the standards of the previous season he seemed off the pace. He still scored nine goals in his first twenty-three games, but was just that tiny bit less imperious than he had been. Instead it was new signing Dimitar Berbatov who seemed to win the plaudits.

In spite of a lukewarm beginning to the season, his heroics the previous season were further rewarded in December 2008, when Cristiano Ronaldo felt he had realized a childhood dream by being recognized as the best player in the world, winning his first Ballon d'Or. 'It is one of the most beautiful days of my life. To gain this trophy is something I dreamed of as a child,' said Ronaldo at the ceremony.

At that time the prize was not based on a worldwide survey of fans, nor even of football professionals, but of ninety-six journalists. Nevertheless, it is a prize with a big marketing projection, and Ronaldo glowed in its aura of celebrity. Of the top journalists polled by *France Football*, seventy-seven voted the Portugal winger as their leading player that year, and every one placed him in their top five. Ronaldo polled 446 points from a maximum 480, finishing comfortably ahead of second-placed Messi (281) and third-placed Fernando

Torres (179), who grabbed that spot after scoring thirty-three goals in his debut season for Liverpool. Torres had also been named man of the match in the Euro 2008 final after scoring the only goal in Spain's 1–0 win over Germany.

Ronaldo was, however, widely seen as the deserving winner of the Ballon d'Or, as Henry Winter, one of the journalists who voted for him, later commented:

> Dominating our thoughts was a player who has enriched so many games, scored so many goals and made so many kids fall in love with football. Ronaldo is special.
>
> From astonishing free kicks against Portsmouth in the Premier League to imperious headers against Roma and Chelsea in the Champions League, Manchester United's magnificent winger is worth the admission fee like no other.[1]

Ronaldo's triumph made him the first Manchester United player to claim the award since George Best in 1968, joining Denis Law and Bobby Charlton in United's golden ball pantheon, and the third Portuguese winner after Eusébio and Luís Figo.

But even after the award, it felt as though there was something missing.

There were still displays of brilliance, as when he scored vital goals in the away legs of both the Champions League quarter- and semi-finals. The first was in Porto on 15 April 2009, when he put United through after a 2–2 draw in the first leg. United still needed a goal to help them progress when Ronaldo let fly with a missile from so far out – forty yards – it seemed foolhardy to even attempt it. But straight and true it flew, soaring into the top corner and leaving goalkeeper Helton stranded.

Then Ronaldo excelled when Ferguson played him as a lone striker in the second leg of the semi-final tie against Arsenal at the Emirates. He traumatized the defence, nearly scoring five goals but settling for two and an assist. The latter came first, in the eighth minute, when Ronaldo's perfectly weighted low cross played in Ji-Sung Park. A long-range, wobbling free kick three minutes later beat Manuel Almunia at his near post. His second goal came in the sixty-first minute, the product of a Nemanja Vidić clearance followed by seven passes in a movement that also involved Park and Wayne

Rooney, but had Ronaldo bolting the length of the field and stretching to thump Rooney's low cross over Almunia and into the top corner. The *Guardian*'s Rob Smyth called it 'a goal of undeniable greatness.'[2]

Yet there were fewer spectacular moments and goals than in the previous season, and Ronaldo showed off some of his old theatrics and petulance, earning him a red card in a Manchester derby and heckles from United supporters during a match against Aston Villa, where he was seen to protest too much. Even those who didn't doubt his professionalism, like Gary Neville, thought he was counting down the months until he could leave.

In his speech collecting the Ballon d'Or, while Ronaldo paid generous tribute to the runners-up and the other strong candidates voted for that year, he also made it clear that, while a dream may have come true for him, his story was far from over. 'This is one that I want to win again because it is so good. Therefore, I will wake and I will say to myself "I want to be even better."'

In so doing, the twenty-three-year-old Ronaldo had thrown down the gauntlet not only to himself, but also to the one player destined to compete with him for the ultimate prize for years to come – and who was already beginning to snap at his coat-tails: twenty-one-year-old Lionel Messi. At the press junket on the day of the award, Messi once again cut an understated figure off the pitch in his very ordinary jeans and cartoon T-shirt, and was evidently ill at ease with all the media razzmatazz. Perhaps his shyness and awkwardness could also be attributed to a desire to get back to work – by then he was in the middle of an extraordinary season himself, which would culminate in that showdown against Ronaldo in the Champions League final that would have a huge impact on the Portuguese's career and bring the next phase of their rivalry to a head. But for that to happen, Messi had to get there.

23. THE GUARDIOLA REVOLUTION: MESSI

The omens weren't good. In July, Messi's influential mentor Ronald-inho left Barça and signed for AC Milan.

His increasing individualism had put him on a collision course with Guardiola, a disciplinarian who had a clear vision of team ethos and players in synchronicity. If there was the definition of a loose cannon, somebody that did not follow any plan other than his own, it was Ronaldinho.

So keen were FC Barcelona to offload him, and so determined was he to join a traditionally big club, even if they had failed to qualify for the Champions League, that they had to cut their losses and accept Milan's offer, which was about €9 million less than the only other bid received, from Manchester City.

Barça had learnt the hard lesson from the Maradona era, and when the Ronaldinho problem emerged, they were ready to nip it in the bud. The appointment of Guardiola as manager was part of the solution.

For all his lack of experience in managing a top team, Guardiola ticked all the right boxes. Politically a Catalan nationalist, his involve-ment with Barça dated from his days at La Masia. As a player and football thinker, he had been moulded by Johan Cruyff as part of the Dream Team. In his first season as a coach, he led the B team to pro-motion from the third to the second division.

As well as experiencing, as a Spanish international, the peaks and troughs of an underachieving national squad, Guardiola had also learnt a lot about emerging talent, tactics and strategy at one of the world's biggest football clubs. Barça was in Guardiola's DNA. 'OK,' he told club president Joan Laporta on being offered his new job in the spring of 2008, 'but only if I can do it my way and with my people.' He promoted the midfielder Sergio Busquets, whom he knew from the B team, and brought back Gerard Piqué, who had played with Messi in the Baby Dream Team but left to sign for Manchester United.

Barça had a history of Brazilians providing one or two seasons of magic, but then losing momentum because of an aversion to discipline and an inclination to enjoy themselves off as well as on the field. And they had had Argentine star players before Messi, who they had let slip out of control. Maradona being a case in point, whose drug-ridden lifestyle had begun in his last months in the city, before he moved to Napoli. When the reports had reached Laporta, who himself had no small reputation as a party animal, that Ronaldinho had drawn the younger, less wordly Messi into his wild nightlife, a red-alert button was effectively pushed.

Even without Laporta's intervention, Guardiola instinctively knew what was happening and what he had to do. He was an obsessive of the game, and very little escaped him about his players, especially those with evidence of promise, like Messi. He believed the face was the mirror of the soul. In other words, he put the person before the footballer, and was constantly on the lookout to ensure their welfare off the pitch as well as on it.

And yet, from the moment Guardiola took over at Barça, he showed himself to be ruthless with those he lost faith in. Ronaldinho is the most famous example, but Deco was also shipped out of the club that summer and Samuel Eto'o would follow a year later. Later, Zlatan Ibrahimović would be sold one season after he was signed, at a club where his individualism was frequently at odds with Guardiola's precise tactics.

By contrast, with Messi, Guardiola did not hesitate to act in a way that recognized the investment the club had made in the player since the age of thirteen, and knew that the Argentine would reach his potential of becoming one of the club's all-time greats, if properly managed.

At the start of Guardiola's first season as Barça's manager, Messi found himself summoned to his office for what turned out to be a critical encounter. Guardiola had been informed that Messi had been drawn into Ronaldinho's hedonistic lifestyle. Guardiola confronted Messi and asked him straight out, with an air of Catalan sobriety, what his dream was.

'To be the best football player in the world one day, better perhaps than Diego,' Messi answered in the high-pitched, fumbling Argentine intonation that characterized his speech, his head inclined downwards, seemingly submissively.[1]

Guardiola responded by telling the young charge that he faced two choices: either continue his off-pitch activities in the wake of Ronaldinho and risk having no future at the club, or else adapt to a more disciplined lifestyle focused on his football, an option that could hold the key to unrivalled excellence. Messi agreed to recommit himself to a regime of early nights, a healthy diet and carefully monitored training.

And yet, on other issues, Guardiola found Messi less compliant, but the coach was willing to compromise, not least when he found that the Argentine commanded considerable respect among the other players, and had the full support of Laporta and his governing board.

Messi made it known that he wanted Eto'o to carry on in the new season, which he did, initially proving Guardiola wrong in his belief that Eto'o considered himself the leader and was not willing to share the role with anybody else. Next, Messi insisted he wanted to be exempt from playing in a Champions League qualifier in order to play with the Argentine squad in the Olympics in China that summer.

The tug of war between the Argentine Olympic Federation and FC Barcelona over Messi became a cause célèbre, not least when Messi, without waiting for a decision from his club, boarded a plane and left to join the Argentine training camp in Shanghai, in his own unilateral declaration of independence. It seemed an unusual gesture, if not an unwitting act of gross indiscipline, by a player not known as either an extrovert or a rebel, but Joan Laporta rightly calculated that to force Messi to return would be to risk losing him for good – even though he had signed a new contract that July for an annual salary of €7.8 million, making him the club's highest-paid player.

Guardiola understood that a positive, solution-focused therapy was the one he needed to apply, one that recognized Messi was a player who lived for his football, felt a patriotic duty to his native Argentina, and carried the weight of Maradona on his shoulders. Guardiola rang Messi in Shanghai and told him to go ahead and win the gold medal.

Messi returned just as the new La Liga season was starting. He was given the number 10 shirt, after wearing 30 in his first games with the first team and later the number 19. The number 10 is, of course, charged with symbolism, not least at Barça, given the place in the club's history of those who had previously worn it, among them Maradona and Ronaldinho.

When Maradona left Barcelona, Bernd Schuster refused to put the number 10 shirt on when asked to by his teammate Steve Archibald. As the Scotsman later told me:

> It was then that I understood the Maradona factor. It had finally entered my head not only what Schuster was thinking, but the whole team was thinking – the influence Maradona had had on them, this world-class player with the magic at his feet. And I realized that for Schuster to change into that shirt was going to mean a much bigger thing for him than for me. Because in the end I thought, I don't care if Maradona and his granny have worn that shirt. I can respond to the challenge.[2]

Messi's thinking seemed more akin to Archibald's than Schuster's. No one in the Barça dressing room challenged him for the number 10 shirt that summer of 2008. In truth, it already seemed that the only young player who could also lay claim to being the best of his generation, and among the best of all time, was alive and well and living in Manchester.

But back in Barcelona, Guardiola's firm ideas about leadership, including how to handle Messi in a way that allowed the player to play to the best of his ability, with a special attention to his psychological and physical characteristics, began to bear fruit.

In Messi, Guardiola saw a player whose only real passion was his football, and thus needed to count on the necessary human support to be able to live and breathe it and to be happy within himself.

Guardiola's decision to let Messi go and play in the Olympics was a hugely important gesture of accommodation to the Argentine's needs. The decision placed the relationship between coach and player on the level of mutual respect, with Messi at the centre of Guardiola's transformative project for FC Barcelona.

Messi, never a man of many words, would years later pay tribute to Guardiola in comments that left no room to doubt what a key role the manager played in moulding team and player into one of the most exciting spectacles in the history of football. In an interview with Martin Souto of TyC Sports in March 2013, Messi described Guardiola as the man from whom he had learnt the most: 'Not only because he knew so much, but because he took me under his wing during a stage when I was developing, the stage at which I grew and learnt the most.'[3]

Guardiola had taken over as manager of the first team when FC Barcelona had not won anything in two years, and found a broken dressing room, in a bad state mentally. 'It was his way of working, transmitting his message, and the trust he built up, that helped change everything,' Messi told Souto.

For his part, Guardiola was clear in his head about Messi's personality. As he told Guillem Balagué after joining Bayern Munich in 2013, and breaking with his rule of not giving one-on-one interviews: 'What I learnt about Leo at that time was that he would vindicate himself on the pitch. That's where he did the talking. He does it through actions, when he gets on the pitch it is as if he were saying "Now I speak", scoring two or three goals, every single day . . . This is what he teaches us, this is his great value: he demonstrates that he doesn't have to be anything else apart from a footballer.'[4]

The changes Guardiola insisted on were not just mental and tactical; undoubtedly the team as a whole benefited from the new dietary and nutritional regime introduced to improve performance and prevent muscular injuries. As related by Guillem Balagué, it was Juanjo Brau, Messi's personal physical trainer, who developed a tailor-made regime for the player – ordering him to cut back on his consumption of Argentine meat and pizzas, suggesting specific warm-up exercises and stretches, and recommending a careful expenditure of energy during matches, including a period of walking after sprinting to minimize the physical demands on his particular muscular typology.

'Leo is more susceptible to injury than most players. He has "fast-twitch muscle fibres" [good for rapid movements like sprinting but contract fast as they consume a lot of energy] so we had to work a lot on his elasticity,' Brau told the Barcelona-based Argentine journalist Leonardo Faccio.[5]

But Messi was his own best motivator. Having been coaxed out of his box by Ronaldinho when the Brazilian was at his zenith, Messi could now mature and flourish on his own terms, bringing his best to the team, and the best of the team to him.

The Guardiola 'revolution' went far beyond tactics. It involved a generational and philosophical shift, which drew from the Cruyff legacy and reinvented it to meet the challenges of a more competitive and demanding era, with a team of highly disciplined, motivated and talented homegrown players. Messi was the star foreigner who had been moulded in the Barça way, and was entering the best years of his footballing career.

Thus was born the most successful and brilliant synergies in the history of modern football, involving Messi and two players in particular – Xavi Hernández and Andrés Iniesta, both of whom had come up through La Masia and had just starred in Spain's victorious Euro 2008 campaign.

So who are these players who nourished Messi's genius?

Iniesta was born 11 May 1984 into a relatively poor Spanish family in Fuentealbilla, a small village near Albacete, in the province of Castile, a stark and punishing rural environment.

While the overland distance separating Barcelona from Iniesta's home town was small compared to the transatlantic crossing which separated the Catalan capital from Rosario, the sense of initial separation was no less traumatic. Iniesta later recalled how he 'cried rivers' the day he left home for La Masia. He measured 1.71 metres in adulthood, compared to Messi at 1.70, and was three years older. Unlike Messi, who was allowed to live in a private apartment with his father, Iniesta was a boarder, along with the vast majority of La Masia's pupils.

Xavier Hernández Creus, better known as Xavi, was born into a lower-middle-class Catalan family on 25 January 1980, in Terrassa, a town near Barcelona famous for its textiles and mechanical industries, Catalan nationalism and Roman ruins. The town takes pride in its Catalan cultural and political identity with the festival displays of *castellers* – the skilful and creative human towers formed by men of all ages, symbolizing national solidarity.

As the son of a former professional soccer player – his father had played for Catalan club Sabadell in the Spanish first division – Xavi demonstrated impressive athletic abilities at an early age and entered La Masia aged eleven, where he felt culturally and socially at home from the outset, speaking fluent Catalan as well as Spanish.

During his days under the media spotlight, Xavi was happy to talk in some detail about Barça's football as a creative form, as well as his unique philosophy of life, while also reaching out to emerging young talent, from whatever country they came. Despite his unique individual talent, Xavi saw himself first and foremost as part of a team ethos. He measured 1.70 metres, a little smaller than Iniesta, same height as Messi.

While born in different countries and into different social contexts, and with different demands put on each of them by their respective families, Messi found in both Iniesta and Xavi kindred spirits. He respected them professionally and as human beings. Messi was the youngest. All three had been educated at La Masia and, although they never played together there because of the difference in their ages, they felt an enduring bond based on shared values, discipline and training.

Alongside the more flamboyant Ronaldinho, the Argentine had looked up to these two elders – the Castilian Iniesta and the Catalan Xavi – with reverential respect since he broke into the first team. With the Brazilian out of the picture, they became his mentors as well as trusted colleagues. The three of them, together during the halcyon days of the Guardiola era, produced some of the most glorious football ever played by any troika in football history.

It was Iniesta's simplicity and calmness on and off the pitch that Messi admired. As he told Iniesta's biographers, Ramon Besa and Marcos López: 'Andrés does his work, trying not to hurt anybody, careful with what he says in public, so that everyone loves him, even his rivals. He wins their respect.'

As for the way Iniesta played football: 'I have always seen him with the ball stuck to his feet. He makes it all look so easy. At times you think he is not doing anything, but it turns out he is doing everything. The most difficult thing in football is to make every move look simple, easy, as if it didn't involve any effort.'[6]

Such comments might as easily have been applied to Messi himself, and therein lies the key. The Argentine and the Castilian reflected each other's genius, understood and complemented each other to the point of perfection. On a good match day, they played to each other's strengths in glorious harmony.

As Messi told Besa and López: 'We are most like each other in the way we don't talk much. He is usually in one corner of the dressing room, and I am in the other. We pass by each other, we acknowledge each other, we meet up. It just takes one look and we know what we need to know. There is no need for anything more. Out on the pitch I like to have him nearby, particularly if a match gets difficult and rough. Then I say to him: "Get close, come on, come by my side." And then he grabs hold of the team, shakes it up, looks for me and then brings me in.'[7]

For Xavi the Argentine would reserve his greatest accolade, for when the Catalan prepared to retire from full-time football in the summer of 2015, Messi called Xavi the greatest Spanish player ever. 'Xavi is a player who controls the pace of the game, and the passing of the ball, who knows how to read games really well,' Messi told a group of journalists on the eve of the Champions League final in Berlin.[8]

Xavi's retention of possession and quick and accurate use of the ball became the trademark of Barça's style in the Guardiola years, a badge of identity that ran through the team.

Messi would be one of the greatest beneficiaries of Xavi's extraordinary vision. As Sid Lowe put it in 2009, 'It is not just that he sees the movement first, it is that he often sees the movement before it has happened, that rather than passing to the movement, he passes in such a way as to oblige the movement. He makes players' runs for them.' Or, as Dani Alves expressed it, 'Xavi plays in the future.'

Lowe concluded: 'At Euro 2008, Xavi had been named player of the tournament, completed over 100 passes in the semi-final when Russia didn't even see the ball, and provided the assist to Torres in the final. When the inevitable question is asked about why Messi has not played as well for Argentina over the past year as he has for Barcelona, it is tempting to give a one-word answer: Xavi. The last week has reinforced the belief that Barcelona are the best side in the world and that Messi is the best player on the planet. Without Xavi, they might not be.'[9] As the quote implies, Barcelona's 2008–9 campaign is one that bears remembering.

Messi's first season under Guardiola was his first with an extended period in the team that was largely uninterrupted by injury, evidence of the positive impact of his improved diet and refined training techniques, as well as the motivation he felt under the new coach. The once fragile Messi – nicknamed 'the flea' and 'the dwarf'– developed the strength and stamina of a top athlete, to better exploit his natural talent. It was a season during which Guardiola quickly learnt to handle Messi's psychology – 'to manage his silences', as Guillem Balagué put it.

That first season began with Messi playing on the right wing, with Eto'o in the centre and Thierry Henry on the left of the attack. As the season progressed, Messi was allowed by Guardiola to play more as a 'false' winger, with the freedom, as he did in all matches, to cut inside and roam in the middle from where he could, with Iniesta and Xavi, help influence the movement of the whole team.

The season in fact got off to an inauspicious start, with FC Barcelona losing 1–0 to Numancia, and the impatient, easy-headline-grabbing sports media both in Barcelona and Madrid immediately raising question marks over Guardiola's suitability for the job. The new coach had inherited a protracted crisis at Barça; fans were impatient to have it sorted out.

After Numancia, Barça drew with Racing, and found themselves at the bottom of the La Liga table. They subsequently beat Sporting Lisbon 3–1 in the Champions League group stages, which lifted the mood, even if the media remained to be convinced about the beginning of the Guardiola era.

Then Barça played away in Asturias against Sporting Gijón and won an emphatic 6–1 victory that showed the team recovering some of the magic of Rijkaard's first season, only with Messi now central to the show. The team played a high-tempo game of possession, pressing and quick recovery of loose balls, so that most of the game was played in opposition territory. Messi was the man of the match.

With Barça increasingly in control of the game, and corners mounting, it was Messi's mentors who finally opened the scoring in a brilliant sequence of combination play that was to help define Guardiola's 'dream team'. In the thirty-second minute, Iniesta turned Sastre inside out then chipped the ball to an unmarked Xavi, who headed home from eight yards.

The second half had Messi looking even more dangerous than he had in the first. An early move saw him skipping past two defenders in the box only to drag his shot across goal. Moments later he scooped the ball to Iniesta, who took the ball in his stride with a glorious first touch but saw his shot deflected. There followed an own goal by Sporting's defender Jorge off a shot by Xavi, after a solo run by Messi had beaten five players.

Then, after Gijón's Maldonado snatched one back, Eto'o made it 3–1 to the visitors. It seemed game over, but Messi had life in him yet. In the seventieth minute he produced an exquisite chipped through-ball for Iniesta to score. Messi then made it an emphatic win with two goals in the last ten minutes, the first a thundering volley off a deflected Iniesta cross, the second a header which showed how he could make up for his small height with impeccable timing and pinpoint accuracy.

It was a match in which Messi showed what he was capable of at his best. Barça had now clicked and settled into a rhythm. With the quality of their other players and a coach like Guardiola, the team began producing masterclasses in creative, attacking football. Barça were back, and a new star was shining bright.

But it was not just goals that made Messi so special – it's easy to forget that Samuel Eto'o was top scorer in the League that season – but it was also his close control, acceleration, vision and creativity that contributed to the team's success. His footballing brain seemed to be developing rapidly.

Messi helped steer Barça to the top of La Liga and was also at the heart of the team's successful Champions League campaign, playing a key role in helping demolish Lyon and Bayern Munich in the knock-out stages. After a 1–1 draw away in the first leg of Barça's last-sixteen fixture with Lyon, the scene was set for a tightly fought second leg. But in front of a rapturous Nou Camp, Henry's quickfire brace had the Blaugrana in control.

Barça put on a mesmerizing display, with Iniesta's return from injury giving the midfield its very special edge of ball possession, quick passing and link-up play. But the moment of pure individual magic in the game came later in the first half, when Messi chested the ball down on the right, bamboozled three defenders, played a lightning quick one-two with Eto'o and then stroked the ball into the far corner. Barça went on to win 5–2 (6–3 on aggregate), with further goals by Eto'o and Seydou Keita.

On 8 April 2009, Messi also starred in an astonishing quarter-final first leg against Bayern Munich. The German side had beaten Barcelona's group-stage opposition Sporting Lisbon 12–1 on aggregate in the previous round, but had just lost 5–1 to Wolfsburg, who would go on to win the Bundesliga that season.

In the run-up to the game, senior Bayern officials talked of a 'mission impossible'. That could have been a typical mind game, but then the Germans really were up against it, not least because Barça had a midfield that had improved on the possession domination Spain had shown against Germany in the final of Euro 2008. Guardiola's FC Barcelona were approaching the game having enjoyed an average of 62 per cent possession in their games, with only one side succeeding in stopping them from scoring in forty-five matches.

Other stats were equally awesome. Barcelona had scored eighty-five goals during the season so far, on their way to racking up twenty-three wins in twenty-nine games. That was more goals than any team in any of Europe's other top leagues; at least thirty more. More than Ronaldo's Manchester United (fifty-two), more than Torres's Liverpool (fifty-five), more than Inter (fifty-five) and more than Marseille (forty-eight).

In La Liga, Barcelona had scored eighteen more goals than Real Madrid. Messi had already scored thirty goals by that stage in the 2008–9 season, compared to the seventeen he had scored in the whole of the previous season with Rijkaard. By the end of Barça's historic campaign, the club's formidable trio would have scored 100 goals between them, with Messi in the lead with thirty-eight, followed by Eto'o (thirty-six) and Henry (twenty-six).

For Messi, it was as if something had clicked that nobody had realized was missing. Always able to beat players, Messi was now leaving them in his dust. He was stronger, quicker, able to ride ever wilder challenges. Players were finding that, if you tried to kick him out of the game, he'd just get up and keep running. It gave Barça a permanent out-ball as they could pass to him in the opponent's half, knowing that however many players there were around him, the ball would stick and they'd begin an attack. And the goals. Delicate chips, free kicks before the opposition team were ready, top corner, bottom corner, with placement or with power.

Despite the well-documented stats, nothing could have prepared the German team for the mauling they got in the first leg at the Nou Camp, courtesy of Messi, who defined the character of the match. Within nine minutes he had opened the scoring, skipping clear of

Bayern's shambolic defence and stroking in an Eto'o pass. He then assisted Eto'o for the second and tapped in Henry's cross, before the Frenchman made it four. Messi then nearly scored a fifth, which hit the woodwork after beating the keeper Hans-Jörg Butt.

It was a game in which Messi personified Barça at their most creative and effective. He kept up the pressure, was slick in possession and tenacious whenever he had to win back the ball.

Barça's 4–0 victory gave them a comfortable leg in Munich. A 1–1 draw there left them 5–1 winners on aggregate. A semi-final against Chelsea awaited, the legs to be played either side of a visit to the Bernabéu on 2 May.

Only later would it emerge that – even at this stage – Guardiola still considered Messi, however effective his link-up play in attack, a player who was well short of his full potential.

Guardiola had noticed that on occasion his team had shown itself vulnerable to counter-attacks on their right flank. Part of the problem, as Guardiola told his biographer Guillem Balagué, was that Messi did not do his 'defensive duties'. Guardiola also didn't think that, out on the right, Messi was enough a part of build-up play. He realized that Messi was a player who needed to play in a position where he saw more of the ball.

In that first season, though, when the team won every title, Messi played on the wing for 95 per cent of the games. So what went right? 'Sometimes the analysis is simple; as simple as realizing that this guy [Messi] could do something each time he touched the ball, that something would happen,' Guardiola told Balagué. 'And if you put him in the middle, he would touch it more than on the wing. I mean: if he is convinced he has to play in the centre of midfield in the future, he will become an amazing midfielder.'[10]

While Messi played mainly on the right wing, like he had under Rijkaard, he was already a false winger, with the freedom to cut inside and roam the centre.

Under Ronaldinho, Messi had played a subordinate role, his stardom still trailing in the wake of the Brazilian's genius. Eto'o had shown a tendency to want to be seen as the other star player, treating Messi as an underling.

As the season progressed, Messi was continually moved into a more central position, with Eto'o moved out to the right wing.

Guardiola's decision on how to play Messi was not just tactical but also hugely symbolic, not only of his own authority as a manager, but of what role he saw for Messi. Guardiola was, in effect, relying on Messi to be the axis of the team as a false centre-forward. Play would revolve around and for him, and he would score goals.

During the Clásico on 2 May 2009, he was played as a false 9, positioned as a centre-forward but dropping deep into midfield to link up with Xavi and Iniesta.

As the Clásico neared its end, the Real Madrid fans began to leave the stadium. It was half empty by the time the referee had blown the final whistle, a protest aimed at the team's perceived poor performance. In fact, FC Barcelona had been deserving victors.

The gap between the clubs, not just in terms of ethos, but talent and efficiency, could hardly have been clearer.

And Messi – supported by Iniesta and Xavi – had been in the thick of it.

It was Madrid that started as the more aggressive of the two teams, with Gonzalo Higuaín heading in the first goal after fourteen minutes. And yet, four minutes later, Messi placed a perfect pass for Henry to slot past Iker Casillas. The assist helped to turn the tide of the match and it was all one way from there: Barça were 1–3 up by half-time and retained complete control, but for a brief closing of the gap when Sergio Ramos headed in early on in the second half to make it 2–3.

At times, it seemed Barça were trying too hard to score the perfect goal, as when Iniesta and Messi teasingly played a one-two on the edge of the Madrid six-yard box before Messi carelessly put his shot straight into the arms of Casillas. When Messi did score, after thirty-six minutes, it followed a goal by Barça captain Puyol, and was the result of a precise Iniesta assist. After Ramos's goal, Henry scored his second, as did Messi when he collected a fine pass from Xavi, dummied Casillas and stroked his shot in with typical assurance. Piqué finished things off with the sixth. The impact of a 2–6 final score was felt across the country and the continent. The La Liga title was effectively Barça's. A few days after that, a late goal at Stamford Bridge saw them into the Champions League final. Guardiola's Golden Era was well under way, with Messi its star attraction.

Over the next fifteen days, showing his increasing versatility across positions, Messi returned to the wing when he helped his team win the Copa del Rey against Athletic Bilbao and, three days later, helped officially secure the La Liga title.

FC Barcelona now faced the challenge of securing the treble, in the Champions League final against Alex Ferguson's Manchester United in Rome's Olympic Stadium, on 27 May.

The Red Devils were hoping to make their own mark in the history books by successfully defending the European crown they had won in the final against Chelsea the previous season. They too had secured the League title, with twenty-six-goal Cristiano Ronaldo the undoubted star of the team.

Minutes before the match began, Messi and his teammates were gathered together by Guardiola in the changing room. To their surprise, he played them a short video clip before they went out to play. It showed scenes from the film *Gladiator*, complete with rousing musical score, intercut with shots of Barça players, led by Messi, in playing action, putting in their best performances.

The message to the team was that, although they were up against the most formidable of historic English clubs, managed by the most experienced boss in the game, they should face the coming contest without fear, sticking to their style, for therein lay the prospect of glory in the Roman arena.

And so it came to be – the most stunning display yet achieved of the quick, short-passing, possession and movement game, a style that had evolved since the Cruyff days of Total Football and morphed into *tiki-taka*.

The 'showdown between Messi and Ronaldo was billed as the spectacular subplot' within the main showpiece, but as the BBC's Phil McNulty noted afterwards, 'there was only one winner, as Barcelona's play maker terrorized United throughout.'[11]

The match began looking as if there might be a different outcome. With two minutes gone, Ronaldo's free kick nearly beat the fumbling Barcelona goalkeeper Victor Valdés, and Gerard Piqué just managed to prevent Ji-Sung Park from turning in the rebound.

Ronaldo was twice narrowly off-target, before Barcelona made their first serious incursion into United territory and took the lead. Messi was *a* star if not *the* star of the Barça show. Swapping sides with Eto'o, the Argentinian darted down the middle, drawing the United defence. Iniesta moved into space and released the ball down another unexpected channel, for Eto'o to pick up and score.

From there on, Manchester United were systematically outplayed, as Messi, Iniesta and Xavi helped produce a stunning display of Barça's choreography, players constantly swapping positions while linking with each other, touch after touch after touch in a flowing display of poetry in motion.

Egged on by Rio Ferdinand, United tried to rally but to no avail, and while their Portuguese star never stopped running, he was increasingly frustrated, earning a yellow card for a late barge on Carles Puyol. Messi in particular was on fire, a master of multiple tricks and resilience, as he rode tackles and dodged every attempt to stop him. It was quite simply a sensational display by the player and the team, culminating in a movement of sublime artistry in the seventieth minute, when Messi received a perfectly angled cross from Xavi and, despite being one of the shortest players on the pitch, looped a header over United's van der Sar, securing a 2–0 victory. Barcelona were champions of Europe and as Henry Winter, the veteran *Telegraph* journalist, wrote that night: 'Messi, so small of frame yet so immense of talent, industrious as well as inventive, ended the debate over who was the best player on the planet.'[12]

During his first uninterrupted campaign, the 2008–9 season, Messi scored thirty-eight goals in fifty-one games, contributing to a total that set a new record at the club. Although they had won the competition the year before, Manchester United were made to look like yesterday's men, blown away by the speed and intensity of Barcelona's play.

The season that saw Messi beginning to show his genius at Guardiola's FC Barcelona also effectively brought an end to Cristiano Ronaldo's successful time at Manchester United. The biggest rivalry in modern football was about to enter its definitive stage.

24. GOODBYE OLD TRAFFORD, HELLO BERNABÉU: RONALDO

In terms of its collective sentiment, the Bernabéu initially looked at Cristiano Ronaldo like a stranger, if still brilliant, body within the group – a player whose mind was focused more on the opposing net than in linking up with the rest of the team. And that meant there were some who took time to warm to him, who resisted his presence. But from day one he set out to win them over and it was not long before the goals statistics showed what a phenomenon he was.

Jorge Valdano[1]

Defeat in Rome had proved a cathartic moment for Ronaldo. The realization had come to him with full clarity that night Manchester United lost the final to Barça. While a jubilant Messi was the first to hug Guardiola like a beloved father before he celebrated with Barça colleagues, Ronaldo looked orphaned and utterly despondent after a match that showed his growing frustration with playing in a team that seemingly overnight had passed its peak. Other clubs were on the march, and Ronaldo believed the United squad were not skilled enough to help him win the prize he craved again – the Champions League. Without challenging regularly for that prize, it would be almost impossible to make the case for being the best player in the world. To combat Messi and the all-conquering style of play that Barcelona and the Spanish national team seemed to represent would need deep pockets and a starry supporting cast. The only team capable of that were Real Madrid.

The summer of 2009 was the final chapter of a very public courtship that had been unfolding for a while. Real Madrid had first become aware of Cristiano Ronaldo back in 2003 when Carlos Queiroz, who had just been appointed coach of the Spanish club, let his employers know of his potential. Manchester United were already well into their negotiations, though, and their move did not provoke any rival offer from Spain.

A two-way channel of communication between Real Madrid and Jorge Mendes, Ronaldo's agent, was established as early as 2005, when José Ángel Sánchez, the chief executive of the club and a key architect of president Florentino Pérez's *galáctico* project, let it be known that Real were waiting for the player if and when he decided to make a move. At the time, Ronaldo was two years into his time at United, and thriving, and the *galáctico* structure itself was coming in for criticism. Pérez resigned as president in February 2006, in order to look after his wife, who was undergoing treatment for cancer, and his business interests. He would successfully run for president again in 2009, unopposed and promising to reboot the glamorous transfer policy of his first term. Ten days after he was sworn back in as president on 1 June 2009, Ronaldo was confirmed as a Real Madrid's newest *galáctico*.

The timing and symbolism suited both the player and the boardroom, but in reality the line of communication between the club and Mendes had never been closed. The deal came after over a year of mounting pressure on United from both Ronaldo and Real Madrid, almost immediately after Ronaldo extended his contract in April 2007, signing with the English club until 2012. The new deal included a €75 million release clause; as Guillem Balagué put it, 'in case Real Madrid or another big club decided to splash out on him'.[2]

Meanwhile the Madrid sports media, in a strategy seemingly approved by Mendes and senior executives at the Santiago Bernabéu, published an interview with Ronaldo's mother Dolores in the summer of 2008, expressing her dream of seeing her son play for Real Madrid one day, and reported that the club was willing to pay as much as his release clause stipulated, or more. United tried to fight back by strongly denying the rumours, officially requesting that Real Madrid desist from pursuing Ronaldo and insisting that the player was more than happy staying where he was. Still, Ramón Calderón, Real Madrid's president in Pérez's absence, had made it clear that Ronaldo would become a Real Madrid player sooner or later.

In fact, after United won the Champions League in 2008, Ronaldo and Mendes reached a gentleman's agreement with Alex Ferguson and United to stay at the club for another year, after which, if Real Madrid came through with a world-record offer and the player still wanted to go, Ferguson would not stand in his way. For Ferguson, it was a way of wresting back some control of a process that was damaging United's image, while preserving some personal honour of his own. He was pragmatic enough to know that Ronaldo's time at United was reaching a natural end. As he later recalled in his autobiography: 'I knew full well that if they [Real Madrid] produced the £80 million, he would have to go . . . The reality of managing Ronaldo, as of other talents who came to Manchester United as teenagers, was that you could oversee the early years fairly comfortably, because they were not yet global idols, they were on the way up. At the point they became mega-stars, as Ronaldo did, you asked yourself a question that Carlos Queiroz and I discussed all the time: "How long are we going to be able to keep Cristiano Ronaldo?"'[3]

In terms of mega-stars, there was the Beckham precedent. Queiroz brought in his own cultural perspective, as Ronaldo's fellow countryman. He knew there was no precedent for a Portuguese player going to another country at eighteen years old and staying more than five years. Ferguson and United had achieved more time than that with Ronaldo.

Confirmation that his days at United were over came with an announcement on 11 June 2009 that the club had received a world-record, unconditional offer of £80 million from Real Madrid and that, after discussion with Ronaldo and Mendes, all involved had agreed to conclude the deal within a month.

The new transfer record, coming as it did following the crash of Spain's overheated economy and a deepening financial crisis, proved controversial. Then UEFA president Michel Platini said that such astronomical deals were a serious challenge to the idea of fair play and the concept of financial balance in football competitions. By contrast, FIFA president Sepp Blatter described it as an 'example of a fantastic investment'. He added: 'There may be a global financial crisis, but football is still on the rise.'

Florentino Pérez had made securing Ronaldo an essential part of his project for his second term in office, and was convinced that he would be his main weapon in countering the Messi phenomenon and Barcelona's dazzling football, and thus worth every euro. The transfer itself and the fees involved were an act of faith as much as a calculated financial risk, brilliantly executed by his agent, Jorge Mendes, who was as ever able to strike the best deal, even with the president of Real Madrid, one of Spain's most astute and ruthless businessmen.

In his autobiography, Alex Ferguson claimed that one of the reasons he managed to delay Ronaldo's transfer to Real Madrid was that Mendes was 'the best agent I dealt with, without a doubt', and that Mendes was anxious about the player going to Real Madrid 'for the obvious reason that Real Madrid might just swallow him up'.[4]

Mendes was, of course, no new boy in the big business of football. He had in fact been circling Spain's two big clubs for nearly a decade, and had developed strong links at the highest level both in Barcelona and Madrid, earning a reputation as a tough and skilful negotiator who knew how to strike the best deal possible for his clients; one of the best in the business, with prime assets in his charge. He manoeuvres expertly through the complex business of football at the highest level, and as such has always had more than one card up his sleeve.

This was the case even with Ronaldo's protracted move to Madrid. As we have seen, FC Barcelona had been offered Ronaldo as a teenager, before his move to United. As one would expect, this was a dialogue that Mendes had periodically reopened in the intervening years, often with Sandro Rosell. Rosell is a man whose network of interests, not all of them transparent, also extends across the big business of football. Indeed, when he was at Nike he signed the company's first endorsement contract with Ronaldo – a fact not widely known.

According to Alfons Godall, a Barça executive at the time, the club was approached again by Mendes, with a teasing offer of Ronaldo, when Joan Laporta was re-elected as president in 2006. Barça declined to make any offer, having judged Ronaldo not only surplus to requirements but also, even at that stage, unaffordable. Mendes likely suspected as much, and the offer appeared to be a strategy to ensure a later bid from Real Madrid – if there's one thing guaranteed to pique either club's interest in a player, it's the alleged interest of the other.

In fact, Mendes timed Ronaldo's transfer in a way that would maximize his price and take his career to another level. The player left behind him a Manchester United that, in the last years of the Ferguson era, had surrendered to the glory that was FC Barcelona, while joining, in Real Madrid, perhaps the only club with the willpower and resources to mount a serious challenge for the slot as top club in the world.

As Mendes told his official biographers, Miguel Cuesta and Jonathan Sanchez, the agent had celebrated Cristiano Ronaldo's first Ballon d'Or in 2008 as both the achievement of an objective but also a step on a ladder to a pinnacle that lay beyond Manchester United. 'I thought from the beginning that Ronaldo was going to be the best player of all time, of everything he had fought for, because of how professional he was . . . He is the best, of that I have no doubt. There is no one like him. But then you have to look at the team because that has an influence, and Cristiano was now playing for the best team in the world.'[5]

At Barça, Messi was already the star of the show, and being talked of as the greatest player in the world. Behind Cristiano Ronaldo's transfer to Real Madrid there was an obvious commercial motivation: the promotion of a contest that had the attention of a global audience – between Real Madrid and FC Barcelona – and, at the heart of it, an iconic rivalry between two apparently very different players, who were considered the best in the world.

Far from throwing money away, Real Madrid's president Florentino Pérez had made a carefully calculated investment. He had a high regard for Cristiano Ronaldo both as a player and a business proposition. Or, to put it another way, he considered the player capable of bridging the dichotomy between those who loved the game and those who simply wanted to make money from it. Hand in hand with expanding revenues and asset growth would come on-pitch success, as had initially occurred with his first superstars at the turn of the millennium.

Pérez had returned to the presidency in 2009 after convincing voting members that the club's sporting standards and finances had suffered during his three-year absence, and that he alone had the passion for good football and business acumen necessary to make the club prosper. Pérez was Castilian-born and was a life-long Madrid fan and member. He was also extremely rich, with extensive influence in media, business and politics. While his construction company, ACS, faced stormy waters as Spain entered a prolonged recession,

Pérez was nevertheless re-elected uncontested, having backed his candidacy with a guarantee of 15 per cent of the Real Madrid budget – equivalent to €55 million – a stipulation aimed at preventing an incompetent president from sinking the club, but also restricting the competition.

Pérez saw Cristiano Ronaldo as essential to the club's sporting success and financial interest. His hope was that Ronaldo would raise Real Madrid's marketing and merchandising revenue in the way David Beckham had done in the middle of the decade. He had watched Ronaldo's marketing and sporting profile turn global at Manchester United, and saw in him a personality and a talent that he hoped could easily rival – if not surpass – that of Messi, once he started playing in La Liga.

In that summer a record-breaking £200 million was spent on new players. Kaká had already been signed for a world-record fee from AC Milan before Madrid broke their own record by signing Ronaldo. Karim Benzema would be added a few weeks later, but one of Pérez's first acquisitions was that of Manuel Pellegrini as manager. The Chilean came to Madrid with an impressive track record coaching top teams in Chile, Ecuador and Argentina, and more recently Spanish club Villarreal, where he had moved after spells in charge of San Lorenzo and River Plate.

Pellegrini was expected to bring stability as well as style to Real Madrid, and also re-establish the club's reputation as a winner, after FC Barcelona's glorious treble the previous season. Since coach Vicente del Bosque had been sacked by Pérez in 2003, after winning two Champions Leagues and two League titles, the club had never repeated such success. They had seen Carlos Queiroz, José Antonio Camacho, Mariano García Remón, Vanderlei Luxemburgo, Juan Ramón López Caro, Fabio Capello, Bernd Schuster and Juande Ramos come and go in the dug-out.

If Barça had evolved a style that was admired globally and based on internal development, and which increasingly placed Messi at the centre of its claim to being the best team in football history, Pellegrini and the big-money imports, especially Cristiano Ronaldo, were seen by Pérez as the start of a fightback. One he hoped would reclaim the glory of the Di Stéfano years in the 1950s, when the club had won five European Cups in a row. The club would define itself against its own past and Barcelona's present. As Guillem Balagué put it: 'Ronaldo had not only to compete against himself. He had landed in a League inhabited by his nemesis – a small, quiet guy who pointed to the sky when celebrating his goals rather than to the ground, as Ronaldo did.'[6]

Pellegrini was not consulted on the players coming in or going out. He also found himself having to navigate potentially stormy waters in the dressing room, with youth-team product and club idol Raúl reaching his sell-by date, and the team having to adapt to the arrival of Ronaldo, a much younger player with a huge ego. But from the outset Pellegrini recognized in Ronaldo a talented athlete and an extremely hard worker, and also a person of great self-belief. As Pellegrini commented later, when at Manchester City: 'I saw from the first moment his desire was to be the best player and to play every game. You could see that desire in every game and every training session.'[7]

One of Pérez's advisers on player quality was Jorge Valdano, who had played alongside Diego Maradona in the Argentine team that had dispatched England on their way to the World Cup in 1986. Valdano saw his fellow Argentine Messi as Maradona's natural successor, but Ronaldo as a player who had the potential to have as great an impact on Real Madrid as club legend Alfredo Di Stéfano. As Valdano put it to me, 'The force of the present, the psychological disappearance of frontiers, the universality of idols – everything leads to the colossal figure of Ronaldo.'

Valdano tells the story of how, a couple of months after Ronaldo had been transferred to Real Madrid, a young female friend of his asked if she could be personally introduced to the player. Valdano agreed and, on the way to the stadium told her, teasingly: 'You know, Kaká is more attractive.' She replied: 'Sure, Kaká might make me a good husband, but Cristiano – he is something else, something special.'

As Valdano remarked to me in 2017:

Boys, women, fans of every background . . . there is no one who doesn't admire the 'superstar' of Real Madrid. And he deserves it because he has not lost sight of his sense of duty despite all the confusion that the modern game of football generates . . . Cristiano personifies football in the twenty-first century. He is a superhero seemingly conditioned for the game in a laboratory.

> We had been waiting for him. From his robotic appearance, unravelling into a gesticulation that is more mechanical than artistic, until that moment of the great stride, leap, and ultimate strike at goal of supernatural power – everything about Ronaldo takes us back into the future.

However, even for the futuristic Cristiano, things were tough to begin with.

Firstly, they were a team surrounded by many strong characters. 'In that moment we had Florentino's ego wanting to be seen as the club's saviour; his two protected "children", Kaká and Benzema; the dressing-room bosses – Raúl, Casillas and an emerging Sergio Ramos; and then the arrival from Liverpool of Xabi Alonso, a strong personality in any team. Faced with all this, Ronaldo didn't have it easy finding his space, to justify his presence, win the respect he felt he deserved,' recalled Cristiano Ronaldo's friend, the Spanish sports journalist Manu Sanz.[8]

However, seemingly at ease with the media attention and fan adulation not seen since the early days of Beckham, it took little time for Ronaldo to show that he had shrugged off the blues of his last season at United. In peak fitness, which contrasted with the post-holiday weight loss required by others in the team, he hit the ground running during an extended pre-season campaign mainly designed to maximize his impact on Real Madrid's international marketing projection, including games in the US. 'Ronaldo goes at warp speed. He is taking the team to another level,' commented the veteran Real Madrid player and Spanish international Míchel Salgado, before moving to Blackburn Rovers later that summer. Pellegrini was impressed that Ronaldo was the first to turn up for training and 'was completely down to earth and unassuming, with no superstar pretension.'[9] He quickly bonded with his teammates, finding it easy to have Spanish as the main common language, given its similarities to Portuguese. His colleagues too would be won over by the hours he put in to his preparatory and recovery work before and after matches – in the gym, doing exercises with weights, and swimming in hot and cold water in his home pool – when other players were following a less strenuous regime. They tended to head out to supper with family or friends – a practice that a succession of coaches had accepted as part of the club culture, as long as it did not provoke scandal.

Ronaldo scored three goals in eight friendly matches over the summer, and showed off his repertoire of bicycle kicks, step-overs and lightning runs, making many more goals for his teammates. He got off to an impressive start competitively as well, scoring a penalty in his first appearance in La Liga against Deportivo de La Coruña at the Santiago Bernabéu and raising his fists to the stands as if to say, 'I have arrived!'

In his Champions League debut against FC Zürich on 15 September, he showed his dexterity with the dead ball, scoring from two free kicks, two of the nine goals that helped Real Madrid win their first nine La Liga and Champions League games, including a thumping brace against Xerez.

But then he picked up an injury to his right ankle in a Champions League match against Olympique Marseille in September. He was playing again before he had fully recovered and as a result he suffered a recurrence eleven days later, within half an hour of kick-off in Portugal's World Cup qualifier against Hungary. This kept him sidelined for over a month and a half.

It was his longest absence due to injury since an operation on his right ankle in July 2008, during his final season at Manchester United, when it had taken him over three months before returning to match fitness.

Now, in his five-match absence, Real Madrid suffered three defeats, including a humiliating 4–1 aggregate defeat by third-tier side Alcorcón in the Copa del Rey, which was treated as a footballing scandal by the press. In spite of an embarrassment of attacking riches, a fully functioning Ronaldo, it seems, was already becoming integral to the team's success.

He was deemed just fit enough to return for the first Clásico of the season in December at the Nou Camp, a typically frenetic battle in which there were nine yellow and two red cards before Barcelona triumphed 1–0 from an Ibrahimović goal on his Clásico debut. There had been chances for Madrid and Ronaldo, but it hadn't quite worked for them. In a game pitched as the battle between the new *galácticos* and the homegrown talent of Barcelona's '*cantera*', Barcelona had drawn first blood. To add insult to injury, Messi was then crowned the best player in the world, winning that year's Ballon d'Or with more than double the points Ronaldo had received.

While Ronaldo had had to endure the pressure of the English tabloid press, he now had to cope with Madrid fans and Madrid mass-circulation sports media groups almost exclusively dedicated to covering in every detail the eternal rivalry between Real Madrid and FC Barcelona. It was a rivalry in which the Catalans had established a clear advantage. 'Barcelona have won everything this year so have to be the best club at the moment,' Ronaldo had conceded just before Christmas 2009. 'Barcelona have a style of play and players who have been playing together for many years, so they are an outstanding team.'[10]

Such generosity of spirit towards the arch rival was not reciprocated by FC Barcelona fans, who regarded Ronaldo as another Portuguese mercenary like Figo, but with an image that made him not just the butt of xenophobia in the Nou Camp, but also of homophobia. The chant '*puto Português*' – 'Portuguese whore' – was a distinctive variant from '*hijo de puta*' – son of a bitch. Behind the abuse was a widely held belief that Ronaldo had been brought in with a specific brief of ending FC Barcelona's golden era and displacing the club from its throne of global popularity. That was a belief shared by Real Madrid's fans, but many of those same fans were suspicious of his celebrity status and doubted he was the player to do it.

In the following game against Almería, Ronaldo played his first home match in more than two months following an ankle injury and was at the heart of most of the action in a 4–2 win for Real, with mixed results. He set up Madrid's first goal, scored their last, won and then missed a penalty, before being shown a red card. This followed two cautions, which did not exactly win him hearts and minds among the Real Madrid fans – the first came after he removed his shirt while celebrating the goal, alone. The second yellow card was for kicking out at Almería's Juanma Ortiz, which – had he been a veteran homegrown player – might have earned him a medal or two for sheer '*cojones*', but in his case was viewed by home fans as an unnecessary consequence of prissy petulance.

This was not how Ronaldo had been sold to Real Madrid. It seemed as if there was something not quite right with the shinily assembled gears in the Real Madrid machine.

The Madrid coach Pellegrini believed in attack, attack and more attack, and his philosophy, allied to Madrid's transfer policy, meant that they were regularly steamrollering the lesser sides in the League, racking up scores of four, five and six goals against them. But it was against Barcelona, and the tough-to-crack Sevilla, that they capitulated and lost vital points.

In the Champions League, too, they made short work of the lesser teams, but lost away to AC Milan in the group stages and went out in the second round after Lyon rode their luck and went through 2–1 on aggregate.

'I came here with high hopes and great pride. Unfortunately, I wasn't able to do what I wanted to do and I had differences from the beginning of the season,' Pellegrini said after his sacking by Pérez. 'I missed having a debate on sporting issues, with the coach included.' Pellegrini then concluded: 'Florentino's project is extraordinary but I think he's got it wrong.'[11]

He complained later: 'I didn't have a voice or a vote at Madrid. They sign the best players, but not the best players needed in a certain position. It's no good having an orchestra with the ten best guitarists if I don't have a pianist.

'Real Madrid have the best guitarists, but if I ask them to play the piano they won't be able to do it so well. He [Pérez] sold players that I considered important. We didn't win the Champions League during my season there because we didn't have a squad properly structured to be able to win it.'[12]

Pellegrini's severely unbalanced squad didn't allow him the option to play Ronaldo in a more roaming role as a modern number 9, as Messi had been evolving at Barça, playing on the wing but with freedom to cut in. But the system he had inherited and players he had foisted on him restricted Ronaldo, in that season, to a more orthodox winger's role – when he was not injured, that is.

Whether the unrest and frustration in the dug-out really affected Ronaldo, however, is open to debate. Indeed, in Jorge Valdano's opinion, one should not overrate the importance of the manager or his influence: 'Managers are important in the formative years of a player – as Ferguson was – but Cristiano Ronaldo came to Madrid from Manchester United as a fully formed player. He was more important for the managers than any one of them were for him. Put another way, look at Cristiano's career – without taking into account the managers

– and you will see a fairly coherent line of progress without big highs or lows. With some managers he got on well, with others less so . . .'[13]

After the Barcelona defeat, Ronaldo helped himself to thirteen goals as Madrid went on a winning run of sixteen victories in eighteen games, with only a single draw and defeat blotting their copybook before the return Clásico in April.

His importance to the team, and the otherworldly aura he brought to the field, were displayed in another La Liga match that season. On 22 February 2010, Ronaldo showed his full destructive power as Real Madrid thrashed Villarreal 6–2 at a thrilled Bernabéu, a win that narrowed the gap to Messi's Barça at the top of the table, above them in terms of goals scored, and which was Madrid's twelfth home win in a row. Ronaldo's spectacular performance led to a deification few players had seen before him:

> God moves in mysterious ways. Theatrically, dramatically. Beautifully, brutally. Head held high, neck extended, shoulders back, spine straight, lips pursed. Chest heaving. Up, pause for effect, down again, air escaping His lungs, blowing sailboats to shore.[14]

This is Sid Lowe's description of Ronaldo just before scoring a magisterial free kick that day, belted in after he scored his first by picking up the ball on the halfway line, setting off on one of his trademark runs, full acceleration with step-overs and feints, beating three defenders, then scoring. In a game in which everything clicked for him, he went on to help create three of Real Madrid's four other goals: the third, a perfect first-time cross to Higuaín; the fifth, passing beautifully to Kaká after sliding through Villarreal's defence; the sixth, proving such a menacing presence as he cut in from the right that a Villarreal defender resorted to cutting him down. Xabi Alonso scored the ensuing penalty. *El Mundo* provided perhaps the greatest compliment, comparing him to Di Stéfano.

As they faced up against Barcelona for the defining game of the season, they were top of the League by a point. Dethroning Barcelona was within reach in his first season. In reality, however, Xavi bossed the midfield throughout the game and as Barcelona reached their hypnotic peak of short passing moves, Messi and Pedro scored the goals that won them the game. Ronaldo was criticized for trying to prove he was the best player in the world and lacking discipline and connection with his teammates.

So, despite Ronaldo's brilliance in a gifted side, Real Madrid drew to the end of their first season with him in the team and without a trophy, but he insisted he was content with how things were progressing. 'I really enjoyed my season, but what's missing is winning a title,' he said. 'I'm very happy here in Madrid and my teammates have helped me a lot, but the team has not won anything. We have to keep fighting and I am confident we will win many titles [in future].' He had scored an impressive thirty-three goals in all competitions, with the stats boys pointing out that his combination with Gonzalo Higuaín accounted for fifty-three, making them the highest-scoring duo in the club's history.

The club had broken their own points record in La Liga with ninety-six, but FC Barcelona overtook this and ended with an extraordinary ninety-nine – an all-time La Liga record. Thus Barça retained the title, with Guardiola in charge and Messi, Iniesta and Xavi again among the key components of his 'dream team'.

Real Madrid ended the season trophy-less, a result that cost Manuel Pellegrini his job as manager after just a year in the post, the latest in a long line of short-lived managerial reigns, unable to withstand the pressures of club president Florentino Pérez's business model and the restlessness of the most demanding fans in La Liga, if not all Europe.

'It was very bad, very difficult, but the circumstances must be taken into account,' he told the Spanish television programme *Punto Pelota*. 'We have new players, a team under construction, a different coach and we know that success does not come straight away – you have to slide a bit.'[15]

Ronaldo recalled his first two years in Manchester, when the team did not win either the League or a European prize, and acknowledged that these things take time. But that was the Premier League, Manchester United, and the regime of Alex Ferguson. It was not La Liga, Real Madrid, and the regime of Florentino Pérez, with a powerless manager in Pellegrini.

Seen from Pérez's perspective, Pellegrini had not only failed to unsettle Guardiola's Barça, but had also been unable to exploit the full potential of the club's prize asset, Cristiano Ronaldo. Moreover, the successful and hugely ambitious José Mourinho, whose aim was to become the first manager to win championships in England, Italy and Spain, was ready for a call from Pérez after winning the Champions League – in Madrid – with Inter. It was an opportunity that Madrid could not miss, and Pérez made Mourinho an offer he was more than happy to accept. He had very personal reasons for relishing the challenge of unseating Barcelona which, after their astonishing season of 2009–10, seemed an extraordinarily difficult task.

25. UNTOUCHABLE: MESSI

While the noise around Real Madrid in the summer of 2009 was about a new team, a new superstar and whether they would be able to gel, for Barcelona and Messi the issue was one of continuity and harmony. After that brilliant first season for Guardiola, which left them entering his second with six trophies to play for, Guardiola swapped Samuel Eto'o for Zlatan Ibrahimović, one of the world's most gifted but strong-willed players. Beyond that, however, the strategy seemed to be 'same again, but better'. For a coach whose mantra was simplicity repeated – he once summed up his strategy as 'receive the ball, pass the ball, receive the ball, pass the ball' – and who prided himself on his coaching, the defining quality of this season was in players improving, or becoming more efficient at what they did.

Messi's excellence in this season, perhaps in response to the noisy neighbour who had just moved into the Bernabéu, was to reach ever new heights. After scoring nine goals in fifteen games before Christmas, and being awarded the Ballon d'Or over the winter break, he returned to score twenty-six goals in the next twenty-three League games. As the season went on, every time a Madrid victory asked a question, a Barcelona performance answered it.

The loss of Eto'o for Ibrahimović and the declining legs of the veteran Thierry Henry meant that they were less dynamic, less overwhelming than they had been the season before, but increases in performance elsewhere meant that this mattered less than anyone could have predicted. Ibrahimović himself would view his season in Barcelona as a failure, mainly because of a falling out with Pep Guardiola that left his future at Barcelona untenable. But other players stepped up to compensate. Victor Valdés, who up until that point had often been the butt of the joke that he was a local winner of a competition to play for Barcelona, began to make claims to be the best goalkeeper in the League, as his distribution and shot-stopping both improved. The Brazilian Dani Alves, whilst continuing to be an astonishingly effective attacking outlet, seemed to get caught upfield less, and Gerard Piqué, the youth team pin-up who had come home, grew into an imperious ball-playing centre-back. There were games, such as against Arsenal away in the Champions League, when the opposition team could hardly get out of their own half.

The youth team player Sergio Busquets supplanted Yaya Touré in the centre of the midfield, and his discipline and simple short passing became the foundation for so much of the creative play built ahead of him. Another youth team product, Pedro, who the previous season had played a bit part, was suddenly seen as a key performer all across the front three. And Messi was more flexible during the season, playing on the right, as a false 9, or sometimes playing off a central striker like Ibrahimović or Henry.

Overall, Guardiola had seemed to add more variation to the way the team was set up, introducing a kind of 4–2–4 formation, which created uncertainty when teams played them. In fact, the only thing to complain about as a fan seemed to be their lurid pink away kit.

The only real bum note in the season had come when they had been knocked out in the Champions League semi-finals by José Mourinho's Inter Milan side. And even then they'd had to contend with a two-day coach journey, due to a volcano eruption in Iceland halting all air travel. It seemed that season that it was only Mourinho, with a little help from God, who could halt Barcelona. As the world looked towards South Africa for the World Cup, the Real Madrid chairman knew what he had to do.

26. WORLD CUP 2010: MESSI

Messi entered the 2010 World Cup light years away from where he'd been at the previous one. He was the newly crowned best player in the world. Debate had raged over whether he was ready four years ago, whereas now the issue was how they could build a team around him.

By that point, with Maradona as Argentine coach, Messi was the undisputed number 10, that shirt whose cultural heft had weighed heavily on the shoulders of other Argentine internationals like Ariel Ortega, Marcelo Gallardo, Pablo Aimar and Andrés D'Alessandro, but if anyone could take on that mantle, it was Messi.

Maradona had come in a little less than two years previously, after increasing pressure had mounted on Alfio Basile's struggling attempt to qualify. Basile had been forced out in October 2008 after securing only four wins in nine months, the crunch point coming when Argentina were defeated 1–0 by Chile, the first time they had lost to their Andean neighbour in thirty-five years.

After that match, a complex network of vested interests had contributed to intensify the lobbying in support of Maradona's appointment as national coach, despite fears that his personality was ill suited to the demands of the job. The campaign included personal phone calls applying various degrees of pressure to the president of the Argentine Football Association, Julio Grondona, by three Latin American presidents – Hugo Chávez of Venezuela, Evo Morales of Bolivia and Argentina's own head of state, Néstor Kirchner, all of whom had been seen to ally themselves politically with Maradona during his latest anti-US phase.

Ever since the player's expulsion from the 1994 World Cup in the USA for failing a drugs test, there had not been much love lost between Maradona and Grondona, but Grondona was made aware of the extent to which the commercial value of the Argentine squad would be boosted with Maradona as coach. For example, the Renova

Group, owned by Russian billionaire Viktir Vekselberg, which had brought the television rights to twenty-four Argentina exhibition matches for $18 million in 2006, forecast a doubling of profits as interest soared as a result of Maradona's latest resurrection.

Within the footballing world, Gabriel Heinze and Sergio Agüero had already led the equivalent of a dressing-room revolt against Basile, persuading other players in the Argentine squad to vote with their feet in favour of Maradona. It was, as one AFA insider described to me, 'the equivalent of a palace coup'.

There is no evidence that Messi himself participated in the plot. He had deliberately chosen to escape from the inner conspiracies of Argentine football by settling in Barcelona, and had been keeping a low profile off the pitch after his meeting with Guardiola, maintaining close links with his family, particularly his father, and a small circle of friends.

But the Maradona coup took shape and turned into a public controversy. While many of the manoeuvrings back in Buenos Aires took place behind the scenes, they were only too evident to Riquelme, a key player in Basile's squad and the only member of the team to take a public stand against Maradona. In truth, ego was mixed with principle. This was in part because Riquelme feared losing his influence in the team under Maradona's tutelage, but also because he genuinely objected to the underhand way in which Basile's removal was orchestrated. Riquelme quit the national squad, saying of Maradona: 'We don't think the same way. We don't share the code of ethics. While he is the coach of the national team, we can't work together.'[1]

His decision to quit followed Maradona's publicly aired suggestion that the national squad worked better without Riquelme.

By contrast, and unsurprisingly, Maradona's attitude towards Messi proved more psychologically complex and ambivalent, suggesting not so much a tension between egos – since Messi didn't seem to demonstrate one – but rather a scarcely veiled Freudian rivalry between a forceful father and an understated son, competing not for the love of wife or mother but for the admiration of a nation, with a sense of legacy a lingering obsession, at least on Maradona's side.

As the World Cup in South Africa loomed, Maradona's veiled criticism of Messi, his questioning of his character, of whether he was too quiet, had been replaced by an open courtship, as Argentina's new coach struggled to put together a coherent team and system that would ensure qualification.

The era of Maradona as national coach got off to a promising start. Argentina won three games, including friendlies against Scotland and France and a 4–0 World Cup qualifying victory over Venezuela, with Messi a key player, scoring the first goal, assisting in the second, and contributing throughout the game to an attack that included Tévez and Agüero. But then Argentina lost 6–1 to Bolivia in La Paz, the whole team struggling with the high altitude, including Messi, who vomited on the pitch during the match.

Facing increasing criticism from the media, the squad just beat Colombia before losing away against Ecuador and then at home against Brazil. Argentina seemed to play not as a team, but as a collection of individuals out of touch with each other, with Messi seemingly the cause as well as the victim of the dysfunctionality. Viewed as the most important player by Maradona, but without the captain's armband – this was worn by Javier Mascherano – Messi was unable to lead by example.

It had never been easy for him with the national team. No matter that he still returned to Rosario for yearly visits, retained his Argentine accent when speaking Spanish and, despite the dietary strictures imposed on him to ensure optimum performance, had never lost his love of pizzas, sweet puddings and Milanesas, the breaded steaks that were his mother's specialty. He was still considered an exile from his own country, having moved to Barcelona as a young boy and grown up there, and choosing to take his summer holidays in his favourite resort, Ibiza, almost every year since. There was also the fact that he rarely raised his voice on the field and was too introverted to belt out the national anthem, which was seen as unpatriotic by the more extreme exponents of Argentine nationalism. He had always been made the scapegoat if they lost, blamed for not inspiring his colleagues to glory as he did in Barcelona. Even if he considered some of his fellow Argentines not to be of the same quality as his club mates, or felt he was inhibited by them not interacting with him in the same way, they were of better quality on the whole than those who had played alongside Diego in Mexico.

But Messi found neither the tactics nor a team that could play to and draw from his talent, unlike at FC Barcelona. The former national coach César Menotti, who had coached Argentina to World Cup victory in 1978 and had been in Barcelona with Maradona, summed up the mess as kindly as he could. 'He [Messi] is not a strategist, he finishes off the strategy. In Argentina, everything is confusion and he is caged in. Messi, at Barcelona, he plays; with the national team, he runs.'[2]

Maradona's Argentina were hugely fortunate to qualify for the finals after losing to Paraguay, only squeezing through after beating Peru and Uruguay in the last two matches of the qualification rounds. And yet for all the disastrous experience of the build-up, Argentina still found itself the focus of attention before the finals, not least because Messi had won global recognition for the major part he had played in FC Barcelona's brilliant season.

There had also been a widely reported 'summit' in the Catalan capital between Messi and Maradona, in which player and coach had agreed on a change to the tactics and system to give him more protection and more access to the ball, when he could best make use of it.

As the football journalist Simon Kuper wrote in May 2010, in the final days before the start of the tournament: 'Usually the main suspense before a World Cup concerns who will win it. This year, people are just as eager to know whether in South Africa we will see the full Messi. If he can match some of the moments he has given us with Barcelona, but in football's ultimate setting – well, the game doesn't get better than that. This World Cup is in large part about Messi. But to understand him you have to understand his Argentine football ancestry.'[3]

I owe thanks to the Argentine football writer Julio Marini for the recommendation that I should watch *Pelota de Trapo* (The Rag Ball) to gain a better understanding of that ancestry, and in particular the mythical figure of the *pibe*, or streetwise child footballer. Argentine fans had been waiting to see the figure resurrected ever since the fall of Maradona as a player, when he was expelled from the 1994 World Cup in the USA following his failed drugs test. As we've seen, many had come close, but the rebirth remained elusive in the national consciousness.

The film, made in the late 1940s, tells the story of a group of kids in a poor Argentine urban neighbourhood who form their own street team, Sacachispas (the Firecrackers). They play their first matches with a ball made of rags, because they cannot afford a leather one. But their natural trickery, skill and fighting spirit, as they control and pass the ball over rough, unmanicured land and take on bigger opponents, is soon evident, with one boy, Eduardo Díaz, emerging as their natural captain.

Díaz starts the film with the nickname *come-uñas*, or 'nail biter'. While indeed he does bite his nails, his understated, almost shy character is transformed when he plays, inspiring the team as a play maker and goal scorer. As Díaz and his team's self-confidence grows, they organize a fundraising campaign to buy a leather ball, which draws the support of hardworking, low-income parents and a local priest. Diaz himself is eventually scouted to play as a professional footballer, and becomes the star of the national team, achieving hero status for playing despite being diagnosed with a potentially life-threatening genetic heart condition.

The film used amateurs as well as professional actors and drew on the advice of one of the great legends of Argentine football in its earlier years, Guillermo Stábile. A player with Huracán who became the first Argentine player to score a goal in a World Cup in 1930 (he scored eight goals in four games in the tournament), Stábile went on to successfully coach the national team between 1939 and 1958, during which he won seven Copas América and one Pan-American Championships.

First released in 1948, when Argentina was undergoing a social revolution in favour of the working classes under the populist military president General Juan Perón, *Pelota de Trapo* became an instant box-office hit in the country, and later secured a large South American following on YouTube. The story of its *pibes*, of what it means to be quintessentially Argentine in football, is a story of national identity, represented by the roving creative tricksters who discover their talent in the bumpy urban spaces, or *potreros*, born in Argentina from immigrant backgrounds. It is this destiny – this romanticized journey from the shantytown to realizing a national dream – that Maradona self-consciously fulfilled. It is also a role in which Messi was miscast – for some Argentines, Messi was not and could not be a true *pibe*.

Maradona wanted to help the lad so much that he asked him to sketch a system that he believed would increase his chances of lifting his first World Cup trophy in 2010. Messi suggested replacing the 4–4–2 system – two wingers, two centre-midfielders and two forwards – that Maradona had shown a preference for and replacing it with a

4–3–1–2, or a 3–4–1–2 system, with play focused on the attacking front three, but with enough players to defend.

The new formation proved effective at the start of the tournament against opponents Nigeria, who offered plenty of space. A partying crowd at Ellis Park, the majority Argentine, showed their appreciation for the entertainment on show; an overweight and slightly self-conscious Maradona gesticulating from the touchlines, and a slimmed-down Messi. Messi was the standout performer, creating opportunities for others and having several shots at goal thwarted by the superb Nigerian goalkeeper, Vincent Enyeama, before Heinze headed in Argentina's winning goal.

During the next match, against South Korea, Messi once again excelled in his play-making role, participating in all four goals of his side's 4–1 victory. As their place in the knockout phase was guaranteed, most of the starters were rested during the last group match against Greece, except Messi, who had acceded reluctantly to Maradona'a request that he put on the captain's armband after resting Javier Mascherano.

For the first time, members of the Argentine squad saw Messi evidently nervous the day before a match. It was not that he feared he would not play well, but that he was terrified about the prospect of having to make a speech to his teammates, as was the captain's traditional task. The next morning, Messi was incoherent when he tried to say a few words to the circle of the starting eleven, leaving it to veteran Juan Verón to shout a few words of encouragement, as he could be heard amidst the tribal chants of thousands of Argentine fans in frenzied mode. They bounced and bobbed during and after the national anthem, they thumped drums, and their rhythm provided an effective counterpoint to the honk of the African vuvuzelas reverberating round the stadium.

As things went, Messi had a frustrating evening playing against a very mediocre and unambitious side. Despite dominating possession, Argentina struggled to find a way through Greece's nine-men-behind-the-ball defence, and even Messi, named man of the match nevertheless, struggled to wriggle free of the attentions of his man-marker, Avraam Papadopoulos. Argentina managed to secure a 2–0 win in the last quarter of the game, with Martín Demichelis scoring the first and substitute striker Martín Palermo the second, after Messi's strike had been palmed by the goalkeeper into his path.

'Exactly twenty-four years after scoring his infamous "Hand of God" goal against England at the 1986 World Cup, coach Diego Maradona leapt for joy in his technical area,' noted the BBC.[4]

'I think we're showing what we are able to do,' Maradona said afterwards, before hitting out at the Spanish-speaking media he considered had been too critical of the squad and his management. 'It's a matter of fair play,' he shouted. 'If every time Messi gets the ball the Greek players bring him down, you should award a yellow or red card and it's over. I mean the Greeks were just pushing Messi. If I tell the fourth official and he doesn't react, what I am supposed to do?'

Maradona claimed to be happy with Messi's performance. 'People should relax,' he insisted, with typical bravado. 'This team is going to show everything it has.'[5]

He spoke as if victory in the tournament was a given, but the fact that Greece's defensive wall proved difficult to smash down for an attacking Argentina with Messi as captain should have given him cause for concern, as there was much better opposition to be faced in the days ahead. In the round of sixteen, Argentina defeated an underperforming Mexico 3–1, with Messi assisting their first goal by Higuaín, a controversial strike that stood despite being offside, and Tévez scoring two. But then came the game with Germany, and Argentina's national disaster.

Joachim Löw's team may have been less star-studded than Maradona's side, but from the outset proved more disciplined in defence and more dangerous in attack. Messi, together with Tévez, tried to step up their tempo in a bid to undermine the German back line, but found little to exploit. As Simon Kuper remarked after the match: 'It turned out in South Africa that there is a way to stop Messi, and Maradona himself stumbled on it. All you need to do is ensure that the boy keeps getting the ball 50 yards from the opponents' goal. Then the opposition can form a nine-man screen to stop him getting through. The Germans did.'[6]

Argentina's unstructured defence had proved a liability throughout the World Cup and finally led to their elimination at the same stage of the tournament and by the same opponent as four years earlier. Their 4–0 loss was their worst margin of defeat since 1974.

FIFA subsequently identified Messi as one of the tournament's ten best players, citing his 'outstanding' pace and creativity and 'spectacular and efficient' dribbling, shooting and passing. But the fact remained that Argentina had failed to get beyond the quarter-finals, and Messi had finished the tournament goalless.

Back home, Messi received harsher criticism than Maradona. As the perceived best player in the world, he had been expected to lead an average team to the title, as Maradona arguably did in 1986, but he had failed to replicate his performances at Barcelona with Argentina, leading to renewed accusations that he cared less about his country than his club.

When Argentina crashed out of the World Cup in South Africa it left Argentine football, not for the first or last time, with a sense of humiliation as well as loss. There was a belated realization that Maradona was human after all, and that Messi had yet to earn his mythological status as the nation's hero.

One key witness, the team's physical trainer Fernando Signorini, at least had a sweeter memory of Argentina's 2010 World Cup campaign when I caught up with him in Buenos Aires in 2016. Sweeter certainly than the nightmare moment in the US World Cup, where he personally had to deliver the news to Maradona that the drugs test had gone against him and that he was being expelled from the tournament, effectively bringing to an end his playing career.

Signorini, who had been close to Maradona for a long time, was rarely surprised by anything he did, but the scene he had witnessed that day – an international star reduced in an instant to a human wreck – was not one he could easily forget. 'It seemed as if Diego's whole world had come apart. He was crying from the deepest depth of his soul, completely out of control.'

Sixteen years later, Signoroni was party to no such hysteria by either Maradona or Messi, perhaps because the former had not that much to lose personally this time, and because the latter had a future assured of stardom, with a better team and manager in his support once he got back to FC Barcelona.

As Signorini told me, he himself overcame the disappointment of not winning the World Cup in South Africa because of the unique circumstances that brought Maradona and Messi together during the campaign. 'It was a marvellous experience while it lasted: Diego, whenever he was out of the media spotlight, showed real tenderness and respect for the much younger Messi when they talked with each other. All that idea that there was somehow a rivalry between them was an invention of some sectors of the media.'

Then, as Signorini chain-smoked and we sheltered from the rain beneath an awning outside La Biela, one of Buenos Aires' most popular cafeterias, he told me the story of a training session.

'We had been training for about forty minutes when Diego shouted out, "That's it, let's all get back to the dressing room". And as everybody heads off, I notice that Leo picks up the ball and puts it in front of the open goal on the left-hand side of the penalty-area D. He hits the ball and it flies to the left, three metres above the bar. Messi makes a gesture of resignation and then starts walking despondently towards the dressing room, shoulders crunched, head bowed. So I catch up with him, put my arm round his shoulder and tell him, "You are on your way to becoming the best player in the world and you are walking to the dressing room having hit that shit ball . . ."

'At that point I hear Diego say, "Hang on, lad, come here . . ." Then Diego puts the ball in exactly the same spot, steps two metres back and, putting his hand on Messi's shoulder, tells him: "Look, when you go in and hit the ball, don't take your foot away so quickly. Because without it the ball doesn't know what to do . . ."

'And at that moment Diego steps up, and kicks the ball straight into the net. There and then I felt the history of Argentine football summarized, in those two guys. It contradicted what some people claimed – that Diego was jealous of Leo. No way was that true, because someone who is jealous of another has nothing to teach him.'

27. WORLD CUP 2010: RONALDO

Off the back of a campaign that in almost any other year would have led to a League title but which was thwarted by the unremitting excellence of Barcelona, Cristiano Ronaldo captained the Portuguese national team in the World Cup in South Africa. The team, coached by Carlos Queiroz, the man who was responsible for drawing Cristiano Ronaldo to Alex Ferguson's attention when the player was at Sporting, and who had helped smooth his transfer to Real Madrid, had got off to an unimpressive start in the group stage with a drab goalless draw with Ivory Coast.

Then, with Cristiano Ronaldo as a key figure, Portugal had put on a display of ruthlessness and verve to defeat a motivated North Korea 7–0. Although he scored only one of these goals, it broke a two-year drought: the last one he had scored with the national team had been in Euro 2008.

There was less cause for celebrating the next match. For all the marketing hype of Cristiano Ronaldo being the new Pelé of the Portuguese-speaking world and Portugal as proponents of the beautiful game, the match between Portugal and Brazil failed to live up to expectations and ended in a goalless draw, which nonetheless allowed both teams to progress to the next round.

Against Brazil, Queiroz opted for a more defensive strategy to stifle the opponents, and its efficiency resulted in an anti-climactic and bad-tempered game, where the number of bookings outweighed clear-cut chances.

Ronaldo, playing in a lone attacking role, struggled to make any impact on the game, failing with a series of long-range efforts at goal. Only once did he really threaten when, fifteen minutes into the second half, he outpaced two Brazil defenders on a run from the half-way line, before being intercepted by Lúcio, with the ball crossing the face of the goal for Pepe, Ronaldo's Real Madrid teammate, to hit wide of the left-hand post.

Then, in the last sixteen of the tournament, Ronaldo again

captained his well-drilled side and threatened with his free kicks. But he was unable to avoid defeat at the hands of Vicente del Bosque's Spain, on their way to becoming world champions two years after winning the European crown under the management of Luis Aragonés. Although Messi wasn't on this pitch, his ghost was, conjured up in Spain's movement, their tiny, skilful players moving in that familiar Barcelona way, and with a team owing so much to players who'd received their education at La Masia.

It was recognition of – as well as a generous tribute to – the extraordinary achievement of Pep Guardiola in building a team ethos and a style that had entertained as well as mesmerized millions of fans around the world, with supreme artistry and vision on and off the ball that demoralized and exhausted the opponent.

Del Bosque had seen what the *galáctico* era had done to Real Madrid, and was not impressed by celebrity or super-egos or waste. But his plan to have Spain follow up their success by retaining their European crown in 2012 would face a threat he had never imagined could emanate from a manager at his beloved Real Madrid.

For, on 31 May 2010, as the La Liga season reached its end, José Mourinho, fresh from winning the Champions League with Inter Milan after eliminating FC Barcelona in the semi-final with an impressively stifling performance, had been appointed as Manuel Pellegrini's replacement at Real Madrid.

28. ENTER MOURINHO

Following on from the World Cup, the summer of 2010 marked several converging moments in Cristiano Ronaldo's career. The first was the departure of Raúl González from Real Madrid, an icon of traditional values, paving the way for the succession by a very different character and player in the number 7 shirt. The second was the news that the usurper of Raúl's shirt, Cristiano Ronaldo, had become the first person in the history of sport to reach 50 million followers through social media.

No matter that Raúl had long been considered a hero by traditional Real Madrid fans and millions of similarly patriotic followers of Spain's national team. Cristiano Ronaldo was a marketing phenomenon and a celebrity of the digital age, a key element in Real Madrid's development as a global business.

Ronaldo's digital history had begun on 23 October 2005, when the Cristiano Ronaldo YouTube channel was launched. It currently has 850,000 subscribers and its videos have been watched over 65 million times. On 6 May 2009, a verified Facebook page for Ronaldo was launched, which gathered upwards of 87 million 'likes' over the next five years. In June 2010, Ronaldo joined Twitter, where he garnered more than 27.2 million followers within two years. On 31 October 2012, Ronaldo created a feed on Instagram. At the time of writing, his followers on that platform number 120 million.

It was certainly Ronaldo-as-brand who had announced, on 4 July, through his personal Twitter and Facebook pages, that he had become a father to Cristiano Junior shortly after Portugal had been knocked out of the World Cup by Spain. It was as if the celebrity had chosen to raise his head to divert attention from the defeated player.

But this was no ordinary announcement of a new family arrival, more a definition of a brand that reached out to parents regardless of marital status or gender, and which reflected Ronaldo's egocentricity: 'It is with great joy and emotion that I inform I have recently become a father to a baby boy. As agreed with the baby's mother, who prefers to have her identity kept confidential, my son will be under my exclusive guardianship. I request everyone to fully respect my right to privacy (and that of the child) at least on issues as personal as these are.'

The statement would lead to inevitable questions as to the identity of the mother, and the nature of the child's conception, with media speculation covering possibilities ranging from the baby being the product of a surrogate mother to the outcome of a casual affair.

To some of Madrid's more traditional fans, the contrast with their soon-to-depart homegrown hero Raúl's personal life was stark. Every Real Madrid fan knew who the mother of Raúl's children was, and the conventional circumstances of their births. Raúl and his wife Mamen Sanz were among the most discreet of couples in the football world, their natural good looks and stylish clothes inseparable from an uncontroversial, enduring marriage. The couple had been teenage sweethearts, and Mamen had taken a ten-year break from a promising modelling career to look after their children, five in number. Early in 2010, just as her husband's career dipped, Mamen reappeared in various fashion magazines, looking stunning and expressing marital bliss four months after giving birth to their latest child.

'Sure I married a very popular player, but I've led a very normal life like any other mother of a family . . . He is an excellent father, and is very involved in the education of his kids, and we always tried to teach them the importance of respect, of not abusing their privileged status,' she told one magazine.[1]

Raúl had reached the age of thirty-three, having played alongside and outlasted the likes of Zidane, the Brazilian Ronaldo, Figo and Roberto Carlos. The Madrid captain was given an emotional farewell by a club that he left as all-time leading scorer, and as the all-time leading scorer in the Champions League. Florentino Pérez paid this tribute to the veteran on his final day at the club. 'We will never forget Raúl,' he said. 'There are many men who form part of the legend of Real Madrid, but few that are chosen to embody the club – Raúl is one of those.'

But those traditional values were perhaps less marketable in a globalized, celebrity-obsessed digital age. Cristiano Ronaldo's arrival had signalled that the club was entering a new phase, with a much younger player who had already generated a global following at Manchester United and whose marketing potential was being realized on a hugely ambitious scale under the direction of one of the most powerful and successful football agents in the world.

With his personal life entering a new phase and his succession to the number 7 shirt giving his CR7 brand a new coherence, Ronaldo began the season with the only coach in world football who could genuinely lay claim to his own cult of personality.

Though Mourinho's arrival had been announced on 31 May, serious negotiations between Mourinho, Mendes and Madrid had been under way months before the Champions League final, early on in what would turn out to be Mourinho's last season with Inter. Mourinho and Mendes had met senior Real Madrid executives secretly at one of the least visible of Mourinho's residences, a mountain retreat in Portugal. As the Real Madrid officials' cars turned up, Mourinho was struck that none of them contained Jorge Valdano, the club's sporting director. When he asked one of the executives why he hadn't come to the meeting, he was told that Valdano hadn't been informed about it and that it had nothing to do with him. It was a signal that Pérez was preparing to accommodate the club's staffing arrangements to meet Mourinho's needs.

Hitherto Valdano had played a dominant role inside the club, with a hotline to the president, advising on transfers and also on media relations. Mourinho, with a strong personality of his own, was not coming to Real Madrid to play second fiddle. He had demanded full control and top billing, and from the outset made it pretty evident he regarded Valdano surplus to requirements, sidelining him and eventually forcing him out.

In Mourinho, Pérez felt he had found a manager with sufficient personality and talent to help take Ronaldo to another level, one that would show he was even greater than Messi, and with a proven record of having taken on and beaten the club's historic rival at its best moments.

Ever since emerging from under his mentor Bobby Robson's shadow to take on the top job at Porto in 2002, Mourinho had developed a controversial style, attracting followers and detractors in equal measure. His critics saw him at his worst as an abrasive, unstable and destructive character, who showed insufficient respect for his opponents and was a bad loser. His admirers thought he had matured since his period at Chelsea, and had retained the ability to undermine his opponents and motivate his players, to team-build while at the same time drawing the best out of players like Ronaldo, who needed special treatment.

While Mourinho and Ronaldo had been in the Premier League, coach and player had had occasional verbal run-ins, but that had more to with finding themselves on either side of club rivalries in highly competitive Premier League matches than any individual problem between them. By the time both of them found themselves at Real Madrid, they had long ago made their peace. Mourinho considered Ronaldo, like himself, an important figure among the Portuguese diaspora, worthy of respect and recognition.

As Ronaldo matured into an ever more important player, and Mourinho endured as the 'Special One', the coach recognized in the player a fellow spirit, one whose insatiable desire to win, coupled with his arrogance and supreme self-belief, mirrored his own; shared characteristics that in the same team could produce a formidable double act capable of getting one up on even the best opposition.

Real Madrid's 2010–11 campaign seemed set to revolve round the manager rather than any of his players, the controversies he generated a distraction as much as an excuse. Years later, in the spring of 2017, as he found himself struggling to break into the top four of the Premier League, Mourinho observed that winning anything in England was particularly difficult because all the top clubs could afford to bring in big players.

'In England the clubs are so powerful economically that the market is open to everyone,' he told *France Football*. 'No club in England can dominate. Power is divided and everything is harder: buying, winning, building.'[2]

It was hard to know whether he had a point or was simply trying to get his excuses in early. But at Real Madrid he had no such excuses. The economic and political power of the club had no rival in La Liga except for FC Barcelona, and both clubs had the pick of the top players domestically and from around Europe. Their hold on revenue from TV rights and marketing amounted to a duopoly. But the fact was that both Real Madrid and its star player, Cristiano Ronaldo, had yet to undermine the reputation of Guardiola's FC Barcelona as the best team in the world, or Messi's as the best player.

José Mourinho had added to his success at Porto and Chelsea by making Inter the first Italian club to win the treble – it was the Champions League achievement that convinced Florentino Pérez that he was the manager that had the key to finally breaking FC Barcelona's golden era. For he did it impressively, with a team that was robust in defence and effective in counter-attack, defeating a strong Bayern team after eliminating Guardiola's Barça in the semi-finals. The latter, in the eyes of Pérez and his club's fans, was the most important, because it showed that the great rival was not invincible; that Guardiola could be beaten, and Messi too.

Behind the latest manoeuvrings at Real Madrid loomed the *éminence grise* of elite modern football – Jorge Mendes, for Mendes was Mourinho's agent as well as Ronaldo's. He also represented four players whom the club signed up to reinforce its squad by the end of the transfer window, after the 2010 World Cup: the Germans Sami Khedira and Mesut Özil, Portuguese defender Ricardo Carvalho and Argentine winger Ángel Di María.

If there was a defining method after Mourinho's arrival in Madrid, it seemed that it was in speaking the loudest and in provoking confrontation. As the sports journalist Jonathan Wilson has noted: 'He is a manager who thrives on conflict, someone who is never happy unless there is something to be unhappy about . . . Tension is simply how he operates. If it isn't there, he has to create it and he isn't too bothered whom he hurts in doing so'.[3]

At Real Madrid, Mourinho picked a fight with the popular young winger Pedro León after a game at Levante in September 2010, 'seemingly just to create an atmosphere of uncertainty and prevent complacency setting in,' wrote Wilson. He would eventually go on to publicly humiliate long-serving and much-respected captain Iker Casillas by relegating him from the first team, largely to curb his competing authority in the dressing room.

Given his proven track record, one would have thought that Mourinho no longer had any need to make clear who was boss, no need to demonstrate his authority, but by picking on León and Casillas it reinforced the message that no one, as Wilson put it, 'is too big, no one too iconic, nobody too close to Mourinho to be safe'.

The exception was Cristiano Ronaldo. While differences in their personal lives and the egos of both men fuelled occasional fracas and loomed large enough to obviate a close relationship, Ronaldo was nevertheless subject to privileged status when it came to the politics of Real Madrid.

It was not just that President Pérez valued Ronaldo as his project's best asset in commercial and sporting terms; Mourinho also considered Ronaldo the best player in the team, while the agent he shared with the player thought of him as the best in the world, a reputation that needed to not only be preserved, but also enhanced by success at Real Madrid.

As Jorge Mendes told his biographers in 2015: 'A very special moment for me was when Cristiano won his first Ballon d'Or [when at Manchester United] in 2008 . . . It was the first step, although I already knew from the start that Ronaldo was going to be the best player ever. For me he is and I have no doubt . . . Cristiano was not playing in the best team in the world [at Manchester United]. But he is the best without doubt. He is the best on all levels: quality, professionalism, human.'[4]

It's hard to separate marketing hype from genuine conviction. The point was that Mendes had convinced Pérez that it was so, and Mourinho had no choice but to do his best to prove it. It was a tough assignment, even for Mourinho, and one that tested his psychological and tactical skills like never before. His signings in the summer of 2010 had been intended to support Ronaldo. Özil and Di María were there to supply him with assists and support running, while Khedira and Carvalho freed him up from defensive duties. The stage was all set for the two of them to take down Barcelona.

Star footballers are not normally the butt of popular comedy, but Cristiano Ronaldo's early playing years with Real Madrid became an easy target for the satirists of one of Spanish TV's most popular comic series of modern times.

Crackòvia had originally been launched in 2008 as a spin-off of an earlier series called *Polònia*, which used lookalike actors in a sharp satire targeting the country's political class. Using the same formula, the new series focused on La Liga, with a special focus on FC Barcelona and Real Madrid, picking up on the larger-than-life characters at the clubs. References to Poles had traditionally been used as a form of baiting Catalans by Spanish fans, on account of the 'foreignness' of their language and culture.

Produced initially by the Catalan official channel TV3, the satirical football series went on to register a strong following of retro-active viewers on YouTube, and by the summer of 2011 would easily surpass the popularity of its more political precursor, *Polònia*. The series' fan club extended across Spain to include many viewers in Madrid, largely thanks to the evolving nature of the rivalry between the country's two clubs, and the relentless media coverage of their two star players – Ronaldo and Messi – who were lampooned with varying degrees of intensity.

While the laughter of viewers at Messi's expense was largely limited to his pronounced Argentine-Spanish accent and seeming inability to string more than a couple of sentences together, the portrait of Cristiano, also heavily accented, seemed to draw on a richer seam of personality traits which the Catalan programme makers evidently relished making fun of, the ridicule contrasting with the reverential tones of some sports writers.

Cristiano Ronaldo was portrayed in his first two seasons at Real Madrid as narcissistic, arrogant and hypocritical, at odds with the rest of his colleagues, and barely tolerated by his first two managers, Pellegrini and Mourinho.

Hilarious scenes mocked Cristiano's image as an athlete and his alleged obsession with Messi at its most exaggerated: they showed him endlessly stepping over the ball without going anywhere, doing press-ups in the middle of a game, and constantly looking at himself in the mirror while blaming his colleagues for their lack of support and appreciation. 'I don't want to play with these players. I am the best. I want to score as many goals as Messi!' he screams hysterically at a Pellegrini lookalike. 'I am rich, I am handsome, and I am the only one who knows how to play.'

In one episode, Mourinho is shown protecting Ronaldo from a dressing-room revolt as the players object to his claim that he has scored all the goals, which he celebrates by removing his shirt and flexing his bronzed, perfectly sculpted torso. In another notorious episode, an off-the-field scene shows him posing, again, in front of the mirror. This time he is in the dressing room, in his briefs, with a Brazilian Carnival male model cooling his naked back with a large ostrich feather – the camp insinuations of the scene could hardly be clearer.

But the most biting spoof is reserved for a scene in which Ronaldo makes a self-interested appeal on behalf of a charity fundraising campaign for those who suffer from jealously of people who 'are rich and beautiful like us'. He urges those watching the advertisement slot, 'If you are ugly and cheap, accept it. If you are jealous of me, just say NO.'

Managers as well as players are targets of the satirists. Mourinho is portrayed in a later episode as a devil, complete with red leotard, tail and horns. He is seen haunting a terrified Guardiola in his bedroom at night, threating the Barça coach with eternal damnation. Lest they stand accused of bias against Real Madrid, the programme makers lampoon Guardiola in another episode as a self-important, fashion-conscious, pseudo-intellectual Catalan, who presides over his 'dream team' in an Armani suit.

For Mourinho, the rivalry with FC Barcelona had an extra personal dimension. The Catalan club had interviewed Mourinho for the post left vacant by Frank Rijkaard in the summer of 2008, after the Portuguese had left Chelsea for the first time. Mourinho had a love–hate relationship with the club, where he had worked as an assistant for Bobby Robson and later Louis van Gaal. He had not endeared himself to everyone during that period, with Barça purists considering him too brash and not in sync with Catalan culture, and some of Robson's household staff among those complaining of his arrogance and rudeness whenever he came to visit the Englishman at his home in Sitges, near Barcelona.

For his part, Mourinho resented the fact that Catalans showed a distinct lack of respect for him, with Barça fans continuing to chide him as a mere '*traductor*', or translator, in reference to one of the jobs he had had when at FC Barcelona under Robson. Hostility towards Mourinho had grown during his management of Chelsea because of his controversial allegations of unethical behaviour against Rijkaard and some of the Barça players, including Messi, whom he claimed play-acted to get Asier del Horno red-carded during that stormy Champions League tie that caused such enmity.

Despite all that, Mourinho wanted the Barça job so much that he presented the club with a twenty-seven-page PowerPoint document outlining his vision, including his plans for revolutionizing the club's traditional 4–3–3 system and his views on the current squad.

As revealed by Marc Ingla, the Barça executive who interviewed him, Mourinho planned to keep Deco, another player represented by Mendes whom he had coached to Champions League glory at Porto, and ended his presentation with the words: 'I know what Barcelona are like.' Whether he was referring to its politics, its culture, its style, or its occasional alleged cheating was unclear. Laporta and some other Barça senior executives rated Mourinho very highly, but in the end were persuaded to go for Pep Guardiola on the advice of the man Laporta treated as his guru, Johan Cruyff. It's fair to say that Cruyff never was Mourinho's greatest fan; they differed in their football philosophies, and both had big egos which left little room to accommodate the other.

With the key cast assembled, Ronaldo firmly ensconced as Madrid's talisman, Mourinho nursing both his own grievances and ambitions, and Guardiola and Messi still dazzling the football world, the stage was set for an extraordinary season of rivalry.

29. CLÁSICOS: RONALDO AND MESSI

The previous season Barcelona had won La Liga by three points. Although they had dropped points to other teams, if one of the Clásicos had gone the other way then it could have been Madrid who'd lifted the trophy. To that end, all the talk was about how they would match up against each other in the Clásicos, with the first scheduled for 29 November at the Nou Camp.

Both teams began the season at a sprint, as if in a hurry to get there as soon as possible. Barcelona won ten of their first twelve games, dropping only five points along the way. Messi and the newly signed David Villa seemed to be on the scoresheet every week. But Real Madrid were even better, going unbeaten and dropping only four points. The fixture beforehand saw both Ronaldo and Messi score hat-tricks.

For Messi and Cristiano Ronaldo, the most glittering of stars in a match featuring eleven world champions, there was a sense of this being a definitive test of who was currently in the ascendant. Ronaldo had never scored against Barcelona; Messi was yet to get a goal against Mourinho. The last two winners of the Ballon d'Or, they had scored against everyone else. Ronaldo reached fifty goals for Madrid faster than anyone in the club's history; Messi had struck seventy in his last seventy-one games.

The game was played on a Monday by mutual agreement. The decision fitted in with the wish of the newly elected Barça president – pragmatic, commercially minded Sandro Rosell – to have Barça judged for its sporting quality first and foremost, and not as an adjunct to a political party, as his radicalized predecessor, pro-independence Joan Laporta, had tried to do.

To have held the game on the Saturday or the Sunday would have coincided with the staging of the highly emotive Catalan regional elections, thus guaranteeing the event being turned into a potential political battleground.

It was a frenzied atmosphere at the Nou Camp nonetheless.

Officials hoping to 'defuse' the latest Clásico were engaging in wishful thinking. In the aftermath of the Catalan elections, and with Mourinho present, it always threatened to be combustible. Politics and history is of course partly responsible for making El Clásico one of the high points of the football season, but it's also about two great football teams – arguably the world's best – and at this point the two undisputed best players in the world, playing against each other.

The game started with a piece of pure poetry in motion, courtesy of Messi and Xavi, the architect of Spain's 2010 World Cup success. As the clock approached eight minutes, Messi, dropping from his false 9 role into midfield, combined with Xavi then passed the ball to Iniesta, who picked out Xavi on the run into the box to nudge a volley past Iker Casillas. The assured possession and quick passing transition from midfield showed Guardiola's Barça at their best, gracefully finding their way through Mourinho's rugged defence.

For Barça it only got better, as, accompanied by shouts of '*Olé*' from the home crowd, Messi, Pedro, Iniesta and Villa played out of the tightest of corners and moved the ball around as if El Clásico had momentarily turned into a mere training session, with Real Madrid players, including Ronaldo, shown up as ineffectual sparring partners. Then, just when Barça looked in danger of over-elaborating and losing the ball, Villa connected with a cross from Xavi, which Casillas just managed to deflect, only for Pedro to stab home the rebound.

Madrid had little of the ball, but when they did recover possession they broke rapidly and with murderous intent. Ronaldo saw a shot flash wide and a free kick dip past the post, and just before half-time had his appeal for a penalty turned down after falling over Valdés. The referee, Iturralde González, felt Ronaldo had dived. The Barça fans packed into the Nou Camp had no doubts that he had.

When Ronaldo next drew attention to himself it was for all the wrong reasons, provoking a twenty-man brawl after shoving Guardiola in response to the Barça coach picking up a loose ball and throwing it past him on the touchline. Both incidents were only of academic interest, although Ronaldo did not emerge from this, the most important encounter of the season, with his reputation enhanced.

With Real Madrid fans still murmuring about a biased decision that had been influenced by the home crowd, the referee exercised Solomonic judgement by disallowing as offside a Messi goal just after the start of the second half. Four minutes later Messi, terrier-like, was back threatening Casillas, with an angled through-pass to Xavi, who hit the outside netting.

Three minutes later Messi repeated the move, only this time with Villa scoring a goal, quickly followed up with his second of the match off another clever Messi pass. Real Madrid fans up in the gods were reduced to an icy silence, a tiny island of humiliated inhabitants amidst a roaring ocean of more than 90,000 supporters in the Nou Camp.

In the midst of the magnificent manicured park, the men in white looked as stunned and diminished as their most loyal fans, and had to suffer the humiliation of hardly touching the ball for another half-hour, Ronaldo and Mourinho's miserable night signed off with a fifth Barça goal in stoppage time by Jeffrén, just three minutes after he had come off the bench. In those final moments, Real Madrid's Sergio Ramos was sent off after scything Messi – a pointless gesture other than in summing up his team's impotence.

The Spanish sports media – in a rare break of their traditional bias in favour of one club or the other – were unanimous in praising the superiority of Barça and holding up Real Madrid to the ridicule they lent themselves to when their arrogance was not matched by perform-ance.

For both Ronaldo and Mourinho, the game proved a particular humiliation, with Mourinho taunted by Barça fans for staying inside the dug-out in the second half, having seemingly declared the game over after the first three goals. As Mourinho finally emerged, a chant of 'Mourinho, go to the theatre!' resonated around the stadium.

As for Ronaldo, he struck an increasingly forlorn and frustrated figure in the midst of Madrid's collective disintegration. By contrast, Messi was one of the shining lights of brilliant choreographed team-play by Barça. Compared to the accolades for 'Super Messi', Ronaldo barely earned a mention in the media the next day. While neither player ended up scoring in Mourinho's first Clásico as a Real Madrid coach, one of them clearly shone above the other. Messi may not have scored goals, but he assisted in two of them, nearly scored one him-self, and was a key figure in Barça's creativity, playing simple and complex passes and keeping the ball moving. Ronaldo stumbled and slid; Messi glided.

Six weeks after seeing his Real Madrid team lose 5–0 to Barça, Mourinho tried as best as he could to raise the morale of the men in white at a gala evening in Zürich, which some journalists dubbed a Barça love-fest, given Messi's recent Ballon d'Or prize and the Argentine's tribute to his colleagues, Xavi and Iniesta.

And few could have held it against him on the basis of the self-effacing way he accepted the 2010 prize on that night in January 2011. A true sportsman, flanked on the stage by Sepp Blatter and Michel Platini, FIFA and UEFA presidents respectively, whose reputations as worthy football figureheads were destined to be less enduring.

The last player to win the Ballon d'Or award twice in a row had been Dutch striker Marco van Basten in 1988 and 1989, while Messi's former Barça colleague Ronaldinho had won the FIFA prize in 2004 and 2005, before the two were briefly merged.

Many thought Iniesta and Xavi, who were the lynchpins of the Spanish side, were favourites to win the Ballon d'Or at the glittering ceremony in Switzerland. Spain's manager, Vicente del Bosque, believed that it had been Iniesta and Xavi who had been most successful in translating their achievement at club level with Barça into helping the Spanish team's transformation from Europe's great underachiever to European and World Cup champions, and deserved recognition. Messi seemed to share that sentiment when he was announced as the winner.

'To be honest, I didn't expect to win today, but it was already great to be here next to my two mates,' said Messi, turning to Xavi and Iniesta, who shared the platform with him. 'To win it makes it even more special. I want to share with all of my friends, my family, all the Barcelonistas and the Argentinians.'

The modesty with which he accepted the prize and his generosity of spirit in his comments seemed genuine enough. It was typical of a player whose only real passion was football played at its best, a man without any conscious obsession with fame or its associated razzmatazz. But it was also Messi's sign of respect towards FC Barcelona, a way of playing football that owed much to the Cruyff legacy.

As the Barcelona-based journalist Graham Hunter puts it in his tribute to Cruyff: 'Without him [Cruyff], there would be no Pep Guardiola, no Leo Messi, no Xavi and no Andrés Iniesta. They would have been judged to be too slow, too small – table footballers. The genius from Amsterdam created the conditions which allowed these incredible players to be recognized and to become central to FC Barcelona's values. Without Cruyff, this story simply wouldn't exist.'[1]

Messi had no wish to dispute this judgement. On the plane back to Barcelona after the awards ceremony, the Barça contingent who had travelled together were treated to a celebration courtesy of the club. Bottles of cava – Catalonia's answer to French champagne – were distributed in generous quantities. Surrounded by his Barça teammates, Messi – his gala jacket discarded, his bow tie hanging loosely round his neck like a sixth-former celebrating the end of the school year, turned and rose from his seat. He lifted his glass, and with an expression of genuine gratitude – less the complicit expression of the street kid than the thanks a boy gives to his elders for a helpful lesson – once again dedicated his prize to Iniesta and Xavi.

Del Bosque, not a man known to bear a grudge in public, would share his disappointment with me during a conversation we had in September 2016, after he had retired as national coach and felt it easier to unburden himself of certain issues that had nagged him.

'Although we won the World Cup, no one on our side won the Ballon d'Or. And it wasn't because Iniesta and Xavi didn't deserve it but because they were competing against two huge monsters of the game – Messi and Ronaldo – who took turns to win it . . . But we won the World Cup after Barça won the Champions League. Iniesta and Xavi accompanied their individual success with a collective success . . . the logic would have been that they should have got the prize.'

Messi was indeed a 'monster'. He had scored a remarkable sixty goals for club and country in 2010. He was the most voted-for on the night, as well as the first player to come first in a World Cup year without having won the tournament since 1994, when Hristo Stoichkov became the first Bulgarian national to win the award. Mourinho's speech when winning a coach of the year award couldn't help sounding hollow in comparison.

'I was lucky too, to come to Real Madrid and find another group of fantastic players with which to round off a year that was packed with incredible victories,' Mourinho said on picking up the prize, a reference to that run of wins in the early weeks of the La Liga season after his Champions League victory with Inter. No mention of the drubbing at the Nou Camp, of course.

He skilfully sidestepped being drawn into a public comment on Messi's Ballon d'Or – his second in a row – or addressing the question of whether he was the best player in the world, given that Ronaldo, who had won the prize two years before, was now his responsibility. Mourinho did call Messi a 'fantastic player', who had won a prize and thus deserved his congratulation. But he came pretty close to being a party-pooper by lamenting the absence from the ceremony of Cristiano Ronaldo. 'It's a shame for Cristiano [Ronaldo], because both in terms of his playing ability and his performances he definitely ought to be among the candidates.'

A blushing Messi, aged twenty-three, looking somewhat trussed up in his gala suit and bow tie, struggled as best he could with the occasion, and found the only additional words that came naturally to him, paying a brief but emotional tribute to his family. 'They were always present when I needed them and sometimes felt even stronger emotions than me.'

Then he added: 'It won't be easy to [repeat] after a year like the one we just went through. I hope the next one will reach the same standards. But to win the Ballon d'Or two years in a row is not an easy thing.'

It seemed he had, unwittingly perhaps, thrown down his own gauntlet, and only Ronaldo was capable of picking it up.

In the spring of 2011, Real Madrid and FC Barcelona prepared to play each other in a run of four games in just over a fortnight – on 16 April in La Liga, on 20 April in the Copa del Rey final, and on 27 April and 3 May in the Champions League semi-final.

Any Clásico is among the most hyped-up sporting events on the planet – the biggest clubs with the biggest stars battling it out with the weight of history and politics on their shoulders. But this was not one battle, it was more like an all-out Spanish Civil War fought over a concentrated period – Madrid, Jarama, Belchite and Ebro all rolled into one.

Only in the middle of the Great War, in 1916, when Spain was neutral and football carried on as usual on its territory while millions died fighting north of the Pyrenees, had the two teams played each other over four games in such a short period. But in 1916, while each team boasted some legendary players, such as Real Madrid's Santiago

Bernabéu and FC Barcelona's Paulino Alcántara, and Barça fans blamed biased refereeing for defeat in the defining game, just a few hundred fans watched the encounters in a rivalry that had years to go before taking on an epic dimension.

Into a new millennium, the unprecedented schedule of four Clásicos over a period of just over two weeks opened up the mouth-watering prospect of a veritable global treat, courtesy of satellite TV, for millions of Messi/Ronaldo aficionados; an extended festival of football played at its highest and most competitive level, each game with more at stake than the last.

Since defeating Madrid 5–0 on 23 November 2010, FC Barcelona had remained unbeaten and were destined to lose only one La Liga match on the way to their third consecutive title. Thus the first game had less potential drama. The second, the Copa del Rey final, was a big but secondary tournament, less rated by Catalan republican nationalists than unionist Madrileños. The last two games were the ones that promised to be most fought over, for the ultimate prize in club football, a place in the European Cup final and a shot at its crown.

Nevertheless, the first was expected to set the tone for the rest.

One excited British sports journalist, Oliver Brown of the *Telegraph*, savoured the occasion, saying that although four portions of any one fixture so close together would normally be more than enough, 'every purist is a glutton where these two clubs are concerned.'[2] The only complaint anyone had was that they weren't meeting in a European Cup final.

On the eve of the first of the four encounters, Mourinho already stood accused of a total lack of respect by the media for refusing to speak to them at a pre-match conference. But you could argue there was as much caution as arrogance in his stance, in contrast to the nobility and self-assurance of Pep Guardiola's pre-match comments praising the Real Madrid team. My own recollection of the match went as follows:

> The second La Liga encounter of the season at the Bernabéu is not short of atmosphere at its outset, with close to 85,000 fans in the stadium roused by a soaring rendition of Puccini's 'Nessun Dorma'. It is an apt choice of anthem, for the start of a sequence

of games that will hold the attention of a large swathe of the world's football audience. Illuminated to a point of surrealism by massive floodlights, the players blink. A majority of the fans are waving white flags, with 2,000 hardcore Madridistas leading with their tribal chants. Boos for Barça as soon as they are on the ball.

Any doubts that Messi and Ronaldo are considered the danger men by either side and that this is a grudge match, even of the highest order, are dispelled soon after the opening whistle, with each player tackled unceremoniously within minutes of each other. Messi first as he picks up a ball on the left touchline, then Ronaldo as he tries to dribble forward, also on the left. As Ronaldo falls, Mourinho looks animated and holds up two fingers to the referee, claiming a card which is not given.

Ronaldo is the key to Mourinho's counter-attacks and when Özil is later brought on for Benzema he becomes Real Madrid's centre-forward. From the outset he is looking keen to sweep into the Barça area and is the first to fashion a shot of any value. The opportunity comes with a free kick at thirty yards. Pepe ducks and opens up a gap in the wall but the shot finds Victor Valdés's midriff.

Two minutes later Messi has dropped deep to look, with no less sense of hunger or responsibility, for the ball. He has been tasked with carrying the main Barça threat to Real. He picks up the ball and runs with it towards the penalty box but his pass to Iniesta is cut out by Pepe. Then Ronaldo combines with Di María and Benzema, but his curling outside of the foot pass to Khedira is just blocked by Puyol on the side of the penalty box.

Whistles break out around the Bernabéu stadium as Barça, with Messi, Iniesta, and Xavi at the heart of the rondo, keep the ball and play with it, in a sequence of fifteen passes. The protest from the home crowd seems aimed as much at Barça's grandstanding as Real Madrid's apparent refusal to break out of its defence and go for it. The Bernabéu evidently has yet to absorb the meaning of Mourinho, and want to see more of Ronaldo, attacking, scoring goals.

On nineteen minutes it is Barça that gets its first real chance of the game when Messi, just onside, connects with Iniesta's chip over the top and brings the ball down just before the right-hand touchline. As Casillas advances he chooses not to take the simplest option but to show he can beat the captain of the World Cup winning side. On this occasion, he doesn't. His attempted lob ends in Casillas' hands.

During a first half of missed chances, Ronaldo rises high to meet a loose ball but powers a header over the bar from the near post. He ruffles Piqué on the edge of the box, but gets no further, and is successfully tackled by Alves when he is just about to pull the trigger.

Real Madrid defend very deep and effectively while Guardiola's boys dominate possession, shifting laterally across the midfield, with Messi showing off his magical trickery with two neat one-twos – one with Iniesta, the other with David Villa – teeing him up to test Casillas. But it's goalless at half-time.

The second half starts without incident but not for long. Ronaldo wins a free kick five yards outside the D. His shot flies up and over the wall and easily beats Valdés, but then veers off after hitting the base of the keeper's right-hand post.

Then, with Mourinho's team resorting to some roughhouse tactics to contain Barcelona, Messi is gifted the first goal of the match. A penalty and red card is awarded after Villa has drifted goal side and is pushed down by Albiol. With trademark accuracy, Messi lofts the ball beyond Casillas to bring him one goal away from a record-breaking half-century of goals for the season – a Spanish record, going past the tallies of Ferenc Puskás, the Brazilian Ronaldo, and Messi himself in the previous campaign.

In the second half Mourinho, playing with ten men, is facing a second consecutive home defeat by Barça after lasting nine years without one. Eight minutes from time, Real Madrid's Marcelo tumbles to earth after tussling with fellow Brazilian Dani Alves and a second penalty is awarded. Ronaldo takes it and scores with the same precision as Messi earlier, easily putting it past Valdés. On replays, the penalty decision looks harsh, with Marcelo going down too easily. It provokes outrage from Barça fans, but Ronaldo had taken it in his stride, as if the two idols had agreed to share the first blood. It raises the tempo of the game in the final minutes, end-to-end, edge-of-the-seat stuff.

Within a minute of Ronaldo's penalty, Messi picks up on a

wonderfully angled pass from Xavi and charges into the box, only to have his run smothered by Casillas. Then it's Ronaldo who gets involved in a flowing exchange of passes with Özil before his final one is brilliantly intercepted in front of goal by Iniesta. Almost on full-time, Messi nearly assists a second goal but his angled pass to Maxwell, who is in space to the left of the area, is cut out.

Then in added time, the fouls pile up. Messi shows his frustration, kicking the ball into the stand. It is a rare act of petulance by a player not known for theatrics. Seconds later, on 94 minutes, it's almost game up. The last move is Barça's but Xavi's long ball is too much even for Messi and the Argentine miscues.

That night I go to bed with two competing chants ringing in my ear – one 'Así, Así gana el Madrid', the other 'Madrid, Madrid, Madrid'.

From a radical Barça perspective, FC Barcelona had been robbed of victory at the Bernabéu by two failed referee decisions: his refusal to give a penalty when Villa was taken down early on in the match, and his willingness to give one to Ronaldo when Marcelo dived.

From a radical Madridista perspective, the penalty scored by Ronaldo was not only justified (if unfairly lacking a red card), but just recompense after a series of lightning counter-attacks that failed to find the net through sheer bad luck.

Well, as I blogged at the time, I found it a pretty even match, whatever the statistics might have suggested. Barça had most of the possession but only rarely created threatening opportunities out of their neat passing in crowded spaces. Real Madrid were a much better team than the one that had played earlier on in the season at the Nou Camp – tighter in defence, and more threatening on the counterattack. They also gained value from Mourinho's perfectly timed substitutions, Özil and the on-loan Emmanuel Adebayor, who helped him salvage points and pride from the game, as did Ronaldo.

'Eleven against ten and it was practically mission impossible,' said Mourinho. 'Especially against a team that – with possession of the ball – are the best in the world. We drew and nearly won but, with the circumstances of the game, it's a draw you have to be happy with.'

Barça's Pep Guardiola said: 'We should have attacked Casillas's goal more when it was 1-0, but it's natural to sit back some when you're in the lead.'[3]

Johan Cruyff said: 'This game confirmed that José Mourinho is a negative coach. He only cares about the result and doesn't care much for good football. His decision to play seven defenders and three attackers was kind of extreme. It was also remarkable to see that Barcelona played with eight players who had come up through the ranks of the club's youth academy, while Madrid fielded only one youth-academy product. The different football philosophies of both clubs were very clear to see.'[4] Ouch.

These are the further observations I wrote in my notebook: Messi showed himself a more complete player than Ronaldo, but Barça remained in desperate need of strikers who could score; Pep's decision to bring out the injury-prone veteran Puyol smacked of a tactical human sacrifice – noble but suicidal; Valdés and Casillas were great keepers who saved their teams; Piqué shouldn't lose his cool so much now that he has Shakira; the result left things wide open for the following Clásico match, although part of me suspected that Mourinho now had the psychological edge.

Four days later the two teams faced each other again, this time in the Copa del Rey final. The stands of Valencia's Mestalla stadium rise up sharply, bowl-like, containing and accentuating sound. It is a pulsating atmosphere.

Although a popular neutral venue for Copa del Rey finals, as well as the Spanish internationals which the Nou Camp has never hosted for political reasons, it is the first time the Mestalla has had a Messi–Ronaldo encounter. The presence of the stars ensures that its packed stands vibrate with cultural and political bias as well as tribal football allegiance. It also ensures an estimated global TV audience of 500 million in 140 countries.

The presence of the King of Spain, Juan Carlos, divides the stadium between royalists and republicans, unionist Spaniards and pro-independence Catalans, who cheer and whistle in equal measure when the Spanish national anthem blasts out through the loudspeakers. It has no words, because a majority of Spaniards have never agreed on any, but the Real Madrid fans accompany it anyway, with a boisterous 'Lo Lo Lo' and 'Viva España'.

Mourinho seemed up for the occasion, knowing from his time

with Bobby Robson that the King's Cup, like the Generalissimo's before it, had always meant more to Real Madrid than FC Barcelona. He had also learnt that Barça was the most political of the two clubs and possibly of any club in the world – and that could be a handicap if you had an opponent that just wanted to play football and win at all costs. In that sense, Mourinho and Real Madrid were made for each other.

That day, Mourinho showed he could be a tactician as well as a psychologist by starting with a strong three-man midfield shield of Pepe, Khedira and Xabi Alonso, and by restoring Özil to ensure a strong offensive edge to a team led by Ronaldo, playing up front with Di María.

As they pressed forward, Los Blancos gave Barça's dangerman Messi, together with Iniesta, Xavi and Villa, little breathing space. As soon as Messi tried to receive the ball, two Real Madrid players would be on top of him to dispossess him by fair or foul means. The tactics made Guardiola's Barça's usually fluid midfield and attack look constipated. At no point in the first half did Messi come anywhere near to scoring his fiftieth of the season, but it was a different story for the other goal-machine on the pitch – Ronaldo. The Portuguese, who had scored his forty-first of the season with his penalty against Barça the previous Saturday, had three chances to make it forty-two in the opening half.

It was Ronaldo who came close to giving his side a lead after twelve minutes, when he beat Barça's second-choice goalkeeper Pinto from close range and a tight angle, only to have Javier Mascherano clear the ball off the line. His second missed chance was when he failed by inches to get a connection on Özil's dinked ball from six yards out. His third came when Özil again provided him with an inspired assist, sending him clear on the right, only to have his shot at goal deflected with one hand by Pinto.

Guardiola tried to rally his troops and Barça began the second half on the front foot, stepping up a gear, with Messi blasting an early shot at goal over the bar. On sixty-eight minutes he nearly scored after brilliantly dribbling his way through three defenders, but this was not destined to be Messi's day. His pass to Villa was converted, only for the Spanish international to be ruled offside. Iker Casillas then denied a fine shot of Messi's own. Madrid weathered the final Barça storm and at ninety minutes the score remained level and goalless.

In the first period of extra time, Barça as a team regained possession of the ball, but it was Ronaldo as an individual who shone on his own terms by racing clear down the right flank and charging into the area, before flashing his low, angled shot just wide of the target.

Five minutes later Ronaldo scored what turned out to be the winning goal of the match, rising imperiously to power home a header at the far post. He remained energized enough to attempt another goal two minutes from the final whistle, although this time he was a victim of his own selfishness, holding on to the ball for too long and seeing his shot blocked when a pass might have proved more productive.

But it was his goal that mattered. It ensured a famous win for Mourinho's Real Madrid, the first time they had won the cup since 1993, ending a spell of almost three years without a trophy. It also drove a wedge into the hitherto seemingly invincible armoury of Pep Guardiola's Barça.

Five months is evidently a long time in Spanish football. Those of us who had watched FC Barcelona's 5–0 victory over Real Madrid the previous November could have been forgiven for wondering at the Mestalla whether it had all been an illusion.

Barça, in the first half of the King's Cup, had put on one of their worst exhibitions under Pep Guardiola's governance. Messi was eclipsed, in shadow. And without him, his was a team that seemed to have lost the will to play, let alone win. They seemed to have no rhythm or strategy, while their vision and energy resembled that of a group of individuals suffering from bad hangovers.

Mourinho's men, led by Ronaldo, had done as they were instructed – playing rough and tough, they defended and disrupted and occasionally counter-attacked with lightning speed in a way that showed up, by comparison, the woeful shortcomings of their opponents when it came to scoring options. An uneven duel for a Clásico, but one that nonetheless enhanced Ronaldo's reputation without denting Messi's, who was judged simply to have had an off-day.

Some images will endure from this lacklustre final. The squabbling that broke out at one point between Barça's front three – Pedro, Messi and Villa; the ruthlessness of Pepe all over the pitch – Mourinho's special emissary; the way that the Barça fans failed to rally round their team after Real Madrid scored their goal; and the contrast between the whistling of the national anthem by the more fanatical Catalanistas and the extended embrace that Casillas and King Juan Carlos gave each other just before the Spanish international raised his first major trophy since the World Cup. This was a night when FC Barcelona showed rather less nobility than it could have done, on or off the pitch, as if it had been infected by a Mourinho bug.

The third Clásico of that legendary spring series, the first leg of the Champions League semi-final, had the two sides facing each other before a crowd of 78,000 at the Bernabéu on 27 April 2011. One banner, unfurled as Cristiano Ronaldo lined up with his teammates, summed up what the home fans expected from their idols: 'We Live for You – So Win For Us', it proclaimed.

Mourinho picked up the thread of the series, deploying similar tactics aimed at disrupting Messi and Barça's flow of play, and having Ronaldo as his key man up front. But his attempt to impose his narrative proved a double-edged sword. Much nobility went by the wayside in a tempestuous game that had Mourinho's enforcer Pepe red-carded in the sixty-first minute for a reckless high tackle on Alves, and the coach himself sent to the stands for sarcastically mouthing 'well done' to the fourth official in protest.

Tension between the sides translated into a half-time fracas on the touchline, which saw Pinto, the substitute Barça goalkeeper, red-carded, and subsequent skirmishes in the tunnel, none of which involved Messi or Ronaldo. In a graceless and ungenerous post-match statement, Mourinho asked rhetorically why it was that Barcelona always received favourable refereeing decisions against his teams. The '¿por qué?' or 'why?' would come back to haunt him, as Barça fans later picked it up as one of their favourite taunting chants against the coach.

For all the melodramatics off the field, there was still room for magic on it, with Messi recovering some of his normal rhythm and effectiveness and scoring a winning brace in the final quarter of the game. 'Two moments of beauty stood out amidst the beastliness of the Game of Shame,' the journalist Henry Winter wrote later.[5] Everything was at stake when Messi, operating like a busy bee around the fringes of Madrid's final third, dealt a huge blow with a goal after seventy-six minutes, skilfully breaching the defence and effortlessly turning in Ibrahim Afellay's cross at the near post.

The second was the kind that defined Messi's genius on the ball. It had the elements of trickery and skill of the streetwise Argentine *pibe* – call him Diego or Leo. Picking up the ball inside Real Madrid's half, Messi dribbled thirty yards, skipping past Lassana Diarra, Raúl Albiol and Marcelo, before slotting the ball past Casillas. It was his fifty-second of the season and what could prove to be the decisive goal of the tie. The context and circumstances considered, it was one of the biggest goals in Champions League history.

'That wasn't a dribble, that was an odyssey,' commented the *Telegraph*'s Henry Winter from the press box.[6]

Mourinho's tactics of sitting back and trying to frustrate not only angered Messi but also provoked the first row between Ronaldo and his coach, as if the two consecrated Gods of Football felt threatened by its Antichrist. From early on in the game, Ronaldo could be seen gesticulating to his virtually non-existent supply line of Mesut Özil, Xabi Alonso and Ángel Di María to push forward and play the ball to him more, rather than focusing so much on their defensive duties.

When Real did finally test Victor Valdés, it involved Ronaldo dropping deep, picking up the ball and then venturing forward before launching a trademark long-range drive that the Barça keeper just managed to deflect. But for the length of the shot, it was Messi-like in its build-up, as if the players were not only chasing each other's goals, but mirroring each other's skills.

It was a humiliating defeat for Real Madrid, and a frustrating one for Cristiano Ronaldo, who felt his talent and image being squandered by Mourinho's tactics. Mourinho's negativity and abrasiveness was by now stirring deep resentment in fans, staff and senior executives in Barcelona. He was also provoking deep concern more widely within the Spanish Football Federation, and those responsible for Spain's national squad such as Vicente del Bosque, himself a loyal Real Madrid fan. For del Bosque he was threatening to cause division between Madrid and Barcelona in the national squad, for others he was simply turning Real Madrid into the most disliked team in La Liga, thus threatening its marketing appeal.

Ronaldo was so enraged that he openly criticized Mourinho in the dressing room for leaving him so isolated for much of the match, and blamed him for the fact that he hadn't managed one shot on target. Although he later defended Mourinho's tactics and blamed the referee when he met the media, he let slip he didn't like the way he was being used. He was dropped from the next match against Zaragoza. Ronaldo was furious, but the message went out to the team that Mourinho was not a manager who tolerated dressing-room rebellions, and player and coach soon made it up.

As for Messi, his star seemed firmly in a special place in the galaxy. If nothing else, we had Pep Guardiola's word for it. As he told the world media after the match: 'He has wonderful ability to take on players, and he's only twenty-three, and already the third highest top scorer at Barcelona! Third! At a hundred-year-old club! It's absolutely incredible. That's the beauty of our football and the way we play.' Messi had once again reminded fans around the world what football should be about.

By contrast, Mourinho faced a suspension. The Special One emerged less loved by traditional fans of Real Madrid, nine-times winner of the European Cup, and as a coach seemingly without virtue, behaving like a thug when dealing with a team that demanded respect, like Messi's Barça. The machine-gunned post-match allegations that scattered from Mourinho's mouth were not just the latest in an enduring campaign of assault on FC Barcelona's integrity; it was a rallying call for hooligans.

While in free flow in alleging his conspiracy, Mourinho seemed unable to produce any proof other than alluding to questionable circumstantial evidence obscured by subjectivity. Thus we were meant to believe that the German referee came to the Bernabéu with the deliberate intent of penalizing Real Madrid, that Pep Guardiola's pre-match talk was focused on telling his players to dive and protest and pick a fight at half-time, and that UEFA somehow wanted FC Barcelona in the Champions League final and not Real Madrid, because their players are sponsored by UNICEF and Qatar.

Whether what Mourinho said was true or not was not really the issue. He said what he said as a tactic to divert and destabilize. On and off the pitch, Mourinho was football's agent provocateur – he planted seeds of insidious rumour and incited his players to play rough, as a matter of style as well as tactic. He had been loved at Porto, at Chelsea and at Inter, and in his first months back in Spain had similarly won the admiration of a different brand of Madrid traditionalists. Mourinho personified aspects of their culture and that of Spanish national football of times past, when aggression on the pitch, so beloved in Franco's days and known as *La Furia* – the Fury – was the order of the day. That style continued to be admired by some political conservatives and traditionalists of the game, who saw *tiki-taka* as an effeminate diversion, La Roja a socialist perversion and Messi an Argentine mercenary who had sold himself to the cause of Catalan nationalism.

Spain had quickly returned to its divisive politics after the temporary euphoria surrounding the 2010 World Cup victory. It had taken Mourinho less than a season to stir up deep-seated rivalries between the country's two major clubs and to undermine the harmony of the World Cup-winning team, coached by the personable Vicente del Bosque and made up largely of Barça and Real Madrid players. Mourinho had provoked gang warfare among them.

Mourinho was a bad loser, and his arrogance denied him the ability to admit to his own shortcomings as a human being and tactician, as he refused to accept criticism even from his own star player. This contrasted with Guardiola's refusal to be provoked, and to see to it that his star player persevered through the distracting sideshows, to produce football played at its most creative. FC Barcelona's overwhelming possession of the ball for much of the game was a testimony to their patient endeavour as much as to the negativity implicit in Mourinho's fortification.

True, Messi's goals came after Real Madrid were down to ten men. But both goals were sublime moments, epitomizing between them Guardiola's real achievement at Barça – his faith that football at its best was Messi.

Still banned, Mourinho was not present in the Nou Camp on 3 May, when Ronaldo and Messi walked out with their teams to a boisterous reception from 90,000 fans. Torrential rain gave the start an air of foreboding, but as things turned out the match had none of the theatrics and bad blood of the previous encounter.

According to Diego Torres, a Spanish journalist with a well-informed inside track on the Real Madrid dressing room, Mourinho had given Ronaldo another dressing down in front of the other players prior to the match for complaining about tactics, while telling him that the formation was designed for him, to make him feel more comfortable, so he didn't have to run so much, just score goals.

Mourinho was forced to watch the match from his hotel room. Some Barça fans celebrated his exorcism from the Nou Camp but, as Henry Winter put it, 'he still haunted the occasion like Banquo's ghost,' springing a surprise by picking a more adventurous team than expected.[7] Real Madrid came out and played with a different formation, with Kaká and Higuaín in the starting line-up to support Ronaldo and give the team a more attacking edge. Ronaldo started with a spring in his step, moving menacingly forward from the midfield with Marcelo on his left, but he soon faded and had a disappointing night.

The slippery surface soon seemed to favour Barça's play. Messi constantly troubled Real Madrid with his lightning-quick anticipation and dribbles into the heart of the opponents' half, as ever combining well with Iniesta and Xavi. All three kept the ball moving with staggering accuracy and speed, provoking another round of '*Olé*' from the crowd. During a mesmerizing five minutes of intricate play, Messi led the main assault, twice forcing superb saves from Casillas, while dragging another effort off target. The score ended level, with goals by Pedro for Barça and Marcelo for Real Madrid. Ronaldo, as if prompted by Mourinho, later complained that a forty-seventh-minute effort from Gonzalo Higuaín was ruled out wrongly by the Belgian referee Frank De Bleeckere.

But the post-match stats told their own story. Messi suffered eleven fouls during the game, more fouls than any player in a single Champions League game during the season. Before this match, Messi had been fouled twenty times in eleven Champions League games. Real Madrid committed twenty-nine fouls, the most in a Champions League game that season. In their five meetings with Barcelona that season, Real had committed 112 fouls; an average of just over twenty-two a game. Cristiano Ronaldo failed to have a shot for the first time in a Champions League game since he joined Real. It was Messi, not Ronaldo, who was through to the Champions League final, Barça's third in six seasons. Those stats told their own story, yes, but not the whole story.

I watched the second leg of that Champions League semi-final tie in a bar in Móstoles, an ugly, sprawling satellite town south-west of

Madrid. A camera crew from Spanish TV had beaten me to it – and I could see why they had chosen this godforsaken neighbourhood, of all places, to find 'atmosphere'. They were accompanied by a technician with a digital invention that measured the 'level of passion', or at least the soundwaves recorded during each critical incident in the match.

The bar was a convivial lion's den. It was shared, in a rare stand-off, between an FC Barcelona fan club and a smaller contingent of Real Madrid followers, each occupying their own space and watching separate plasma TVs.

The 'atmosphere' was dominated by the chants of the majority Barça fans, defiant in the knowledge that this was a space they felt reasonably secure in. I sat in the Barça section, sharing beers, ham and cheese with a group of fans. My companion on the night was Carlos, an enduring Anglo-Spanish friend from childhood who split his tribal loyalties between Chelsea and Real Madrid.

The game, as it turned out, was one that in the main restored two of world football's greatest clubs to a stage where each was allowed to play to its strengths and a wealth of talent and skills translated into entertainment. Despite the modesty of the final scoreline, the game's key moments brought into sharp relief the central role of the team's respective icons. Messi, as with the first leg, once again seemed ahead of Cristiano Ronaldo in terms of his overall impact as an individual, but also weaving his talent as part of an extraordinary team of players, working in harmony, heading towards the final at Wembley.

Sure, there was one questionable referee decision – the disallowed Madrid goal after Piqué had been manhandled by Cristiano Ronaldo – but this match would be remembered for something other than loose fouls and easy diving.

There was some riveting bold and open attacking football by both sides – and missed chances. There were mighty duels between individual players. There was magic in some of the passing and running with the ball. There were some spectacular saves by Casillas in particular – a Móstoles kid – and two good goals, one by each side. This was a Real Madrid that was unshackled and a Barça that had rediscovered its harmony. It was interesting how the Spanish TV cameras at one point focused on the veterans Jorge Valdano, Emilio Butragueño and Zinedine Zidane – the civilized ambassadors of Real Madrid –

watching the game. No gesticulation or badmouthing there, just respect.

This was a game where artistry shone through the mud, when it was hard to tell whether the players' shirts were soaked with sweat or rain, such was the commitment shown by both sides. The sight of players slipping and sliding through the water and still managing to control the ball underlined their brilliance.

Madrid used everything they had in their armoury to try and stop the sublime little Argentine. None of Real Madrid's twenty-nine fouls were major, despite Messi being on the receiving end of eleven of them, his low level of gravity and nimble feet allowing him to suddenly switch direction or skip over the opponent.

For much of the match, Messi was at his elusive best, while also devastatingly present, even if the heroism and the nobility of this encounter found its maximum expression in the last two minutes, when the stadium rose as one to pay tribute to Éric Abidal as he took to the field, just months after being diagnosed with cancer and just days after being given the all-clear to play.

For the first time in that season, a Clásico finished with eleven players in both teams, but the joy unconfined belonged exclusively to FC Barcelona at the final whistle, as Xavi led Messi and the rest of the team to the centre circle to celebrate, with Messi evidently overjoyed.

Barça went on to face Manchester United at Wembley, a repeat encounter of the final in Rome two years earlier, and won the trophy again, along with that third consecutive La Liga title. Of all the chants resounding round the Barça section of Wembley, few proved as popular as '¿Por qué, por qué, por qué?'

Why do Barça win, was the question Mourinho had asked, insinuating – as only he would – that the answer lay in diving and deranged referees. Well, Mourinho had to eat his hat that day. The answer, as Alex Ferguson recognized, was blowing in the sweet air of a team's collective genius, which made an opponent of the quality of Manchester United struggle to keep in the game for much of the match. Ferguson described Barça as the best team he had ever played against, and Messi as the best player in the world.

I can't remember a match in which my natural instinct as a fan to jump and chant struggled with the wish to follow every detail of Barça's performance, such was the mesmerizing impact of the players' movement around the pitch once Pep Guardiola's team got into its stride. They won 3–1, with Messi scoring the decisive goal.

Until then, I couldn't remember a match in which Messi celebrated a goal with such frenzied abandon, almost Maradona-like. And one couldn't blame him for that. History reawakened basic patriotic as well as club instincts. This was the site of Rattín's humiliating red card before Argentina's defeat by England in the 1966 World Cup. And this was the site where Barça won their first ever European Cup in 1992.

But in the new Wembley, Messi not only conquered history, but also made a bold statement about a style of football that had already marked an era in the twenty-first century – to that extent he personified a collective achievement.

A season which began with so much promise for Ronaldo and Madrid ended with them finishing four points behind Barcelona, one more than the previous season, and going out to them in the Champions League. That they stopped them doing the treble by winning the Copa del Rey was scant consolation to anyone. Likewise, Ronaldo's personal success in scoring sixty goals in all competitions vs Messi's fifty-three wasn't fooling anyone – it was clear to all who had triumphed that season.

Victory at Wembley was arguably the culmination of a process that was set in motion by Cruyff, and finessed by Guardiola during one of the most bruising seasons in Spanish club football. One dream team had metamorphosed into another.

Mourinho was left to brood on his touchline bans and the media love-in for Barcelona, and plot some way of stopping the unstoppable Messi and his club.

30. MOURINHO STRIKES BACK

For those who hoped that the new season would be a relief from the animus between Barcelona and Real Madrid, things began in an ignominious fashion. Before the summer of 2011 was out, the second leg of the Super Cup encounter between Real Madrid and Barça at the Nou Camp ended in a nasty brawl, as – with Barcelona leading 3–2 on the night and 5–4 on aggregate – Marcelo was sent off for a wild tackle on Fàbregas, who was making his debut after being re-signed from Arsenal. Meanwhile Mourinho was caught on camera reaching through the melee and hooking his finger into the eye of Guardiola's friend and assistant, Tito Vilanova. Not for the first time, the enmity between the two sets of players threatened to overshadow the football played. Across both legs there had been plenty to celebrate, as Ronaldo fizzed with energy and purpose, scoring his hundredth Real Madrid goal. However, he was yet again trumped by Messi's goals and assists, which always made Barcelona the more likely team to win the day.

Yet Mourinho continued not only to be tolerated but ever more supported by the Madrid president Florentino Pérez. When Jorge Valdano had been unceremoniously paid off for the final two years of his contract in May, José Mourinho was made 'head of football operations' as well as head coach, which was a massive strengthening of his power base. In some quarters this was viewed with alarm, as a rejection of the dignified, Real Madrid way of doing things, suggestive of a Faustian pact to win at any cost, but most Real Madrid fans greeted the news with a gleeful shrug, because his psychological tactics were showing themselves to be only one small part of the team he had built up.

Easy as it was for Barça fans and the Barcelona media to caricature Mourinho as a hooligan, there was no doubting that Real Madrid began the new season much better than they had the previous one, and were playing with style, cohesion and a real hunger for goals. They had brought in Nuri Şahin, Hamit Altintop and Fábio Coentrão.

Their League season began with a 6–0 away win over Real Zaragoza, which included a hat-trick from Ronaldo. Although they had a mini blip, losing to lowly Levante and drawing with Racing de Santander in their next two games, they went on a run of ten straight victories in the lead-up to the first Clásico, with Ronaldo scoring fourteen goals, including three hat-tricks. Barcelona, on the other hand, had already dropped eleven points by the time they met, with costly draws against Valencia, Sevilla and Athletic Bilbao. In spite of this, Messi was still in sparkling form, scoring seventeen goals in fifteen games, also including three hat-tricks. So ludicrous had the levels of performance that these teams reached become that Barcelona's aggregate score of 49–4 over those fixtures left them looking dour and defensive, in the face of Madrid's 57–9 over the same period.

The only really important stat was that Real Madrid were three points clear at the top of the table with a game in hand, the early season momentum with them, and the story was that Mourinho was finally in the right place to properly land a blow on Barcelona. This, after all, was a man who kept a picture of himself celebrating his win over Barcelona hanging over his desk.

There had already been the sense that he'd got into Guardiola's head. Whether it was questioning Barcelona's relationship with UEFA, or UNICEF, or referees, it had eventually got through. Though Barcelona had ultimately triumphed in their Champions League showdown the season before, it had been noted that Guardiola lost his cool, referring to Mourinho as the 'f***ing chief' on live television in a furious interview. Bit by bit, the story went, Mourinho was dragging Guardiola out of his comfort zone and into the place where the Special One thrived. A word bandied about was that Barcelona looked 'frail'.

The counter story to this, of course, was that Barcelona's players were only human. They had operated at the peak of performance for two seasons, in an intensely physically and mentally demanding system. If there was a dip in their performances, it was only to be expected. Yet even with this dip, they were going into this first game very much in touching distance of Madrid. No need to panic.

Within twenty-one seconds, Madrid were ahead, as a sliced clearance from Valdés pinballed its way around various players, before Benzema looped the ball in. In pouring rain, Barcelona seemed to have forgotten how to play football, as they slipped and slid around the pitch, Valdés continually punching when he should have been catching. The whole team seemed infected with nerves and doubts. Suddenly the rumour that they had closed off Plaza de Cibeles, an area of Madrid where fans gathered to celebrate national team victories, in case of a Madrid win, didn't seem so outlandish.

However, half an hour in and Barcelona equalized, completely against the run of play. Messi drove through the centre of the pitch, Madrid players drawn to him as if to a magnet, before he released Alexis Sánchez, who drilled the ball into the net.

Now it was Madrid's turn to shrink from the ball and Barcelona whose touch and passing had suddenly returned. Eight minutes into the second half, and a massive deflection on a speculative Xavi shot saw Casillas wrong-footed and the net bulge.

Just after the hour, Ronaldo missed a clear chance when unmarked eight yards out, but his header went wide. Almost immediately, Barcelona went up the other end and scored from a Fàbregas header. Celebrations for Barcelona, heads in hands for Madrid. The rest of the game petered out with Madrid unable to force matters.

Real Madrid had had Barça where they wanted them, but two big misses from Ronaldo had let them off.

After this result, both teams then embarked on another sequence of phenomenal performances, as Barcelona dropped seven points in the next seventeen games. Real Madrid however dropped only six in the next eighteen.

As the autumn turned to winter in the 2011–12 season, Mourinho went relatively quiet all of a sudden, and adopted an air of civility that had been lacking just a month earlier, when he had become an easy target for his detractors. His relaxed mode reflected confidence in his young players and their ability to play good football without resorting to thuggery. He had also been asked by Pérez to try and win hearts and minds, rather than risk losing Real Madrid any friends it had ever had. Soon Mourinho was being judged by his results, not by his words. The chorusing of Mourinho's name by Real Madrid fans was unprecedented. No manager or coach in the club's history has secured such popularity.

By then the definitive main attraction in La Liga was the performance of its two rival stars, Messi and Cristiano Ronaldo, both of whom had begun to make a habit of breaking records, not least their own. Spanish sports journalist Santiago Segurola described the unfolding drama of world football over this period to me thus:

> FC Barcelona with Guardiola had won six titles with a team that captured the imagination of a global audience and with a quite spectacular player called Messi. So Real Madrid counter-attacks with a claim that not only is it the most successful club in Spanish football history, but it now has one of the best players in the world . . . so we have the battle ground set between Cristiano and Messi, players who have very different characteristics and yet some similarities – in football terms they are players that can define games, they are both goal scorers . . . In Cristiano's case you have a player who, properly managed, can fit in with Real Madrid's identity – a complete singlemindedness, and an extraordinary capacity to pillage the opponent. Cristiano inherits the mantle of Di Stéfano, a player who is irresistible in front of goal, who wants to win at all costs, and who refuses to be second best.[1]

The decades-old, see-sawing rivalry between the two clubs was increasingly being defined by the tit-for-tat record-breaking of their star players.

Watching the sheer volume and quality of their goals over this period is to wonder at just how their rivalry has driven them on to ever greater heights. You can trace it in the pattern of their goals: a brace by one sees a hat-trick by the other the following game, matched by another hat-trick by the other.

In the period between the two Clásicos, Messi scored twenty-three goals in seventeen games, Ronaldo twenty-four in eighteen. There were other players making extremely valuable contributions in both teams, but here was a parallel championship, narrowed to these two players.

By the time of the return Clásico in April, some damaging recent draws by Madrid had left the gap between them and Barcelona at only four points, the difference having been ten points just a few weeks before. Mourinho had won only one of ten previous Clásicos. If Barcelona won, as the Clásico form book suggested they would, then it would be only one point.

There was all to play for in the final Clásico of the season, with

Guardiola knowing that the Special One was not only laying siege to the football Camelot that the Catalan had nurtured and developed over three seasons, but was potentially about to breach its defences before pillaging and plundering the system and style of play that for a while had been the wonder of the world.

Guardiola had reminded Messi and the other players that they only had one option, which was to win. Lose or draw and Real Madrid, given the number of points that had opened up between them, would be League champions. Ronaldo sprinted around Busquets, winning a free kick, which led to a shot by Ángel Di María which went behind for a corner. Valdés made a mess of judging the flight of the corner; although he made a save, the ball bounced around the goal line and Khedira managed to poke the ball home. Barcelona were out of sorts. Xabi Alonso was expertly denying Messi the space he needed and Iniesta looked off the pace. They looked sluggish out wide and predictable in their passing through the centre. Even when they did get a sight on goal, they wasted the opportunity. Madrid, on the other hand, looked poised and potent, ready to spring forward whenever they won the ball back. In the second half, the two best chances fell to that season's youthful hope, Cristian Tello, but he miscued one and blasted the other over the bar. The pressure was building but Madrid were holding firm. Suddenly their patient passing seemed ill suited to the pressure of the clock. By contrast, Ronaldo was as energized with the ball at his feet as a greyhound chasing a hare.

Barcelona brought Alexis Sánchez on as a last roll of the dice with twenty minutes to go, and within two minutes he had equalized, bundling the ball over the line after Casillas had made two smart saves.

But whatever hope had been raised in the Nou Camp by Alexis Sánchez's goal was extinguished within three minutes, courtesy of Cristiano Ronaldo.

As the Nou Camp roared its support for the home team, Ronaldo took a pass from Mesut Özil and ran at an angle, coolly clipping the ball around the Barça goalkeeper for his forty-second goal of the season. As he ran to celebrate he motioned downwards with his palms and could be seen mouthing 'Calma' and then gesturing to himself. Whether it was mainly aimed at the Barcelona fans, himself or his teammates, the message was clear: on the biggest stage of all, it was business as usual this time. The Barcelona fans could be heard cursing him long into the night.

Less than a week later, in front of a clearly emotional phalanx of Barcelona players, Guardiola formerly announced that he would not be renewing his rolling one-year contract. After four years, the Guardiola era was over. He spoke of needing to rest and recharge, of it being 'his time'. And looking at him, it was hard to argue. The last two seasons, in their different ways, had taken their toll. He seemed physically diminished, at various points no longer untouchable, above the tit-for-tat of the grinding week on week of La Liga. After rapturous applause, Barça sporting director Andoni Zubizareta announced that Tito Vilanova would be taking his place.

Messi didn't attend the press conference. Instead he made a statement on Facebook, saying: 'Because of the emotions I feel I preferred not to be present at Pep's press conference and to stay away from the press because I know they will look for the pain on the players' faces. It is something I decided not to show.'

Real Madrid won their remaining games, delivering the League title to Real Madrid by nine points, and securing Mourinho's seventh League championship title in four countries. How the tables had turned since the humiliating 5–0 Clásico defeat that Mourinho's Real Madrid had suffered during his first season as manager in La Liga. They had won La Liga in record-breaking form. They achieved a record thirty-two wins, a record sixteen away wins, reached a record 100 points, and set a new goal record of 121, to finish with the highest-ever goal difference.

During the 2011–12 season, Ronaldo surpassed his previous goal-scoring feats to achieve a new personal best of sixty goals across all competitions, and became the first player in history to score against all other nineteen clubs in a single Spanish top-flight season.

And how different were Cristiano and Leo's moods as they went into summer. Under Mourinho's management, Ronaldo had found his compass, recovering the drive and motivation that had defined his best years at Manchester United. Ronaldo had been confirmed as the undisputed star of the team with a series of virtuoso performances, rising to the challenge week after week, showing off the athleticism, multiple skills, commitment and goal-scoring ability that had Madrid aficionados finally warming to him, not so much as a person, but as a player who knew how to sweat for the shirt and win. His and Mourinho's future seemed unified and pointing in one direction: up.

Ronaldo's only disappointment that season was that he was held responsible by Real Madrid fans for the elimination of his team in the semi-final of the Champions League, when his penalty against Bayern Munich was saved by Manuel Neuer. Even here, though, there was some relief that Messi had missed his penalty against Chelsea, sending Barcelona out of the Champions League. As Mourinho put it in the press conference after the game: 'The best footballers miss penalties the same way that the best tennis players don't always win their match points. Ronaldo missed a penalty just as Messi missed a decisive penalty. People act like they are Superman, but Superman is a film.'

Even in his moment of adversity, Ronaldo had Mourinho in his corner, fighting on his behalf; Messi, on the other hand, was contemplating a season ahead without the manager who had done as much as anyone to develop him as a player. Even still, it was clear Ronaldo was as focused on Messi as ever.

In an interview in May 2012, Ronaldo displayed a certain frustration at being asked about Messi, instead of being judged on his own terms.

'Sometimes it makes me tired . . . for him too because they compare us together all the time,' he told CNN World Sport. 'You cannot compare a Ferrari with a Porsche because it's a different engine. You cannot compare them . . . He does the best things for Barcelona, I do the best things for Madrid, so the number [of goals] . . . everyone says "it's incredible". For him and for me because we beat our own records, so it's amazing. I think we push each other sometimes in the competition, this is why the competition is so high. This is why Madrid and Barcelona are the best teams in the world because everyone pushes each other.'[2]

Messi, on the rare occasions he gave interviews, also tired of being asked about Ronaldo, but then he didn't really like being asked about anything. Unlike Ronaldo, he didn't need to press his case. He let the football do it for him.

'It's only the media, the press, who wants us to be at loggerheads but I've never fought with Cristiano,' Messi told the sports daily *Olé* later that summer, a period during which reports about their rivalry intensified.[3]

Messi also said there had never been 'any kind of quarrel or anything' with Ronaldo, whom he called 'a great player', while speaking in Frankfurt before a friendly between Argentina and Germany in August 2012.[4]

But while Messi has never let slip any particular irritation, and always insisted he has no quarrel with Ronaldo, he is viewed as a nemesis by the Portuguese star, as a permanent point of reference, in his view, all too often used to unfairly misjudge him. Ronaldo had stayed away from the FIFA Ballon d'Or ceremony for 2011, which many people read as a public sign that he resented his rival being considered better than him. No one thought he was going to stay away from the 2012 ceremony.

As Ronaldo left for the European Championships in Poland and Ukraine, he could be forgiven for thinking the pendulum was swinging as far in his favour as it ever had done.

International Break

31. EURO 2012: RONALDO

Ronaldo entered the championship in the form of his life. But Portugal's first opponents were Germany, a team that had got the better of them in tournament football before. In the end, a tight game where chances were at a premium was settled by a Gómez goal for Germany. Despite hitting the woodwork, Portugal were nullified and Ronaldo subdued.

In their next game against Denmark, Ronaldo missed a series of opportunities as Denmark came back from 2–0 down to draw. With three minutes of the game remaining, it was left to Silvestre Varela to win the game with a low strike after mishitting his first shot. Ronaldo played better than he had in the first game, causing problems throughout, but he didn't put his chances away when given the opportunity.

His profligacy in front of goal delighted the Danish fans, who repeatedly taunted him with chants of 'Messi, Messi'. After the game, Ronaldo angrily reacted when questioned by the press. 'Do you know what he [Messi] was doing this time last year?' he asked. 'He was going out of the Copa América in the quarter-finals.' As things panned out, he might have wished he'd phrased things differently.

In their final group game against the Netherlands, Ronaldo had a lot to do to convince people he was the best player in the Portugal team, never mind the world.

It looked as though things weren't going to plan in the first ten minutes, as the Netherlands moved the ball well and took the lead in the eleventh minute from a van der Vaart curler.

Five minutes later saw Ronaldo cutting in from the left and clipping the outside of the post with a low, curling effort. Another five minutes and he was aiming a bullet header down the throat of the Dutch keeper.

Five more minutes, and after a reverse pass from Pereira took out the Dutch back line, Ronaldo coolly clipped the ball past the keeper. Now it was as if he was everywhere, bursting into the centre of the field before stinging the goalkeeper's palms with a thirty-five-yard drive, leaping to plant a header just wide of the post. It was as if he had heard the criticism and decided to put things right in one game. As the Netherlands had to press forwards to chase a win by two clear goals, he found himself time and again with space to run at the creaking legs of the Dutch defence. In forty-five minutes, Ronaldo was hailed as having put in the best individual performance of the tournament so far. And there was still forty-five minutes of the match left. Although they only needed a draw to go through, Portugal scented blood.

The first twenty minutes of the second half were disjointed, as several heavy tackles went in and as the Netherlands gradually began to lose self-belief. Ronaldo set up a couple of chances with his trademark runs, including a miss in front of an open goal from Nani, but seemed to have reined in his energy from the end of the first half.

Then, in the seventy-fourth minute, van der Vaart lost the ball and Portugal broke forwards at pace, first Nani carrying the ball forwards, before swinging it across the pitch. Ronaldo controlled the ball, cut inside the Dutch full-back, van der Wiel, leaving him dumped on his backside, before hammering it into the bottom left corner. There was still time for Ronaldo to go for his hat-trick, but the ball came back off the far post. Two goals, questions answered: Portugal were into the next round.

In the quarter-final, a resolute Czech side were finally taken apart by a Ronaldo goal, as he hit the woodwork twice and peppered Petr Čech's palms throughout. And yet, he found himself once again up against Spain, the team that had come almost to assume the position of Messi's proxy in European football.

Though he tried his best over the course of 120 minutes, the game finished goalless. Portugal were much more effective than they had been in any previous recent games against Spain.

When it came to the penalties, it would later transpire that Ronaldo gave himself the final penalty, in what some saw as an attempt to hoover up the glory for himself. However, in the event, two missed penalties meant that Spain won, without Ronaldo getting to take one. He had to watch as Barcelona's Fàbregas tucked his away to put Spain through into yet another final. The fans who had been chanting 'Messi, Messi' to taunt him were left laughing long afterwards.

32. LIFE AFTER PEP AND WITH MOURINHO:

MESSI AND RONALDO

It was fair to say that no one quite knew what to expect from Barcelona as the new season began. Even in an era in which they defined themselves by finding solutions from within, still Tito Vilanova would in no way have been the bookies' favourite for the Barcelona job. Extremely well liked, Vilanova had come with Guardiola as they'd made their journey from managing the Barcelona reserves in the third tier all the way to the first team. He'd famously responded to Guardiola's question, 'Are we ready?', while he was deciding whether to take the job with Barcelona B with, 'You are.' Guardiola had dedicated his coach of the year award to him at the beginning of the year, in Catalan, after his friend had undergone an operation to remove a tumour. The man whom Thierry had once called 'Pep's twin brother' had the full approval of Guardiola and the club. The most high-profile new signing, Jordi Alba, had played in the Barcelona youth team before being released and making his career elsewhere, but was now returning to the fold. Vilanova also had the requisite antagonistic relationship with Mourinho who, after poking him in the eye the previous season had repeatedly referred to him as 'Pito Vilanova', changing his name to the Spanish slang for penis.

Real Madrid, on the other hand, were entering a period of what passed for stability in that neck of the woods. It was the beginning of Mourinho's third season. The signing of players Luka Modrić and Michael Essien for Nuri Şahin and Hamit Altintop felt like upgrades. Although the muttering over Ronaldo's penalty order choice continued, in Spain it was assumed that he would be back to business as usual.

Barcelona started as they'd left off the previous season, winning 5-1 against Real Sociedad. Madrid, on the other hand, seemed out of sorts, drawing 1-1 against Valencia at home. The Spanish Super Cup first leg was a pulsating affair in which, it was largely agreed, Barcelona played all the football, but Real Madrid scored two priceless away goals.

Barcelona were like a caricature of themselves at their dizzying, passing best. Iniesta seemed to be able to see round corners and to move his feet twice as fast as anyone else. Messi was running from deep, bursting past challenges and slipping passes all over the pitch, smuggling the ball past Real Madrid players who didn't quite seem to know where it was a lot of the time. However, it was Madrid that took the lead from Ronaldo's powerful header, their first attempt on goal. Pedro's impeccable finish from a lofted Mascherano pass made it 1–1. Then Iniesta's dancing feet won a penalty which Messi dispatched. 2–1 to Barça. When Xavi scored a third after good work again from Iniesta, it seemed as if Barcelona would be taking a comfortable lead into the second leg, but then Ángel Di María scored and with two away goals the balance swung back towards Madrid.

Madrid lost their next League fixture against lowly Getafe, so that when the return leg came around, there was already talk of a mini crisis. Without a win in three games, it was the worst start Mourinho had ever made to a season. He admitted that he had doubts about their mentality after losing the previous Sunday. Meanwhile, Barça sat serenely at the top of the table.

When the return leg started though, Barcelona were a mess. A simple ball over the top allowed Higuaín to score and equal the score on aggregate. Then another long ball from the back was flicked neatly over Piqué and his deflected shot beat Valdés. Suddenly Real were in the driving seat. Things got even worse when the Barcelona defender Adriano was sent off for tugging back Ronaldo when he was through on goal.

Barcelona were in tatters. As one match reporter remarked, we were used to seeing Real Madird do this to small teams, but not to Barcelona!

In the thirty-seventh minute, Messi tried to single-handedly drag his team back into the game when he scored a wonderful free kick into the top corner. The second half was cagey, as the game was so finely balanced. Madrid seemed happy to sit back and allow Barcelona the ball, who with ten men seemed unable to ever really trouble Madrid without running the risk of a counter-attack. Messi had the chance to win it in the ninety-second minute, but his shot was just wide. Real Madrid had won on away goals.

However Real Madrid's travails in the League didn't improve. After they lost 1–0 against Sevilla, Mourinho lamented the fact that he was only able to make three substitutions and said he wished he could have made seven. Their German play maker Mesut Özil, so influential in the previous season, was banished to train with the reserves. After only four matches, they were eight points behind Barcelona, who had made a perfect start to the season. The whole Madrid team seemed frail, conceding from free kicks, not fit enough in midfield, or creating enough chances. Ronaldo in particular seemed off the boil, muttering darkly about feeling 'sad' and suggesting that those at the club knew why. People suggested it was simply a ploy to get an enhanced contract.

The first Clásico of the season came early that season, on 7 October, and it received more attention than it normally would. A massive pro-Catalan independence gesture was planned: Barcelona fans would shout for independence on the seventeenth minute and fourteenth second of each half, to commemorate 1714, the date Catalonia lost many of its historic rights. Real Madrid had always been the old enemy, but suddenly the fact that Real meant Royal seemed to mean even more. Sandro Rosell, the club president, regularly went on record as being in favour of self-determination, saying, 'When Catalans decide their future, Barça will be at their sides.'[1]

If all the talk was dominated by events off the pitch, the game was a startling reminder of how explosive a fixture it could be, with the Nou Camp a cauldron of noise and the ground a sea of red and yellow – the Catalan colours. At the heart of it was an astonishing personal duel between Ronaldo and Messi.

The game began with half-chances for Madrid, until the ball was flicked in to Ronaldo in the box, who cut across the ball with brilliant disguise, sneaking it past the keeper at the near post. Then Messi sneaked in on a terribly miscued clearance by Pepe and slotted the ball home.

Just past the hour, Messi curled an extraordinary free kick over the wall and into the bottom corner, only for Ronaldo to beat the offside trap five minutes later and score to equalize. In a game in which so much felt at stake, the two players at the heart of it did what they always did. Scored goals. Between the two of them they had scored 100 club goals in 2012. At the age of twenty-five, Messi was one goal behind Alfredo Di Stéfano's Clásicos record.

For the first time, the sports paper *AS* gave its best player award jointly to them both. *MARCA* said: 'Just when you think they can't do anything more, they do. Every time.'

After the game, Mourinho took a break from complaining about bad decisions to say: 'Talking about who the best player in the world is should be banned because they're so good.'

Vilanova showed he was picking things up quickly by using it as an opportunity to land a glancing blow on Ronaldo, saying, 'Ronaldo would probably have had greater recognition if it had not been for Messi.'

In January 2012, it was Messi who was awarded his fourth Ballon d'Or. He looked more self-assured than on previous occasions, in a polka-dotted dinner jacket and matching bow tie, dedicating his prize to his childhood sweetheart and soon-to-be wife Antonella, and his young son. He was still a man of few words and a somewhat goofy expression, but no longer the introverted, disorientated child of the past. Success had matured him, even if he seemed not to have been spoilt by the fame that went with it.

He certainly seemed a planet away from the celebrity aura that surrounded the most carefully made-up and manicured couple present that evening – the tanned, gelled Ronaldo, in a silk double-breasted dinner jacket, accompanied by his model girlfriend Irina Shayk, who's on-off relationship with the player featured in news kiosk magazines.

Messi polled 41.60 per cent of the votes, with Ronaldo in second place taking 23.68.

As Messi's colleague Piqué summed it up, 'Cristiano Ronaldo is the best of the humans but Messi is an extraterrestrial.' Although he had missed out on both the La Liga and Champions League crowns, Messi had scored fifty goals in the League season and a record fourteen goals in the Champions League season, and had become the first player to net five times in a Champions League match. He had also gone some way to shattering the myth that he couldn't play as well for Argentina as he did for his club by scoring twelve goals for his country in nine games. By early December 2012 Messi had scored his eighty-sixth goal of the year, surpassing Gerd Müller's eighty-five goals for

Bayern Munich and West Germany in 1972, and claiming the record for most goals scored by a player in a calendar year. Unless there was a remarkable turnaround in the second half of the season, he was laying the groundwork for his fifth Ballon d'Or already.

They reached the halfway point in the season having scored fifty-five points from a possible fifty-seven with Messi scoring a barely believable twenty-nine goals from nineteen games. The only points Barcelona had dropped in the League were those two against Madrid in October.

Madrid, though, had continued to stutter, in spite of sixteen goals from Ronaldo, and found themselves fourteen points behind Barcelona.

On 20 December it had been announced that Vilanova had undergone another operation to remove a tumour, which would be followed by chemotherapy. In a twist of fate, Éric Abidal, who had been out since the previous year after a liver transplant following a cancerous tumour, played in training. His statement on Facebook said: 'I hope to come back soon on the fields, but I can't stop thinking of our coach, Tito Vilanova: I wish him and his family a lot of courage!'

Meanwhile, throughout the autumn and winter, Mourinho continued to blame his players for the team's poor form. In one bizarre episode in October, Sergio Ramos had put on Özil's shirt under his own after the German was substituted, in what people interpreted as a defiant gesture of solidarity with the player who Mourinho seemed to be blaming for the entire team's problems. There were rumours of a divide on the team bus between the Spanish and Portuguese players. Mourinho, the master of creating a siege mentality, seemed here to be the one stuck on the outside, his team inside the fort. People began to wonder if Ronaldo, playing for himself, was somehow a hindrance, a weakness that other teams could exploit.

And still someone – many were sure it was Mendes – was leaking stories that Ronaldo felt sad, that he didn't want to link his long-term future to Madrid until he had atoned for the poor start to the season. The super-rich Paris Saint-Germain were said to be waiting in the wings. With perfect timing, Messi quietly signed a contract extension that would keep him in Barcelona until 2018. Reports said Mourinho was said to have agreed to leave in the summer. The news broke that Guardiola would manage Bayern Munich next season.

At the end of January, Madrid and Barcelona were drawn against each other in the Copa del Rey semi-final.

The first leg felt like a retread of every recent Clásico, as Barcelona, in their trademark style, moved the ball about, working Madrid all over the pitch, whereas Madrid seemed content to try and break at pace. Barça eventually took the lead when Messi stabbed a poor clearance back through the lines and Fàbregas found himself onside and swept the ball underneath the goalkeeper. There were good chances for each side, before the teenage defender Raphaël Varane, making his Clásico debut for Real Madrid, headed down and powerfully into the net from a recycled corner. It seemed a game mercifully lacking in controversy until the Madrid winger, José Callejón, claimed to have heard Messi call the Madrid assistant coach, Aitor Karanka, 'Mourinho's Muppet' in front of his wife.

In between the two legs, Ronaldo had the little matter of a visit from Manchester United in the Champions League to contend with.

He scored from a hanging header but, more importantly, won huge plaudits for the intelligence of his performance, as his movement around the pitch pulled Man United out of shape, so desperate to contain him that they left his talented teammates with space. Though United had their away goal through a Welbeck effort, the game felt finely balanced, and all the talk was of Ronaldo finding his form at just the right point in the season. His comments that Real Madrid were a better team than Manchester United seemed realistic rather than disrespectful.

Barcelona, on the other hand, were dreadfully disappointing in their game against Milan as they lost 2–0. With Vilanova undergoing treatment for his cancer, it was left to his assistant Jordi Roura to take charge of the team. It was a night where nothing worked for Barcelona. They couldn't find space and get their passing rhythm up and going. Messi was as anonymous as he had ever been. It was clear that the team was feeling the effects of their manager's illness. As Roura spoke of his 'total confidence' that Barcelona would turn things around, it rang hollow. *AS* reported on the match, calling them '*pardillos*', naive country bumpkins, thinking that what they did in the League would work automatically in Europe.

Barcelona managed to pull a result out of the bag against Sevilla in the League three days later, with Messi finding the net, but next up was Madrid at the Nou Camp.

For Madrid, it marked the start of eight days, with games against Barcelona and Manchester United that would decide what Mourinho's legacy at Real would be. Though they had conceded the League months ago, knocking Barcelona out of the Copa del Rey and keeping on track for their tenth European Cup would go some way to making his time there an historic period of triumph, rather than up for debate.

In the end, Madrid swatted Barcelona aside in the second leg of the Copa del Rey, with Ronaldo scoring a goal early in each half, as Madrid won 3–1. Diego López, the Madrid keeper, made several routine saves, but in the end Real Madrid kept Barça at arm's length with something to spare. The Madridistas sang 'Goodbye to the Cup, Goodbye' long into the evening.

According to Sandro Rosell, Vilanova's cancer was the thing that none dared discuss publicly but which explained the downturn in Barça's fortunes, as personified in the unarticulated sadness Messi fell into for a while.

> All the players loved Tito, but particularly Messi . . . so it was personal and professional. It affected the team's motivation – they kept thinking how much he was suffering . . . I remember the day I went to the Barça ground, the Ciudad Deportiva, to explain to the players what was happening, that he was going to have treatment for cancer . . . It was difficult to play football, it was really a tough time for everyone. The thing was that it wasn't exteriorized and most of the media didn't know and those who did didn't know how or didn't want to explain it . . . It was good that it was kept inside the house, under wraps . . . I've always said that grieving is best done behind walls. It wasn't our way to make a big deal of it . . . The problem was that people looked for a reason why Barça were playing so badly and couldn't find one.[2]

For Messi, who had flourished under his replacement mentor after Guardiola had left, it had become increasingly hard to focus. Vilanova had been Messi's coach when the Argentine was in the Barça youth teams, and had then been assistant coach of the first team during the Guardiola years. He had learnt that Messi was the key to Barça's success, and that the best way to treat Messi was not to bark orders at him but to trust in his vision and dexterity with the ball. The mood swings and communication blocks that affected Messi now and then off the pitch were ones that the personable if low-key Vilanova had learnt to manage with patience and empathy.

In the second La Liga Clásico of the season, Mourinho made clear what his priorities were by starting Ronaldo, Higuaín, Khedira and Özil on the bench.

Messi started but was largely quiet, as it felt as if both teams were conserving their energies for the second leg of their European ties. Benzema converted at the far post with an early Madrid attack and that seemed to suck the life out of the game. Barcelona kept the ball but were largely toothless; Madrid were happy to let them have it. After a long passage of Barcelona possession, Messi beat Ramos with a change of direction and slotted the ball under the advancing goal-keeper. But still the game felt lacking in urgency. Messi was popping up all over the pitch with neat flicks and interplay but there was no penetration.

Ronaldo was brought on after an hour and transformed the game. He was all purposeful running, urgency and power. He drew fouls, got up to take the free kicks. The brief calm that had descended over Barcelona was punctured and it looked as if Madrid were the only team going to win. And they did when Sergio Ramos rose to thump in a header from a Modrić corner. The Barcelona players surrounded the referee to demand a penalty but it was not awarded.

Ronaldo had been efficient and clinical, changing the game; although he scored, Messi looked washed out, like someone doing an impression of the player in the first months of the season.

Real Madrid's game against Manchester United on 5 March 2013 was Ronaldo's first trip back to Old Trafford, a return that dominated the pre-match discussions. The first half flashed by, all half-chances and blood-and-thunder challenges. Madrid had a goal wrongly disallowed for offside, but United were doing well, containing Madrid, and could argue they had had the better chances. Five minutes in and Ramos scored an own goal, after Nani's dangerous cross was slid in. However, five minutes later he was sent off after a high challenge with a raised foot was judged to be a red card. Mourinho immediately took off the defender Arbeloa and brought on Modrić. Just over five minutes later, he had equalized with a stinging drive that went in off the post. Three minutes later, Ronaldo slid home a dangerous cross to give Madrid the lead. They played out the rest of the game and went through. There had been times in the past when Ronaldo had been obsessed with showing how he had moved on, and had ended up playing only for himself, but here he was calm, disciplined and decisive. He might not have dominated the game, but he played his part and had a big say in the result.

With Vilanova still not well enough to take his place in the dugout, and the form book against them, on 9 March Barcelona faced Milan in a Champions League match with many fearing the worst. Crisis, never far away, was said to be fully blown.

Messi's performance that day was one of those that legends are built on. Conditioned as we are by the archetypical Rocky narrative, the punch-drunk fighter up against the ropes, all hope fading until that moment when the fightback begins.

That moment came within five minutes when, after a period of neat passing interplay in between the Milan defence, he took the ball into the box and somehow scooped out from under his feet an unstoppable shot into the top corner. It had seemingly no backlift, like a hockey shot, curled from the wrist. His teammates enveloped him. Barcelona roared onto Milan, asphyxiating them, pressing them all over the pitch, winning the ball back and tearing into them, but always with the note of caution that a Milan goal would almost certainly swing things the other way entirely because of away goals. Hearts stopped when Milan's M'Baye Niang struck the post. But only two minutes later, Messi was played in by Iniesta and struck a low shot through Mexès's legs and past the keeper's despairing dive. As the half-time whistle went, pundits around the world wondered if Barcelona would play with more caution or double down in the second half.

The answer came quickly – Barcelona kept pouring forward, with Milan still sensing they had a chance on the break. First Villa curling in a peach of a left-foot strike and then, in the very last minute of the match, the left-back Jordi Alba found himself sprinting forwards into the box, controlling the pass from Alexis Sánchez and finishing neatly. There could be no more fitting tribute to the style of play that Guardiola and Vilanova had perfected and encouraged. Barcelona had done it and they had done it their way.

The remainder of the season didn't quite go as planned for either team, though Barcelona would drop only four more points in winning the League, ending on 100 points. Madrid limped home, fifteen points behind them. Barcelona beat Paris Saint-Germain over both legs on away goals, as Messi came on and revivified them, while Madrid went through 5–3 against Turkish side Galatasaray, despite losing 3–2 in the away leg. Ronaldo scored three of their five goals. They were kept apart in the semi-finals, where they both lost in the first leg to German opposition – Barcelona to Bayern 4–0, a shocking result as a clearly unfit Messi gamely ran around the pitch but couldn't shake off the effects of a hamstring injury. Madrid lost 4–1 to Borussia Dortmund. Madrid made a game of it in the second leg, winning 2–0, but Dortmund went through. However Barcelona were a shadow of their usual selves as they lost 3–0 in the second leg, 7–0 on aggregate. It was an awesome display by the German team that sent shockwaves through Europe and caused the Spanish press to write endless pieces about a global 'changing of the guard', describing Barcelona as needing 'every removal van in Barcelona to help with the clear-out'.

Real Madrid, for their part, lost in the final of the Copa del Rey to a resurgent Atlético Madrid team, with Ronaldo, Gabi and Mourinho all sent off in a fractious encounter.

Both teams finished the season in flux and with questions to be answered. Cristiano and Leo continued their own astonishing personal form, but there was the sense with both that, when it had come down to it, they had been let down, by their bodies, by their inability to focus. Perhaps it was foolish to expect two players to play perfectly always; after all, whatever others said, they were only human. The uncertainty over their managers had clearly had an impact on their concentration. Mourinho slunk away, muttering darkly, unable to dethrone Barcelona domestically for more than one season and, more tellingly, unable to deliver the tenth European Cup that Real Madrid demanded.

Both teams moved quickly in the transfer market, Barcelona securing the exciting Brazilian Neymar and Real Madrid gaining Gareth Bale, for a fee some claimed was higher than Cristiano Ronaldo's previous world record.

On 25 June, Real Madrid announced that Carlo Ancelotti had joined as manager.

Just under a month later, on 19 July, Barcelona announced the sad news that Tito Vilanova's cancer had returned and he would be stepping down from his role at Barcelona. As the staff and players sat in the press conference, Messi sat with his arms crossed, staring into space. He made a statement on Facebook: 'Strength Tito! We are all with you in this fight!' Tragically Tito would die in April 2014, and a visibly tearful Messi would attend the memorial service conducted by the Archbishop of Barcelona, with the entire first-team squad in attendance.

33. KING CRISTIANO: BLACK DOG MESSI

Jorge Valdano recalled the groups of excited Real Madrid fans walking with a spring in their step on their way to Gareth Bale's presentation at Real Madrid in 2013 with 'great smiles, as if they had won the lottery.'

He went on to note: 'But they hadn't won anything. They were going to the presentation of Gareth Bale, a player with not a huge record of achievement outside England and Wales until the eleven games played in the Champions League, without any relevant trophy, and having never played in a World Cup . . . The majority of those who walked by in procession had no idea a year earlier who this new planetary idol was. But in recent months Bale had not done anything but be the new player that was about to land in Madrid. With each media report, his price kept rising without him having to play a game. A summer inflation without any football underpinning which allows us to understand certain coordinates of the sport today, above all one: money rules.'[1]

And it was this expectation that clashed with the reality of what was to be a mildly tortuous integration into a Real Madrid squad. Bale, quiet and down to earth, was faced with the big characters and high profiles of Cristiano Ronaldo and the other Real Madrid players.

Indeed Bale's initial encounter with Ronaldo at Madrid's luxurious Valdebebas training ground showed him looking timid, almost awestruck, when welcomed by the man with the biggest social media following in the world and the looks and attitude to launch a thousand commercials.

Some people who had followed Bale's career closely feared that – despite his ability as a player – he might lack the mental strength to cope with such a big transfer and the immense spotlight that would be put on him in Spain.

In his first season there were some glaring examples of the lack of chemistry between him and Cristiano Ronaldo, as Real Madrid's latest coach Carlo Ancelotti tried to find a way of accommodating them both with his strategy for the team.

Ancelotti was a famously safe pair of hands. A quietly authoritative, cosmopolitan Italian, who had won championships with whichever clubs he had managed over a varied career. He had won a reputation as a pragmatist, able to find the system best suited to the players. After a summer of more expensive acquisitions, this was thought to be essential. Moreover he was well liked throughout the football world, and Real hoped that the often poisonous atmosphere that had developed towards the end of the Mourinho years might dissipate, as fans had booed the Portuguese several times before games.

Madrid were solid if unspectacular in La Liga, in the build-up to the first Clásico at the end of October 2013. Bale seemed to lack fitness, and though Ronaldo was still scoring with a regularity that most players would regard as the peak of their careers, there was something not quite on the boil.

In one incident that achieved a certain notoriety, Bale and Ronaldo were clearly not on the same page when deciding who was going to take a free kick during a game against Sevilla. As Guillem Balagué recalled it, the award of the free kick 'gave rise to one of those moments of subtle gestures and revelatory glances whose outcome affects the entire balance of the team.'

Both players had a proven record of turning dead balls into goals. On this occasion, Ronaldo set the ball down with the intention of taking the kick, only to have Bale come over and ask to take it himself. Ronaldo was evidently reluctant, but his appeals to Ancelotti to mediate from the bench went unheeded. The Welshman took it, much to the Portuguese's evident disgruntlement. Worse still was Ronaldo's visible reaction when Bale's strike failed to hit the back of the net and instead sailed over the bar.

The relationship between Ronaldo and Bale was just one of the many difficult man-management tasks facing Ancelotti in this team stuffed full of egos.

Meanwhile, at Barcelona, Gerardo 'Tata' Martino had taken over as the new coach in the third week of July 2013, with a keen sense of the enormous challenge he would face to recover some of the living poetry of the Guardiola years. In their search for a replacement for

Vilanova, Barcelona had spoken to former midfielder and B team coach Luis Enrique, but he had committed to Celta de Vigo for the coming season. They had also talked to Ernesto Valverde, but he had agreed to join Athletic Bilbao. Both would later end up as managers of Barça's first team.

As it was, Vilanova's decision to quit in late July 2013, when the new football season was about to start and most top coaches were settled in the jobs, with the bulk of the summer transfers signed and sealed, meant that Tata Martino had been brought in not as first or even second choice, but as a necessary emergency service. The club board had decided at an early stage, on humanitarian grounds, that Vilanova should be given all the moral and financial support possible, and that he should be allowed to continue in his post for as long as he felt he had the spirit and the strength to do so. Now Tata Martino was being trusted with the task of trying to free Messi from the black dog of depression.

Martino was someone Rosell knew from his days as a Nike executive in the 1990s, when he had developed close business ties in South America. He subsequently became more widely known in Spain when he managed a spirited and well-organized Paraguay side that nearly beat del Bosque's La Roja in the World Cup in 2010. But it was Rosario-born Martino's long association with Newell's Old Boys, Messi's childhood club, and his huge admiration and respect for someone he had a year earlier called 'the best player in the world' that proved a key factor in his appointment.

Personable, and with a reputation for good man-management of players, Martino was, like Pep Guardiola, an admirer of the eccentric but brilliant Rosario-born coach Marcelo Bielsa, under whom he served as a player for Newell's. But he was thought more pragmatic. He favoured tactics that had been popular at Barça since the Cruyff period and which had adapted themselves to Messi, to ensure that he played where he felt most comfortable and effective.

'Any coach that comes to Barça with Messi has to be clear that he can't introduce a system of play that isn't accountable to him as the leader, that gives him freedom on the pitch . . . We had to find someone who understood this way of playing, and Tata had that,' said Rosell.[2]

Martino was sold to the Barça media as someone who would

bring continuity as well as stability. But within months of his arrival, the club seemed beset by deepening problems, not all of his own making. In his first season, he also risked having several key players focused less on the club than on international duties.

A World Cup in Brazil lay ahead, which threatened to make or break their international reputations. The tournament in Brazil had Vicente del Bosque's Spanish squad – with several Barça players still key to its collective sense of identity – defending their world crown. Among the countries most determined to dethrone Spain were the South American powerhouses Argentina and Brazil, whose stars were both Barça players: the Brazilian Neymar, recently transferred from Santos, and, of course, Lionel Messi.

If Ronaldo and Messi were football's present, then Neymar perhaps represented the future. He was already a well-developed marketing machine by the time he arrived in Spain, and seemed at least as engaged as the Portuguese was with his own celebrity. He also had the on-field talent to back up the hype. The stats showed that on his arrival at FC Barcelona in June 2013, aged twenty-one, Neymar had scored 156 goals in 257 games for Santos and the Brazilian national squad, which was over 100 goals more than those scored by either Ronaldo or Messi at the same age.

Former Nike man Sandro Rosell, the Barça executive who had negotiated his controversial transfer from Santos, believed his marketing potential among a new generation of football fans was even bigger than Messi's or Ronaldo's. His arrival represented a leap into the future.

In fairness, Neymar remained a seemingly modest guy when it came to interviews. Asked by a Portuguese-speaking journalist on the eve of the World Cup how he rated himself, Neymar replied: 'It's an honour to be compared to the incomparable Pelé. The fact is that Pelé, Messi, Cristiano Ronaldo are players that defy comparisons. Right now, in my opinion, Messi is the best in the world.'

And yet he took time to settle down at the Nou Camp, where his habit in his first season there of interrupting play to change his brightly coloured, Nike-branded boots during matches annoyed fans. They suspected a marketing ploy and accused him of being narcissistic, like Ronaldo. In the midst of so much flux, Messi had now become not just the star but the effective captain of the team, a point of reference for all the players for their performance on the pitch, and the person to whom club executives turned to settle agreements over bonus payments, and even to consult over transfers.

As former president Joan Laporta recalled: 'Once we were flying back from a Champions League match in Paris, when some of the players, including the notional captain Carles Puyol, raised the issue of bonuses. I suggested a figure and Puyol went off to see Messi. He then came back and told me: "OK Presi, I've talked to Messi, and he says it's OK with him, what you're offering. If it's OK with him, it's OK with us" . . . I realized then, as if I had ever had any doubt, that Messi was in charge in the dressing room.'[3]

Yet this was a player who had no natural inclination to lead others. Whereas Maradona would take to the field, chest all pumped up and head raised, Messi had, over the years, developed a hangdog look. He stepped out on to the turf looking downwards, as if avoiding the glare of flashlights and any eye contact with spectators.

This also contrasted with Real Madrid, where the captaincy in recent years had passed from Raúl to Casillas to Sergio Ramos, all extroverted characters who knew how to raise their voices during a match as effortlessly as they did in the dressing room, the inner sanctum of every major football club. All three captains had managed to develop a compromise arrangement with Ronaldo, showing him respect and not ordering him around in return for his loyalty.

And yet, as those who worked closely with Messi agreed, his leadership was not conveyed in words, let alone speeches, but simply by example, on the pitch. Barça were happiest and at their best when Messi was happy and his best, but all bets were off when he was injured or he failed to find form. The team absorbed Messi's glow, just as it was thrown into turmoil by his darker moods, which came and went, usually beginning when he disappointed himself – for he was his own biggest critic, despite what the press might think.

He and Barcelona began the first few games of the season in good form, only dropping two points in their first nine games and topping the table. Messi scored eight goals but there was something not quite right. There were rumours of a recurring hamstring injury, of black moods and silences. His manager didn't seem outwardly worried: 'He set the bar so high that when he doesn't score it feels like it's a problem. But it's not a problem.' But still the statisticians said he was touching the ball fewer times, making fewer runs. Messi's father had only one word for the press: 'relax'.

The first Clásico of the season passed both Cristiano and Leo by, with both players involved but much less influential than they had been previously. Instead it was Neymar who took the headlines with his first Clásico goal, and a wonder strike from Alexis Sánchez gave Barcelona a 2–0 lead. Jesé pulled a goal back, but Barcelona took first blood, winning 2–1.

Only a few weeks later, the press were reporting that Messi was unhappy with the terms of his contract, after it had been announced that Ronaldo's new contract was reportedly worth 1 million euros more a year than Messi's. It was the first time that a story had shown Messi caring about that side of things, and it felt like a shift had occurred.

Both teams made light work of their Champions League fixtures but then as November turned into December, Barcelona lost 2–0 to Ajax and then 1–0 to Athletic Bilbao in quick succession. Messi was injured, believed back in Argentina, and towards the end of the Bilbao game, as Xavi and Iniesta were taken off, Gerard Piqué was pushed up front. It felt like a very public losing of their identity. Martino said he was willing to swap control for penetration. What they got was neither.

Bale seemed to be finally coming to life for Real Madrid whereas, without Messi, Barça struggled to keep a semblance of form. The announcement that Ronaldo had won the 2013 Ballon d'Or was greeted with very little dissent. (Apart from Franck Ribéry, who believed he deserved to win.) Ronaldo had found a whole new set of gears, whereas Messi had merely been excellent compared to every other player in the world.

Ronaldo's acceptance speech was that of someone professionally and privately happy with their life.

'First of all I have to say a great thanks to all of my teammates with the club and the national team,' he said. 'Without all of their efforts this would not have been possible. I am very happy, it is very difficult to win this award. Everybody that has been involved with me on a personal level I have to thank. My wife, my friends, my son. It is a tremendously emotional moment. All I can say is thank you to everybody that has been involved.'

A few weeks before, Messi had made a rare statement about Ronaldo, telling *MARCA*: 'He is always there scoring goals in all the games and taking part in his club and national side. He has been doing that for many years and whether he is at his peak or a bit below it makes no difference.'[4]

Between the teams' return from the winter break and the second Clásico in March, Barcelona dropped thirteen points, while Madrid dropped four. Messi scored two goals on his return in January, but wasn't fooling anybody. This season, the new challenge to both Real Madrid and Barcelona came from Atlético Madrid who, under the permanently combative Diego Simeone, continued to make great strides and were threatening to break the duopoly.

Atlético Madrid just kept on winning: 2014 saw them become what some wags called the third horse in a two-horse race.

Rumbling on in the background was the crisis surrounding Rosell's presidency that the investigation into Neymar's transfer had caused, and which ultimately would result in his resignation, after it was revealed that the announced transfer fee was much smaller than the actual payments that had gone to various parties.

Prior to the Clásico in March 2014, some media commentators suggested it could be an era-defining match, with Real Madrid players determined to give FC Barcelona such a thrashing as to leave no doubt that supremacy had shifted back to the men in white for the first time since the pre-Laporta era. It was the kind of hype, not entirely unbiased, that one expected from the Madrid and Barcelona media in the run-up to any El Clásico.

Although the confidence of Real Madrid players proved misplaced, it was a thrilling spectacle nonetheless, with Ronaldo and Messi in the thick of it. The goal scoring began with Andrés Iniesta shooting into the top corner, before Karim Benzema's brace put Real ahead. Messi restored parity soon after, only to have Cristiano Ronaldo restore Real's lead from the penalty spot. After Sergio Ramos was sent off, Messi won the game with two penalties. It was described as the Clásico of the century. And for once it felt as if the football, rather than the rivalry, was the main talking point. It was breathless, exhilarating stuff, as Barcelona made light of the form book and reminded Real Madrid that they weren't finished yet. The teams traded the lead, the game swinging one way and then the other: 0–1, 2–1, 2–2, 3–2, 3–4.

In the midst of a 'crisis' in his form, it was Messi's second hat-trick in a row as he became the second highest scorer in La Liga history, moving ahead of former Real Madrid striker Hugo Sánchez on to 236 goals. The Argentine also became the all-time top scorer in Clásicos, with twenty-one goals, surpassing Real Madrid legend Alfredo Di Stéfano. Martino became the fifth Barça coach to win on his first trip to the Santiago Bernabéu. More importantly, they were back within one point of the top of the League.

If they hoped that would be the catalyst for title-winning consistency, though, much as Messi tried to drag them onwards, a damaging defeat away at Granada and three successive draws to close out the season left them second, level on points with Madrid but behind on goal difference. Above them both was Atlético Madrid.

In the midst of Barcelona's spring woes, Atlético had also put them out of the Champions League, with a bruising 1–1 draw at the Nou Camp, followed by a 1–0 victory at home, where Atlético also hit the woodwork three times. Barcelona were crowded out of the game all over the pitch, and Messi could do nothing to drag them back into it.

A week later, they lost the Copa del Rey final to Real Madrid, as a strangely subdued performance saw Messi utterly peripheral. Ronaldo was out injured, but Bale came up with the goods, sprinting from the halfway line, slipping the ball around the Barcelona defence and outpacing everyone before coolly sliding the ball past Pinto, the Barcelona keeper.

While they were third best in the League, Madrid cruised through their own Champions League qualifying group, with Ancelotti crafting just the right balance between attack and defence, often with devastating results. Ronaldo was in imperious form and became the first player ever to score nine goals in the group stage. In their 9–2 aggregate defeat of Schalke over two legs in the first knockout round, Ronaldo had scored another four goals. They survived a scare against Borussia Dortmund in the next round, after winning the home leg 3–0 but losing the second 2–0, and in the semi-final, they found themselves up against a familiar foe in the opposite dug-out as they drew Pep Guardiola's Bayern Munich, with the first leg at home.

It was a classic mix of styles, as Bayern Munich looked to control the ball, attempting to pass Real to death. However, the goal when it came was a classic bit of Madrid counter-attacking, as when a Bayern move broke down, first Ronaldo and then Fábio Coentrão carried the ball forwards at pace before Benzema passed the ball into the net from six yards. It wasn't a perfect performance, Ronaldo grimaced in disgust at himself as he missed an easy chance from twelve yards, but Guardiola's words that he was proud of his team rang hollow. Ancelotti certainly wasn't getting complacent, saying, 'We have a bit of an advantage, but nobody can say what is going to happen.'

What happened was exactly what Pérez would have hoped when he hired Ancelotti. In the face of Guardiola's patented brand of possession football, Madrid simply kept compact and then hit them with ruthless counter-attack after counter-attack. Even before their first goal, Bale had sliced through the midfield. Sergio Ramos, who had missed his penalty two years before in the semi-final shootout, scored two thumping headers within the first twenty-five minutes, to leave Bayern Munich with a mountain to climb.

As they tried to put pressure on Real, without ever really threatening their goal, a lightning-fast counter-attack just after the half-hour saw Di María and Benzema exchange passes and release Bale, who found Ronaldo and he drove it with power from just inside the area: 3–0 to Real Madrid. For most of the second half, Madrid let Bayern have the ball, keeping them at bay with ease. Then, with a minute to go, Madrid won a free kick twenty yards out. Ronaldo bent the ball under the wall as they jumped and into the net.

The *tiki-taka* style, so often behind Barcelona's dominance over Real Madrid, had been defeated, to such an extent that some wondered if it would ever recover. Guardiola was vanquished; Ancelotti had taught him a tactical lesson. Real were in the final of the Champions League and the Decima – the club's tenth European title – was on.

If there was a moment that Cristiano first experienced the possibility of realizing his dream of unconditional respect from his Portuguese compatriots and Real Madrid fans it was when he walked out in the Champions League final at the Estádio da Luz in Lisbon on 24 May 2014.

The game started slowly, with Atlético seemingly happy to sit deep and deny Bale and Ronaldo the space they'd used to such good effect against Bayern.

Half an hour in and the only real chance had fallen to Bale, when he'd shot just wide of the goal under pressure from Tiago.

Then Madrid found themselves behind when a poorly cleared corner was swung back in and Godín, challenging on the penalty spot, looped a header backwards that Casillas saw pass over him and into the net. It was Real's turn to be taught a tactical lesson, as Simeone's team kept Madrid unbalanced with strong challenges, denying them time and space. They seemed all set to keep Real at bay when, in the ninety-third minute, two corners in quick succession left Ramos stretching to guide a low header into the bottom corner.

As the first period of extra time played out, Ronaldo seemingly couldn't do a thing right, as his extra time consisted of scuffed shots and improbable runs. Five minutes into the second period, a low shot from Ángel Di María bounced up off Thibaut Courtois' legs and there was Bale to head home. Five minutes later, a very tired Atlético side failed to close down Marcelo and his long shot made it 3–1. And then, in the last minute of extra time, Godín bundled down Ronaldo. Ronaldo stepped up, powered the penalty into the back of the net and took his top off to stand shining under the lights. An image dutifully captured by a special camera that was filming an authorized documentary on his life. Player and brand perfectly synchronized, in a display that had his detractors cringing because of its narcissism.

Even the Real Madrid official website recognized that Cristiano Ronaldo was far from being the man of the match, choosing to pick Sergio Ramos and Ángel Di María as the stand-out players instead. But if there was one personality trait that Ronaldo never lacked, it was self-belief.

Real Madrid's Decima had an epic quality about it, even if the first hundred-odd minutes didn't really justify it. A club that had always viewed its abundant silverware as a mark of global superiority had finally won the title it believed it carried in its DNA, after a twelve-year drought, and a recent period where it had struggled to impose its hegemony domestically. They had also done so against their city rival Atlético, who had lifted the La Liga crown earlier that month.

It was certainly a sweet victory for Ronaldo, played out in a stadium filled with ghosts from the past that had always threatened his ambition to be considered the best player of all time. For this stadium belonged to Benfica, a club that had always resisted the idea of their legendary player Eusébio being surpassed in greatness by the Madeiran upstart, who had entered the international hall of fame after playing for rival Sporting. In 2004, it had also been in the Estádio da Luz that the final of the European Championships was played. The Portuguese national team's failure to win a match in which Ronaldo played was a national humiliation if ever there was one.

Now, ten years later, Ronaldo had succeeded in expunging the demons, despite being marginal for much of the game because of a lingering hamstring injury.

But, as Atlético coach Diego Simeone remarked later, in these kinds of games no one remembers the loser. Nor do memories endure about the game itself beyond the winning goal, not least when it is scored by Ronaldo, the ultimate narcissist, celebrating his own image.

Real Madrid had shown a consistency as the season had progressed that had been lacking in their rivals, looking increasingly impressive on an upward curve, while Barça had been on a kind of rollercoaster of limited peaks and embarrassing troughs. And while Real Madrid seemed to have found a certain stability and cohesion, not to mention an ethical compass, post-Mourinho under Ancelotti, FC Barcelona seemed to have been hoisted on the petard of its own mythology – that it was more than just a club, destined to be more deserving of support than its historic rival. As well as Rosell's resignation, the club faced a season-long ban from FIFA for breaching rules on the transfer of underage players; Qatar, FC Barcelona's main sponsor, become embroiled in fresh allegations about bribes linked to its Word Cup bid; and Messi, along with his father, was investigated for tax evasion. Every way you looked at it, the 2013–14 season ended in failure for FC Barcelona.

'My Barça was an utter failure. Normally failure means not winning. My view on that is different,' Martino later told the Spanish football magazine *Panenka*. 'If Barça had played their own style but not won the title, it wouldn't have been a failure. But we didn't win and we didn't play well either.'[5]

Martino believed Barça had fallen into a deep collective depression, a prolonged grieving over the much-loved Tito Vilanova, which had a profoundly demoralizing impact on Messi, the player around whom the team revolved.

But Martino too was held responsible.

He did not shine as a coach, seemingly overwhelmed by the adverse circumstances, while lacking the personality and vision to deal with them. At a critical stage in the season, there was no consensus of opinion as to which of Barça's various potential line-ups worked best, not least in attack, where star signing Neymar had to fit in with Messi, but had yet to earn the right to claim that he was worth leaving Pedro and Alexis Sánchez on the bench for. What was worse, whatever the scoring statistics said, Messi often seemed strangely peripheral. For a coach who had joked in his first press conference that he was sure Messi and his father had 'put in a good word for him', one of his apparent strengths was his undoing.

In May 2014, Martino and Barça announced that they were parting ways after just one season, during which the first team had failed to win any trophies for the first time since 2007–8, and had ended up playing some uncharacteristically listless football, which often seemed to keep Messi on the fringes of games. It was not ideal preparation personally or professionally for Messi, as he sought to lift the World Cup on the continent of his birth.

International Break

34. WORLD CUP DISAPPOINTMENT, NATIONAL EMBARRASSMENT: MESSI AND RONALDO

In 2014, Argentina had gone to the World Cup in Brazil convinced that it would emerge victorious on the home territory of its historic continental rival. Argentine fans arrived in their thousands, enthusiastically accompanying their team. The joke was that they planned to put Messi on a pedestal, up on the hill with Christ the Redeemer. As had been the case for a while, all the talk was of whether Messi would finally win the prize that would anoint him a national legend.

Carlos Bilardo, coach of the Argentine national team in 1986, told me about the World Cup in Mexico: 'There was Diego, and then there was the rest of the team.'

Bilardo considered Maradona an exceptional creative talent who required completely different – and indeed very privileged – handling compared to any other member of the squad. Bilardo's indulgence included allowing Maradona to stay up later than the others, be surrounded by his own clan of friends, hangers-on and relatives, and dealing with his own personal life as he thought fit.

While no evidence has been produced that he took drugs in Mexico, by 1986 Maradona had already walked very much on the wild side in Barcelona and Naples, with a looming paternity suit back in Italy. Nonetheless, that World Cup will always be remembered as the high point of Maradona's unrivalled genius, and one of the high points of football history.

Undoubtedly, Messi went to the 2014 World Cup with a cleaner personal image, but with a pending case for unpaid tax filed against him by Spain's Inland Revenue. A Spanish financial prosecutor had lodged a legal filing in 2013, accusing Messi and his father of committing tax fraud, with the alleged offences being committed from when Messi was just seventeen.

As it was, the case initially barely registered in the concerns of football fans, who marvelled at the magic he was producing with Barça, even if the previous season had probably been the most subdued of his senior career. As for his fellow countrymen, until he won a World Cup, the jury was out on whether Messi deserved to take his place as a national legend. The national mood was optimistic, though, particularly after the euphoric reaction by Argentines to the election in March 2013 of one of their number, the Cardinal Jorge Bergoglio, as the first ever Latin American Pope.

Within weeks of his election as Pope Francis, both Messi and Maradona had separately made their way to Rome to attend charity matches, and their meetings with the Pope were widely publicized back home. While Messi settled for shaking hands with the pontiff along with all the other members of his team, Maradona managed a one-to-one meeting, from which he emerged claiming his Catholic faith had been restored. Thus did the hand of God appear once again to be laying its blessings on Argentine football.

The parallel between Maradona in Mexico 1986 and Messi in Brazil 2014 was that both had managers who believed they had special status and therefore required special treatment on the field as well as off it. Both Bilardo and Alejandro Sabella, the Argentina coach in 2014, built teams around their VIPs, with the rest of the players filling the role of a supportive if functional cast. It was a tactic that bore fruit for both squads, as the 2014 vintage, backed by vociferous support, initially seemed the right decision. A dour opening game against Bosnia-Herzegovina was lit up by a brilliant individual goal from Messi, who weaved into the box, beating three challenges before placing the ball into the corner.

The second game against Iran was overshadowed by rumours of Messi's displeasure at the 5-3-2 formation in the first game. So here they lined up in a 4-3-3 formation like Barcelona. Iran managed to keep them at bay and could even have caused an upset by scoring, until the ninety-first minute when Messi curled in a brilliant winner. In the final group game against Nigeria, with both teams already through, Messi scored two goals: one an early rebound from an Ángel Di María free kick and the other an inch-perfect free kick. In the last sixteen, Messi wasn't able to add to his tally against the Swiss, but set up Ángel Di María for the winning goal. Against Belgium in the quarter-finals, in the game that brought him level on caps with Maradona on ninety-one, he produced his most complete performance of the competition, making runs throughout and spraying long passes about the pitch. Though his performance wasn't as attention-grabbing as that one in 1986, he was spoken of as the most influential single player at the competition.

Two days before Argentina's semi-final against the Netherlands they watched, as stupefied as the rest of the world, as Germany beat Brazil 7–1. So the Argentina–Netherlands game began with an almost conscious effort from both teams not to be turned over in that manner, and consequently the game was 120 minutes of almost totally dull football. Messi was assigned a permanent man-marker and, though this blunted the Argentinians, it left the Dutch completely blunted as an attacking force. As the game went to penalties, Argentina scored all theirs, including a decisive Messi effort, and went through to the final.

The main difference was one of outcomes: while in Mexico Argentina had, by the quarter-final stage with England, wowed people with the brilliance of Maradona and how much the team owed to him, Messi was in shadow throughout much of the tournament in Brazil, including the final, where a run down the wing petered out like a damp firework, and he fluffed a crucial free kick. When Mario Götze arrowed his left-foot volley into the net in extra time, 112 minutes into the final, few commentators doubted that Germany were worthy champions.

Argentina had played with width and penetration earlier in the match, but the gods were not on Messi's side. It would be hard for Messi to forget – as indeed it would be for Argentine fans – that moment two minutes into the second half when Higuaín broke through the German defence and placed the ball at his feet. With only Neuer in the German goal to beat, Messi put his shot wide.

In truth, it was the supporting cast of Argentina's defence – held together by Messi's Barça colleague Mascherano, a *de facto* captain as opposed to the *de jure* captain, the evidently diminished Messi – and the attacking auxiliaries Higuaín and Di María who truly delivered for Sabella. All of this might have proved academic if Messi had scored or contributed to an Argentine victory in the final, but the fact was that he didn't.

Instead, Argentina were justly beaten by a Germany that showed skill, flair and determination as a unit, showing that their manager, Joachim Löw, had absorbed and improved on the quick-passing attacking football played by previous champions, Spain's La Roja.

The Argentine team had been so confident that they had taken to singing bawdy songs in the dressing room, like conquering gauchos. But Argentina's national sense of frustration and humiliation after the defeat found its escape valve in blaming Messi.

Messi had won four man-of-the-match awards for his perform-ances early in the competition against Switzerland, Nigeria, Iran and Bosnia-Herzegovina, and he was chosen from a ten-player list of can-didates for the tournament's Golden Ball, who were announced on the eve of the final.

Frustration that Messi had failed to produce the perfect narrative in the final itself soon gave way to anger, when the losing captain was asked to receive the Golden Ball as FIFA's outstanding player of the tournament. The prize was sponsored by Adidas, the German sports-wear company Messi had switched to after his father had ditched Nike. Messi appeared embarrassed, and took the award with little grace, let alone pride. To make matters worse, Maradona would claim, not without justification, that Messi had only been awarded the prize as a marketing ploy, given that the trophy was branded by Messi's principal sponsors, Adidas.

How different would Messi have felt had Argentina won the World Cup in Brazil. Many observers who watched Messi, both at Barcelona in 2013–14, and in Brazil, noted he still didn't seem physically right. Indeed, some say he was even taken ill during the final.

The contrast between the unqualified veneration Messi had received at FC Barcelona, and the trophies won, and his disappoint-ing performances in his national colours continued to raise questions about just how great he was or wasn't.

The 2014 World Cup also seemed to lack the aura of the 2010 tour-nament, when Maradona had managed the national squad. In 2010, Maradona had faced scathing attacks from non-Argentines for his inept team planning and coaching skills, but his enduring mythology briefly morphed into Messi's for some Argentine commentators, who idolized both. 'There was a concerted effort by the likes of Juan Sebastián Verón to publicly defend Messi from the hard time he was being given. This, in conjunction with an obvious bonding with the supreme ego that was manager Diego Maradona, helped turn around the press's attitude. Some way into the tournament, the love conquered all, and although the country didn't win the trophy, snippets of the fun Messi and Maradona had with their talent delighted us all,' recalled Maradona's English translator, the journalist Marcela Mora y Araujo.

There were those nonetheless who argued that Messi suffered in 2014 as he did in 2010 from not finding the same skills and team ethos in the Argentina team as he had grown up with in Barcelona. There were no Argentine equivalents of Xavi Hernández or Iniesta or Sergio Busquets. The ball possession, passing and transition that had developed to a fine art form, from the early days of La Masia and then under Guardiola's management, moulding itself to – and bringing out the best of – Messi's talent, had no equivalent in successive Argentine squads.

Moreover, Argentine football had been characterized by an enduring endemic corruption that impacted on the morale of players, and tested their loyalty.

Such corruption was personified in the figure of Julio Grondona, whose presidency of the Argentine Football Association and key position in the executive structure of FIFA had straddled a succession of military and civilian governments in his country, allowing him to build up a network of influence and patronage unrivalled by any Argentine politician or businessman.

Under Grondona's long-running regime, Argentine club and national football had become deeply embroiled in political conspiracies, subjected to intervention, and controlled by vested interests, including protectionist rackets run by fanatical rival groups of fans, some with links to the drugs trade. Such gangs were rife in Rosario, the city from which the Messis had emigrated, and the city had developed a particularly bad reputation as the 'Chicago' of Argentina.

Grondona, only belatedly recognized by his fellow countrymen as a deeply controversial figure, was for decades barely questioned by the local media and politicians, let alone the judiciary. His death from an aortic aneurysm in July 2014, just weeks after Argentina and Messi had been beaten by Germany, saved him from almost certain indictment as part of the US FIFA-gate action, as he was posthumously named as one of the key figures allegedly involved in bribes and vote rigging.

While Catalans rallied round him, Messi faced the wrath of his fellow countrymen, with Maradona continuing to cast a long shadow over Messi when it came to judging which of them held the better claim to greatness on the field in defence of the national colours.

The stats boys resurrected the fact that Messi had created more chances than anybody at the 2014 World Cup, and only Andrea Pirlo played as many through balls. Messi gave us more – a lot more – completed dribbles than any other player, with his tally of forty-six taking him well clear of Arjen Robben's twenty-nine.

'In fact, Messi's dribbling success bears closer comparison to Diego Maradona's total of fifty in his annus mirabilis of 1986. That seems to sum it up. Messi's good, but he's not quite Diego. When it comes to being regarded as the greatest player of all time, naturally, the demands are exacting,' reported Sky Sports' Adam Bate.

'If the statistics leave you cold,' Bate went on to comment, 'just recall the manner in which Messi danced away from his markers for the decisive assist against Switzerland, or the imagination required in conceiving let alone executing that pass against Belgium. It's cruel to be compared to Maradona. It's crueller still to be adjudged a disappointment due to an unfavourable comparison with your own self.'[1]

But, in the end, what endured in the memory was that Argentina had lost in the final to Germany. It seemed almost the final dice from the player in the prime of his career. Messi would be thirty-one when the World Cup next came round, and in the national squad he was struggling to be a director of a less than brilliant orchestra.

If there was any consolation for Messi, though it was a very slim one, it was that Ronaldo had endured an even more disappointing World Cup than him. Portugal were mauled 4–0 by eventual champions Germany in their opening game, with Ronaldo subdued apart from a fierce free kick that was saved. Suffering from tendonitis, it then took an injury-time equalizer from a Ronaldo cross to draw 2–2 with the USA. They then needed to win by four clear goals against Ghana to stand any chance of going through. In the end, Ronaldo scored to make it 2–1 but it wasn't enough.

35. ENRIQUE VS ANCELOTTI

Cristiano and Leo entered the 2014–15 season united by a disappointing summer of international football but with a very different mood around their club sides.

Barcelona, which had limped to the end of that traumatic season under Martino, announced they had finally got their man when former player and Reserves manager Luis Enrique agreed to join them as manager on 19 May. He was tasked with helping Barcelona rediscover their mojo, and with rescuing Messi from the dark hole he found himself in after the trauma of the summer. A managerial challenge that Adoni Zubizareta admitted was a 'sizeable one'.

Barcelona had a busy summer, as amongst others, Cesc Fàbregas left for Chelsea, Alexis Sánchez for Arsenal and Victor Valdés left on a free transfer; iconic club captain Carles Puyol retired and joined the backroom staff. In came goalkeepers Marc-André ter Stegen, Claudio Bravo, defenders Jérémy Mathieu and Thomas Vermaelen, the Croatian midfielder Ivan Rakitić, and the controversial Uruguyan forward Luis Suárez, who would be unable to play until 26 October after being banned for biting Giorgio Chiellini during a World Cup group match against Italy. In an absurd state of affairs, his banning by FIFA from 'all football activity' meant that Barcelona's lawyers advised them not to publicize his medical or allow pictures of him to be published.

Watchers speculated about how Barcelona would play, how it would be different, more like the Barça of Vilanova. Would they be more direct, what did the signings mean, how would they work together, and – always central to the conversation – where would Messi play – false 9, number 10 – and how close to the Messi of before would he be? Johan Cruyff predicted that it would all end in tears, with the stars, like divas, fighting among themselves for the leading role, but with a fast-maturing Neymar and the current European Golden Boot, Suárez, to come, they certainly wouldn't be light on firepower. It was hoped that Suarez would have taken advice from a good psychologist, and had learnt to channel his energy. Luis Enrique saw him as a player who had that competitive urgency that Barcelona had missed the previous season. It was noted that 26 October, the day after Suárez's ban was due to come to an end was, neatly enough, the first Clásico of the season.

But first they had to play nine League games and begin the first half of their Champions League campaign. They started well, winning seven and drawing one of their games, with Messi scoring seven goals in the League. He seemed refreshed, seeing a lot of the ball and seeming to relish playing with Neymar, the two of them constantly looking for and finding each other in and around the box. But it was their defence that was most impressive, not conceding a goal in nine games. If there was one attack that might threaten them though, it was Real Madrid's, who were riding out a bumpy start to their season.

In many ways, Madrid began the season with a much clearer sense of what they needed to do: more of the same. With Ancelotti still riding the wave of the Decima, Madrid sold Ángel di María, Álvaro Morata and Xabi Alonso, let Nuri Şahin go out on loan, and brought in the top scorer at the World Cup, Colombian attacker James Rodríguez, for big money and World Cup-winning German midfielder Toni Kroos. They had lost a legend as Alfredo Di Stéfano had died on 7 July 2014, but living legend Zinedine Zidane joined the staff as coach of the reserves.

Madrid began the season by beating Sevilla in the European Super Cup. Both goals were scored by Ronaldo: the first slid in from a Bale cross, and the second was a powerful drive from just inside the box, which the keeper got hands to but could do nothing about. Ronaldo was given the man-of-the-match award by Alex Ferguson, who said that he had made it easy for him with his performance, and Ronaldo in turn thanked the coach who had taught him a lot.

Then they were on to the first leg of the Spanish Super Cup, where they drew with Atlético in a typically rugged game where both goals were scored in the final ten minutes. However, three games into the season and they were in crisis. A 2–0 win over Córdoba in their first game was quickly forgotten when they lost the next two games against Real Sociedad and Atlético Madrid. Suddenly questions were being asked about why Xabi Alonso had been allowed to leave, how the attack looked dysfunctional without Ángel Di María to knit things together. Madrid looked unfit, vulnerable at the back, as Casillas's form continued to decline, and they seemed out of ideas going forwards. So, of course, they won their next game 8–2. Cristiano scored a hat-trick, Bale and Javier Hernández, who'd been loaned from Man United, a brace apiece, the Mexican's two coming in three minutes at the end of the game. After their consecutive League defeats, their record in the run-up to the Clásico read: played five, won five, goals for – twenty-five, goals against – three. Ronaldo scored thirteen of those goals in an astonishing burst of form. Among them was a physical-law-defying header against Deportivo in which, as the cross floated behind his run, he somehow managed to generate the power to beat the goalkeeper from the penalty spot, as he was being clattered by a defender. It was the only place he could have put the ball to score, a superlative piece of skill, made to look utterly routine. Indeed, as Messi continued his move deeper on the pitch, he seemed to have lost that explosive first couple of yards: was it not now Ronaldo who was the better goal scorer, certainly the more explosive player?

As the first match-up between them approached that October, yet again it was put to Ronaldo that his rivalry with Messi was again central to the upcoming Clásico. His response was simply, 'I'm not going to play against Messi, I'm going to play against Barcelona.' His warm-up was to be given a standing ovation by Liverpool fans as he scored in a 3–0 victory at Anfield.

All the talk before the game was dominated by the sheer weight of attacking talent in the combined line-ups. Though Bale was out injured, they included the joint European Golden Shoe winners, the World Cup Golden Ball, the World Cup Golden Boot, plus the winner of the last two years' Ballons d'Or. In fact, the winners of the last six Ballons d'Or. In a fixture already swimming in hyperbole, much was made of the sheer scale, the transfer fees, the combined goals, the audience figures, the TV money, even the number of journalists. The biggest game in the world had never felt bigger. If Stoichkov had once – and only half-jokingly – said, 'Go to the moon ... Madrid, Barcelona', it felt as if even further afield the game might still be being talked about. Ancelotti joked that he was lucky enough to have a seat to watch the game, and he didn't even have to pay for a ticket.

Barcelona began at a sprint when Suárez cut infield and fizzed a pass across the area to Neymar, whose shot bent into the bottom corner.

Back came Real Madrid, tearing into the opposition at pace, with only the frame of the goal saving them twice in quick succession. Barcelona seemed to have braved things out and Messi's shot was saved when he should have scored. The game seesawed back and forth until the thirty-fourth minute, when Piqué slid in to block a cross and handled the ball in the area. Ronaldo dispatched the penalty with ease.

The game swung further towards Madrid when Pepe scored a powerful header from a corner. Barcelona tried to put Madrid under pressure and conceded again when a mistake between Iniesta and Mascherano let Madrid in for a third scored by Benzema. For the remaining half-hour, Barcelona were neat on the ball without really appearing threatening, whereas Madrid looked dangerous every time they came forward. The Madrid fans were chanting *Olé* by the end of the game. Luis Enrique admitted they hadn't deserved anything from the game, whereas Ancelotti praised the 'unique professionalism' of his players, who sacrificed themselves for the team. Although Ronaldo didn't take the headlines this time, he'd played his part flawlessly. When it had been put to him earlier over the summer that losing Xabi Alonso and Di María wasn't ideal, he had conceded the truth of that, as he had reportedly reacted with anger and frustration when Özil had been sold to Arsenal the season before. But his trust in Ancelotti never wavered. 'The mister knows what he is doing. We just have to let him work calmly.'

When the dust had settled, the gap had been narrowed to a single point.

Barcelona proceeded to lose their next game to Celta Vigo and suddenly all the talk was of Barcelona again losing their identity. They had chances, Messi had three to himself, but they all ultimately came to nothing.

The star attacking trio, soon dubbed 'MSN', didn't seem to be clicking. Indeed, some said it was this reliance on superstar imports that was eroding their identity. It was as if Madrid and Barcelona had swapped their traditional roles of legacy and stability vs *galácticos*.

Over their remaining six games of the year, Madrid won all six, scoring twenty-two goals, of which Ronaldo got nine. Barcelona won five and drew one, with Messi scoring eight. On Saturday 6 December 2014, Ronaldo scored the twenty-third hat-trick of his career, overtaking Alfredo Di Stéfano's record. On Sunday the 7th, Messi scored his own hat-trick, and surpassed 400 goals for Barcelona. He even scored two with his right foot.

Still people discerned problems in the team's interplay. Neymar seemed to lack maturity as a team player, with a tendency to frown and protest too regularly like a spoilt school kid, lacking the grace and sheer fun that Ronaldinho had given fans in his heyday. Suárez beat his chest and the turf with frustration whenever his passes went astray or his teammates failed to convert a chance that he laid on. Xavi, meanwhile, cut a distinctly tragic figure on the subs bench, the ageing veteran no longer in charge of the team on the pitch. And Messi – well Messi, in spite of his continuing goal scoring, seemed to have temporarily lost his capacity to transform a team into something better, to bring his teammates onto his wavelength and make spectators feel they were watching football for the first time.

Barça, in short, seemed to be a team still struggling to be coherent, suffering from an excess of rotation – Luis Enrique played twenty-three different starting line-ups in his first twenty-three matches – and playing with unseemly haste, over-elaborating in the final crucial seconds of attack, when one touch would have done. In the team's determination to push the ball upfield as quickly as possible, and engage the MSN triumvirate, there was no intricate geometry, other than the occasional one-two. Barça's midfield had disappeared as a creative entity, and its defence, as ever, remained vulnerable to a well-organized counter-attack, be it from Real Madrid or Celta Vigo.

An ominous silence from the Barça fans accompanied Luis Enrique, for all his animated gesticulations. Then, on 4 January 2015, Barcelona lost away to Real Sociedad. Luis Enrique kept Messi and Neymar on the bench and Suárez was awkward and ineffective.

The Nou Camp had a depressed feel about it, the fans evidently lacking belief in what they were witnessing. This was a club struggling to hang on to the credibility of its motto – '*Mes que un club*' – and what it signified in terms of artistry, solidarity and democracy. Politics were a dead weight round its neck, with former presidents facing criminal charges, and some of its longest-serving members questioning the ethics of maintaining Qatari money as the club's main sponsor – a country criticized by Amnesty International for its human rights record, and a suspected financier of the head-cutters of Islamic State.

FC Barcelona is a club that has spent most of its history, for better or worse, affected by Spanish politics, both national and regional – and now the landscape was far from stable. Those crying for 'Independence Now' in the Nou Camp seemed increasingly vocal, while having little impact on the quality of the play. Barça was playing badly, losing, and – worst of all – Real Madrid seemed serene.

The day after the Real Sociedad defeat, Barcelona announced that they had sacked Andoni Zubizarreta and that his assistant Carles Puyol had resigned. Two days later, Luis Enrique was forced to deny that he had been given an ultimatum. There were also rumours that Messi's absence from the traditional annual open training session – suffering from 'gastroenteritis' – might have more to do with a bust-up with Enrique, who had left him on the bench. There were reports of arguments, of Enrique wanting to discipline Messi for returning late from his winter break but being overruled. Suddenly old quotes were being resurrected from over a year previously, when Messi had called Barcelona's financial vice president, Javier Faus, 'someone who knows nothing about football', after he had made a statement about Messi's contract renewal not being urgent. Before the World Cup Messi had been quoted as saying: 'Barcelona is my home, but if they don't want me or doubt me, I'd have no problem in leaving.' And only a couple of months earlier, in an interview with an Argentinian newspaper, he said: 'Although I have said I'd like to stay at Barcelona for ever, things don't always turn out how you want them to.' In this climate, journalists seemed to ascribe mystical significance to his following two Chelsea players on Instagram. When Enrique was asked if Messi wanted to stay, his reply was 'I'm not the right person to answer that.'

In January 2015 there was an online story that Barça fans had taken to looking for old DVDs of Ronaldinho, of Messi, of Iniesta and Xavi, of Guardiola, and of Johan Cruyff, in an exercise of nostalgia for those halcyon days when a team came together under a manager and a president, striking a harmonious note.

As Barcelona were undergoing their winter break *horribilis*, Real Madrid were being crowned the best club side in the world at the Club World Cup, as they defeated Argentinian side San Lorenzo in Marrakesh. In a game in which the players kicked each other at least as much as the ball, a visibly frustrated Ronaldo tried everything but didn't score as the team won 2–0.

While Barcelona's manager was being forced to defend his position, Madrid's president announced that they were planning on extending their manager's contract that summer. The role reversal seemed complete.

But then, in their first League game back after the break, Madrid lost to Valencia, with Bale receiving criticism for not passing to Benzema, as Ronaldo's penalty wasn't enough to stop them losing 2–1. Then, in their next match came the absurd situation of the Real Madrid fans booing Gareth Bale as they won 3–0, because he chose to shoot instead of squaring to Ronaldo. Ancelotti was forced to defend his players, saying, 'Bale is a fundamental player like Cristiano and for that the fans demand much.'

The Ronaldo vs Bale controversy even made its way to the Ballon d'Or ceremony that January, where, in spite of winning the award by his biggest ever margin over Messi, Cristiano found himself discussing the booing of Gareth Bale.

'They are very intense, they show what they feel, they aren't liars. But I think the things with Gaz are normal because they know that Gaz is a very important player for us, a key player.'

He also spoke about his own ambitions, saying, 'I want to be one of the greatest players of all time and this requires a lot of effort but I hope to get there.'

In the midst of their off-field turmoils, there was respite for Barcelona, as they beat Elche 5–0 in the Copa del Rey on 8 January. However, they faced defending champions Atlético Madrid in the League, still reeling. In the end it was a performance full of skill and bravado, as all three of the 'MSN' scored. When Messi scored the third goal, the three of them ran towards the corner arm in arm, the kind of image that football marketing departments dream of. By that point Messi had given away a soft penalty, but the crowd roared his name long after the final whistle. If there was any doubt as to where the crowd's loyalties lay, their reaction made it abundantly clear.

In the following days, Messi gave a strident interview where he attacked rumours of a rift with Luis Enrique and his father having contact with Manchester City and Chelsea as 'lies' coming from people who claimed to love the club. He called for the club to be more united than ever. A visibly annoyed Messi (or as visibly annoyed as he gets) said he was sick and tired of the rumours that he had had players and staff kicked out of the club, insisting that he was 'just another player in the team'. Two days later, Luis Enrique gave an interview where he said that Barcelona without Messi was not something they could contemplate, and that Messi would be at Barcelona for many years.

Sometimes in football, things just click. Throughout the spring of 2015, as they headed towards the Clásico on 22 March, Barcelona played nine games, dropping only three points in a shock defeat to Málaga. They scored thirty-one goals, conceded seven. Messi scored an astonishing sixteen goals.

But those statistics cannot convey the increasing and infectious joy of a team finding their range. Barça seemed transformed. They played with a style and strategy that seemed to be more overtly in competition with Real Madrid's high-octane forward play, rather than with its traditional trademark style: the intricate, patient midfield play that had characterized Guardiola's heyday had been replaced by fast-moving transitions focused on delivering the ball to the front trio of Neymar, Suárez and Messi. What had seemed hurried and inelegant in the first half of the season had been transformed into something vibrant and direct, not least because that forward trio had found a way of working together better, and taking turns to score goals. In the midst of it all, they even began to pass the ball around a bit more.

Messi was once again showing off his magic. It was my wife, not a football fan, but with me on the night, who summed it all up. 'Messi is beautiful to watch.'

As I blogged at the time, the player is not exactly an Adonis, we all know. He is short and scraggly, long-nosed, walks with a stoop, and has a tendency to clear his throat by spitting or, on a bad day, seemingly throwing up. Nor does he set you on fire when he speaks in his squeaky Rosario accent, far less musical and evocative than that of Buenos Aires – but then he often has very little to say anyway.

But, at his best, his transformative presence on the pitch defines his football intelligence. Messi touches and plays the ball and moves around the pitch like few other players can, with an extraordinary sense of anticipation and resolution, with absolute focus and inventiveness of rhythm and shape. Tactics and strategy mould into one, teams become inspired, matches defined.

This happened at the Nou Camp when FC Barcelona played Manchester City in the second leg of the last sixteen of the Champions League on 18 March 2015. Already 2–1 up from the first leg in Manchester, Messi's utter control of the game showed in his pace and timing. The entire stadium paused whenever he stopped dead in his tracks to draw opponents to him before swerving and sliding his way through them, leaving them frustrated and with little option other than to try and hack him down. He turned City's star players into roughnecks, and turned his teammates into supportive knights.

This poetry in motion was what made Barça's second-leg victory a particularly memorable occasion, the English champions outclassed by a Barça that was galvanized by the brilliance of their little big man.

Messi failed to hit target with his free kicks, but this paled into insignificance compared to his overall performance, for each Barça attack – and there were many – had Messi involved in its conception. It was not just his attempts at goal, but the sheer havoc provoked in Man City's midfield and defence, whenever he ran with the ball, creating space and endless opportunities for other attackers. For Messi's nobility lies in his selflessness.

'*Messi, Messi, Messi, Messi,*' a packed Nou Camp chanted repeatedly throughout the game. It was that kind of night. Beautiful indeed. Afterwards, Messi's Argentine Barça colleague Javier Mascherano simply said, 'Football controls us all but Messi controls football. He is a legend, doing things mere mortals cannot aspire to.'[1]

Real Madrid, however, came into the spring Clásico with the wheels well and truly falling off.

Their twenty-two-game unbeaten run disappeared in the first game after the winter break, as they lost 2–1 to Valencia in a bruising, bad-tempered game in which Ronaldo missed a couple of good late chances to avoid the defeat. Then they lost 2–0 to Atlético in the Copa del Rey. They won their next League games at Espanyol, Getafe and Córdoba, but Ronaldo was sent off for petulantly kicking out at an opponent. He took to Twitter, saying, 'I apologize to all and especially to Edimar for my reckless act in the game today', but he was banned for two games. They won the next two games, but there were injuries, to James Rodríguez and to Sergio Ramos. They came into their February game against Atlético Madrid out of sorts, and they were torn apart. The touch and poise shown by their rivals was astonishing as they demolished Real 4–0. Ronaldo couldn't get into the game; the players seemed shell-shocked, second to every ball, playing as if they were wearing flippers. After the game, Ancelotti said there wasn't a single player who had played well. Ronaldo was then criticized for being caught on camera singing karaoke as he celebrated his thirtieth birthday on the night of the game. In a press conference, despite calling for calm, the birthday boy became irate at a journalist asking about his sending off at Córdoba, saying, 'If you were an intelligent journalist, you'd ask me about the game today. You are not intelligent. Sorry.'

Jorge Mendes stepped in to defend his client saying, 'He decides games, he does everything. But when he goes through a spell when things don't go as well, people should stand behind him because we are talking about the best player in the world.'

Madrid were still a point ahead in the League, but the mood was fractious; there were rumours that the players were unfit, that Ancelotti was too hands-off, too in thrall to his stars. Even as they won against Deportivo, they were booed by their own fans.

In March they drew with Villarreal and lost to Athletic Bilbao, then lost 4–3 at home to Schalke in the second leg of their Champions League last sixteen game. They went through 5–4 on aggregate, with Ronaldo scoring twice, but footage emerged of Ronaldo allegedly mouthing 'disgrace' towards the end of the game, and he refused to talk to the media until the end of the season. Against Levante, although Real won 2–0 thanks to two goals from Bale, Ronaldo failed to score and was whistled by some supporters, causing him to nod his head in disbelief.

It was a full-blown crisis. Florentino Pérez was forced to defend Ancelotti publicly.

The pendulum had well and truly swung towards Barça. There were articles written about the turnaround in both teams' and players' form since the Ballon d'Or award in January, when Ronaldo had stood, flanked by Sepp Blatter and Thierry Henry that night, and said, 'This is my third Ballon d'Or but I am not going to stop here. I want to catch Messi.' Perhaps the little Argentinian guy in the red velvet suit and bow tie had decided then and there he was going to have something to say about that.

Among the more telling insights that emerged from Anthony Wonke's documentary, released in November 2015, was Ronaldo's and his agent Mendes's evident obsession with winning the Ballon d'Or, rather than with beating Messi specifically. Authorized by both in anticipation that he was going to be awarded his gong that year, the documentary, made by the company responsible for the acclaimed *Senna*, skilfully picks up on some revealing – if unwitting – indiscretions which survived the final cut.

At one point, Mendes and one of his associates are filmed watching a match from an executive box at the Bernabéu, talking in coded Portuguese about the threat that 'the other guy might destroy everything', in an apparent reference to Messi.

'It's a card inside an envelope that can change so much,' Ronaldo says at one point of the Ballon d'Or award ceremony. 'To see Messi win four in a row was difficult for me. After he won the second and third I thought to myself: "I'm not coming here again."'

The overwhelming image that comes across is of a person obsessed with himself over and above any obsession with Messi and, but for a very close circle of family and friends, lacking the generosity of spirit for real human engagement and trust. 'I'm not going to lie to you,' he says, explaining why he went to the 2014 World Cup with an injury. 'If we had two or three Cristiano Ronaldos in the team I would feel more comfortable. But we don't.'[2]

As the *Guardian*'s Daniel Taylor remarked, 'Watching this film, it becomes clear just how difficult it must be for Gareth Bale, signing for Madrid as the most expensive player in history, to deal with that planet-sized ego.'[3]

Now, it seemed as if the gravitational force of that ego was pulling the entire team into a black hole.

On the eve of the Clásico in late March 2015, Messi had become even more of a team player, contributing assists and twenty goals already in that calendar year. Ronaldo had scored nine and seemed withdrawn, petulant, at war with his teammates and the media.

The Clásico was hyped as the game that yet again would settle the title. In the event, Madrid played pretty well for the first fifty minutes of the game. They went behind to a Jérémy Mathieu header from a Messi cross, but got back into the game through a wonderful goal, when they raced forwards from a saved Neymar shot and a brilliant sweeping team move saw Benzema fooling the whole Barcelona defence with a back-heel in the area, and Ronaldo driving what almost seemed like a toe-poke in. Again, he celebrated by seeming to gesture to the Barcelona crowd to calm down. Messi seemed relatively quiet and Madrid looked threatening whenever they broke at pace. The ball seemed to be stuck in Barcelona's midfield. So Dani Alves decided to bypass it entirely and chipped a high ball behind the Madrid back line, Suárez ran on, controlled with one touch and slid the ball past the Madrid keeper. And with that, the confidence seemed to go out of Madrid. They gamely chased and had a couple of half chances, but it never felt as if they had it in them. Barcelona played the ball about neatly and seemed much more likely to score.

Barcelona were now four points ahead of Real Madrid.

Madrid's response to this setback in the League was superlative, however, as they won their next game 9–1 against Granada, Ronaldo scoring five goals. In total, they proceeded to take twenty-eight points from their remaining ten games, scoring forty goals. Ronaldo hit a remarkable run of personal form, scoring seventeen goals – but it wasn't enough. Barcelona won the League by two points, Messi having scored another eleven goals.

After grinding their way past Atlético in the quarter-finals of the Champions League, Real Madrid went out over two legs to Juventus, as a goal in each leg from Ronaldo wasn't enough to stop them losing 2–1 on aggregate.

Barcelona continued their progress in the Champions League, following up the Messi masterclass against Man City with a 5–1 aggregate victory over Paris Saint-Germain, as Messi seemed content to play a supporting role to Suárez and Neymar across the two legs.

In the semi-finals, they drew Bayern Munich, under the management of Pep Guardiola, whose Bayern side were setting new records in the Bundesliga.

The build-up to the match on 6 May was dominated by talk of Pep vs Leo, with Guardiola – returning to the Nou Camp for the first time as an opposition manager – admitting there was simply no way to stop Messi if he was in one of those moods. And boy, was he in one of those moods.

Leo delivered one of the great club performances by an individual player that night as the occasion and the opposition demanded that someone should step forward and take the game by the scruff of the neck. On seventy-seven minutes, after a brilliantly enthralling game full of chances for both sides, he finally beat the Bayern goalkeeper Manuel Neuer with a low drive from just outside the penalty area, but it was his second goal three minutes later that reminded all of us why we love watching football. A ball slipped inside left him one-on-one against Jérôme Boateng and, as he shuffled as if to go inside, he instead flicked back outside Boateng, leaving him floored by the change of direction, then delicately chipped the ball over the onrushing goalkeeper. It was vintage Messi, one of those moments when it seems as if he is operating outside the boundaries of normal physics. The change of direction and pace at the same time, the ability to find the only finish capable of scoring from that angle. You couldn't imagine another player in the world scoring that goal in that way; indeed you almost imagined the Ronaldo version of that goal, bludgeoned in low and hard.

FC Barcelona beat Bayern Munich 3–0 on the night and Guardiola had one word: 'unstoppable'. Even Mourinho said that any of the big teams in the world would win the Champions League with Messi. This was a game played by two great sides, charged with emotion, but delivered with grace once more by Messi, who worked his magic amidst giants of the game. This was a semi-final first leg that should have been a final, and that would endure in the memory of any true football fan as a masterclass.

In spite of an improved Bayern performance in the second leg, which they won 3–2, Barcelona went through to the final against Juventus.

They warmed up for the Champions League final by beating Athletic Bilbao 3–1 in the final of the Copa del Rey, with Messi scoring another couple of goals, adding another extraordinary goal to his collection as he ran from just inside the halfway line, beating four players as he twisted inside and out and then finished low past the keeper at his near post. It was extraordinary, a distillation of everything he seemed to stand for, as he rode challenge after challenge, twisting his body, sometimes raggedly, but ultimately he was able to score from a position that no one else in the ground was able to understand. In what was to be Xavi's final game for the club, it was a fitting tribute.

The 2015 UEFA Champions League final against Juventus was a

thrilling spectacle in which the brilliance of Barça as a team was evident from the outset.

Barça's perfectly choreographed opening goal within the first five minutes seemed to hark back to the team ethos that had made the club both so successful and respected by fans around the world – with nine players involved. The final passes involved Neymar playing the ball to Iniesta, who picked a perfect pass to Rakitić inside a packed penalty box, and the Croat beat Gianluigi Buffon. Juventus came back in the second half and scored a brilliant goal of their own from Morata. Just as the game seemed poised to go either way, Messi went on a brilliant run, and his rasping shot was only pushed out by Buffon to Suárez, who showed his predator's instinct by drilling the ball high into the net.

And then it was Neymar's turn, scoring the third and decisive goal on the breakaway in the ninety-seventh minute.

Barcelona had won the treble, again, with Messi's genius supplemented by brilliant contributions from Neymar and Suárez.

While the purists and nostalgics came to lament the break-up of Barça's intricate transition game, contrary to Cruyff's dire warnings, Neymar adapted to a supporting role for Messi, as did Suárez, covering for him when necessary while delivering on the goals he helped create with increasingly impressive results. The three struck up an understanding on a personal and professional front, with Suárez moving into Messi's neighbourhood in Castelldefels and becoming a regular companion off-pitch as well as on it.

Messi and Neymar also got on well, although the dynamic of the relationship was very different to that which he had enjoyed with Ronaldinho. While in the early years the young Messi had deferred to the advice and support of the older Ronaldinho, now Neymar looked up to Messi as a player with greater experience than him and still at the top of his game.

For all the developing strategic focus on the trio, team tactics and the way Neymar and Suárez combined still revolved around the figure of Messi, as play maker and main goal scorer, and the man with a global following that only Cristiano Ronaldo could claim to easily surpass. Both Neymar and Suárez upped their game and played their part alongside Messi in becoming La Liga's most successful front three, scoring 122 goals between them by the end of the season. They overcame the adversity of the first months of the season to rewrite the record books again.

Real Madrid had fallen apart when it mattered, the stability that the beginning of the season had seemed to offer proving a thin veneer, with all the old politics over pecking order always ready to capsize their season. Central to this was whether it was possible for any world-class player to find their way around Ronaldo's ego. After so much promise, yet again the season ended with massive doubts over the manager, who – trophy-less – appeared to be a dead man walking.

Though the statistics would show he had come back strongly and won the Golden Shoe, Ronaldo had disappeared when his team needed him, retreating into petulance and criticism, suspended, and then not making the difference when it counted. Simply put, no one could imagine that Messi would have found solace in an individual award if the roles were reversed, but it was possible to imagine Ronaldo doing so. It was tempting to see the difference between the two of them summed up in their different attitude to the Ballon d'Or. In an interview towards the end of the season, Messi had explained that everything had changed with the birth of his son, saying, 'Above all, how I think. Now it is [Thiago] first, then everything else after that. It has changed the way I see games, too. Before, if I missed a chance or I had a bad game, I would not speak to anyone for three or four days.'[4]

As Barcelona lifted the Champions League trophy again, there was one man who would have been sadder and angrier than anyone else.

36. THE 2016 COPA AMÉRICA: MESSI

Messi only made it to the bench for Argentina's first game against Chile after injuring his back, and in the end they didn't need him, as a Di María-inspired side won 2–1. Indeed, much of the pre-tournament talk had been about where it was possible to play Messi in this Argentina side, with so much attacking talent. Whereas at Barcelona, the team and his best performances had seemed to come when Messi was just allowed to be Messi, dropping deep, playing false 9 or number 10 from moment to moment. For Argentina there wasn't the same flow. Martino had shunted him out to the right wing when he had taken charge, the position Messi had started at as a young player at Barcelona. But whereas one of the first things Guardiola had done was to play him more centrally, here he was left out of much of Argentina's approach play. There were those who said that he should play as a number 10, mimicking the role he'd played so successfully as supplier to Suárez and Neymar. After all, if there were two finishers more suited to those roles than Higuaín and Sergio Agüerro, it was hard to imagine them. It was a perennial problem with Argentina, who seemed constantly to be trying to fit their attacking talent into a system. But it was hard to square Messi's lack of international success with his club career.

He was still only fit enough for the bench in their next group game against Panama and sat watching as Otamendi scored from a header and then Panama went down to ten men. Messi was brought on with half an hour or so remaining and scored a hat-trick in nineteen minutes, with a brilliant free kick, a low finish and a delicate chip blowing a tired Panama away. There was still time for Agüerro to make it 5–0. The Panama manager, Hernán Darío Gómez, called Messi a 'monster'.

That hat-trick left him one goal away from equalling the record of Argentina's all-time leading goal scorer Gabriel Batistuta, whose response was to say, 'It will annoy me but I will have the consolation that I lost my record to a player of another dimension.'

In a stadium full of US football fans in Barcelona shirts with 'MESSI' on the back, he equalled the record, as Argentina beat Venezuela 4–1, setting up a semi-final against the hosts, USA.

They outclassed them, with Messi scoring a brilliant free kick and setting up two goals. The issue of where he should play suddenly seemed absurd and the answer obvious: 'anywhere he liked'. They went into the final against Chile, buoyant and confident. After all, they had beaten Chile once without Messi; now they had him in inspirational form.

In the end, what will be remembered of this final would be Messi announcing that he was retiring from playing for Argentina. He had just missed his penalty in the shootout and watched as Chile had gone on to win. He was inconsolable in the dressing room, unable to rouse himself from his disappointment. All the good things he'd done in the previous games seemed forgotten as that ball looped up over the bar.

As he announced his retirement, he said, 'I tried my hardest, it's been four finals but I was not able to win. I tried everything possible. It hurts me more than anyone but it is evident that this is not for me.'[1] He was unable to meet the eyes of those journalists around him. He had obviously been crying.

The pressure of playing for Argentina; the self-fulfilling narrative of the bottler, who couldn't do it when it counted. In his third summer of international football, he seemed wiped out, spread too thin. Four final losses were too much for him. He had said he would swap all his Ballons d'Or for one tournament win with Argentina. The team returned to Buenos Aires to find banners urging him to change his mind and Maradona added to the chorus, saying that Messi had been 'abandoned' by certain teammates.

Perhaps he meant it, but all it did was to make it seem as if Messi was cursed, while Maradona would for ever more claim that God was on *his* side.

37. REBUILDING: MESSI AND RONALDO

As ever, Madrid and Barcelona's identity seemed to be defined in opposition to the other. Barcelona quietly renewed their contract with Luis Enrique. Ancelotti was hurried out of the door and replaced by Rafael Benítez.

In truth, club president Florentino Pérez had been questioning the Italian's judgement for a while. Even as far back as January 2015, Ancelotti had substituted Gareth Bale in the seventy-first minute in a match against Valencia. Real Madrid had won a record twenty-four consecutive victories before that game, but Pérez criticized Ancelotti for his substitution anyway: 'To take off Bale is an attack on me. He is a strategic player for us,' Pérez was reported to have told the coach.[1]

According to Ancelotti, he was told by Pérez that the Welsh international's agent, Jonathan Barnett, was displeased with the way the coach was treating the player, in his view playing him in the wrong position and seemingly underestimating his potential contribution to the team's success. Bale had generally played on the right side of a three-man attack since joining Madrid from Tottenham for €100 million in summer 2013, with Cristiano Ronaldo and Karim Benzema also part of the front line. When Pérez asked Ancelotti what he was going to do about Bale and his agent's concerns, the Italian replied, 'Nothing.'

As Ancelotti later related in his book, *Quiet Leadership: Winning Hearts, Minds and Matches*, the issue was over whether Bale played centrally, as he wanted to, or out wide. Ancelotti was clear that he knew better than Bale's agent, better than the president, what Bale's qualities were and how to get the best out of him. His position was that he wasn't willing to adapt the whole system to fit Bale.

Pérez was also stung by UEFA statistics which showed that, under Ancelotti, the players' fitness record had deteriorated because of a somewhat laissez-faire attitude towards training, feeding into a suspicion within the club that the coach was not fully in control of his players on and off the pitch.

And yet Pérez took a risk in sacking him, for the Italian was popular with fans and some key players, not least Cristiano Ronaldo, who tweeted his support for him after the last game of the season. The respect was mutual. Ancelotti would later publicly describe Cristiano Ronaldo as a leader and someone who cared about the team. He decried those who had been obsessed with his image, how he looked. He described a player who liked to be with his teammates, to discuss how the game had gone and who liked to joke.

Of Ronaldo's relationship with Barcelona rival Lionel Messi, Ancelotti believed the pair pushed one another to achieve greatness through their competitive spirit. As he saw it, 'Perhaps they would not have flown so high without the other pushing them on.'

Onlookers wondered, with good reason, how this team of *galácticos* and their galactic egos might respond to Benítez's famously authoritarian, hands-on management style. It had seemed to those who had followed the previous season that the rot had set in at around the time that stories of tension between Bale and Ronaldo had started to gain traction.

Despite having to deal with a succession of managers in his time at Real Madrid – Pellegrini, Mourinho, Ancelotti – there was not one with whom Cristiano Ronaldo had a major public falling out, largely because they were under orders from club president Florentino Pérez not to provoke him.

In terms of personal relations with his managers at Real Madrid, Ronaldo got on best with Pellegrini and Ancelotti, and developed a working relationship with Mourinho. It was fair to say that Benítez's policy of treating no player as bigger than the team – and by extension that meant Ronaldo too – was bound to run into problems.

Meanwhile, in Barcelona, Luis Enrique had to tread delicately around Messi after his summer of international disappointment.

The sting from his missed penalty didn't take long to surface, as Messi was lucky to stay on the pitch against Roma in a friendly, after aiming a headbutt at a defender and grabbing him by the throat.

Both Barcelona and Messi's form was patchy, leading up to the first Clásico in November 2015.

Barcelona had won the Super Cup 5–4 after they'd needed extra time to get past Sevilla; they'd been leading 4–1 at one point, before being pegged back to 4–4. Messi scored two brilliant free kicks and it was his saved shot that was poked home by Pedro. They'd then been hammered 5–1 over two legs in the Spanish Super Cup by Athletic Bilbao, in games where Messi looked tired and some of his teammates not up to the task without him at his best.

In the League, they dropped six points in their first eleven games, as they lost to Celta Vigo and Sevilla. Messi scored three goals, including a vital winner against Atlético, which he dedicated to the birth of his second son, Mateo. But he was then injured in September and only returned for the Clásico.

Madrid, on the other hand, with a new head coach who'd joined saying football was 'just about winning', had drawn three and lost one of their first eleven games and there were already mumblings of discontent about their style of play. Ronaldo's form was patchy, too, as he had scored five goals in one remarkable game against Espanyol and a hat trick in their 4–0 defeat of Shakhtar Donetsk, but only another three in the other ten League games. Madrid came into the game off a damaging 3–2 defeat against Sevilla.

In the background were a bungled goodbye ceremony for club legend Iker Casillas, ongoing bad press over Sergio Ramos's contract renewal and their failure to get a transfer deal for David De Gea over the line at the last minute.

Benítez's claims that Ronaldo was the best in the world smacked of Jorge Mendes's hotline to Florentino Pérez and a swift reminder of hierarchies, rather than a genuine change of heart. He was forced to defend Ronaldo's form before the Clásico, calling him a 'fundamental player' and saying he was certain the goals would come. For the first time in a long time, both Messi and Ronaldo entered the game not quite fully centre stage.

Ronaldo seemed unsettled, apparently annoyed at his manager for trying to give Gareth Bale a role in the team that appeared to compete with his, and also trying to give Ronaldo suggestions about how to play better – the Portuguese believed Benítez had nothing to teach him. During an emblematic training session, Ronaldo was caught on camera and recorded swearing at Benítez for having a goal he had scored disallowed as offside by the coach. The sequence developed a popular following on YouTube.

Messi had been out for eight weeks injured and, while he was gone, Suárez and especially Neymar had coped admirably.

In the end, Messi sat out most of the game on the bench, and Ronaldo probably wished he had done, as an Iniesta-inspired Barcelona tore Madrid apart, winning 4–0. Benítez had second-guessed himself, picking an attacking line-up, only to have his team outplayed all over the pitch. When Messi came on for the final half-hour, he touched the ball more than Ronaldo did in the entire ninety minutes. The defining image of the game is of Ronaldo grimacing in disgust while Benítez writes in his notebook. The player who needed an arm around his shoulder was ignored by the tactician, while Real Madrid fans clapped Barça's Andrés Iniesta as the man of the match.

In the fallout from the game, it was widely reported that Ronaldo was so convinced that Benítez was to blame for the team's lack of cohesion and morale that he told Pérez, 'Either you sack him or I go.' '*O Benítez o yo*' went the headline in the Spanish media. Benítez, in fairness, seemed caught between a rock and hard place: damned if he surrendered to his critics, damned if he didn't. In El Clásico he chose to try and get his players to play a more attacking football than he characteristically favoured, and found his team comprehensively beaten. The men in white were simply unmotivated by the dour Benítez – not least Ronaldo, a player who liked to win and to play a starring role in any victory.

In the eyes of his less than sympathetic critics, Benítez looked as if he was clutching at straws when he blamed the media for hatching a 'campaign' against Real Madrid, president Florentino Pérez and himself. It was reminiscent of his 'facts' rant about Manchester United and Sir Alex Ferguson while manager of Liverpool, and left the Spaniard pointing fingers without acknowledging the mistakes he had made himself. Even his attempts to calm the situation made things worse. 'Cristiano is a very hard-working and an important player to our team. But we will try not to rely on the individuals.'

What, went the thinking, was the point of bringing together the most expensive squad of star footballers in history, and then pretending to be some sort of collective? If you couldn't rely on Cristiano Ronaldo, who could you rely on?

Luis Enrique claimed the result was 'historic'; it certainly seemed as if there was only one team who were going to kick on and take control of the League. As the year came to an end, and Barcelona won the Club World Cup, a recurring theme was the unity that MSN felt. At first, it had seemed like a joke, a mildly mocking nickname that drew attention to how hard it was going to be for them to play together, but no one was joking about that any more. When they crunched the sums in December, it was worked out that since Messi had been shifted out wide and Suárez moved more centrally, their record read: played sixty-seven, won fifty-four, won four trophies; Neymar had scored forty-two goals in fifty-two games, Suárez forty-three in fifty-eight and Messi fifty-three in fifty-four. But as ever those statistics only really contained the ghost of what it was to watch those players revel in the movement and the space that the others afforded them. Suárez had added what Barcelona had hoped he would: teeth, in the right way; he constantly hustled and ran, giving defenders no rest and his finishing was brilliant. Neymar had added end product to his graceful runs and was probably the closest challenger after Ronaldo that Messi had ever had to being the best player in the world. Messi, well, he continued to be both the conductor and the star violinist, lifting up the players around him. No one was talking about the various scandals that had rocked Barcelona in recent months; they just wanted to talk about the goals.

The next Clásico was set for 2 April 2016, and over the next seventeen League games Barcelona won forty-six from a possible fifty-four points, drawing only three games. Messi scored nineteen goals.

After the Clásico defeat, Benítez and Madrid limped on, but seemingly from one mini crisis to another.

Florentino gave Benítez a public vote of confidence at the end of November, blaming everyone, including Carlo Ancelotti, the media and radical ultras for the boos in the stadium. He explicitly denied that Ronaldo had a problem with Benítez.

However, the club was kicked out of the Copa del Rey for fielding a player who had been given three yellow cards in the competition the previous season while on loan. There was a respite in the Champions League as Ronaldo scored four goals in an 8–0 victory over Malmö and took the opportunity to defend Benítez, saying that he had a good relationship with him.

The season began to resemble a slightly sickening rollercoaster, however, as they went from the lows of a defeat against Villarreal, to the high of a 10–2 victory against Rayo Vallecano. As the year 2015 finished they were in touching distance of the top of the League. In their final game of the year, Ronaldo scored twice as they beat Real Sociedad 3–1. Benítez thanked him for carrying the team 'on his back'.

Finally, it was a 2–2 draw against Valencia that did for Benítez, and on 4 January it was announced that he had been sacked, with club legend Zinedine Zidane stepping up from his reserve team manager role. The early signs were positive, as Madrid began with a 5–0 and then 5–1 victories at home. There were encouraging noises from players, as the atmosphere lifted. Zidane – as one of the most popular players ever – had a vast store of credit with the fans. When he was asked in February who the best player in the world was, he answered without hesitation that it was Ronaldo, whereas Benítez had famously equivocated and compared the choice to asking his daughter whether she loved her mother or father best. Zidane understood just how important a motivated and happy Ronaldo would be to his and Madrid's fortunes. At the end of January, a radio station broke the mischievous story that Madrid had tried to buy Messi three times, with the most recent offer being only the year before.

At a fractious press conference before Madrid's first-leg game against Roma in the Champions League, Ronaldo walked out angrily in response to a question about whether he was worried about not scoring in his last four away games. He addressed the assembled journalists, asking them who'd scored more away goals than him since he'd been in Spain. When there was no answer, he excused himself and walked out, but not before hoping that his 'bad form' continued until the end of the season. There would be a couple of draws and a damaging defeat against neighbour and title rival Atlético, but in Zidane's first twelve games in charge before the April Clásico, they dropped only seven points. Out of their thirty-six goals, Ronaldo scored fourteen. They also saw off Roma 4–0 on aggregate, with Ronaldo scoring in both legs. They seemed to have ridden out the controversy of Ronaldo's statement after the Atlético game that, 'If we were all at my level, maybe we would be leaders.' He had immediately apologized to his teammates on WhatsApp and then gave an interview to *MARCA*, saying, 'I was referring to the physical level, not level of play. I am not better than any of my teammates.'[2]

The talk before the match was dominated by the tribute to Johan Cruyff, the man who had done more than anyone to make Barcelona who they were. On the fourteenth minute – in tribute to Cruyff's shirt number – there was a round of applause and a huge mosaic of cards held up by fans read, 'Gràcies, Johan'. But what everyone wanted to see was how Zidane's Madrid would stand up to Barcelona, what they were made of.

Barcelona started brightest and took control of the ball, nearly scoring several times, as Madrid seemed lost. At one point, Ronaldo tried to find Benzema with a pass on the counter-attack and Benzema slipped onto his backside. He threw his hands up in disgust on the sideline, as Barcelona broke back at them. The second half was more of the same, until a Messi chip was saved for a corner, from which Piqué buried his header. Five minutes later, though, and Real were level from a Benzema volley. With only five minutes to go, Sergio Ramos saw red for a second booking and the signs weren't good for Madrid, but then a brilliant cross from Bale found its way to Ronaldo, who chested it down from a tight angle and hammered his shot under the goalkeeper.

It hadn't been close to some of the most classic of Clásicos, but Madrid had shown guts, Ronaldo and Bale had combined when it mattered and, for the first time in six months, Barcelona were beaten. The Real players celebrated by posting a dressing-room selfie where, on one side, straining his fabulous torso into the most flattering pose and wearing the smallest, whitest pairs of briefs you can imagine is Cristiano Ronaldo.

After the Madrid game there was a worrying run of form for Barcelona as their first defeat in thirty-nine became four in five, as they lost to Real Sociedad and Valencia in the League, either side of crashing out of the Champions League quarter-finals 3–2 on aggregate to Atlético Madrid. Suddenly the title race was wide open, with the slightest stumble ready to be seized upon.

In their next game, they won 8–0 against Deportivo as Suárez scored four and set up three other goals, as if deciding enough was enough. They won their remaining five games 24–0 on aggregate and were named League champions on the final day of the season.

They also won the Copa del Rey 2–1 in extra time.

Real's season ended with the Champions League final against Atlético Madrid again.

Two images endured for me in the aftermath of that final in Milan, both taken in the final minutes of a less than memorable encounter.

The first was that of beaten finalists Atlético's Juanfran, the other of Real Madrid's Cristiano Ronaldo, just after the two had taken their respective shots at goals during the penalty shootout.

Juanfran's shot hit the bar and his subsequent drowned-dog look and pose was that of a man who would forever carry within him the memory of defeat. Ronaldo, by contrast, did what Ronaldo liked to do best – show the world that he is the best; not just the best goal scorer, but the physically most beautifully crafted human being. After converting the winning penalty, he once again revealed his sculpted pectorals and biceps, displayed in a shimmering golden tan, relegating the priestly, unshaven and pale Juanfran to the level of ordinary mortal.

And lest we forget, Ronaldo told us that he had always known he would score the winning goal, which is why he had asked Zidane to have him take the final penalty. A man of destiny, the foot of God.

No matter that up to and including extra time, Ronaldo had utterly underperformed, barely touching the ball during much of the game and making a hash of his one previous shot at goal. No matter that Juanfran had assisted in Atlético's equalizer and worked his socks off for the rest of the game, helping defend against Bale's relentless assaults, and who would have been a candidate for man of the match had his team won. Bale had a more effective performance, and yet Ronaldo was able to control the narrative. A season of coherent excellence from Messi and Barcelona as they did the double was overshadowed by yet another Champions League. Ronaldo had been definitive when it mattered. As Ronaldo limped into a summer of European Championships with Portugal, who would bet against him doing the same again.

International Break

38. EURO 2016: RONALDO THE MANAGER

After Spain had won the European Championships two successive times either side of the World Cup between 2008 and 2012, the label of Europe's great football underachievers had shifted, not for the first time, to its neighbour. Despite boasting some star players in leading European leagues, Portugal had never won any trophy of any significance.

If there were golden memories of the national team, they were of brilliant football without trophies – led by that of Eusébio, who had starred in the Portuguese side that played in the World Cup in 1966 after staggering through the qualifying group stage.

By contrast, Portugal's moment of maximum humiliation and tragedy was losing Euro 2004 on home territory in the final against Greece, after starting the tournament as favourites. Ronaldo's tears after the final personified a nation's sadness, endearing him to many of his countrymen – but not all.

For a nation that had long ceased to be a great power and had no political clout internationally, and yet had always loved football, it was a very bitter defeat. After a series of quarter- and semi-final defeats in subsequent tournaments, their reputation as 'nearly men' had become entrenched. Portuguese participation in the 2014 World Cup proved disappointing once more, with the team eliminated in the group stage, despite featuring Ronaldo at the peak of his powers. The 'nearly men' had become 'nowhere-near men'.

Against this background, Fernando Santos, the national coach for Euro 2016 in France, was asked before the tournament about when he thought he would return to Portugal. Almost no one believed him when he replied: 'I am only coming back after the final.' Where there's a will there's a way, in other words, and Portugal was going to win, an attitude that seemed perfectly in tune with Cristiano Ronaldo's self-belief.

But the tournament got off to a less than encouraging start. After their opening game, a 1–1 draw with Iceland in which he failed to score, Ronaldo accused Portugal's opponents of being 'lucky' and 'small'. He then missed a penalty and had a goal ruled out for offside in the goalless draw with Austria.

The gods were in his favour in Portugal's final Group F match against Hungary, however, with Ronaldo scoring twice, his first goals of the championship, to secure a 3–3 draw. Portugal squeezed through as one of the best-ranked third-placed teams. Such was the frustration of not winning more convincingly, Ronaldo took against a journalist for his line of questioning and threw his microphone into a lake.

From then on, things started to go right. Narrow wins against Croatia and Poland saw the Portuguese into a semi-final against Wales, where Ronaldo scored in a 2–0 victory. They would start the final against host nation France as underdogs, but this was a competition that Ronaldo was destined to play a key role in winning. As far as his Portuguese compatriots were concerned, it also secured legendary status for a player who had struggled until then to make a major impact on the country's underwhelming national team.

For all his success at club level – mainly playing for non-Portuguese clubs – Ronaldo had struggled to establish a reputation among his fellow countrymen as the best, let alone most loved, Portuguese footballer ever.

According to one of Portugal's most respected football commentators, André Pipa of Bola TV, even when Ronaldo won his first Ballon d'Or at Manchester United, his earlier years as a Sporting player made it difficult for rival Benfica fans to accept the displacement of their icon Eusébio, much as they found it hard to go crazy over Figo, another Sporting man.

As Pipa told me when we met in Lisbon in the spring of 2017, 'Benfica claims 6 million fans compared to Sporting's about 3.5 million. So you are talking about a good proportion of the population of Portugal [10 million] and a great deal more than metropolitan Lisbon [2.8 million] that had serious misgivings about Cristiano Ronaldo earlier in his career.'

And then there was an issue of personality. Portugal had evolved as a modern European society since its entry into the EU, but certain prejudices dating back to the long years of the dictatorship had endured in some sectors of the population. As Pipa put it, 'There is a surviving cultural trait among some Portuguese, which is that of mean-spiritedness, an unhealthy envy of those who are successful – we are a "small-minded" people.'

Ronaldo, then, was disliked not because he won prizes, but because he openly declares his right to them. 'When Kaká won the Ballon d'Or in 2007, Ronaldo was unable to hide his anger in public that he had come in third behind Messi. That's because he is hyper-competitive and has a monumental ego. Ronaldo works hard to be number one. He feels he has to be. He is like some of the early Portuguese discoverers of the fifteenth century, somewhat egocentric and possessed with an enormous sense of self-belief,' said Pipa.

And yet all changed with Portugal's victory in the European Championships of 2016, when Ronaldo achieved something for his country that neither Eusébio nor Figo had ever achieved – a major tournament title, playing an epic role. As Pipa put it, 'There the doubts dissipated . . . more and more Portuguese began to recognize the absolute primacy of Cristiano.'

So what accounted for Portugal's success, I asked Raquel Vaz-Pinto, a fanatical football fan and Lisbon academic:

In my view, the key figure was the coach Fernando Santos and players like Ronaldo, Pepe and Quaresma. But if I had to choose one player I would go for Pepe. He was magisterial and a general in defence, which was the basis of our strategy. The main idea was that we couldn't allow a goal and then built it from there. For a player who had such a poor performance in the 2014 World Cup [Pepe was sent off against Germany], it was his great and last chance to redeem himself. The same goes for Quaresma, one of our most talented players ever but who never quite made it to the very top, and he knew this was his last chance to have a place in history.

Fernando Santos was able to bring out the best of these older players. Quaresma has always been a very tough ego to manage and it was wonderful watching him enter the game at seventy or eighty minutes completely focused and . . . scoring. You wouldn't hear a single moan about why wasn't he in the starting eleven, and so forth.

Eder, the player who scored the winning goal in the final, was twenty-eight at the time and until that goal was not a decisive player. At the same time, the team was able to integrate younger players like Renato Sanches and to maintain several players from Sporting, which gave the team some degree of stability. As to the former, the younger players like Renato had recently been promoted to the squad for the first time. They had real talent and much to prove.[1]

But rising above them all it was Cristiano Ronaldo whose role proved decisive. Although worn out after a tough season with Real Madrid and carrying injuries, he was utterly determined to lead the squad to victory.

Nine minutes into the final, Ronaldo went down in pain after a collision with Dimitri Payet and needed treatment. He then resumed playing in evident discomfort until the seventeenth minute, when he sank to the ground in tears and went off the field for further treatment. Three minutes later he was back, only to slump to the ground again in the twenty-fifth minute, to be taken off on a stretcher. The captain's armband was passed to Nani who told the other players to win it for Cristiano.

After he was injured, Cristiano – already the most capped and prolific player in Portugal's history with sixty-one goals in 133 caps – did not renounce centre stage. Instead, like a wounded, heroic commander still rallying his troops, he urged his teammates to victory from the touchline. He became as motivated off the pitch as on it, as Vaz-Pinto explains:

> He was our captain off the pitch when we needed him the most. I was watching the game with my husband Duarte and our niece Maria and I remember turning to them, after the foul committed by Payet on Ronaldo, and saying: this is the moment. The team is going to rally and deliver to Ronaldo and to all of us. In the final, coach Fernando Santos stepped back from his frontline duties as coach and allowed Ronaldo to voice his encouragement and support from the touchline after he had been injured. What

might have in different circumstances and with a different coach
been interpreted as a dereliction of duty became engrained in
the imagination of Portuguese fans as an act of tactical and strategic intelligence by someone who showed huge personal skills
in managing his players, not so much indulging in their idiosyncrasies but giving free rein to their creative talent, thus allowing
Ronaldo to lead the players as if he was playing.[2]

When victory came, 1–0, after Eder's speculative shot in extra time, the
celebration showed a nation in touch with and at ease with its own
sense of collective identity as a multicultural society. At a time when
most of Europe had experienced an upsurge in anti-immigration votes
and racist ideologies, the mixed origins of the Portuguese team was a
non-issue. The Euro 2016 winners included players who were born in
the Portuguese-speaking African countries, like Eder, immigrant families in Germany or France, like Cédric Soares and Raphaël Guerreiro,
people with gipsy origins like Quaresma, and those born in Brazil like
Pepe. Captaining them all was Cristiano Ronaldo, born in Madeira
with ancestors from Cape Verde.

Ronaldo had now played in more European Championship
matches than any other player, was the only player to score in four
different Euros, and was level with Michel Platini as the competition's
all-time leading scorer, with nine goals.

Despite this achievement, Ronaldo's emotional display from the
touchline during the final did not meet with universal approval.
Among his fellow Portuguese, the veteran international António
Simões and José Mourinho echoed each other in their veiled criticism
of what they saw as Ronaldo's continued egocentricity.

'I've been in football for fifty years, and never seen anything like
that. None of the great world players would have done something like
that. I knew players, great leaders, Pelé, Eusébio, Cruyff, Maradona . . .
Maradona, even with his personality, never did anything like that. I
believe that Ronaldo let his huge nerves take him over – he wanted to
win and show he was a leader. Doing that does not make you a leader,'
said Simões.

Among the tributes that Ronaldo received after the victory, however, was one that claimed to sum up the feelings of the team, from
his Real Madrid colleague Pepe: 'It was tough to lose our main man,

the man who could at any moment score a goal,' he said. 'We said we would win it for him and we managed to do that.'

Those Portuguese who put Ronaldo on a pedestal inadvertently made him part of mythology. Overall, Euro 2016 was, in purely competitive terms, a rather lacklustre tournament with a similarly underwhelming final.

As J. J. Bull, a columnist with the *Telegraph*, summed up the drama:

> For 109 minutes of this final, it looked like all we were going to remember of Cristiano Ronaldo's night would be the moth that settled on one of his finely sculpted eyebrows as he contemplated the pain in his left knee that not even the best-developed quad muscles in world football could disperse.
>
> Then, deep into extra-time of the worst final in living memory, the Portugal striker Eder, who was not good enough for Swansea City, scored the kind of goal Ronaldo has been burying all his life, and on the touchline the real Ronaldo celebrated it with even more intensity than he usually reserves for his own hat-tricks.[3]

It was probably not too far away from the worst nightmares that Ronaldo had suffered – Portugal winning but him being completely sidelined. Instead he was able to put himself front and centre by effectively managing the team through extra time and then stripping off at the final whistle. You could almost see the thoughts in his head as he lifted the trophy with Messi still effectively retired. *Beat that.*

39. ON TRIAL: MESSI

Four days before Ronaldo lifted the trophy at Euro 2016, Messi faced up to an opponent who steadfastly refused to be beaten.

Since starting his professional career, Lionel Messi had had his low points – poor passes, lost balls, squandered opportunities, missed penalties – but nothing had quite prepared him for the public humiliation he experienced on 6 July 2016. Not in a stadium but in a court of law, and in Barcelona, of all places. It also offers a fascinating glimpse into the world of Messi and his family.

Feeling intimidated by the crowds gathered to hear the sentence, and awkward and diminished by the oppressive functionality of the court room, Lionel sat peevishly on a bare wooden chair, alongside his father Jorge – looking less a benevolent patriarch than an overprotective older brother – and heard a judge sentence them both to jail terms of twenty-one months and fines for defrauding the Spanish state of €4.1 million. Had he been sent to jail at that moment, he might have been saved the ignominy of what followed.

As both walked out of the court room on probation – Messi first, followed by his father – and made their way to a waiting car, closely observed by policemen, they ran the gauntlet of photographers, TV crews and football fans. Some of them were as supportive as when he scored a goal; others were accusing them of being common thieves, as if more than ten years of stardom on the pitch had been negated there and then.

The scene was the culmination of protracted legal wrangles involving Messi, not all of them so publicized, and related to earnings from image rights that had been channelled through various shell companies set up in tax havens across the world. Messi Junior stated from the beginning that he 'knew nothing' about his financial affairs and left that to his father. Messi Senior said that he had been told by a financial adviser that there was nothing illegal about the practice.

There were interesting parallels with another legal process that had occurred eight years previously, when the Messis had walked through the iron gates off a busy shopping street, leading to a small picturesque tropical garden and into the whitewashed court building in Gibraltar. There, lawyers and judges received them politely and dealt with the case before them, as tradition demanded, speaking through translators in English and wearing starched white collars and white curly wigs.

It was in the UK colony on the southern tip of the Iberian peninsula in 2008, where British policemen spoke with Andalusian accents, and pubs serving English beer and fish and chips shared space with Moroccan grocery stores, Italian-style coffee shops and Spanish tapas bars, that a civil action had been taken by trustees of the Belize-registered Sports Consultants Ltd (SCL), who handled Messi's image rights, to establish who deserved to make money from their exploitation.

There were two sides in the dispute and the case hung on their credibility as witnesses, given the contradictory content of their statements, which included those taken earlier in another unpublicized court case in Belize.

According to court documents, an Argentine ex-footballer turned agent, Rodolfo Schinocca, claimed that he had been assigned a majority shareholding in a company that had been set up to exploit Lionel Messi's increasing commercial value as he was fast-tracked into FC Barcelona's first team as a hugely talented teenager.

Over the years, Jorge Messi had come to the conclusion that agents, particularly those emanating from the endemically corrupt world of Argentine football, were not to be trusted, and that his son's career was better protected as part of a firm controlled by the family rather than contracted out to any of the numerous third-party sharks pitching for a deal in the cut-throat business of football.

In fact, Jorge Messi had rarely lost sight of his son since Lionel's early days as a schoolboy footballer. While his wife had subsequently chosen to stay behind in Rosario and not move in with her son in Barcelona, Jorge spent as much time as he could in the Catalan capital.

The court in Gibraltar heard various pieces of contradictory evidence as to how much Messi earned at the time. Messi was piggy in the middle, if – by his very nature – a silent one. It was football not money that absorbed him, in such an obsessively focused and verbally inexpressive way that some observers speculated he might be suffering from Asperger's syndrome – a developmental disorder characterized by significant difficulties in social interaction and non-verbal communication, along with restricted and repetitive patterns of behaviour and interests.

The Argentinian writer Leonardo Faccio later caught up with Schinocca in Buenos Aires in 2013, where the agent had escaped being charged with any criminal offence and sworn his innocence. Faccio asked him if Lionel Messi took an interest in his contracts.

'Yes. He was interested. It was part of his professional career. But he wasn't involved in the negotiations. He left all that in the hands of his lawyers, with me, with his family. He just got on with playing football and giving his personal guarantee that he would do whatever advertising that was specified [in the contract],' Schinocca replied.

The Gibraltar case heard evidence that the player was still an immature teenager when he found himself unwittingly in the crossfire of those claiming to represent his best interests, and those tempted to exploit him for their personal gain.

Jorge Messi told the court that the relationship with Schinocca broke down when the latter received payments from Adidas but failed to transfer the sum to the company or account for it.

As the presiding judge in Gibraltar saw it, there were inconsistencies in evidence produced by both the Messis and Schinocca but, in weighing it all up, he found the Messis the more credible witnesses, though neither side emerged from this case squeaky clean.

The judge noted that the Messis were 'not beyond criticism' because of the inconsistencies in the way they had advanced their case at different times. 'Mrs Messi's absolute ignorance of the commercial relationship and Mr Messi's inability to even identify documents central to the case was certainly strong cause for dealing with their evidence with circumspection,' the judge said.

Eight years later and it seemed that not much had changed.

When he was later forced to give a witness statement to the Catalan court in 2016, Messi found himself temporarily separated from his father. He struggled to express the feelings of genuine love and gratitude he had felt for him from childhood. 'My old man rarely used to say when I was a kid, "you played well." As a boy I would score four goals and he still found something to criticize. That made me always want to be better,' he told the judge.

From the beginning, the twenty-nine-year-old had always denied any knowledge of his tax affairs, saying he 'only worried about playing football', while his father claimed he left it all up to financial advisers.

During the four-day hearing into the case, Messi insisted he had 'never' discussed tax on his image rights with his father or lawyers.

'So, you signed all contracts with your eyes shut?' the district attorney asked him.

'I signed them because I trust my father and it never entered my head that he would try to cheat me,' Messi replied.

But, summing up the case, the presiding judge, Mercedes Armas Galve, said of the five-time world player of the year: '[His] avoidable ignorance, which was derived from indifference, is not an error, and it does not remove responsibility. The information that the accused avoided having was, in reality, within his reach via trustworthy and accessible sources.' Indeed, as it later emerged, Spanish prosecutors pursued the case against the Messis after father and son had already paid a 'corrective payment' of €4.1 million in 2013 after they had admitted filing incomplete tax returns for the years 2006 to 2009. Under Spanish law, sentences of less than two years for first offences are usually suspended, and neither the Barcelona star nor father Jorge were expected to serve time behind bars. However, they were fined an additional €1.7 million and €1.3 million respectively by the court in Barcelona. And they were subjected to the humiliating gauntlet of onlookers outside the court.

Discovering that the best-paid Barça player was using the disputed jurisdiction of the British enclave to set up a 'tax efficient' corporate structure was the equivalent of a red rag being held before a bull – and, to make matters worse, the investigating Spanish judge turned out to be a Real Madrid fan.

In the aftermath of the guilty verdict against Messi in a Catalan court, FC Barcelona rallied round the player, insisting that he was in no way criminally responsible.

Among some Barça senior executives, there was concern that the judgement would lead to Messi feeling so demoralized as to want to quit the club and Spain – a move he had considered in 2013 when the tax authorities first caught up with him.

Yet, not all of them agreed with the suitability of a social media campaign, launched after the judgement in the summer of 2016 with the blessing of club president Josep Maria Bartomeu, and the enthusiastic support of thousands of football fans. The club urged their supporters to demonstrate their unconditional support for the player by taking to social media and using the hashtag #WeAreAllLeoMessi, as well as asking for fans to take photographs holding 'both hands open' in a gesture of solidarity.

The campaign proved hugely controversial, damaging Barça's self-projected image as a club proud of its ethical and civil values. Critics saw its echo of the campaign in protest at the murder of French journalists at the magazine *Charlie Hebdo* by Islamic terrorists as inappropriate and in bad taste. There was also a sense that the business of football was governed by an 'anything goes' mentality, with star players not held accountable for their misdemeanours to the extent that most sectors of society were.

Inevitably, given the tense relations between Catalonia and the Spanish government, the Messi case became politicized, with sectors of the Catalan media and Barça supporters alleging a huge conspiracy aimed at deliberately destroying the iconic player's reputation.

It was pointed out that other elite sports people had had tax problems but that they had all been settled administratively, as was the case with Real Madrid players Xabi Alonso and Iker Casillas and tennis star Rafael Nadal (a Real Madrid fan). By contrast, Messi was the only one to be put in a very public dock and given a suspended prison sentence, as well as a huge fine, even after he had settled the unpaid tax. Somewhat outrageously, the prosecutor, state attorney Mario Maza, compared the player to a boss of a criminal network – stronger language than any ever used in a Spanish court of law against a star footballer.

Much was also made by Barça fans of one of the main state prosecutors in the Messi case being a well-known Real Madrid fan, even if the judgement against him was made in a Catalan court.

At the end of that summer, Messi returned a peroxide blond, sporting an overgrown reddish beard and with a dark intensity in his eyes, Beckham style. There was a touch of absurdity – if not uncharacteristic vanity – displayed in his new hairstyle, for Messi was no Cristiano Ronaldo, needing to augment his natural talent with celebrity branding.

While it was hard to take the roughneck look seriously at first, it became clear that it reflected a maturing as well as a resurgence; as if he had lost the innocence but none of the self-belief associated with his youthful self.

The court experience had proved an ordeal and he had willed himself to survive it. While he still trusted his father, he also understood that he had to fight for his own interests, his young family's interests, for the freedom to do what he still considered the only thing that really mattered in his professional life – play football.

The young *pibe* had turned into a sharper, harder personality, all innocence lost – a warrior as well as a magician, determined to show he was still the best, even if he had a rival who refused to lie down.

Messi had cut his holiday short that summer in order to prepare for the new season, and he soon showed his extra levels of resilience, picking himself up from the worst setback of his life and showing renewed passion for the game. That August, writing in *El País*, the journalist Jordi Quixano noted that the health of FC Barcelona depended on Leo Messi's smile as well as the excellence of his football.

Watching Messi play in a pre-season warm-up game against Leicester City, I was not alone in feeling elated. The crowd in Stockholm's aptly named Friends Arena evidently relished, as did TV viewers around the world, his ability to raise the occasion to something worthwhile. It was indeed a necessary tonic after a summer marred by an insipid European Championships and the dark menace of terrorism. The Messi tonic came in the sheer creativity and vision of his play, with the precision of his passing contributing to all three Barça goals.

He might have been one of the smallest players on the pitch, and might no longer have the speed to always outrun opponents, but this 'little big man', as the Spanish journalist Alfredo Relaño put it, 'saw the game with a periscope and placed the ball with mechanical accuracy'. The stadium chanted '*Messi, Messi, Messi*', and gave him a standing ovation when he was substituted in the sixty-second minute. As Gary Lineker later commented: 'Thank you for the joy, Leo.'[1]

As the season began, with a summer in which Ronaldo achieved his dream of another European Cup and international success, and Messi's private life was raked over in a personal nadir, as always these two players seemed to be ever more linked, the pendulum swinging one way and then the other.

40. LEGENDS: MESSI AND RONALDO

It was a season in which both Cristiano and Leo at first seemed to return to the realm of the mere mortal. In their first ten League games in August, September and October, Messi scored seven goals and Ronaldo five, with their teams dropping eight and six points respectively. The two players were both injured and then not fit in the autumn; when they came back, they still scored, but it was left to others – Bale and Benzema at Madrid, Suárez and Neymar at Barcelona – to score the goals that really mattered. Though Messi racked up hat-tricks in the Champions League group stages, even there, Ronaldo seemed somehow subdued.

They entered the first Clásico in December with Barcelona trailing six points behind Madrid, who were unbeaten in thirty-two games. In the end, it was a disjointed game, where both teams were so focused on cutting down the time and space for their opposition creative players that there was no room for anyone to operate. Barcelona were leading 1–0 from a Suárez header in the fifty-third minute but Ramos equalized at the death. It felt like a fitting Clásico for Ronaldo and Messi's current mood. By the standards that any other player on earth is judged by, they were having respectable – even good – seasons. But for them it wasn't quite enough.

In the final game before Christmas, Messi flared into life with one of his classic dribbles, as he swerved through a packed defence, changing direction in that familiar, soft-shoed way, as players seemed to fall down around him. But when it came to the finish, he could only manage a weak toe-poke and it was left to Suárez to sweep in the rebound. Later, he beat another four Espanyol players and set up Alba to score.

Ronaldo was away in December, winning Madrid the Club World Cup with a hat-trick but, although it may sound absurd, it was a performance of very little else. Gone were the eviscerating runs, it seemed; now he operated as the still, extremely sharp point at the top of the pitch, his job to score and little else. The goal statistics were as impressive as ever, but it felt to those fans who enjoyed the sight of Ronaldo in full flight as if there should be a brief period of mourning. For two players who used to be able to do it all, it felt as though they were being forced to do one or the other at this stage of their careers.

He wasn't able to collect it in person, but in December Cristiano Ronaldo was announced as the winner of the Ballon d'Or for the fourth time, leaving him only one win behind Messi.

They both began the year 2017 in stronger form, but with their teams still not performing consistently well, both dropping ten points over the first four months of the season, but with Messi shading it in the League, scoring seventeen goals in seventeen games as against Ronaldo's nine in sixteen.

Real Madrid were efficiently getting the results, with match reports using verbs like 'scrape' and 'grind', but with some grumblings that they weren't actually playing that well. In April, just before the Clásico, there was the absurd spectacle of some Madrid fans whistling Ronaldo in a game against Bayern Munich in which he'd just scored a hat-trick in the second leg of a two-legged tie they won 6–3 on aggregate, with Ronaldo scoring five of the goals.

In the middle of that run, Messi played a key part in an epic game and one of the most dramatic fightbacks seen in the history of football – in the second leg of the Champions League tie against Paris Saint-Germain. The first leg in February had finished 0–4, with Barcelona's performance deemed so bad that it had caused an existential panic at the club. Iniesta looked old and unfit, Busquets looked past it, even MSN couldn't get hold of the ball – and the few times they had it, they didn't seem to know what to do with it. It was a result that made people realize how Messi's goals were papering over the cracks in a team functioning way below its previous level. As the sports newspaper *AS* put it: 'It is not that Barcelona are out of Europe; it is that Barcelona are out of Barcelona.'

They stumbled along in the League, Messi digging deep and scoring a late penalty against Leganés, without celebrating, and then in the next game scoring very much a messy goal, rather than a Messi goal, against Atlético Madrid to go top of the table. He scored another goal against Sporting Gijón in a 6–1 victory, after which Luis Enrique announced he was leaving Barcelona at the end of the year. A manager who had won eight of the ten trophies he had competed for, won the treble in his first season, the double in his second and whose team, in the middle of a crisis, were still top of the League and had reached the final of the Copa del Rey, was hardly mourned. Commentary focused on the timing of his departure, rather than the fact of it. Though he had taken Barcelona from the low point he had found them in, there were those who claimed that he had sold Barcelona's soul by bypassing the homegrown midfield and implanting expensive imports up front.

For the return leg against PSG in early March, it was the kind of night when the Virgin of Montserrat, San Jordi, Messi's granny and the spirit of Catalan pride past, present and future converged on the Nou Camp, as Barça faced what seemed the impossible task of overcoming the four-goal deficit.

As it turned out, it was Neymar who was truly the defining player in the match. Leading 3–1 on the night but needing three more goals in the final two minutes plus injury time, Barcelona scored three times in seven minutes and seventeen seconds, and Neymar was involved in all three.

He scored a stunning free kick, bending the ball over the wall and into the left-hand corner from thirty yards out. Once he had scored, the Brazilian picked up the ball, held it close to his chest and then ran back to the middle of the park, as if he intended to ensure that it stayed with him for the rest of the game.

And up to a point it did, just as it had done until then, for if Barça's fightback was a collective effort, Neymar's relentless movement on and off the ball presented PSG's defence with its most disruptive element. One minute into injury time, it was Neymar who made it all square on aggregate with a successful penalty kick, giving players and supporters a final glimmer of hope that the impossible might just happen, even if PSG were still ahead on away goals.

And so it was that faith, as Luis Enrique put it afterwards, prevailed, with Sergi Roberto scoring the winning goal five minutes into injury time, from Neymar's floated cross.

This was a match that temporarily redeemed the controversial Luis Enrique as a tactician, for it involved the whole team pursuing a ruthless pressing game for all of the first half and much of the second, which succeeded in locking PSG down.

But for some occasional quick passing in midfield, and a simply sublime back-heel by Iniesta that contributed to PSG's own goal, Barça – in their relentless hounding of the ball and determination to fight back – played more like a traditional Real Madrid or Man United of Ferguson's heyday than a Barça of the Cruyff/Guardiola brand. Even Mourinho would have approved, as the tactics were a means to an end, not an end in itself. From the outset Barça played to win – it was edge-of-the-seat stuff but not beautiful to watch, even if when it was over you felt, in the words of Piqué, like making love – if you were a Barça supporter, that is.

Messi's face showed just how much he had matured, particularly in his expression of leadership before he pounded his penalty kick into the net. With his ruddy reddish beard and maniacal eyes, he looked less an Argentine *pibe* and more like a stocky warlord about to deliver the ultimate beheading on a bloody battlefield. No grace or enjoyment or trickery, just silent, cold focus and utter determination.

At the end of the match it was Messi who created another enduring image by leaping onto the advertising boards at the north end of the Nou Camp, and holding his arm up triumphantly, as the fans, at his feet, surged round him. Within two days, 70 million people had seen the picture online, and it was claimed by its photographer, Santiago Garcés, as the most-viewed picture in Barça's history.

But it was an image taken on an evening when Neymar believed he had played the best game in his career, and on which it became clear to him he would never be the main man so long as Messi kept playing.

Compared to the heroism of the comeback against PSG, FC Barcelona's quarter-final defeat at the hands of Juventus over two legs on 19 April 2017 was a huge anticlimax. Barça were crushed in their own stadium. You don't expect that in the Nou Camp, let alone in the Champions League, and what was worse was that Messi was unable to do anything about it.

With his rusty beard and face bloodied after crashing to the ground under Miralem Pjanić's heavy foul, Messi may have briefly morphed once again into the warrior king defiantly holding off the enemy, but he neither had the support nor the solo inspiration to turn the match around. Barça had long ceased to be the Camelot it was in Guardiola's era.

With the exception of Neymar's brief flashes of brilliance, as when he danced away from four challenges before running into Chiellini, this was a Barça easily thwarted, incapable of scoring, and generally lacking creativity or a plan B. The failure of substitutes Mascherano and Alcácer to have any impact on the game showed up the weakness of its bench. The Luis Enrique era was over, with victory in the King's Cup against one of La Liga's weaker clubs, Alavés, scant compensation for Real Madrid winning La Liga and the Champions League.

The day before Barça were eliminated by Juventus, it had been Real Madrid that battled their heart out effectively against Bayern Munich, raising its performance still further with its substitutions, and having its victory delivered by a Cristiano Ronaldo hat-trick.

Ronaldo's goal scoring that season in the last stages of international club football's pre-eminent tournament broke new records, not least Messi's. After the win against the German champions, Cristiano scored another hat-trick against Atlético Madrid in the semi-final, drawing level with Messi on seven Champions League hat-tricks.

If Messi was unable to lift his team in a quarter-final of the Champions League, it was because the Argentine, over-indulged by Luis Enrique, had doggedly refused to rest all season, while Ronaldo, wisely and tactfully handled by the coach Zinedine Zidane, had paced himself.

The Clásico that followed was the one that began this book, a brief respite for Messi in a season of triumph for Ronaldo and Madrid.

Thus Ronaldo was able to lift the Champions League trophy in Cardiff's Principality Stadium after scoring the 600th goal of his career. Ronaldo had scored twice on another exultant night when he also leapfrogged Lionel Messi to announce himself as the competition's leading scorer for the fifth season running. But he was also part of a collective achievement, for Real Madrid had lifted European football's most coveted silverware three times in four seasons, and consolidated their standing as the most successful club in football history. No one doubted that Ronaldo was on his way to his fifth Ballon d'Or.

In reserving his energy for the final weeks of the season, Ronaldo had shown himself intelligently in tune and receptive to the advice of Zidane, a person he respected enormously professionally. He saw in Zidane a player from a humble background whose career progress to stardom had mirrored his own, both at club and national level, defying prejudice and playing a key part in France's golden age as an international team, before becoming one of Real Madrid's most admired *galácticos*.

Ronaldo had also been able to align the interests of the team with his desire for personal glory. The Madrid press's enthusiasm for him had never reached such heights as they did now. Among the most euphoric was Tomás Roncero – a columnist with *AS*.

> I know a lot of people prefer the dribbling style and magic of Messi. I respect that. What I can't stand are those who pontificate – it is an aberration to compare the two players because Messi is on much higher levels ... Check out the numbers in the last stages of the Champions League ... Cristiano averaging almost a goal per match, Messi only manages 0.50. Cristiano is the perfect example of a man who has constructed his own biography, without anybody's help. An unflagging competitor, he has learnt when to speak and when to be silent on the pitch. They've been predicting his decline for the last two years. Absurd. It's been the best season of his career, and he has scored more than 400 goals for Real Madrid. Let someone else come along and beat that ... *tranquillo*. No one will.[1]

Conclusion

And they – Ronaldo and Messi – despite their advancing years, kept themselves up there, among the pantheon of football gods, each in his own way measuring his ability to carve out a new role for himself within his respective team, and delivering on it in a way that retains the respect and admiration of a succession of managers, colleagues and fans. As I write, they are midway through their 2017–18 season; as the book publishes, it will just have finished. Barcelona are under new manager Ernesto Valverde on a record-breaking run of League games, without Neymar, who has left for PSG, but with Messi, still scoring, still making the magical seem mundane. Ronaldo's Madrid are suffering badly from the downswing after the record-breaking 2016–17 season. They are currently fourth in La Liga but Ronaldo has twenty-seven goals in twenty appearances. Messi has twenty-seven in thirty-four appearances. Having sworn I wouldn't rely on statistics, I found myself quickly overwhelmed with the sheer number of goals. If for no other reason than to give the reader some way of assessing their achievements against their own astonishing benchmarks, I had to relent. Like comparing a dinosaur to a double-decker bus, I needed some sense of scale.

In December 2017, Ronaldo drew level with Messi with five Ballons d'Or. Two weeks later, Barcelona beat Madrid 3–0 in the second Clásico of the season, with Messi scoring his fiftieth goal of 2017. The pendulum swings again. By the time you read this, it will likely have swung again. What we know for sure is that after reversing his decision to retire, Messi brought Argentina back from the brink of missing out on the 2018 World Cup and Ronaldo was able to drag Portugal with him too. A thirty-three-year-old Ronaldo at surely his last World Cup; Messi will turn thirty-one just before Argentina's final group game. What are the odds that they will draw each other? Even if they don't, the question of who is the best will be asked again and again.

In tracing the development of their careers, what has become clear is how the world seems to need them to be opposites: the shy, shuffling introvert vs the brash egotist, the bronzed Adonis vs the pale hobbit. But the depiction of Cristiano Ronaldo as simply a sculpted, athletic, egocentric Robocop in contrast to the naturally talented, scruffy genius Messi has, as the years have passed, become an over-simplification of two lives that have had almost as many cross-overs and similarities as differences.

Both experienced difficult rites of passage as exiles from their childhood roots. They struck lucky – perhaps the demons casting shadows over their respective families were diverted – and both have allowed others to strike hard bargains and lucrative deals on their behalf. They have been helped by inspired coaches and by science (diet, exercise, and in Messi's hormone treatment of questionable ethical justification) to make the most of their talents, and each in their own way has given football fans the world over more sustained joy and entertainment than has ever been experienced in the history of the game. Each has also been challenged and dogged by the endur-ing memory of past legends.

Even this simplifies matters. While Ronaldo perhaps had an objectively tougher childhood than Messi – born into a poorer family with an alcoholic father – and has had to prove his worth at a succes-sion of clubs and cultures, he has never had to struggle as much to be accepted by his compatriots as Messi has. 'Messi always wanted to be more Argentine than the Argentines . . . but he has always been viewed as an incomplete Argentine, one that lives far and away,' says the journalist Santiago Segurola.

They are connected, by the decade-long swinging back and forth, which has left every other player of their generation in their shade. Now, for the first time, with Neymar at PSG, and with 2017 only the second time in seven years that Ronaldo or Messi wasn't the winner of the European Golden Shoe, there is a sense that we might be enter-ing a new era, as their powers wane.

And so the question that follows on – is either of them the greatest player of all time?

The doyen of football writing, Brian Glanville, who began covering FIFA World Cups in Sweden in 1958, provides some historical per-spective. If pushed he ranks Pelé and Alfredo Di Stéfano above the rest, but ultimately dislikes such historical ranking. 'Comparisons are odious,' Glanville said. 'People forget about Di Stéfano. He utterly inspired that Real Madrid team. Ronaldo is essentially a brilliant attacking player. Di Stéfano commanded practically the whole field. One moment he was clearing under his own crossbar in that amazing game against Eintracht Frankfurt, the next minute he was in midfield sending another player through to score. He was total football before anyone else played it.'[1]

We all have our favourite football moments, but for me one stands out more than any other as to this day encompassing the best and most beautiful of the sport. It is that of Bobby Moore and Pelé embracing after Brazil had knocked England out of the 1970 World Cup. There was no sign of anger or resentment on Moore's side, nor of strutting arrogance on the other – just an unconditional expression of mutual respect between one of the most accomplished English defenders ever, and the Brazilian who had already been heralded the best player of all time. Only he and fellow legend Diego Armando Maradona have received the honour of officially being dubbed by FIFA as the greatest players in the history of the game.

Pelé began smashing records at an early age, making his debut for Santos at just fifteen, then making his debut for Brazil at sixteen and winning the first of his three World Cups at seventeen. Pelé had an incredible eye for goal and always glowed with confidence, even at such an early age. He was good in the air and was also a good team player, often laying on assists for his teammates. Pelé's original technique and athleticism were highly praised, whilst his dribbling ability and sharp passing moulded him into an all-round forward. An average-sized man, he was blessed with speed, great balance, tremendous vision, the ability to control the ball superbly, and the ability to shoot powerfully and accurately with either foot and with his head. Yet both played in a different era, with vastly different contexts. As one Reddit poster put it recently in a debate of who was the greatest footballer ever: 'He played against *farmers*!'

It is Maradona who, in the pantheon of gods, lies nestled between the prolific, modern-day achievements of Ronaldo and Messi and the golden age of Pelé and Di Stéfano. It is hard not to argue that the 1986 World Cup carved out a special niche in football history, exclusively thanks to him. He was a hugely talented genius of the game, and charismatic, too, producing moves of great artistry, like Pelé, during an era of football when attacking players, unseen by multiple TV cameras and unprotected by referees, were subjected to incessant fouling. But over a stop-start, twenty-one-year professional football career, Maradona's trophy haul is minimal compared to Ronaldo's and Messi's. Inevitably the self-destructive elements of Maradona's personality add to his fascination for football fans; there is something more romantic about Maradona compared with the remorseless, self-made nature of Ronaldo, and he was always more defiant and rebellious than Messi will ever be. Maradona is a tragic, failed genius. He's very human, this guy who was born in incredibly adverse circumstances in the worst possible shantytown in Buenos Aires. He struggled against the odds. He became, in his time, the best player in the world by a long way.

He has always placed himself on the side of the genuine fan, who still believes there is such a thing as tribal loyalty. 'I am the voice of those who have no voice, the voice of many people who feel represented by me because I always have a microphone in front of me, while they never get the chance to have one in their godforsaken lives.'[2]

What often comes into play when we judge the greatest footballer in the world is what kind of person we judge them to be – what do they represent? And it's here that Ronaldo and Messi operate in a modern space distorted by the forces of global marketing. An earlier biographer, Guillem Balagué, complained that Jorge Mendes and the others who are allowed to stick close to Ronaldo have one role, which is to 'keep criticism at a distance, or control it, create the narrative and keep him on his pedestal.'[3] I was struck by the story I heard from a company source that the crew filming the documentary about Ronaldo were struck by the mystery of one room in his house. It remained from the outset – along with any questions about his private life – strictly out of bounds; as if what it contained was something that might prove too controversial for public consumption or damaging to his massively marketed image. Even if the story is apocryphal, it feels like the ultimate metaphor for players in the modern media glare – have a fly-on-the-wall camera crew following you at all times, but keep one room in your house locked and off limits.

As his unrivalled social media following shows, a different kind of fan relates to Ronaldo, the world's best-paid athlete in 2016 according to *Forbes*. He comes across as an isolated if egocentric figure, but he appeals across cultures and genders in a digital world, so much so that he has built museums and commissioned documentaries in his own honour. By contrast, the most widely viewed documentary on Messi has him discussed by others in a restaurant. It is almost impossible to find anyone from Messi's inner circle who will speak about his private life.

I wanted to try and understand more about this side of Ronaldo, so I arranged to try and talk to the man who claims to understand him better than anyone. For my meeting with Real Madrid president Florentino Pérez, I was waved in by a security guard at the entrance to the imposing, glass-fronted headquarters of construction giant ACS, and then led by a butler, via a fast lift, to the executive upper floor.

An almost funereal silence accompanied us. Not only did the butler, dressed formally in starched shirt and black jacket, not say a word, but I could see no other sign of human activity. The silence was pronounced after the bustle of Madrid's busy main avenues and in stark contrast to the frenzied atmosphere that followed Mr Pérez for much of his daily life, straddling as he does the world of big business, politics and sport – and yet my isolation struck me as being contrived, deliberately diminishing the visitor prior to his audience with the emperor.

When he walked in to greet me in the executive boardroom, Pérez was in a well-tailored blue club suit, of the kind worn by his players, and physically rather smaller than I remembered him – the last time I had spent any length of time with him was during David Beckham's time at Real Madrid, as he presided over the Bernabéu from the presidential box like a Roman emperor at the Coliseum, his stature enhanced.

Now he seemed surprisingly relaxed, given the absence of official press spokesmen or other minders, even if evidently mindful that I was writing a book not just about Cristiano Ronaldo but also the player's main rival for global attention, Lionel Messi.

I knew that behind the personable, unostentatious manner he had perfected to deal with ordinary fans and players, there lurked one of the most politically powerful businessmen in Spain, who personified the scope and scale of modern football at its most ruthlessly ambitious. I knew, via years of closely following the Spanish corporate and political world as a journalist, how expansive were ACS's network of interests, straddling joint ventures and shareholdings in the international construction industry and linked, over the years, via board representations to other big corporations and banks in Spain, including the Barcelona-headquartered savings bank La Caixa and the Catalan motorway developer Albertis – interests never affected by the mutual vitriol that characterized the political rhetoric of the Real Madrid/Barça rivalry.

I had also experienced Pérez, acting out his more public persona in the Bernabéu presidential box, surrounded by corporate hospitality seats that are a microcosm of contemporary, monied Spain, with its network of politicians and celebrities, businessmen and financiers, dealmakers and fixers, all gathered there like bees round honey.

Our encounter was taking place in the spring of 2017, and Real Madrid were going through a palpable uplift in their fortunes; top of La Liga and approaching the later stages of the Champions League, with a strong and cohesive squad of homegrown and foreign talent managed by the one-time *galáctico*, turned able strategist and coach, Zinedine Zidane. The Beckham era – undoubtedly a marketing bonanza but underwhelming in terms of silverware and indeed performance – had long since been overtaken by the Cristiano Ronaldo era, one that had taken on epic proportions in terms of Real Madrid's history, and in the iconic rivalry with Messi that enthused millions of fans around the globe.

It is an era that still, then, has as its point of reference Real Madrid's historic 'enemy' FC Barcelona, which only days earlier had pulled off an unforgettable second-leg come-from-behind victory over Paris Saint-Germain, and where Lionel Messi had long ago achieved legendary status.

And yet, Real Madrid remained world football's unrivalled powerhouse when it came to marketing and influence in the transfer market. As the 2016–17 season reached its final weeks, Real Madrid's much-visited museum boasted eleven European Cups – four more than AC Milan and six ahead of Barcelona, Bayern Munich and Liverpool. Two of these had been won in the last three years, and the club would go on to beat Juventus that May in the Champions League final in Cardiff.

It was in such a context that I asked Florentino Pérez if he could help shed light on the importance of Cristiano Ronaldo to Real

Madrid, football and the universe. And the answer came back unequivocally.

'Cristiano Ronaldo is our symbol; in my view the most important player in the history of football.'

Why?

Context was important, he told me. Pérez, who was born in my birthplace, Madrid, at the same time I was, reminded me that he and I belonged to a generation whose childhood had coincided with Real Madrid's golden decade of the 1950s. It was a period when the dictator Franco's Spain struggled on account of its isolation from the rest of Europe.

Those were the days before mass tourism, when Spain, and Madrid in particular, was still regarded by most foreigners as a sinister, backwards and repressive place. Spain's national football squad was barely respected beyond the Spanish border, but the country exported immigrants, oranges and Real Madrid. For the club produced brilliant football – played by the best foreigners and Spaniards – that defied political and national barriers.

I still remember my first glimpse of the Bernabéu in the winter of circa 1958 – at that time it was on the outskirts of Madrid, bordering open countryside. I recall a giant stadium, glowing in the dark like an illuminated cathedral, dwarfing all the other buildings nearby, and being drawn into the warmth and excitement of the crowd.

My Spanish mother preferred bullfighting to football, as did my British father, so I was led by the hand of an old friend of my maternal grandfather to my first football match. Florentino went at the hand of his father, he told me, continuing his narrative.

'In those days, remember, there was an exceptional player called Alfredo Di Stéfano who changed the history of Real Madrid; who, I think, also changed the history of football. When I watch Cristiano Ronaldo I see he has the same determination, the same self-belief to reach unprecedented heights of achievement. I would say Cristiano is a man obsessed with football, who only lives for football, and who works hard to be the best player in the history of football. With respect to his relationship with Real Madrid, his identification with its values are total: effort, team spirit, humility, that "never surrender" mentality . . . For me he is an example on and off the pitch. He has never behaved badly with our players, with the club, or third parties. He is a phenomenon that is worth analysing. I would sum it up by saying that every child in the world wants their photograph taken with Cristiano Ronaldo.'

Commitment sure, but team spirit and humility are not characteristics that easily come to the mind of Ronaldo's critics. Although it was certainly true that under Zidane he had integrated more with the team, it was partly because of the respect he had for Zidane as a person, as a former great player and latterly an inspiring coach, and also because player and manager realized that advancing age meant diminishing speed and agility, and difficulty playing in every match. It would be at the end of that year that the story broke about Madrid players allegedly having a WhatsApp group with everyone but Ronaldo in it. Although sources were quick to rubbish the claims, it was one of those things that felt right. As anyone who saw the Cristiano documentary knows, the dark muttering about 'the other guy' reveal just how important individual glory is to Ronaldo. As much as he may praise his teammates, thank them for being the wind beneath his wings, there is always that nagging sense that for him, this is what the strategic moves from club to club have been about – finding the place he can become the greatest player ever. Whereas for Messi, one gets the sense that they are the corollary of what he loves best – playing as the central part of a great football team.

One of the most literate and incisive commentators on Spanish football, Jorge Valdano, himself a former player, coach and sporting director of Real Madrid, had talked to me about Cristiano Ronaldo when we had met a few days earlier to discuss the iconic rivalry.

Like Pérez, Valdano doesn't believe in short answers. He answers each question not with a marketing pitch but with a philosophical thesis.

'Cristiano Ronaldo is a worthy representative of our times. He is a rich and famous millennial. An individualist with a sense of perfection that begins with his own body and ends with a professionalism which I have rarely seen in my lifetime. But quite apart from this, he has been a sufficiently long time at Real Madrid and done enough relevant things to have won a position of honour in the history of the club – just look at the statistics. And then look at his charisma . . . but I am talking more of a technical leader than a social one. He dazzles us more with what he does than what he says and his influence is what it is because what he does is exemplary. When the great figure of the team is the first to arrive and the last to leave a training session, works his butt off in the gym and always wants to push himself still further, all this makes him a point of reference that denies all who follow him the right to idleness.

'And when one is talking about a historic reference point, I am talking about his extraordinary potential as a player and his utter professionalism. All the time he has been at Real Madrid, he hasn't provoked one single conflict. We are talking about a legend of our times who nevertheless it is impossible to find anywhere after eleven p.m. other than in his own bed. He has a gym in his house. Sure, he has a narcissistic element which is part of his human condition as a player. He looks after himself, aspires to perfection. One doesn't know whether this is to dazzle himself in the mirror or to dazzle the masses, but what is certain is that he achieves both, which is why I say that it's probably more relevant to talk about him as a genius rather than as a narcissist.'

As for his conduct off the pitch, the available evidence certainly suggests Cristiano Ronaldo has not allowed fame and celebrity to get in the way of his performances on the pitch as has occurred with other stars of the game, although this does not stop the media intruding into headline-provoking areas of his private life.

Some further interesting insights into the man behind the player, if through a soft lens and leaving more questions than answers, were provided in the documentary *Ronaldo*, released in 2015. There are two unrivalled stars of the film – Ronaldo and his son Cristiano Junior. Their idealized father–son relationship verges on the hagiographic, like much of the rest of the film. An intimate scene shows the father with a self-conscious sense of responsibility, lovingly making his son breakfast in an evidently alcohol-free zone. The scene will resonate with many a separated or single dad making up for an absent parent, however futuristic Ronaldo's luxurious homestead outside Madrid.

Other scenes show Ronaldo Junior sharing his father's love of football and luxury cars, and as a natural in front of the cameras, particularly when both attend the Ballon d'Or ceremony.

'I always had a dream of having a son. I wanted to be a young father at twenty-five. Be there to accompany his development, as a father.'

The contrast with Ronaldo's own experience of childhood could not be greater. Ronaldo gives his son the attention his absent alcoholic father never gave him.

And yet, what might have been his fate had he not had the strength of will to draw himself out of the domestic pit is exemplified by his older brother Hugo – a one-time construction worker with a real talent for football, who like his father at one point sold Ronaldo's Manchester United shirts in order to feed his addictions.

Unlike his father, Hugo managed to save himself through rehab, and was subsequently given a job by his star brother managing the Museu CR7, the Ronaldo museum in Funchal, the capital of Madeira – an enduring reminder for Ronaldo and his mother that redemption is possible.

The mother of his first child? 'People speculated that it was this girl or the other or a surrogate mother,' Ronaldo says. 'I've never told anybody and I never will.' No mention of what Cristiano Junior might be brought up being told, about who else or what circumstances he owes his existence to.

For many people watching the documentary, it seemed to suggest something odd about Ronaldo as a father, an egotism that extended into the act of parenthood, as he effectively removed the mother from any central role in shaping his children. Ronaldo recreating himself in Cristiano Junior. In his looks, his cocky bearing, his exercising and love of football, and when he learns, while visiting his dad's garage, how to pronounce the word 'Lamborghini'. And yet, I was far more interested in how his complex attitude to fatherhood might stem from his own relationship with his father. If there was something of the sterile quality of a lab in his life, then one could understand why he might want to avoid the messiness of his own upbringing.

He has been photographed in the company of female models over the years, mainly brief encounters catalogued in photographs at awards ceremonies. Among his most publicized longer-term companions was the Russian model Irina Shayk. She began being photographed with the player soon after they met on a publicity shoot for Armani in 2010, after his arrival at Real Madrid. She and Ronaldo continued to be periodically seen together before their highly publicized break-up five years later, after reports that she had discovered he was seeing other women.

Shayk was followed by another widely reported association with Georgina Rodriguez, a former Gucci employee who met the player at a Dolce and Gabbana party, or so the tabloids claimed. The young Spanish model was first snapped with Cristiano Ronaldo in the autumn at Disneyland Paris. Despite putting on a disguise, Ronaldo was identified, with the player 'cuddling up', as the *Sun* put it, to his 'his new love interest'.

But no one appears in the documentary film.

Ronaldo's mother Dolores has her part to play in the film, as does Jorge. She adds to the image of a fractured family background by recalling her husband's drunkenness, and how she nearly aborted Cristiano. She recognizes that, 'All I have I owe to that son,' although his fame has brought new challenges as well as benefits. She is filmed buying herself tranquillizers in the chemist's, and her son is shown calling to check that she has taken them. 'It's quite complicated to be the mother of a player who needs to win,' Dolores tells us. 'I suffer a lot.'[4]

Money, of course, can't buy happiness. It can, however, buy you adulation, as the documentary *Ronaldo* shows. Consider the scene when a hysterical young girl runs across a training pitch before a World Cup match in Brazil, making a beeline for Ronaldo. He hugs her obligingly, after she has been restrained by a security guard.

'He knows I exist,' she cries. Then, when a TV reporter asks a few moments later what he has said to her, she tells him, 'He asked me to stay calm and stop crying.'

'And what did you say to him?'

'I asked him to follow me on Twitter.'

Ronaldo shows himself most at ease in the company of a small group of friends, including Mendes, while his Portuguese teammates look awkward and not greatly amused when Ronaldo shows off his singing talent with an impromptu karaoke in front of the camera on board the team plane. 'In football I don't have a lot of friends. People I really trust? Not many. Most of the time I'm alone. I consider myself an isolated person,' Ronaldo says. And yet his popularity is measured remotely and at a digital distance via social media, and his privacy only serves to underline that it is himself more than anybody else that is at the centre of his universe.

As for Messi, it would be inaccurate to say that he is indifferent to social media, even if he has a smaller following on Twitter, Facebook and Instagram. He too is aware of its moneymaking potential. He evidently is no natural before the cameras, and remains as uncomfortable and awkward before microphones as he does messaging people he doesn't know. But in amongst the press shots and product endorsements on his Instagram there are intimate photographs of him reading stories to his sons. This is in contrast to Ronaldo, who rarely shares private family photographs, preferring more professionally staged shots of his children. Whether you see this as more of his famed egotism, or a desire to shield his children from the glare of media intrusion is another of the interesting ambiguities at the heart of him.

Messi's ordinary-guy persona masks a very real authority that he has gained. Over the years, the once shy, unassuming kid who was simply one more member of the team has become the most influential component of FC Barcelona's footballing and business project, and that of Argentina's national squad, and the player has imposed his personality not just in the way he plays, but by his periodical petulance. He has also increasingly shown a public awareness of his own 'brand story'. With his tattoos, Messi has experimented with a range of themes, from Jesus Christ to fatherhood, from the iconic number 10 to the 'blackened leg', which superseded all that came before. That tattoo is supposed to evoke the warrior roots of the Maori that has so inspired New Zealand's All Blacks. The concept was developed by Argentine tattooist Robert López, whom Messi flies across the Atlantic to Barcelona whenever he requires his presence.

In the summer of 2017, Messi married his childhood sweetheart and mother of his two children, Antonella, in Rosario. By the standards of some celebrity weddings over the years, including Maradona's infamous one in Buenos Aires back in the early 1990s, the Messis' was a relatively modest affair, if not without its sprinkling of stardust. It was held in a modern casino hotel with the guest list of 250 (Maradona had 1,500) made up of family and friends, with some from the football world.

Born into a middle-class family the same year as Messi, Antonella had grown into an intelligent, good-looking and self-assured woman. She studied odontology before switching to social communications at university in Argentina, and then moved to Barcelona to join Lionel.

Their relationship had blossomed in 2007, after Messi had flown back to Rosario to console her over the death in a traffic accident of a close mutual friend.

In Rosario, the neighbourhood gossip had been at one stage of a tense relationship developing later between Antonella and Celia, based on perceived differences in social background and a stereotyped female rivalry.

But Antonella moved effortlessly into Messi's Barcelona world, initially keeping their relationship out of the media spotlight, with the couple choosing the moment to go public after they had committed to a longer-term future together. By then, the couple seemed to be forged by a compatibility of apparent opposites – his shyness was dispelled in her presence, her intelligence warming to his instinctive passion as a player and his refusal to be seduced by the adulation of others. As he matured and became famous, she happily developed her own line of business in fashionable footwear, and gave birth to their two sons: Thiago, born on 2 November 2012 and Mateo, born on 11 September 2015. (A third son, Ciro, was born on 10 March 2018.)

For their wedding day, Sergio Agüero led a delegation from the Argentine national squad, but it was the Barça stars to whom Messi gave a particular warm welcome in recognition of the pinnacles reached in his career. They were led by the old alumni of La Masia, with whom he had grown up and become a star – Piqué and Fàbregas, with the latter's girlfriend the bride's maid of honour. Messi strictly forbade the carrying of mobile phones and asked that each guest donate money to one of the charities he had set up to help poor kids in Rosario develop their football skills. It was a nice human touch, genuinely motivated with no commercialism attached.

For all the glamour and media siege, Leo and Antonella looked very much an unassuming couple, simply in love, with Messi's look still defined by his elfish ears and goofy grin; still the little big man who seemed to have dropped in, after a quick shower, from playing football, yet glowing in the company of the beautiful and supportive love of his life.

Parents, brothers and sister were all there, including the black sheep of the family Matias, behaving discreetly and looking indistinguishable from other guests, absorbed by a civilized social engagement, as if his dalliance with Rosario's criminal fraternity was now past. Only months before, in September 2016, the local media had reported that a court had dropped a case brought against Matias for illegally possessing a .22-calibre pistol. Instead, he was ordered to coach football classes for four hours per week for a year with a local club, Leones de Rosario. He was also instructed to pay a fine of 8,000 pesos (£350) and to 'abstain from drugs and/or alcohol'.

As Messi was preparing for his wedding, Ronaldo, as if it was part of a process of osmosis in the settling of their personal lives, announced he had had two more children via a surrogate – twins – and celebrated Real Madrid's twelfth Champions League victory with his young son Cristiano Junior and his girlfriend Georgina Rodriguez, amid rumours strongly denied by the player's mother, but later confirmed, that she was pregnant.

All generations of Ronaldo's family seemed to strengthen as his brood expanded. When Real Madrid players had celebrated their tenth European title in the late spring of 2014, few people at the time realized the poignancy of Ronaldo's gesture in the Lisbon's Estádio da Luz. While his teammates danced and cheered on the pitch, he walked over to where his older brother Hugo was sitting and beckoned him to come onto the turf to receive his jersey, before embracing him.

Ronaldo had long ago made a pact with Hugo that if he kicked his drinking and drugs habit, the star would dedicate a Champions League title to him. Ronaldo made good on his promise, after scoring seventeen goals en route to Real Madrid's Champions League triumph in a stadium that had, until then, brought him more professional and personal disappointment than success.

Another interesting link between the two – the struggles of their brothers – is a reminder of what a different outcome there might have been for Ronaldo and Messi if their destinies had not led them out of the environment they were born into. Hugo is the less talented son of an alcoholic father, a father who did little in his life beyond being a conscript soldier. For Ronaldo, his father's failings became a motivation; for Hugo, a burden. Matias had chosen to stay in Rosario and ended up trying to make a living in the corrupt, violent society from which Barcelona had saved his brother. In a sense, someone had to draw the short straw.

The subject of Cristiano Ronaldo's sexuality seems to be of

enduring fascination with a certain sort of football fan and, though it feels rooted in the insults of the terrace chant, I felt I had to ask the question of those who are most closely connected to his brand. Those sources in a position to shed light on it paint an ambiguous picture. At Real Madrid, it was clearly an issue that had been closely examined by people at high levels of the club, with one senior executive telling me that the intelligence held by the club was that Ronaldo had 'slept with women but not with men'. By contrast, a marketing executive not connected with Real Madrid but who had dealt with the player professionally, was convinced he was gay.

Neither source suggested Ronaldo had ever engaged in a serious long-term relationship with anyone outside an intimate family circle, in which his mother Dolores has assumed an increasingly central matriarchal role from his time at Manchester United.

Dolores has shared a house with him in Madrid, and helped look after his son. She has carved out a public role for herself in the Ronaldo narrative by publishing her memoirs, and taking a commanding presence at public events in Portugal, to which Ronaldo's relatives are invited along with the player.

'Dolores features in our highest-rating celebrity TV shows, leading her family up the red carpet, as she is very much the head of the tribe,' Francisco Pinto Balsemão, former prime minister and one of Portugal's media magnates, told me. 'Does Ronaldo deserve to have an airport in Madeira named after him? Sure he does. Portugal is a small country, but I go around the world, and everyone asks me about Cristiano.'

In my encounter with Florentino Pérez, he sidestepped the question when I put it to him that when people speculate whether Cristiano Ronaldo is gay or not, the very ambiguity is a marketing strength.

'People write a lot of things about Ronaldo which are untrue. They are people who envy him. But I stick to the facts. There is nothing more reassuring than his large following on social media. The whole world is with him.'

I must say, the factual integrity of social media struck me as a bold claim to make in the year when the American and British voters were subjected to 'fake news' en masse through the medium. But then this was about the football market, not about gospel truths.

'You might think I am being subjective in my judgement, but there is an objective fact Cristiano Ronaldo has a following of 285 million across social media, the most followed personality in the world,' Pérez said, before handing me a few sheets of information from Real Madrid's marketing department. They showed Ronaldo well ahead of other sports personalities, like LeBron James, Stephen Curry, Tiger Woods, Rafa Nadal, Usain Bolt – and Lionel Messi. In fact, all of them put together still had fewer followers than Cristiano Ronaldo.

'Now don't tell me that is not a phenomenon. I'm not responsible for organizing the world so that it adores Cristiano Ronaldo in this way,' Pérez insisted, pointing triumphantly at the stats before adding that Ronaldo still came out ahead when put alongside singers like Shakira, Beyoncé, Jennifer Lopez and Lady Gaga. He even has more than Barack Obama.

So he is an icon for the millennials; he transcends social boundaries?

'Sure. Social media is like a thermometer and it shows through Cristiano Ronaldo how it transcends all the frontiers of the world,' answered Pérez.

'Really?' I asked.

'Yes. Let me give you an example. It concerns a young Syrian boy who has been in a terrible war situation. We bring him here to Real Madrid, he meets Cristiano, and without any prompting the boy is overwhelmed with tears of excitement and emotion. When the child of a rich American family meets Cristiano, the same thing happens. Cristiano has become the biggest socializing element in the world . . . I genuinely believe this. I have never seen anything like this in the world of science, culture or politics.'

'But what about Pope Francis?' I asked. As the Pope's recent biographer, I had an interest in the subject.

'Eeeerr, oh, I am sure Cristiano has many more followers . . . the Pope is not among the greats, although to tell you the truth he's not in the marketing research we have,' Pérez admitted, somewhat wrong-footed. 'I will have to check.' He lifted the phone and asked for the information to be delivered as soon as possible. When the information came through, it suggested that Pope Francis was running a close second. 'Let's stick with objective facts . . . at Real Madrid Cristiano has scored 391 goals in 382 games [as of April 2017]. In the eight seasons he's been with us, he has become the biggest goal scorer in the history of the club, nineteen trophies in the thirteen years played at two clubs, Manchester United and Real Madrid, four Golden Boots etc. Everyone loves him; for me he is between a son and a friend. I've never had any problem with him and, besides, he has a huge human dimension which is his sense of solidarity with a worthy cause.'

Dozens of other people I interviewed confirmed Cristiano Ronaldo's support for charitable causes, both individual and organizational, much of it unpublicized at his request. Officially, the anonymity is because he doesn't want to be seen to be profiting from his philanthropy in image and marketing terms. There may have also been an element of self-preservation: not wanting to be seen as an easy cash cow, or become the target of a multitude of requests, not all of them of genuine need.

Among the causes Ronaldo was involved in publicly was that of Nuhazet in June 2012, a young boy in Las Palmas, Gran Canaria, who had cancer. The case was initially brought to the attention of Manu Sainz, a journalist with the sports newspaper *AS*, who was an old friend of Jorge Mendes's.

As Sainz recalled: 'I was told about the boy by a friend who was the patron of the Association Against Cancer in Las Palmas. The boy had always had this dream about seeing Real Madrid play in the Bernabéu. My friend rang one day and said, "Manu, I've got this kid who's been told by the local doctors they can't do anything for him and given him three months to live ... his parents have got a flight to Madrid but no tickets for the stadium. I've talked to some of the Real Madrid players, who promised the tickets but failed to deliver. I am desperate," she said. "Can you get me one for the father and the other for the kid?" So I talked to Mendes and Cristiano and they told me to take the kid to meet them in a hotel. Cristiano gave him a signed shirt, and the tickets ... Then they paid €70,000 for his treatment in a Madrid clinic. He lived for another nine months.'

'So what about Cristiano's commercial value?' I asked Florentino Pérez.

'Everything he touches he turns into gold ... in commercial and image terms he has an enormous potential. It's not just that he has overtaken Beckham, he's ahead of everyone else.'

It is here that Ronaldo's more overt commerciality and his physicality seem to tie together. If there is arguably something more endearing, more magical about Messi for many fans – perhaps his small stature and his awkwardness off the pitch makes what he does on the pitch seem transformative – but he is no Maradona, claiming to turn the world upside down. Messi shies away from microphones.

Perhaps it is simply to do with Ronaldo's obvious physical gifts, which separate him from almost everyone on the planet. His footballing prowess seems to be a simpler equation, built on cells and sinew. Every time he takes his shirt off, revealing that body, we can feel the perfect synchronicity of physical and marketing machinery. Whereas with Messi, we can allow ourselves, however naively, to image that his gifts reside in a kind of footballing soul. It was why the tax scandal hit so hard, because it was a reminder that he wasn't some pure footballing sprite, removed from earthly things, but a hugely wealthy sporting star, as enmeshed in complex global financial structures as anyone.

In the summer of 2017, the Spanish inland revenue announced that it was investigating Cristiano Ronaldo for alleged non-payment of €14.7 million in tax due on image rights in the years 2011–14. A statement issued by his agent denied tax evasion, while Real Madrid stated they had full confidence in the player and understood he had legally complied with his tax obligations – a different argument to that used by Messi, whose defence was that he had no idea how his tax affairs were conducted by third parties, as he was not personally involved.

Some Barça fans and Catalan commentators chose to celebrate the announcement, seeing it as long-overdue vengeance for the way that Messi had been prosecuted and fined for a much lower sum of unpaid tax. Ronaldo claimed innocence, issuing a statement that his conscience was clear. Messi had also declared his innocence, but the judges did not believe him.

In January 2019 Ronaldo agreed to settle the case by paying a €18.8 million fine and accepting a suspended jail sentence. What the two cases brought to the surface was the complex structures set up by advisers to both players to minimize what was paid in tax on the large amounts of money each earned. It doesn't feel too hard to tease out the symbolism that in the modern age of the full-spectrum sporting star, it is only through their financial affairs that we gain a sense of what their lives are like.

For his part, Messi was unwittingly caught up in the biggest political crisis to impact on FC Barcelona since the death of Franco – the unilateral declaration of Catalan independence, followed by the imposition of temporary direct rule, after a pro-independence referendum had been declared unconstitutional by the Spanish government and main union parties.

Of the many matches I have attended over the years, few look likely to endure longer in my memory – for its own particular reasons – than that played in the Nou Camp between Messi's Barça and Las Palmas in October 2017.

The match was played behind closed doors, as Catalan fans protested the police brutality used against those who had voted 'Yes' to independence. I watched the game at ground level, alone, except for the team staff and subs and a few journalists who had been banished to the press box.

The match was a surreal affair, with the players evidently unmotivated and detached. And yet, in the huge, cavernous silence of the near empty stadium, I absorbed the privilege of not only being close to the game, but also of being able to hear the players' voices as I had never heard them before.

I was struck by how much they spoke and occasionally shouted to each other, all except for one, and he was the name that seemed to be most uttered by players on both sides, as they either tried to pass the ball to him or foul him. The player at the centre of their game kept utterly focused, without uttering a word himself that night, let alone his own name: Messi.

Messi may well have been deeply affected by the violence and protests of those days, if nothing else because it would have reminded him of darker times in Argentina. But if he did, he did not show it, nor talk about it publicly. Indeed, he was conspicuous in his total lack of public involvement with the Catalan crisis, keeping a distance from a nationalism he had never, as a Latin American immigrant, become emotionally involved with. In contrast, many Barça fans are overwhelmingly pro-independence, as evidenced by the Catalan flags they wave and their chants during home matches at Nou Camp stadium; and no other club in the world was more emotionally affected by the political crisis unleashed in Spain over the Catalan question than FC Barcelona.

Despite his many years of living in Barcelona, Messi, still a Spanish speaker and culturally Argentine, had not felt politically inclined to follow the example of his mentor, Pep Guardiola, or his football brother-in-arms, Gerard Piqué, another well-known supporter of the Catalan cause who, the day after the match against Las Palmas, made an emotional statement of solidarity with those who had been hit by police batons.

It is not just that Messi is apolitical. He plays only for his football and knows where his bread is buttered. For all its Catalan identity, when it comes to the Clásico, FC Barcelona has become a major global business venture, as has Real Madrid, the sponsorship and marketing revenue of the two clubs boosted by their rivalry and the parts played by Messi and Ronaldo.

Speculation at the time of the referendum that Barça might be forced out of the Spanish League or quit of its own volition, with the club joining a minor Catalan League, seemed off the mark.

And hardly surprising given the vested interests involved. About 70 per cent of Spanish club football's commercial value is tied up in the enduring rivalry between the two super-clubs and their non-Catalan superstars.

No matter what happens politically, it's likely Madrid and Barcelona won't score an own goal by severing their ties. But the prospect of either Messi or Ronaldo quitting La Liga for their own reasons one day could spell the end of one of the greatest and most enduring personal rivalries in the history of sport.

As I wrote this conclusion, it was announced that Messi had signed a new contract, aimed at keeping the Argentinian superstar at the club through the 2020–21 season. The buyout clause was set at €700 million. Thus, by the time the new deal expires, the striker will have spent seventeen years with the first team.

FC Barcelona had tried their best to keep details on his thoughts on the matter from public scrutiny, but it was reported subsequently in the Spanish and Catalan media that it had a specific clause, initially kept secret by the club, stating that the player will be free to leave the club in the event of Catalan independence having Barça excluded from any major European leagues, including La Liga.

Within the Messi family, one of the main concerns has been that the younger generation should not be compelled to speak the Catalan language. It was the reason why Messi's mother chose not to live in Barcelona but took herself and her daughter back to Rosario in Argentina.

Meanwhile, the perennial story has broken that Ronaldo is unhappy and looking to leave. It feels for the first time in many years that their remarkable rivalry may be about to shift fundamentally. The goofy skinny kid from Funchal and the little big man from Rosario may be about to enter a very new final act of their careers.

As we look at these two players, it is tempting to look to the future. At the current rate of goal scoring, they will both exceed the totals of Gerd Müller and Pelé in the next three years. At that point, they will sit outside of any context that we have so far seen; two outliers – with only themselves to refer to – will pass beyond the bounds of what we have known and take us somewhere entirely new.

Epilogue
Staying Power

As millions of fans prepared to watch the World Cup in Russia in the summer of 2018, few players continued to draw as much global attention as Cristiano Ronaldo and Lionel Messi.

For ten years of championship club football, Ronaldo and Messi had shared the accolade of best elite footballer in the world, each winning five prestigious Ballon d'Or titles and redefining modern football with the unprecedented scope of their achievements, breaking goal-scoring records as well as showing extraordinary physical resilience and sublime skills that had firmly established them both in the pantheon of sporting gods.

The 2017–18 club season had ended with each player making another important contribution to the history of European football. On 17 May, Ronaldo scored two goals in Real Madrid's match against Celta Vigo, breaking Jimmy Greaves's record as the all-time top scorer in the top five European leagues, and helping secure La Liga, a prize that had evaded the club since 2012. He also contributed to Real Madrid's successful European campaign, scoring a spectacular bicycle kick in the quarter-final first leg against Juventus, before going on to win his own fifth Champions League title in the final against Liverpool on 26 May. He finished the campaign with a total of fifteen goals, and was the top scorer of the tournament for the sixth season running.

No one could claim to better him except, of course, Messi. By the high standards the Argentine superstar had set himself, Messi had a less successful club and international season in 2017–18 than his rival, with FC Barcelona ending runners-up in La Liga, and exiting the Champions League in the quarter-final stage.

And yet Messi was still regarded as one of the greatest, if not *the* greatest player of all time by many fans, and he hadn't given up. On 18 October, in FC Barcelona's 3–1 victory over Olympiakos, he followed Ronaldo in becoming only the second player in football history to score 100 goals in all UEFA club competitions. In La Liga in January

2018, he scored his 366th Spanish championship goal. Only Gerd Müller had until then held the record of so many league goals for the same club in one of Europe's top divisions.

And so to Russia. With Ronaldo aged thirty-three, and Messi turning thirty-one in June 2018, both players approached the World Cup at an age that for most football players would represent the declining phase of their career. In fact, while contributing rather less in terms of running and speed on the pitch than they once did, they continued – more often than not – to single-handedly define games, whether scoring brilliant goals themselves or helping create them for others in their team.

And yet the two players had much to prove in a World Cup that was likely to be their last, certainly the last in which they would be able to compete at the top of their form. And while Ronaldo had been credited with inspiring Portugal to their European Championship win in 2016, the World Cup was a crown that had so far evaded him, as it had done Messi.

Arguably, of the two, it was Messi who had suffered most criticism from his fellow countrymen, because of his failure to match the success of the great legend Maradona with his national team, Argentina. By contrast he remained the undisputed god for Barça fans, with the club showing its own faith in him, following his fourth Golden Shoe award in November 2017, by signing a new contract taking him through to the 2020–1 season with a buyout clause set at €700 million.

Ronaldo too had carved out his own special place in club history, considered by many Los Blancos fans, including Real Madrid club president Pérez, as the greatest achiever since Di Stéfano. Nonetheless, he approached the World Cup with his relationship with the club under strain, facing a huge fine to the Spanish state for unpaid tax, and still feeling personally undervalued by not being among the best-paid players in the world.

As Ronaldo prepared for the World Cup with the Portuguese national team, the Portuguese media reported that Ronaldo had made the 'irreversible' decision to move out of the Bernabéu, with French giants Paris Saint-Germain touted – inaccurately as it turned out – as the most likely destination. Meanwhile, in Spain, the local media reported that Real Madrid had offered Ronaldo a new deal comprising a basic salary of £22 million, with £6.5 million bonus-related add-ons.

The £28.5 million still had him lagging behind Messi, whose salary was estimated at £600,000 a week, equating to £31.2 million every year.

Further fuel was added to the fire of the transfer talk by the publication of the *Forbes* rich list in early June 2018, which saw the Barcelona star edging out his Real Madrid rival by £2.24 million ($3 million). Messi's fortune was estimated at £82.84 million ($111 million) while that of Ronaldo was put at £80.6 million ($108 million).

Prior to that, Ronaldo himself had contributed to raising the stakes in his periodic tug of war with Real Madrid president Pérez. He showed a reluctance to join the team in celebration of its Champions League final victory over Liverpool, a thinly veiled signal that his time at the Bernabéu had finally come to an end, but not before claiming the recognition he had always craved. In characteristically provocative comments that displayed his egocentric side but were guaranteed to make headlines, and to pressurize both Real Madrid and those who might wish to bid for him, Ronaldo told the world's media that he would make a decision within days, and added that the tournament should be named the 'CR7 Champions League' in his honour, after he won his fifth title and finished as the competition's top scorer.

In the end it all came down to ego and money, with various dramatis personae involved. The next big news to be generated by Real Madrid suggested that Ronaldo's future was being negotiated although it was still not clear whether he was staying or going and no one expected any imminent announcement of a move. Two days before the start of the World Cup, Real Madrid's Pérez dropped a bombshell by announcing that he had signed up the coach of Spain's national team, Julen Lopetegui, as the club's new manager, succeeding Zinedine Zidane, who had quit two weeks earlier.

Real Madrid fans were among those shocked at the timing of the announcement, less than four days away from Spain's crucial opening game against Portugal, in which Ronaldo was set to play against some of his own clubmates. Such was the outcry that the Spanish Federation president Luis Rubiales felt no qualms about having Lopetegui summarily dismissed from the national squad, plunging Spain – 2010 World Cup and 2008 and 2012 European champions – into crisis mode.

When I first heard the news, I thought it was an urban myth developing; I couldn't believe it was true. Things could not have been handled in a worse way. It was unbelievable: Real Madrid making their announcement two days before a crucial competition, risking destabilizing the entire Spanish squad. It was, by any sane measure, a complete dog's dinner. As I told Richard Fitzpatrick in an interview with him for the *Bleacher Report*: 'It's a reminder to us. At Barça, Leo Messi calls the shots; at Real Madrid, there's one person who calls the shots more than anyone else – Florentino Pérez, the club's president, and he's done it again. This will have gone down like a lead balloon among many Real Madrid supporters who are also quite patriotic and support the national squad and who are looking forward to Spain doing well.'

Prior to this, football had thrown up examples of several managers who had worked through tournament finals before taking up club positions, including Antonio Conte, who was appointed Chelsea manager before leading Italy at the UEFA Euro 2016 finals.

But the Lopetegui affair was seen in moralistic terms by the newly appointed Rubiales, who was determined to act on a point of principle. He had been on the job less than a month on a mandate of transparency, after his long-serving predecessor, Ángel María Villar, had been arrested the previous summer on suspicion of embezzling funds. Rubiales told the media that he felt Real Madrid's behaviour had been unacceptable, having found out from the club about the appointment of Lopetegui five minutes before it went public. The club disregarded his request to delay the announcement.

It was nonetheless possible to speculate that there was a method in the apparent madness, or least a convergence of interests beyond the Spanish national squad, not least involving the relationship nurtured with Spanish club football over many years by Mendes, the agent who had both Lopetegui and Cristiano Ronaldo among his star clients. But quite where Ronaldo fitted into Mendes's and Florentino's plans only became apparent later, a week before the final of the World Cup tournament, from which the Portuguese Ronaldo, along with his Argentine nemesis, had long since departed. For on 10 June it was confirmed that Ronaldo had signed a €100 million four-year deal, transferring him to Italian champions Juventus.

More on that later. But first it is worth reflecting that the story of

Ronaldo's and Messi's respective exits from the 2018 World Cup in Russia underlined once again the extent to which their lives as players had mirrored each other, as much in their successes as in their disappointments, with their rivalry made all the more intense by the Spanish clubs they belonged to.

As things turned out, the much-anticipated encounter between the two players in the World Cup never materialized, as Portugal and Argentina were knocked out in separate encounters with other teams.

I watched Portugal's opening game with Spain in my favourite beach bar, El Chiringuito Carbonell in Sitges, south of Barcelona, not far from Messi's Catalan home in nearby Castelldefels. There is something about beaches and football that make me feel happy. I kicked my first ball around on a beach in the north of Spain, organized matches on a beach in southern Spain when my daughters were still little girls and excellent players, then later enjoyed watching other potential stars of the future, young Latinos with dancing feet and tanned torsos, from the Algarve to Copacabana. I was on a beach in the Gulf of Cádiz back in 2010 when Iniesta scored Spain's winning World Cup goal, watching the TV on the terrace of a private house where I had gathered with a group of Spanish friends. We celebrated by stripping off and running naked into the Atlantic.

Against this backdrop of good memories, I have to say that feelings were mixed in El Chiringuito Carbonell that night of 15 June. My friends were an unusual gathering of Barça and Real Madrid supporters, their divided club loyalties showing a clear bias of affection for individual players in the Spanish team, and united in their struggle to appreciate Cristiano Ronaldo.

No one missed CR7 looking one way at the camera, as if gazing at himself, when all his teammates were looking away, or making sure that he was captured singing the Portuguese anthem with the self-conscious enthusiasm of a military cadet officer on his passing-out parade. Then came the theatrical reaction to a soft tackle and his sublime curling penalty, and he became momentarily Spain's wrecker and Portugal's saviour.

When Spain equalized, the Spanish TV channel declared that from then on Spain would be in control and go on to win. Spain's striker Diego Costa obliged up to a point, but the Spaniards overlooked the capacity of Cristiano, aged thirty-three and on top form (in contrast to the substituted and exhausted Iniesta), to lift the game almost single-handedly, his third goal, sublime in the power and accuracy of its execution, leaving Spain's De Gea mummified.

Afterwards I looked out at the empty beach, and for an instant thought I caught a glimpse of the Madeiran wonderboy dancing, while giving us all a cheeky wink.

The next day I walked along the beach to another bar staffed by South Americans from the River Plate region to watch Messi. Pre-match reports suggested that Messi – with other senior players – had helped pick the team, accepting their preference for four defenders, although coach Jorge Sampaoli, who favoured attacking football, liked to play with three.

Dysfunction in the Argentine team was only too evident from the outset. Compared to Ronaldo's strutting appearance twenty-four hours earlier, Messi looked distinctly out of sorts, as if struggling with the strain of what was expected of him, even if his teammates went into their first World Cup game against Iceland thinking it would be a walkover. Instead they walked away with their tail between their legs, a leaden Argentina just scraping a 1–1 draw with the tournament's rank outsiders after Messi missed a penalty – his fourth miss in seven attempts.

Whatever the Icelanders were, they were certainly not minnows. 'They are Vikings,' an Argentine friend commented as we watched the game along with several of his compatriots, all long-term residents of Catalonia. What they might have lacked in skill, the Icelanders made up for in height, physical strength, and sheer motivation, more than enough to frustrate an Argentine team that seemed to lack form or method, however much their coach screamed at them.

The biggest disappointment, because the expectation was so high, was Messi himself, let down by his teammates as much as being at fault himself. For much of the match he seemed to be walking, as he does at Barcelona, waiting for the pass that would activate his genius, the difference being that with Argentina he was rarely found, and when he did get the ball at his feet, he either lost it or misfired.

Messi certainly looked fitter and healthier than the watching Maradona, whose bloated face and puffy eyes briefly appeared on our TV screens. He looked less than happy to be a 'live' Word Cup observer and pundit, however much he might have praised Putin on his arrival in Russia. Despite Maradona's present-day shortcomings, Messi did little to convert those Argentine supporters who still believe he has yet to prove that he is better than Diego when it comes to sweating the national colours in a World Cup. As for his enduring rivalry with Ronaldo, the Argentine's one failed penalty and an off-target strike at goal was very underwhelming in contrast to the Madeiran's hat-trick against the quality opposition that Spain showed itself to be on that day, when Portugal managed a 3–3 draw.

'Poor Messi,' I wrote after the game, 'how he must already miss his Barça mates in this tournament, while Cristiano was the Portuguese team which played for him and he for them.'

After Portugal's next game, the World Cup in Russia seemed to belong to Ronaldo as he broke further goal-scoring records, that of Puskás and his own, defying those who had concluded that his less than gracious comments at the end of the Champions League final suggested that an era might be coming to an end. In fact it always seemed only too evident to me that Ronaldo's threat to quit Real Madrid was part of a strategy simply to get more money and more recognition, and that he was entering the World Cup tournament highly motivated to prove, once again, that he was worth it.

And so it proved in his first two games, the undisputed star of a somewhat lacklustre but, so far, with him in the team, undefeated Portugal, bringing to mind the possibility that he might take them to the final just as Diego Maradona did with a similarly mediocre Argentine team in Mexico 1986. But then it was comparisons with Pelé and Cruyff that spun off the lips of one BBC TV commentator that day, not with Maradona – a name that still hung like a dark shadow over Messi.

Not only was Maradona glimpsed grumpily observing Messi's failed penalty against Iceland, but his legend permeated the collective criticism that was subsequently launched by the Argentine media and social media hounds at the Barça player, who was accused once again of badly letting down his nation.

Thus, while Cristiano remained elevated in the pantheon of football gods, Messi awaited what could be a defining match of his career, having to face up to the challenge of rescuing his reputation when Argentina faced Croatia, potentially much harder opposition than Iceland. Like prize fighters, battling it out in every round, it was Messi who was clearly losing by points so far in this World Cup, and by a distance after Argentina was thrashed by Croatia 3–0. It was Argentina's heaviest defeat in the group stage of a World Cup since losing 6–1 to Czechoslovakia in 1958. It was also the first time for forty-four years that they had failed to win either of their opening two matches at a World Cup. Argentine players, in other words, were making history – just not the history that Messi had had in mind when he had come out of international retirement two years previously.

Against Croatia, Argentine coach Sampaoli recalled his good work while managing Chile and then Sevilla, and hoped Argentina would play faster and move more off the ball. And while Argentina hardly had a reputation for developing fluency, their best hope was opportunism. After all, in Messi, as my *FT* colleague Simon Kuper put it, they had the 'world's supreme dribbler and free-kick taker, in a tournament where more goals come from dead balls than from passing combinations.'

And yet Messi was absent for most of the game, played badly, and left the match staring at the ground – as if disconnected from, or worse, alienated by the team he was playing with. The Argentine media were split between those who questioned his mental fortitude, and those who struggled to excuse him because of the inadequacy of the rest of the team and the disaster of goalkeeper Willy Caballero's inexcusable blunder. The fact was that Sampaoli and Messi were let down by Argentina's slow, mediocre defenders and midfielders, and Sampaoli by Messi when the player's genius failed to come to the rescue. Instead Sampaoli spent Argentina's brief, humiliating tournament searching fruitlessly for the right formation that could bring Messi alive.

The greatest drama of modern football seemed set to continue – and it did. We have grown used to Messi speaking through his football (in the match against Croatia he was evidently in inarticulate mode), but in Argentina's next game against Nigeria he showed a less typical, for him, capacity to play the leader. While his opening goal showed the vision, touch, composure and accuracy that has marked his genius for more than a decade, as illustrative of his personality was his talk to his teammates at half-time, and the celebration of Argentina's second goal. The talk just before Argentina walked out for the second half, by all accounts, involved not a huge speech but a few words spoken with sufficient conviction to raise morale in a team that had just had its renewed self-confidence badly dented by the Nigerian equalizer.

It was a typical Argentine rallying call, delivered not by an army general or a Peronist trade-union leader, but by a bearded warrior of the game, uncompromising, defiant and melodramatic, urging fellow players to give it their all, to live or die, to go over the parapet and forward with no other aim but to win.

And what a contrast to the introverted tongue-tied Messi of earlier games, and indeed of previous World Cups, where Argentina had had to rely on more assertive sergeants to lift shattered morale among his under-performing fellow countrymen, and try and make them raise their game to his level, often without success.

Among those inspired to 'keep going forward' was Marcos Rojo, a defender who delivered the match-winning volley in Argentina's 2–1 victory over Nigeria, with the predatory spirit, vision and aggressive advance positioning of a star striker, or a Messi.

It was a goal, allowing Argentina to scrape through to the last sixteen, that seemed then and there to ignite the thousands of Argentine fans who had come to Russia with high expectations of conquest, and provoked Messi's own very special celebration as he piggy-backed Rojo, before himself kneeling down and looking up at the sky, thanking God with open arms.

Both gestures by Messi recalled other legendary moments in football history. One, on 1 May 2005, had Messi, aged seventeen, himself being piggybacked by Ronaldinho after scoring a brilliant rite-of-passage winning goal against Albacete in the Spanish La Liga – 'the goal that started the Barcelona legend', as the BBC reported at the time. The day after that goal, Maradona, still undisputedly the greatest ever player, rang Messi from Buenos Aires to congratulate him. Maradona, living legend of the game, exclusively blessed with the Hand of God, acknowledging the pretender to the throne.

Maradona was there watching Messi again in Russia, a mockery of the legend he once was; less a noble Caesar than a decadent Caligula, presiding over football's equivalent of the Roman theatre. He cut a grotesque image as he watched the Argentine team from a stadium balcony seat, giving us an overdose of his theatrical range, from rolling eyes to abusive two fingers.

But as he celebrated Argentina's first and second goals, Maradona was no longer alone in claiming a privileged line to his fellow countrymen, let alone God. Even if Messi had yet to win the World Cup, his genius of play coupled with his exemplary leadership exteriorized a transformation of character that – if maintained – could not only show God firmly on Messi's side, but promised to be one of the defining themes of this tournament.

It was not to be. Argentina tumbled out of the tournament, outplayed and outclassed by France and its rising young star Mbappé, after Messi had shown himself unable to lift himself or his team out of its renewed mediocrity. And yet, in a rare departure from previous debacles, the Argentine media and fans did not lay the blame on Messi, but rather on his teammates, and the coach Sampaoli, who was identified as the ultimate fall guy, for switching systems and players too often and failing to deliver any cohesive, let alone quality, route to victory.

This was a World Cup that showed Messi trapped in a chaos not of his making and demotivated. And yet the fact that Argentina and Messi had not only lost another World Cup, but that Messi and Barça had not won a Champions League since Berlin in 2015, suggested that the star was suffering from a more enduring crisis of identity in the wake of the departure of a coach like Guardiola and players who had contributed to sustaining his genius – notably Puyol, Xavi, Neymar and, most recently, Iniesta.

As for Ronaldo, his Word Cup stardom declined rather less dramatically after his hat-trick against Spain and scoring the only goal in Portugal's victory over Morocco. Against Iran, he failed to convert a penalty that would have given Portugal first place in the group and perhaps a different destiny. Instead, a below-form Portugal played against an on-form Uruguay that kept Ronaldo under wraps so that he managed only one shot on target.

Nevertheless, it was Ronaldo's best ever World Cup; he scored more goals than he had in all the previous tournaments put together and was evidently Portugal's key player. Other statistics showed the athlete he was still capable of being: a top speed of 33.98 km/hour against Spain was one of the fastest in the tournament, and he completed more than thirty-four kilometres in the four games he played, an extraordinary achievement for a thirty-four-year-old. The World

Cup in Russia fuelled the argument that when it came to international challenges, Ronaldo was more than up for them, Messi less so.

Ronaldo moves to Juventus, Messi stays at Barça

While Florentino Pérez took a calculated risk of boosting his club's coffers after more than realizing his initial investment in the Portuguese player during his time at the Spanish club, both Ronaldo and his agent Mendes believed their own best interests would be met by moving the player from Madrid to Turin.

By contrast Real Madrid fans were not unanimously happy with his departure; many of them felt it was worth paying Ronaldo more to keep him at the club, and in recognition of what he had achieved and what he still had in him, given his unflagging athleticism. In his sensational nine seasons at Real Madrid, he had defined a golden era, scoring 450 goals and helping to win four European championships, easily overtaking Raúl as the club's all-time top scorer.

After an inaugural season in Spain with thirty-three goals, Ronaldo went on to score in excess of forty per season for eight consecutive seasons, smashing a career-topping sixty-one in 2014–15. In total, 311 of his goals came in La Liga, but 105 came against Europe's elite in the Champions League – he was the competition's all-time top scorer with 120 and the first to score 100 for one club. He has also scored twenty-two goals in the Copa del Rey and another twelve shared among the Club World Cup, Spanish Super Cup and UEFA Super Cup.

While his transfer negotiations were going on, Manuel Jabois, a widely respected commentator on Spanish football culture, pleaded in *El País*: 'You don't sell someone who gives you joy . . . there are kids who were six years old when Cristiano came to Madrid; they don't know any other Real Madrid than the Real Madrid of Cristiano Ronaldo. Real Madrid should hang on to him just as Barcelona hang on to Messi . . . you only get rid of a player of his ability when he is missing two legs.'

By contrast, at Barcelona, the club that had adopted Messi as a young adolescent, no one begrudged him his poor World Cup performance, but rather celebrated the fact that he had returned 'home' to

Catalonia, fully motivated to captain Barça with his reputation as the best player in the club's history untarnished.

Despite the loss not just of Iniesta, but before him Xavi and others who had formed part of the golden years under Guardiola, new players like Arthur, Malcolm and Lenglet promised to reinforce the quality of a team that played – with Ernesto Valverde as manager, and Luis Suárez alongside – to Messi's strengths. As the veteran Spanish international Sergio Busquets put it: 'The more time he [Messi] has the ball at his feet, the better for all of us . . . our game has to go through him. This isn't Messi dependence, it is being intelligent and taking advantage of the best player in the world.'

Certainly, as Barça prepared for the new La Liga season in August 2018, Messi showed he had recovered from his World Cup blues by giving an impressively self-confident speech as captain and by being man of the match as Valverde's men beat Maradona's old club Boca Juniors 3–0 in the annual curtain-raiser of the season, the Gamper Trophy.

By contrast, as Real Madrid kicked off the 2018–19 season, losing to city rivals Atlético de Madrid in the European Super Cup, questions intensified as to how and when club president Pérez would find a suitable replacement for Ronaldo, a talisman who held a staggering goal ratio – in excess of one per game – during his time with Los Blancos.

As far as Ronaldo was concerned, he had more than proved his greatness at Real Madrid, as he had done at Manchester United. A move to Juventus, among the strongest clubs in Europe, and champions of the competitive Italian league, was a new challenge he relished, taking him to another level and getting one up on his rival Messi, who has spent his entire club career, as a youth and adult, in Spain. In his pre-season friendly against the Italian club's B team, Ronaldo kept Juventus fans waiting only eight minutes before scoring his first goal. Certainly the Italian club owners seemed to have few worries about recovering what they had paid for Ronaldo. In the first week alone following the announcement of the transfer, they sold 50,000 Ronaldo (Juventus) T-shirts.

But with Ronaldo's departure from Spain ended an aspect of football's most enduring battle of the giants: the war between the two great Spanish clubs for which these two special competitors played.

Not only had Ronaldo and Messi come to personify one of the most politically charged club rivalries in the history of football, but they did so during a prolonged period of time that drew out the best of their talents and produced golden years of club football played at its collective as well as individual best. But while an unprecedentedly brilliant era in the history of football had come to a close, their story was not over yet, and nor was the prospect of the continuing joy they could each give fans around the world.

In October, after Ronaldo's departure, Real Madrid found itself immersed in crisis with the sacking of manager Julen Lopetegui towards the end of October 2018, only 138 days into a job that had cost him his chance of leading Spain in the World Cup. He was sacked in the wake of a 5–1 hammering by FC Barcelona, a result provoked by Ronaldo's absence from Real Madrid as much as Messi's contribution to the team in which he had found a more enduring place. Real Madrid's first post-Ronaldo season couldn't have got off to a worse start. The defeat by Barça was Los Blancos's third in a row in La Liga, and was close on their worst ever run; they had won only one of their last seven matches.

In a debate that would continue under the short and similarly underachieving reign of Lopetegui's successor, Santiago Solari, critics of club president Florentino Pérez suggested he had made a huge mistake, not only in allowing Ronaldo to leave the club, but also leaving the club without a manager or a squad capable of succeeding without the Madeiran-born star. Ronaldo himself stirred the controversy by claiming that a shift in his relationship with Pérez had convinced him to call time on his glittering nine-year spell at Real Madrid. Officially the club had claimed that the transfer had been instigated 'at the will and the request of the player.' But in an interview with *France Football*, Ronaldo said that after his first five years at the club, he had felt increasingly less appreciated. 'The president [Pérez] looked at me through the eyes that didn't want to say the same thing, as I was no longer indispensable.'

In truth there was a combination of push–pull, with Pérez believing that in business terms he had enjoyed an excellent return on his initial investment, and Juventus feeling that if anyone could win the Champions League for them, it was Ronaldo. For the player, it was good not just to feel really wanted, but also to face a new challenge,

that of succeeding in a new league, in a top Italian club with a legendary history, while his rival Messi was still sticking to the comfort zone
he had inhabited since the age of thirteen.

And yet with Ronaldo's departure from La Liga, not only had the
Spanish league lost its most legendary player-rivals, but the two biggest clubs found themselves losing their dramatic edge. As Ramon
Besa, the veteran Barcelona-based sports writer for *El País* wrote in
that first autumn of Real Madrid without Ronaldo, 'La Liga has lost its
definition . . . gone are the days when Barça and Real Madrid achieved
more than 100 points, when Cristiano and Messi played for the Ballon
d'Or in matches played in the Mestalla, San Mamés and Sánchez Piz-
juán. Gone are the days when the personal duel was relentless, with
maximum tension in the pitch and on the bench.'

Just days earlier, those like Besa who lamented the end of an era
seemed to have their argument confirmed when FIFA named Modrić
the best player in the world, followed by Cristiano, and Mohamed
Salah. And yet writing Messi off turned out to be a somewhat premature act of dismissal by world football's governing body, as Tottenham
found in its early Champions League group encounter with the little
big man that season.

Messi had started the season promising Barça fans that winning
the Champions League was his priority that season. Against Tottenham, Messi showed his strength and skill. On 3 October he delivered
what many watching that night considered one of the greatest individual Champions League performances. He was unstoppable for
most of the game, with no less than ninety-six magical touches,
involved in all four goals, scoring two of them, and striking the post
twice. 'Is there anyone who seriously still believes there has ever been
a player better than Messi?' commented Gary Lineker as he watched
it.

The Anglo-Spanish author and writer John Carlin expanded further on this in his column in Catalonia's main daily *La Vanguardia*,
focusing on that enduring debate as to who had won the race to be
considered the best in the world: Messi or Cristiano. According to
Carlin, at this stage in football history only three categories of people
could be excused for arguing that Ronaldo was the better of the two:
his most loyal fans in Real Madrid, his most loyal fans in Juventus, and
those who didn't understand anything about football.

The reality, claimed Carlin, was clear as daylight. As he went on to write: 'Messi plays the violin, the piano, and all the other instruments with the same virtuosity; Cristiano plays the trumpet. Cristiano scores goals; Messi invents them.'

Messi, during the season, went on to show that he still had the capacity to turn even a non-Clásico La Liga encounter into something worth watching, even after Cristiano had long departed. Against Betis on Sunday 17 March 2018, Messi produced not just another memorable masterclass, but a reminder that FC Barcelona's impressive record of league titles over the last decade had increasingly become all of his making, as the club, ten points clear and with ten games to go, appeared to be heading for Messi's tenth La Liga title. He scored a hat-trick, his fifty-first with the Catalan team. He scored his third five minutes before the final whistle, the ball, not so much hit as caressed, rising softy and curving gently, leaving the Betis goalkeeper to watch it float by like a slow-motion replay. As the ball went in, the Betis coach and assistant and striker Loren Morón clapped, as all around them in the Vilamarín stadium – the majority Betis fans – spontaneously rose and applauded before chanting 'Messi, Messi, Messi' in a collective tribute to the conquering genius.

Barça won 4–1, with Messi the undisputed man of the match, despite some touches of brilliance from his friend Luis Suárez. Messi not only scored the goals but also choreographed the build-up play, providing the pass to the player who provided the assist, running into position with extraordinary anticipation and vision, and yet making it all seem so simple. Once again, the stats told of an extraordinary achievement, his goal-scoring totals in La Liga alone – 29 (and counting), 34, 37, 26, 43, 28, 46, 50, 31, 34. In all competitions so far that season he had scored 39, plus 18 assists, in 37 games.

And yet, inevitably, given that Messi and Ronaldo now played in different countries, it was at the highest competitive level of the Champions League that the rivalry came under the greatest scrutiny before the judge and jury of international football fans.

In the second leg of the last sixteen of the 2018–19 season, the Italian champions Juventus came into the game against Diego Simeone's Atlético Madrid at Turin's Allianz stadium, facing a two-goal deficit. Juventus were eight points clear at the top of Serie A, but the club and their star signing were facing unknown consequences were they to leave the Champions League tournament at this stage.

Ronaldo came out of the tunnel and performed a quick on-the-spot run followed by a jump in the air, his trademark display a signal that if anyone was going to inspire Juventus to a spectacular Champions League comeback it was him; and so he proved, becoming the hat-trick hero in his own inimitable way.

With minutes of the game underway, Ronaldo puffed out his chest and gestured to the Juventus fans behind the Atlético box to raise the volume. The game was destined to be that kind of night, full of passion, and full of great, end-to-end football.

And it was Ronaldo who firmly took centre stage, planting a header past the Atlético goalkeeper Oblak. It was his twenty-third goal in thirty-six games he had played against Atlético, and his goal number 122 in the Champions League. The Allianz stadium erupted.

Ronaldo continued to be a threatening presence through the first half, probing menacingly down the left and then, only minutes from the half-time whistle, just failed to head in another goal from a cross by Spinazzola.

With the second half under way, Ronaldo – still the supreme athlete – was off again, running into space and finding his pinpoint-accurate cross to Mandžukić, just deflected by Giménez. But in a follow-up attack, it was Ronaldo in predatory mode again, rising high and heading another goal in. Juventus had levelled up the tie!

Then, on the eighty-fourth minute, Juventus was awarded a penalty. Seemingly unfazed by a lengthy VAR check and attempts by Giminez to distract him, Ronaldo stood his ground and remained totally focused before thumping the ball in. Ronaldo's eighth hat-trick in the Champions League meant he had equalled Messi's record.

Twenty-four hours later, it was Messi's turn to come out fighting from his corner before 99,000 fans at the Nou Camp, when FC Barcelona, the only Spanish team left in the Champions League, were taking on Lyon, three weeks after a goalless draw in the first leg in France.

While in the second leg Messi was unable to match Ronaldo's hat-trick, he still proved that in football he remains a class well above most ordinary mortals, showing not just an amazing talent but a commitment to hard work as well. He scored two goals, and set up two more, playing a key part in ensuring Barcelona's move into the Champions League quarter-finals with a 5–1 win. Once again, Barça's victory was all about Messi.

As it was when Barça played against Manchester United in the first leg of the Champions League quarter-finals at Old Trafford on 10 April 2019. Bloodied after an aerial challenge and a trailing arm from Chris Smalling had struck Messi in the face, the Argentine fought on. Nearly eight years on from Guardiola's mesmerizing victory over Ferguson's Man U in the Champions League final at Wembley, Messi was far from being out of sight. 'The game found him covering parts that the world's outstanding creative players are not supposed to reach. Scrapping with Diogo Dalot to rescue a ball on his own by-line after a Marcus Rashford free kick. Tussling with Paul Pogba in United's midfield,' wrote the *Daily Mail*'s Ian Herbert.

Earlier, when the first and only goal of the match came in the twelfth minute, it was thanks to Messi as the master craftsman. He received a ball that Sergio Busquets had lofted up towards him and then, shifting his centre of gravity, by instinct or a process of osmosis, measured a perfect pass to Suárez, whose header glanced off Luke Shaw and went in.

Meanwhile, in Amsterdam, Ronaldo delivered his own brand of brilliance, scoring an away goal for Juventus in the first leg of their Champions League tie against Ajax with a spectacular diving header, precise and powerful, his fifth Champions League goal of the season. It confirmed Ronaldo as the top goal scorer in the history of the Champions League, 125 goals to Messi's 108. Juventus's head coach Massimiliano Allegri said afterwards: 'Ronaldo showed he is on a different level. His timing and movement is different to everyone else's, there's nothing you can do about it. He's a player who just has a different technique than the others.'

And yet, while Ronaldo remained venerated playing for club and country, Messi still struggled to win over his fellow countrymen. In early March 2019, Messi's return to the Argentine team after nearly a year's self-imposed sabbatical ended in a 3–1 defeat by Venezuela in Madrid's Metropolitano stadium, a result that fuelled renewed controversy about his apparent failure to match Maradona's patriotic example.

'When he plays for Barcelona Messi shows a different attitude to when he plays with Argentina,' complained Daniel Passarella, captain of the Argentine squad that won the 1978 World Cup and part of the squad that had Maradona lifting the trophy in 1986.

No good arguing that Messi may have felt himself let down over the years by a dysfunctional Argentine team of badly coached players and an Argentine Football Association better known for its political in-fighting and corruption than its professionalism. In the ongoing debate among Argentines as to who was the greatest player, Diego or Leo, people remembered Maradona's commitment as a player to the national cause and his winning goals, not his volatility or drug taking. Such is football.

For Messi, winning a World Cup remained an elusive target, his country's and his own fatal flaw, even if most fans around the world considered him, in his Barça colours, the best player in history. The perception didn't look like it would be changing any time soon, despite Messi and Barça crashing out of the Champion League's semi-final second-leg tie against Liverpool.

The result followed an epic performance by the English club known as the Reds, one of the most extraordinary fight-backs in European club history, with Liverpool winning 4–0 at home after carrying what was widely perceived as an insurmountable 0–3 deficit from the first leg at the Nou Camp against one of the biggest and most successful of European clubs and the greatest of players.

Liverpool, despite missing its two star players – Salah and Firmino – and losing a third key player, Robertson, during the match through injury, won thanks to an extraordinary team-spirited performance full of true grit and drive. Credit was also due to inspirational management by German coach Jürgen Klopp, and passionate support – tribal rather than political – by the home fans at Anfield, with their deeply felt rendering of their anthem 'You'll Never Walk Alone'.

By contrast, Messi broke down in tears back in the dressing room after failing to lift his team to anywhere near the quality expected of such an experienced and talented group of players, and later suffered the indignity of being confronted by a small group of disgruntled Barça fans at Liverpool airport before flying home.

And yet such hostility – usually reserved for Real Madrid players – proved a rare exception to the otherwise enduring adulation of the Argentine genius by the vast majority of Barça followers, and respect by fans on a global scale.

While sentiment and loyalty in football, when seemingly struggling to save its soul from the celebrity and money, can often prove ephemeral, few Barça fans blamed Messi for his failure to deliver on the pledge he had made at the start of the season, as captain: that he would win his fifth Champions League with the club. Criticism instead was aimed at the unsmiling coach Valverde and what the purists felt was the absence of players in the team with the creativity and resilience enjoyed in the 'dream team' days when Guardiola was coach.

Many fans clung on to the memory of Messi's extraordinary catalogue of individual performances and contribution to the team's successes over a decade, not least to winning yet another Spanish League championship and his contribution, before the debacle at Anfield, to getting Barça through to the final stages of the Champions League of 2018–19.

On 16 April 2019, in the second leg of the quarter-finals against Manchester United at the Nou Camp, and ten years on from his first Champions League triumph over the legendary Red Devils, Messi showed his greatness, defining the tie by scoring two of his team's three goals.

During the match some Barça fans in the Nou Camp were checking their phones to see how Juventus were fairing in its match against Ajax. A twenty-eighth-minute goal by Ronaldo, his 126th goal in the competition, produced momentary ecstasy in Juventus fans at the Allianz stadium and a murmur of disapproval at the Nou Camp, while seemingly coinciding with Messi raising his game, as if both ties were building up into a telepathic contest between two iconic rivals.

And yet the expectation of such a contest on this occasion proved ill-founded. With the match in Turin ending after a fight-back by the Dutch champions and Ajax winning and qualifying for the semi-finals, Barça fans seemed to have every excuse for a double celebration – Messi's victory and Ronaldo's defeat. Only some had, in common with other lovers of sublime football, looked forward to the two superstars being back together again on Spanish soil, stepping up to the biggest of sporting stages and fighting it out in the Champions League final in Madrid.

For Ronaldo, who had won three successive Champions League finals while at Real Madrid, his first season at Juventus did not go quite according to plan. He went on to help Juventus beat Fiorentina 2–1 to win their eighth successive Serie A title, but his failure to once again win the big prize in Europe had Ronaldo having to defuse speculation that he might quit Italy after just one year of his four-year contract.

But it was Messi that seemed to pull ahead of him in the race to be considered the best player of all time, following up Barça's victory over Manchester United over two legs in the quarter-finals of the Champions League with another brilliant display in the first leg of the semi-finals against Liverpool.

On 1 May 2019, fourteen years to the day since his first La Liga goal for his club against Albacete, Messi brought 98,000 fans in the Nou Camp to their feet and had fans around the world in awe as his left-footed free kick from thirty yards swung round the Liverpool wall and propelled into the top corner of the net, beating one of the best goalkeepers in the world, and making it his 600th for FC Barcelona. It was Messi's second goal in a match that Barça won 3–0 and had the little big man displaying the kind of magic that has brought enduring joy to any lover of football.

Jimmy Burns
May 2019

Acknowledgements

Although this book is not an official history, still less an authorized one, it would not have been possible without the co-operation and insights of various clubs, agents, lawyers, marketing executives, backroom staff, journalists, players and fans who have played a part in the lives of Ronaldo and Messi.

The project sprang from my own experience of living and working over the years in Portugal, Argentina, the UK and Spain, and from the idea for a dual biography conceived by Robin Harvie and Jamie Coleman at Pan Macmillan, whose advice and forbearance have been invaluable.

The following institutions opened their doors to me in different ways: the Madeiran government, the Pestana Group, Blandy's, Club Nàutic de Sitges, Tres Quarts Sports Bar (Sitges), Clube Futebol Andorinha, Penya Blaugrana (London), Clube Desportivo Nacional, Sporting Clube de Portugal, Newell's Old Boys, Manchester United FC, FC Barcelona, Real Madrid CF, and football fan clubs, associations and federations in respective countries.

While the various individuals who helped are too numerous to mention, I would like to extend a special thanks to the following, in no order of priority or seniority:

In Madeira – Adam Blandy, Michael Blandy, Miguel Albuquerque, Peter Booth, Rui Santos, Fernando Sousa, Joao Marques de Freitas, Ricardo Oliveira, Dave Bartram, Andre Abranches, Agostinho Silva, Venetia Welby, Caetano Fernandes, Ricardo Santos, Elda Isabel Chaves, Paulo Neves and Bruno Macedo.

In Rosario – Richard Willmott, Eduardo Bermudez, Maxi Rodriguez, Enrique Dominguez, Rafael Bielsa, Sebastián Domínguez and Marcelo Lewandosky.

In Lisbon – Penelope Abrantes, Peter Wise, Dave Rowlands, Paulo Anunciacao, Francisco Pinto Balsemão, André Pipa, Aurelio Pereira, Luís Sobral, Alison Roberts, Andres Malamud, Raquel Vaz-Pinto and Carol Garton.

In the UK – Simon Kuper, Jim White, Patrick Harverson, Guillem Balagué, Jon Holmes, Marcela Mora y Araujo, Gary Lineker, Jonathan Wilson, Andrew Haynes, Peter Montegriffo, Eduard Manas, Jorge Gallardo at Bar & Co, Jason Pettigrove and Robert Powell.

In Buenos Aires – Fernando Signorini, Luis Ampuero, Ezequiel Fernadez Moores, Ernesto Cherquis Bialo, Ricardo Kirschbaum, Roberto Guareschi, Maria Laura Avignolo, Julio Marini, Carla Rossi, Benedict Mander, Jose Luis Melendez, Eduardo Valdes, Carolina Barros, Mariano Cuneo and Sergio Levinsky.

In Barcelona – Carlos Tusquets, Cuqui Sarrias, Jose-Maria Minguella, Sandro Rosell, Dolores Jaraquemada, Marti Anclada, Edwin Winkels, Eduardo Prim, Alfons Godall, Joan Laporta, Raphael Minder, Jordi Alberich, Chemi Teres, Francesc Orenes, Graham Hunter, Luis Fernando Rojo, Ramon Besa, Gloria Gutierrez, Dorinda Avinet, Dominic Begg, Lluis Canut, Sandro Rosell and Richard Fitzpatrick.

In Madrid – Santiago Segurola, Juan Jose Diaz Clavel, Jorge Valdano, Emilio Butragueño, Raul Rosales, Florentino Perez, Vicente del Bosque, Frank Porral, Jose Angel Sanchez, Carlos Oppe, Tom Burns, Dolores Luca de Tena, Tomas Burns Luca de Tena, Manuela Burns Luca de Tena, Juan Milagro, Angel Altozano, Regino Garcia-Badell, Paco Arenosa, Ana Momplet and Sid Lowe.

My London agent Annabel Merullo of Peters, Fraser & Dunlop together with Laura Williams and Laura McNeill.

And to Kidge, Julia and Miriam, my love and warm thanks for putting up with the trials and tribulations of another book and all those football matches.

Bibliography

Dolores Aveiro & Paulo Sousa Costa, *Madre Coraje* (Testimonio, 2016)

Guillem Balagué, *Pep Guardiola, Another Way of Winning* (Orion, 2012)

Guillem Balagué, *Messi* (Orion, 2013)

Guillem Balagué, *Ronaldo* (Orion, 2016)

Peter Banke, *Neymar* (Cúpula, 2014)

Patrick Barclay, *Mourinho* (Orion, 2011)

Stephen Beasley, *José Mourinho: Up Close and Personal* (Michael O'Mara, 2016)

Ramón Besa & Marcos López, *Andrés Iniesta: La Jugada de la meva vida* (Malpaso, 2016)

Rafael Bielsa, *Rojo Sangre* (Planeta, 2017)

Marcus Binney, *The Blandys of Madeira* (Frances Lincoln, 2011)

Jimmy Burns, *The Land That Lost Its Heroes: How Argentina Lost the Falklands War* (Bloomsbury, 2002)

Jimmy Burns, *When Beckham Went to Spain* (Michael Joseph, 2004)

Jimmy Burns, *Hand of God: The Life of Diego Maradona* (Bloomsbury, 2010)

Jimmy Burns, *Barça, A People's Passion* (Bloomsbury, 2010)

Jimmy Burns, *La Roja, A Journey through Spanish Football* (Simon & Schuster, 2013)

Luca Caioli, *Ronaldo: The Obsession for Perfection* (Icon Books, 2014)

Andreas Campomar, *¡Golazo!: A History of Latin American Football* (Quercus, 2014)

Alejandro Casar González, *Pasó de Todo* (Planeta, 2015)

Johan Cruyff, *My Turn* (Macmillan, 2016)

Miguel Cuesta & Jonathan Sánchez, *La Clave Mendes* (Esfera, 2015)

Leonardo Faccio, *Messi* (Debate, 2011)

Rio Ferdinand, *#2Sides* (Blink, 2016)

Alex Ferguson, *My Autobiography* (Hodder & Stoughton, 2014)

Hugo Gambini, *El Che Guevara* (Vergara, 2016)

Brian Glanville, *The Story of the World Cup* (Faber & Faber, 2010)

David Goldblatt, *The Ball is Round* (Penguin, 2007)

Alberto Granado, *Cón el Che por Sudamérica* (Marea, 2017)

Barry Hatton, *The Portuguese* (Signal Books, 2011)

Ernest Hemingway, *Death in the Afternoon* (Penguin, 1966)

Graham Hunter, *The Making of the Greatest Team in the World* (Backpage, 2016)

Simon Kuper, *The Football Men: Up Close with the Giants of the Modern Game* (Simon & Schuster, 2011)

Simon Kuper & Stefan Szymanski, *Soccernomics* (HarperSport, 2014)

Sergio Levinsky, *AFA* (Autoría, 2016)

Sid Lowe, *Fear & Loathing in La Liga* (Vintage, 2016)

Stephen G. Mandis, *The Real Madrid Way* (Benbella Books, 2016)

Diego Maradona with Daniel Arcucci, *Touched by God* (Constable, 2017)

Gary Neville, *Red* (Transworld, 2011)

Michael Parkinson, *Muhammad Ali* (Hodder & Stoughton, 2016)

Gerard Piqué, *Viatge D'Anada i Tornada* (Ediciones62, 2010)

Cristiano Ronaldo, *Moments* (Macmillan, 2007)

José Saramago, *Journey to Portugal* (Harvill, 2000)

J. R. R. Tolkien, *The Hobbit* (HarperCollins, 2013)

Jorge Valdano, *Fútbol: El Juego Infinito* (Conecta, 2016)

David Winner, *Brilliant Orange* (Bloomsbury, 2001)

Notes

Prologue

1 Peter Shaffer, *Amadeus* (1980; Penguin Classics, 2007).

1. Madeira

1 Barry Hatton, *The Portuguese* (Signal Books, 2011), p. 69.
2 Jimmy Burns, *Hand of God* (Bloomsbury, 2010), p. 9.
3 Hatton, *The Portuguese*, Introduction, p. xii.
4 *Ronaldo* documentary (Anthony Wonke, Spain/UK, 2015).
5 See Dolores Aveiro and Paulo Sousa Costa, *Madre Coraje* (Testimonio, 2016).

2. Rosario

1 Álex de la Iglesia, *Messi*, TV documentary (Mediapro, Spain, 2014).
2 Gerardo Grighini, quoted in 'Las Aventuras de la Banda de Messi', *Perfil*, 29 September 2012.
3 Toni Frieros, quoted in Guillem Balagué, *Messi* (Orion, 2013), p. 45.

3. Rites of Passage: Ronaldo

1 Benjamin Markovits, 'Usain Bolt: Now you see him, soon you won't . . .', *Observer*, 30 July 2017.
2 Nuno Luz in *Planeta Ronaldo*, TV documentary (SIC Notícias, 2008), quoted in Guillem Balagué, *Ronaldo* (Orion, 2016).
3 TV documentary, ElEspanol.com, 22 November 2016.
4 Hatton, *The Portuguese*, p. 204.
5 Ronaldo, 'My Story', theplayerstribune.com, 3 October 2017.
6 Balagué, *Ronaldo* (Orion, 2016).
7 'The real Cristiano Ronaldo: What matters to me? Family, football and money!': mirror.co.uk, 2 July 2011.
8 Balagué, *Ronaldo*, p. 68.

4. Little Big Man: Messi

1 Diego Schwarzstein, quoted in Richard Fitzpatrick, untitled manuscript. Permission of the author.

2 López's ongoing trial on charges of administrative fraud during his presidency of the club was widely reported in official Argentine news media: see telam.com.arg, 9 June 2016.

3 Julio Marini, interview with author.

4 Joan Lacueva Colomer, interview in *El País*: see AS.com, 8 May 2014.

5. Lisbon Star: Ronaldo

1 Cristiano Ronaldo, 'Madrid: My Story', theplayerstribune.com, 3 October 2017.

2 Dolores Aveiro, quoted in the *Sun*, 29 January 2009. See inside-worldsoccer.com, 31 January 2009.

3 Video report, Sport TV, 2001, accessed on YouTube.

4 Jorge Mendes interview, *Jorge Mendes: The Super Agent*, TV documentary (SIC Notícias, 2012).

5 Augusto Lendoiro, FourFourTwo.com, 20 November 2016.

6 Ben Lyttleton, 'Who is Jorge Mendes?', FourFourTwo.com, 26 May 2016.

7 Cristiano Ronaldo interview, *Jorge Mendes: The Super Agent*, TV documentary.

8 Balagué, *Ronaldo*, p. 87.

9 Luis Miguel Pereira and Juan Ignacio Gallardo, *CR7: Los secretos de la maquina* (Prime Books, 2014).

10 Quoted in Pedro Marques, 'Memories of Ronaldo's debut: on this day in 2002', UEFA.com, 14 August 2017.

11 Marques, 'Memories of Ronaldo's debut', 14 August 2017.

12 Quotes from Poruguese media summarized in Marques, 'Memories of Ronaldo's debut', 14 August 2017.

13 Marques, 'Memories of Ronaldo's debut', 14 August 2017.

14 Cristiano Ronaldo, *Moments* (Macmillan, 2007), p. 52.

15 Ibid., p. 53.

16 Luca Caioli, *Ronaldo: The Obsession for Perfection* (Icon Books, 2014).

17 László Bölöni interview in *France Football* magazine, cited by Reuters.com, 13 January 2015.

6. Growing Pains: Messi

1   Figure quoted in Balagué, *Messi*, p. 114.
2   This account based on author's separate interviews with Josep María Minguella and Martin Montero.
3   Jorge Messi, quoted in Sique Rodríguez Gairí, *Educados para Ganar* (Now Books, 2011).
4   Jorge Messi, quoted in Pete Jenson, 'Fabregas, Messi, Pique: Class of 2002', *Independent*, 27 March 2010.
5   Balagué, *Messi*, p. 128.
6   Lionel Messi interview, *Barça Dreams* documentary (Entropy Studio/Gen Image Media, Spain, 2016).
7   Albert Benaiges, quoted in Jenson, 'Fabregas, Messi, Pique', 27 March 2010.
8   Cesc Fabregas, quoted in Fabricio Rinandoni, 'La Masía y su generación dorada del '87', NegroWhite.net.
9   Jorge Messi, quoted in Guillem Balagué, 'Lionel Messi's improbable progression from struggling youngster to world super star', telegraph.co.uk, 2 December 2013.

7. Into the Market: Ronaldo

1   David Goldblatt, *The Ball is Round* (Penguin, 2007), p. 682.
2   Pedro Garcia-del-Barrio and Stefan Szymanski, 'Goal! Profit maximization and win maximization in football leagues', *Review of Industrial Organization* 34 (2006), 45–68.
3   Gary Neville, quoted in Ian Herbert, 'How Manchester United made Cristiano Ronaldo', Independent.co.uk, 11 February 2013.
4   Rio Ferdinand, quoted in Balagué, *Ronaldo*, p. 101.
5   Alex Ferguson, *My Autobiography* (Hodder & Stoughton, 2014), p. 90.
6   Ibid., p. 90.
7   Alex Ferguson, quoted in Frank Worrall, *Fergie: The Greatest* (John Blake Publishing, 2013).
8   Jim Ryan, quoted in Ferguson, *My Autobiography*, p. 112.
9   David Conn, 'The brightest star in Europe and £1m to a mysterious agent', theguardian.com, 19 January 2011.

8. The Dwarf: Messi

1   Sergi Alegre, quoted by Xavi Hernández, 'Gracias, Leo, maqui', ElPais.com, 13 January 2016.

2   Hernández, 'Gracias, Leo, maqui', 13 January 2016.

3   Balagué, *Messi*, p. 191.

4   Lionel Messi, quoted by Sport.es, 23 December 2015.

5   Simon Kuper, *The Football Men: Up Close with the Giants of the Modern Game* (Simon & Schuster, 2011), pp. 205–6.

6   Rodrigo Messi interview, *Informe Robinson* (Spanish TV programme), 13 November 2011.

7   Rodolfo Schinocca, quoted in Leonardo Faccio, *Messi: El Chico que siempre llegaba tarde* (Debate, 2011), p. 120.

8   Schinocca, quoted in Faccio, *Messi*, p. 121.

9   Jorge Valdano, interview with author.

9. The Red Legacy: Ronaldo

1   George Best interview (2003) reprinted in Justyn Barnes, 'George Best on Ronaldo's Debut for Man Utd', Sabotagetimes.com, 15 September 2014.

2   Ryan Giggs, quoted in Herbert, 'How Manchester United made Cristiano Ronaldo', 11 February 2013.

3   Paddy Harverson, this and following quotes, interview with author.

4   Ellis Cashmore, quoted in Jimmy Burns, *When Beckham Went to Spain* (Michael Joseph, 2004), p. 107.

5   Ferguson, *My Autobiography*, p. 108.

6   Ronaldo, *Moments*, p. 86.

7   Ferguson, *My Autobiography*, p. 116.

8   Ibid., p. 110.

9   James Scowcroft, quoted in Herbert, 'How Manchester United made Cristiano Ronaldo', 11 February 2013.

10 Henry Winter, 'Humiliated Arsenal in the dock', telegraph.co.uk, 22 September 2003.

11 Ferguson, *My Autobiography*, p. 110.

12 Carlos Queiroz, quoted in Ferguson, *My Autobiography*, p. 110.

13 Kevin McCarra, theguardian.com, 23 May 2003.

14 Gary Neville, quoted in 'Neville hails Ronaldo', BBC.co.uk, 22 May 2004.

10. Euro Blues: Ronaldo

1   José Carlos Freitas, *Luiz Felipe Scolari: The Man, The Manager* (Dewi Lewis Media, 2008).

2   Freitas, quoted in the *Manchester Evening News*, 13 January 2013.
3   Ibid.
4   Ibid.
5   Luiz Felipe Scolari interview for Omnisport.tv: see Ronaldocr7.com, 3 June 2016.
6   Jonathan Wilson, *Financial Times* (5 July 2004): see si.com/planet-futbol, 4 July 2016.

11. First Team Calling: Messi
1   Iglesia, *Messi*, TV documentary (2014).
2   Ronald Reng, 'Lionel Messi', *Financial Times*, 27 May 2011.
3   Lionel Messi, quoted in Reng, 'Lionel Messi', 27 May 2011.
4   Reng, 'Lionel Messi', 27 May 2011.
5   Lionel Messi interview on MBC, quoted in 101greatgoals.com, 27 March 2016.
6   'The goal that started the Barcelona legend', BBC.co.uk, 1 May 2015.
7   Lionel Messi interview, FCBarcelona.cat, 11 July 2013.
8   Kuper, *The Football Men*, pp. 204.

12. Manchester Days: Ronaldo
1   Ronaldo, *Moments*, p. 100.
2   Ibid., p. 101.
3   Rio Ferdinand, *#2Sides* (Blink, 2016), p. 91.
4   Ferguson, *My Autobiography*, p. 110.
5   Gary Neville, quoted in Herbert, 'How Manchester United made Cristiano Ronaldo', 11 February 2013.

13. The Rise of the Hobbit: Messi
1   Fabio Capello interview, FCBarcelona.com, 14 May 2015.
2   Ramon Besa, ElPais.com, 27 September 2005.
3   Sid Lowe, 'Madrid too ugly for Ronaldinho', theguardian.com, 21 November 2005.
4   Santiago Segurola, interview with author.
5   Thierry Henry interview, Marca.com, 22 February 2005.
6   Balagué, *Messi*, p. 286.
7   Lionel Messi interview, *Barça va recuperar el somriure*, TV documentary (Barça TV, Spain, 21 July 2013).

14. Diego's Shadow: Messi

1   Andreas Campomar, *¡Golazo!: A History of Latin American Football* (Quercus, 2014), p. 458.

2   Jorge Valdano, *Fútbol: El Juego Infinito* (Conecta, 2016), p. 99.

15. World Cup Trauma: Ronaldo the Winker

1   John Vincent, 'Flying the flag: Gender and national identity in English newspapers during the 2006 World Cup,' in *Soccer and Society* 12(5): 613–32.

2   Liz McClarnon comment in *Cristiano Ronaldo: The Story* video (IMC Vision, 2008).

3   Alan Shearer and the *Sun* cited in Andrew Murray, 'Year Zero: The making of Cristiano Ronaldo (Manchester United, 2006/07), FourFourTwo.com, 31 May 2017.

4   Cristiano Ronaldo, quoted in Murray, 'Year Zero', 31 May 2017.

5   Phil McNulty, 'Backlash begins for Ronaldo', BBC.co.uk, 6 July 2006.

16. Kicking On: Ronaldo

1   Rob Smyth, 'Shredding his legacy at every turn', theguardian.com, 31 July 2006.

2   Neville, quoted in Herbert, 'How Manchester United made Cristiano Ronaldo', 11 February 2013.

3   Cristiano Ronaldo, quoted in Herbert, 'How Manchester United made Cristiano Ronaldo', 11 February 2013.

4   Graeme Murty, quoted in 'Ronaldo has last laugh on Reading fans', Telegraph.co.uk, 25 September 2006.

5   Paul Wilson, 'Ronaldo sets tempo for Ferguson's anniversary waltz', *Observer*, 5 November 2006.

6   Ronaldo, quoted on Independent.com, 11 February 2013.

7   Cristiano Ronaldo, quoted in Greg Evans, 'Ronaldo: Sir Alex Ferguson taught me the basis of the game at Man Utd', Squawka. com, 6 November 2016.

17. The New Maradona: Messi

1   Sid Lowe, 'The new Diego: Messi scores Maradona's goal', theguardian.com, 20 April 2007.

2   Alfredo Relaño, As.com, 20 April 2007.

18. Close Encounters: Messi vs Ronaldinho

1 Nani interview with Chris Wheeler, 'Chronicles of Nani: From the crushing poverty of life as an outcast to United hero', dailymail.co. uk, 16 October 2011.

2 Rene Meulensteen interview with Henry Winter, 'The secrets behind the development of Real Madrid's Cristiano Ronaldo, revealed by Rene Meulensteen', Telegraph.co.uk, 29 August 2014.

3 Meulensteen interview with Winter, 'The secrets behind the development of Real Madrid's Cristiano Ronaldo', 29 August 2014.

4 Ronaldo, *Moments*, p. 31.

19. Ronaldinho's Farewell: Messi

1 Bruno Garcia, 'I am Brazilian: I saw the true Ronaldo, I saw the 7–1, I saw 1994, I know things', Quora.com, 25 October 2016.

21. The Beijing Olympics and Maradona

1 Diego Maradona, quoted in Chris Davies, 'Maradona hails his successor', Telegraph.co.uk, 24 February 2006.

2 Valdano, interview with author.

22. Centre Stage: Ronaldo

1 Henry Winter, 'Cristiano Ronaldo deserves to win Ballon d'Or ahead of Fernando Torres and Lionel Messi', Telegraph.co.uk, 2 December 2008.

2 Rob Smyth, 'Golden Goal: Cristiano Ronaldo for Manchester United v Arsenal (2009)', theguardian.com, 5 February 2016.

23. The Guardiola Revolution: Messi

1 Lionel Messi, quoted by FC Barcelona executive source in interview with author.

2 Steve Archibald, interview with author.

3 Lionel Messi interview (2013), TyC Sports, cited in Guillem Balagué, 'Pep and Messi. What they both think of each other', Yahoo! Sport, 19 January 2017.

4 Pep Guardiola, quoted by Balagué, *Messi*, p. 444.

5 Juanjo Brau, quoted in Faccio, *Messi: El Chico que siempre llegaba tarde*, p. 203.

6 Lionel Messi, quoted in Ramón Besa and Marcos López, *Andrés Iniesta: La Jugada de la meva vida* (Malpaso, 2016).

7   Ibid.

8   See, for example, Joshua Hayward, 'Lionel Messi: Xavi is the best player in the history of Spanish football', Eurosport.co.uk, 2 June 2016.

9   Sid Lowe, 'Xavi pulls the strings as Barcelona leave Madrid dangling in despair', theguardian.com, 12 April 2010.

10 Guardiola, quoted by Balagué, *Messi*, p. 453.

11 Phil McNulty's Champions League final match report, BBC.co.uk, 28 May 2009.

12 Henry Winter's Champions League final match report, Telegraph.co.uk, 27 May 2010.

24. Goodbye Old Trafford, Hello Bernabéu: Ronaldo

1   Valdano, interview with author.

2   Balagué, *Ronaldo*, p. 213.

3   Ferguson, *My Autobiography*, p. 108.

4   Ibid., p. 109.

5   Jorge Mendes, quoted in Miguel Cuesta and Jonathan Sánchez, *La Clave Mendes* (Esfera, 2015).

6   Balagué, *Ronaldo*, p. 242.

7   Manuel Pellegrini, quoted on Ronaldocr7.com, 3 June 2016.

8   Manu Sanz, interview with author.

9   Michel Salgado, Manuel Pellegrini, quoted in Caioli, *Ronaldo: The Obsession for Perfection*.

10 Press Association, 'Cristiano Ronaldo happy at Real Madrid but missing Manchester United', theguardian.com, 21 December 2009.

11 Manuel Pellegrini, quoted on espn.com, 27 May 2010.

12 Manuel Pellegrini, quoted in Glen Harrington, 'Real Madrid: Home of the managerial merry-go-round', givemesport.com, 12 June 2013.

13 Valdano, interview with author.

14 Sid Lowe, 'Cristiano Ronaldo smites Villareal to become the new God of Madrid', theguardian.com, 22 February 2010.

15 Cristiano Ronaldo, quoted in 'Ronaldo refuses to rule out future Barcelona move', Mirror.co.uk, 12 May 2010.

26. World Cup 2010: Messi

1   Juan Román Riquelme, quoted in Joel Richards, 'Riquelme can no longer justify Argentina Maradona's means to South African end', theguardian.co.uk, 12 March 2009.

2   César Menotti, quoted on goal.com, 13 October 2009.

3   Kuper, *The Football Men*, p. 201.

4   Paul Fletcher's World Cup 2010 Group B match report, BBC.co.uk, 22 June 2010.

5   Sean Ingle, World Cup 2010 Group B match report, theguardian. com, 22 June 2010.

6   Kuper, *The Football Men*, p. 207.

28. Enter Mourinho

1   Mamen Sanz, quoted in *Europa Press* newsagency report, 24 June 2010.

2   José Mourinho, quoted in Paul Wilson, 'José Mourinho thinks Premier League power is too divided, but is he right?', theguardian. com, 22 March 2017.

3   Jonathan Wilson, 'José Mourinho thrives on tension but after two years it becomes a problem', theguardian.com, 20 August 2015.

4   Mendes, quoted in Cuesta and Sánchez, *La Clave Mendes*.

29. Clásicos: Ronaldo and Messi

1   Graham Hunter, *The Making of the Greatest Team in the World* (Backpage, 2016), extract from Goal.com, 30 December 2011.

2   Oliver Brown's Champions League semi-final match report, Telegraph.co.uk, 16 April 2011.

3   Mourinho and Guardiola, quoted in John Sinnott's La Liga match report, BBC.co.uk, 16 April 2011.

4   Johan Cruyff, quoted in 'Negative Mourinho doesn't care about football! Barcelona hero Cruyff slams Real Madrid manager', Dailymail.co.uk, 18 April 2011.

5   Henry Winter's Champions League semi-final match report, Telegraph.co.uk, 27 April 2011.

6   Winter's Champions League semi-final match report, 27 April 2011.

7   Henry Winter's Champions League semi-final match report, 3 May 2011.

30. Mourinho Strikes Back

1   Segurola, interview with author.

2   Cristiano Ronaldo, quoted in Press Association, 'Cristiano Ronaldo

claims Lionel Messi rivalry improves both players', Independent.co.uk, 18 May 202.

3   Lionel Messi, quoted in 'Barcelona's Lionel Messi blames media for inventing rivalry with Real Madrid's Cristiano Ronaldo', Telegraph.co.uk, 15 August 2012.

4   Lionel Messi, quoted on Sportsmole.co.uk, 15 August 2012.

32. Life after Pep and with Mourinho: Messi and Ronaldo

1   Sandro Rosell, interview with author.

2   Rosell, interview with author.

33. King Cristiano: Black Dog Messi

1   Valdano, *Fútbol: El Juego Infinito*, p. 162.

2   Rosell, interview with author.

3   Juan Laporta, interview with author.

4   Lionel Messi interview with *MARCA*, quoted on Sportsinquirer.net, 21 November 2013.

5   Tata Martino interview with *Panenka*, quoted in D. Piferrer, 'Tata Martino: My Barcelona period was a total failure', *MARCA*, 12 May 2016.

34. World Cup Disappointment, National Embarrassment: Messi and Ronaldo

1   Adam Bates, 'World Cup Final: Was Lionel Messi really a disappointment in Brazil or have we become numb to his greatness?', Skysports.com, 16 July 2014.

35. Enrique vs Ancelotti

1   Javier Mascherano, quoted in Sid Lowe, 'El clásico pendulum swings to Barça and Lionel Messi before Real Madrid clash', theguardian.com, 21 March 2015.

2   Cristiano Ronaldo interview in *Ronaldo* documentary (Anthony Wonke, Spain/UK, 2015).

3   Daniel Taylor, 'Cristiano Ronaldo film captures giant ego and strange, lonely world of being CR7', theguardian.com, 5 November 2015.

4   Lionel Messi, quoted in 'Barcelona's Lionel Messi: I'm back to my best after a difficult year', theguardian.com, 14 April 2015.

36. The 2016 Copa América: Messi

1   Lionel Messi, quoted in 'Lionel Messi retires from Argentina after Copa America final loss to Chile', espn.com, 26 June 2016.

37. Rebuilding: Messi and Ronaldo

1   See, for example, 'Reports claim Carlo Ancelotti was sacked for substituting Gareth BAle', sportskeeda.com, 16 June 2015.
2   Cristiano Ronaldo, quoted in 'Cristiano Ronaldo apologises to Real Madrid team-mates – reports', theguardian.com, 1 March 2016.

38. Euro 2016: Ronaldo the Manager

1   Raquel Vaz-Pinto, interview with author.
2   Vaz-Pinto, interview with author.
3   J. J. Bull, 'A crying shame for Cristiano Ronaldo but Portugal win Euro 2016', telegraph.co.uk, 11 July 2016.

39. On Trial: Messi

1   Gary Lineker, message to the author.

40. Legends: Messi and Ronaldo

1   Tomás Roncero, AS.com.

Conclusion

1   Brian Glanville, quoted in Richard Fitzpatrick, 'Why Cristiano Ronaldo should be talked about as the GOAT', Bleacherreport.com, 1 June 2017.
2   Diego Maradona, quoted on BBC.co.uk, 24 October 2000.
3   Balagué, *Ronaldo*, p. 13.
4   Dolores Aveiro, interview in *Ronaldo* documentary (2015).

Index